**Advance Praise for *Never Give Up the Jump***

"*Never Give Up the Jump* is a unique insight to the wartime experiences of an American hero. Readers will see his war, and that of others, through snippets of incredibly intimate and personal letters, which highlight the effect of war both at the front, and at home. At points in this read it is hard to keep one's emotions in check! This is a fine addition to the existing library of books highlighting the exploits of the American Airborne Warrior."

—Adam G.R. Berry. Author: *And Suddenly They Were Gone*. Overlord Publishing.

"I am most impressed—this is a real contribution to our understanding of the men of WWII airborne units and their families. Histories of World War II continue to appear as new sources become available. This book provides a significant contribution to our knowledge of the 508th Parachute Infantry's service in the European Theater. The existing histories of the 508th focus on the larger view—the strategy—of the Regiment during the War. This book takes to the men of the Regiment and their families, on both the home front and the battle front. The book's descriptions of the 508th's training and combat provide new insights into the Regiment's history. The officers' wives' 'Round Robin' letters area unique contribution showing how the women worked to hold their own morale and courage. In all, this is a marvelous contribution to our understanding of the men and families that were the Army's parachute troopers."

—George Cressman, Jr., PhD, Senior Historian, Camp Blanding Museum.

"*Never Give up the Jump* is an outstanding telling of a World War II story through the medium of saved personal letters—such a rare possession during those climactic years. Sue and Jack have given us a unique peek into love letters, to tell a remarkable story."

—Ron Drez, Author,historian, and combat veteran.

"*Never Give Up the Jump* is a heartwarming, beautiful love story which unfolds in letters sent during WWII between the battlefield and home. It is a glimpse into the thoughts and emotions of those separated by war, and living for the next day."

—Judy Drez, Vietnam war wife.

“The majority of the books on WWII describe the events on the battlefield,but very few deal with the subjects the Talley’s have through more than 1,200 letters and documents. The almost daily exchanges depict the state of mind of George Gurwell and his wife Jeane,but also that of the women officers of the 508th PIR since their entry into the army, the epic of the brand new combat units, and the famous US paratroopers, until their return to the United States in 1945 for the lucky ones. The authors have selected letters representative of the state of mind of this generation which had just gone through the Great Depression and which was going to be sent across the Atlantic to liberate Europe of the Nazi yoke. This book speaks of the sacrifice of the soldiers as well as the sacrifice of the wives of these officers who remained in the USA who built a close bond of real support between them. Hasty weddings before departure, then the pain of these women and families who received a telegram from the War Department announcing the sad news of the death of these heroes who fell in battle in the name of our freedom. These young widows, these young mothers remained with their heads held high despite the hardships. This publication finally tackles one of the things least treated in most historical books of the Second World War; PTSD linked to their prolonged presence on the front line, physical and psychological fatigue, bombardments, and the loss of brothers in arms. These disorders also affected wives who had the heavy task of continuing to manage daily life with the anxiety and stress related to the fear of losing their loved one. These women, some of whom are already mothers, or were pregnant,demonstrated courage and unfailing self-sacrifice even for those who will be hit hard by the loss of their husband. Victory in Europe meant the end of hostilities in Europe but for many veterans the return home will not be followed by any treatment for post-traumatic stress disorder.”

—Eddy Lamberty, WWII Battlefield Tour Guide, Belgium.

"Many a reader will have wondered what it was like to be on the front lines as a paratrooper in WWII, and also how the families back home dealt with the little news they received. *Never Give Up the Jump* brings you into the front lines based on 1100 letters from Susan's parents exchanged in 1943-1945 and wartime letters by the wives of fellow officers, all set in chronological order and placed in historical context. The book provides a unique glimpse into the hearts of American women who lost their loved ones on the battlefield. This book takes you through WWII in a way unsurpassed by any other. Lieutenant Gurwell was responsible for processing personal effects of many paratroopers of the 508th, including many friends who died on D-Day. He suffered from PTSD after the war and Susan and Jack movingly describe their efforts to get him to talk about his war experiences. Their journey into the past continued after his passing in 2004 to meet veterans who served with George Gurwell for missing answers on his WWII service. A book that will leave a lasting impression of gratitude for the 508th PIR in their odyssey to defeat Nazi-Germany, and the authors who enabled you to read it from your comfortable chair."

—Frank van Lunteren, author: *Birth of a Regiment: The 504th Parachute Infantry Regiment in Sicily and Salerno.*

"Susan Gurwell Talley and Jack Talley set out on an amazing mission to document the war experience of Lt. Gurwell, the men of the 508th PIR and their loved ones on the home front. Using an astonishing collection of wartime letters written by Susan's father, mother and other officers of the regiment and their wives, this book gives us a riveting account of their experiences,the struggle for survival, love, loss and trauma. Where the post-war impact of PTSD is often neglected, Jack and Susan break the silence in which so many GIs from World War II carried the pain of trauma. Their journey to find answers, healing and closure, show us amazing parallels with trauma that is experienced by modern veterans and their families. *Never Give Up the Jump* is a moving story that unconditionally gives honor to whom honor is due: the brave Red Devils of the 508th PIR and their families!"

—Thulai van Maanen, Dutch (combat) veteran, granddaughter of a WWII regional resistance leader, WWII historian.

"A trove of over 1,000 letters between a young Lieutenant in the 508th PIR and his wife provide a special lens to read a powerful story of love and war from D-Day through VE-Day in World War II."

—Mark Vlahos, historian and author.

# NEVER GIVE UP THE JUMP

## Combat, Resilience, and the Legacy of World War II through the Eyes and Voices of the Paratroopers, Wives, and Families of the 508th PIR

# NEVER GIVE UP THE JUMP

## Combat, Resilience, and the Legacy of World War II through the Eyes and Voices of the Paratroopers, Wives, and Families of the 508th PIR

**SUSAN GURWELL TALLEY**
*and* **JACK L. TALLEY**

KNOX PRESS

A KNOX PRESS BOOK
An Imprint of Permuted Press
ISBN: 978-1-63758-428-6
ISBN (eBook): 978-1-63758-429-3

Never Give Up the Jump:
Combat, Resilience, and the Legacy of World War II through the Eyes and Voices of the Paratroopers, Wives, and Families of the 508th PIR


Permuted Press, LLC
New York • Nashville
permutedpress.com

Published in the United States of America
1 2 3 4 5 6 7 8 9 10

To the grandest people, the men and
women of the 508th PIR during WWII and all
Gold Star families, may we never forget.

When a Veteran serves, it affects more than just the Veteran. The bond shared by those in service, their families, caregivers, and communities transforms them from a group of individuals to members of the military family. They are related to one another not just by blood, but through sacrifices of loyalty and intimate experiences only they can understand.

—Staff at Purple Heart Homes, established by
veterans Dale Beatty and John Gallina

# CONTENTS

# AUTHORS' NOTE

Susan's parents, 1st Lt. George L. Gurwell of the 508th Parachute Infantry Regiment (PIR) and his wife, Jeane, were prolific letter writers during WWII. The wartime letters of Susan's parents are unique. Their correspondence, numbering over one thousand letters, provides the timeline for their journey through WWII. The collection covers the time frame from the start of the 508th PIR at Camp Blanding, Florida to the final victory and occupation at the end of the war. As an officer in Regimental Headquarters Company (HqHq), Lt. Gurwell was assigned to process the personal effects of soldiers that had been wounded or killed in battle. As such, he had the opportunity and desire to ship personal materials home, such as Jeane's old letters, that few enlisted men or officers had. He also shipped home numerous documents and artifacts. This war-long correspondence provides a glimpse of the give-and-take between a paratrooper officer and his wife.

We used about 350 of Jeane and George's letters. We cataloged nearly eleven hundred of them in an Excel file, assigned them an ID number, entered the date and location of the writer, deduced the likely location of the addressee, made a subjective rating of the importance of the contents from one to five, and summarized the content using searchable keywords. Sorting the writings by date or author proved to be invaluable. We were also able to sort out about two-thirds of the letters that were "routine" and of lesser interest. This file allowed us to find letters by keyword.

There are two formats for dates used in the book. In general, but not always, American civilians in WWII used the month-day-year format. The armed forces generally used the European format of day-month year. The two formats are used consistently with the original documents. Sue's dad used the American format until he left for Europe at the end of December 1943. Following this time, he used the military format during the war. We left the format as in the original letters. The dates of the letters should be clear using either format. They are helpful to the reader in signaling a change in the next letter's author.

The authors and our editor, Gayle Wurst, edited the letters, especially for the numerous salutations and greetings that would make the text cumbersome. Let the reader rest assured there is no shortage of the Gurwells expressing their love for one another. At times we also edited out repetitive content, corrected misspelled words that would leave the text unclear, and used brackets around inserted text.

Using the historical record, George's documents, and the interview we had with him in 2001 was critical in determining the exact location from which he was writing. We did our best with this daunting task. Due to censorship regulations, he had to be at a location for about two weeks before he could write that in a letter home. We used George's timeline, paralleling the history of the 508th's movements to help determine when to present letters from home. Sometimes a letter would take a month or more for turnaround time, leading us to share letters not always in the sequence written, but grouped by which letters answered each other.

The Gurwell letters also provide a framework for understanding the other major component of the book: the Round Robin letters, a circular letter written by forty-eight of the officer's wives of the 508th PIR, including Jeane Gurwell, from January 1944 to May 1945. The wives are a who's who of notable officers in the 508th. Forty-five of the represented husbands dropped into France on D-Day, nearly a third of the officer corps of the 508th. These officers' wives included numerous clippings of articles/photographs from unnamed newspapers. Sadly, most of these clippings are obituaries for husbands killed in action. Unfortunately, we could identify the source for only one of the clippings after trying online, so we decided to use just a few photos from public sources. We are grateful to have access to the most excellent website, in our opinion, of any WWII unit: 508pir.org. This site was our best online resource for information on the husbands of the Round Robin writers. However, we would have been able to identify the rank and company of these officers from documents in the "Gurwell Collection" alone.

Now, we are happy to share our four-year journey producing this book with the reader.

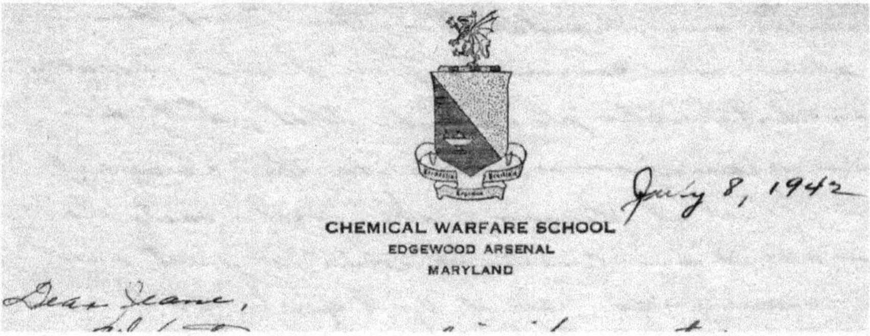

CHEMICAL WARFARE SCHOOL
EDGEWOOD ARSENAL
MARYLAND

July 8, 1942

Dear Jeane,

## INTRODUCTION

# THE JOURNEY BEGINS

### By Susan Gurwell Talley

I'm sitting here in my living room surrounded by nearly eleven hundred letters dating from World War II, dozens of military records, original maps, and documents concerning my dad's unit, the 508th Parachute Infantry Regiment. There is also a slew of my parents' personal effects: Dad's Class A uniform and Ike jacket, a boot that landed in Normandy (yes, there were two, but somehow one mysteriously wandered off), his airborne wings with two jump stars, his Combat Infantryman Badge and other medals, souvenir paratrooper jewelry he gave to my mom, and about a dozen cherished period photographs—and I'm feeling just a little overwhelmed.

How can I ever put this time capsule together in a meaningful way? How do I get started on this journey that my husband Jack and I have proposed to ourselves, the adventure of assembling this immense treasure trove of material to construct a coherent narrative for an inside look at World War II through the eyes and words of those who lived through it?

Over nine hundred of the letters sitting before me were exchanged between my parents, George L. Gurwell and Jeane S. Gurwell (formerly Jeane Roselyn Slonaker), from February 1940 to August 1945. The exchange begins three years before their marriage on April 11, 1943, and ends with a letter my father wrote from Frankfurt, Germany, after serving in all four campaigns of the 508th Parachute Infantry Regiment (PIR), attached to the 82nd Airborne Division (ABD). We also have correspondence from men who served with Dad, and nearly sixty other letters from their wives, most of whom had bonded together as a band of sisters during their husbands' training and continued to support each other during the war. Wartime correspondence from my grandparents, great-grandparents, aunts, uncles, and family friends are also all part of this group, which we now call "the Gurwell Collection."

The sheer number of letters and documents was mind-boggling. The initial attempt at organization entailed arranging the letters by postmark dates and eventually assigning them each an ID number, marked in pencil on the envelope, which we subsequently entered in an Excel file along with the date, the sender's and recipient's names and addresses, and a brief summary of the content. We could now sort the letters by date and author or do a keyword search for essential information. Our next task was to enlarge the letters so we could actually read them. While my parents' handwriting seemed easy enough to follow, scanning now became a priority. Enlargement was especially necessary when it came to the task of deciphering the minuscule print on V-mail[1] and the cursive—sometimes idiosyncratic—handwriting of other correspondents in the collection.

The documents date from May 1942, when my father was first assigned as a second lieutenant with the Chemical Warfare School at Edgewood Arsenal, but the majority cover the daily activities and workings of his second assignment as a paratrooper with the 508th PIR, where he served as the executive officer of the Regimental Headquarters Company (HqHq).[2] This position permitted him to collect, compile, and save the extraordinary range of documentation in the collection on the 508th and on the 82nd ABD in general: orders, a complete roster of the 508th from November 1943, original maps, after-action reports, and the daily newsletters printed aboard the transport ships that carried him to and from Europe.

While training in Florida on January 11, 1943, for example, the regiment's scheduled entertainment included boxing matches and the regiment singing en masse. On the back of the boxing schedule was a song, "Johnny Paratrooper," later changed and now famously known as "Blood on the Risers." One of the most moving documents is a list of all the officers on the ship to England, assigning seats for meals. In his own hand, my dad also entered the status of every man still on the list at the end of the war: OK (not injured), WIA (wounded in action), PW (prisoner of war), and KIA (killed in action).

And then there are the myriad of physical objects, each imbued with personal meaning for my parents, that also say so much about the world in which they lived. We might not have *both* of Dad's jump boots, but we do have the tiny survival compass and survival knife that was sewn into his jumpsuit for concealment when he landed in the flooded plain of the Merderet River near Sainte-Mère-Église on D-Day. I pick up the Colt .45 revolver that he carried as a sidearm throughout the war. One of Grandpa Slonaker's relatives had carried it in World War I, and Grandpa passed it on to Dad just before he headed overseas. Then I lay it back down, next to the delicate, solid gold chain bracelet that Dad gave Mom in 1943. In the center is a pair of airborne wings, flanked with the letters US and AA on either side. Next to that is a piece of the chute that dropped Dad into Normandy, as well as two handles from reserve chutes. We also have a section of the reserve chute that he cut up to make ascots for his men when they served as General Dwight D. Eisenhower's honor guard in the occupation of Germany. There are so many things, yet they are all treasures that testify to the lives of the brave men and women who unselfishly did their part to keep the world safe for those of us who followed.

**Wartime keepsakes from the Gurwell Collection. Top: Garrison hat and Ike Jacket. Center: Jump boot with gold bracelet, silk reserve chute, two rip cords, 82nd Airborne and 508th patches, fragment from D-Day chute. Bottom: Belgian Franc note with signatures, escape compass and knife, Nazi money.**

* * *

I was born and raised in Richland, Washington, just a stone's throw from the Columbia River in the eastern part of the state. Unlike western Washington with its rain forests and pine-covered mountains, eastern Washington is desert land, complete with sagebrush, cactus, tumbleweeds, prairie dogs, and rattlesnakes. Summer is dry and hot, and winter is mild, but spring and especially fall are surprisingly beautiful.

Growing up as the fourth child, I was the "baby" of the family. My older siblings, in order of birth, are Richard (Rick), Linda, and Janell. Rick was born on May 8, 1944, just one month before Dad jumped into Normandy. Linda was born three years after Rick, and Janell two years after Linda. I came along eight years after Janell. Although Janell swore that I was an adopted Indian baby, Mom assured me that out of the four of us, I was the only one they had planned on. The *other* three were the surprises.

Like most kids, I knew the basics about my parents. Dad was born in Idaho, but grew up in Seaside, Oregon. A chemical engineer, he managed a lab at the Hanford Nuclear Reservation, which used to be the old Camp Hanford Army Base where the plutonium was made for "Fat Man," the atomic bomb that was dropped on Nagasaki, Japan, at the end of World War II. After the war, it remained a restricted area with guard houses and large parking areas where workers parked their private vehicles, then traveled by special buses to and from the labs and reactors. For many people across the country, nuclear reactors raised concerns and fears, but for us and our community, they were just a part of our everyday life. One of my favorite T-shirts during my high school days said: *In case of a power outage, grab me. I glow in the dark.*

Then, as now, humor is the best medicine.

My mother's family, on the other hand, moved from Indiana to Oregon, where Mom grew up on the family fruit ranch in Hood River. She was a registered nurse and head of pediatrics at Kadlec Hospital in Richland. It was very reassuring for me to know that if I ever had to go to the hospital, Mom would be close at hand. About the time I was heading to junior high, she was headed to the local community college to begin her career as a nursing instructor.

I can't really say when I realized Dad had served in the war. He never spoke much about it, and as best as I can remember, Mom didn't either. There were little signs, though, one being a set of "Red Devil" water glasses that fascinated me as a young child. The glasses showed a picture of a red devil suspended under a parachute, wearing jump boots, and holding a rifle and a grenade. Kept safely on the highest shelf in the kitchen cabinet, these glasses were *off limits*, and somehow, I just knew that nothing good would come to me if I messed with them. I was told that they were special to Dad and held memories from his time in the army during the war. Not until I was nine or ten did I find out that the Red Devil stood for his regiment, the 508th PIR.

Other things, too, hinted at his service. In summer you could see the scar on his left leg, only visible when he wore shorts. I was told that it came from a wound he had received in the war. Strangely, Dad was not impressed by big July 4 fireworks displays, nor keen on attending the celebrations. He always said that he had seen the largest fireworks ever from behind Utah Beach, and nothing could compare to them. A shake of his head and a stare off into the distance usually followed.

Camping was another activity on his not-to-do list. He insisted he'd had enough of living in a tent during the war to last him a lifetime, and he never needed to do it again. I can't remember ever taking a family camping trip as I was growing up. That said, we kids had something even better—a full parachute canopy to use as a backyard tent. At the time, of course, I had no idea that our "tent" had landed in Holland on September 17, 1944, during Operation Market Garden. I was in junior high before I learned the story, and the significance of our childhood fort began to sink in. Later still, I learned that this parachute was not the one that Dad jumped into Holland with but one that was left behind intact on the drop zone. His chute had actually blown a panel out during the descent, so when he found a good one, he swapped it out. He would later say that parachute kept him alive during the freezing Battle of the Bulge, when he wrapped up in it for an extra layer of warmth inside his bedroll.

**Sue and George with the parachute used by the 508th in Market Garden that George mailed home to Jeane in 1945. Richland, WA, June 21, 2002.**

This very same bedroll also evokes significant memories for me. Whenever we visited my maternal grandparents in Hood River, we carried it along to serve as my sleeping pallet. I also remember coming across a bunch of small, black-and-white pictures at my grandparents' house that showed some men and bicycles lying around on the ground. I was just a little girl and had gotten no more than a fascinating glimpse before grown-up hands snatched them away. "You don't need to see these," I was told. Just why not, I did not know, but what I'd seen remained all the more strongly engraved on my mind because of it. Only in 2001, when Dad told Jack and me the story, did I learn that those men scattered on the ground were dead—German bicycle troops Dad and some others had cut off and killed on D-Day morning. Tellingly, the photos of the dead bicycle troops were missing from the collection when we received it.

Yes, as a child I knew that Dad was in the war, but it took a long time to piece together enough details to understand why he never talked about it. As I got older and learned more about history, my interest in my father's involvement in the war also began to grow. I never pressed him for information, but occasionally I would ask him simple questions, hoping for answers. In his own way and on his own timetable, he eventually shared a bit more about his life in service. The mystery of the water glasses now was solved: he was a paratrooper in the 508th, and his regiment was called the Red Devils. The German soldiers called them "devils in baggy pants." He also jumped behind enemy lines into Normandy on D-Day, jumped into Holland for Operation Market Garden, and jumped out of the back of a truck for the Battle of the Bulge. His leg wound occurred in Normandy, and he was sent back to a hospital in England. About the only information that my mom ever shared was that Dad was part of Eisenhower's honor guard.

Whenever Memorial Day came around, movies like *The Longest Day* and *A Bridge Too Far* would always be shown on TV. Dad would get a long, distant stare and make comments like "It didn't happen that way" or "We didn't fire our weapons while descending during a jump. Our weapons weren't loaded." He would shake his head and mutter about the British stopping to brew tea in Holland, or vent his frustration about how his regiment and the entire 82nd ABD were told to stand down when they wanted to go into Arnhem to rescue the surrounded British paratroopers. Without him saying much, you knew he was not very fond of the British army commander, Field Marshal Bernard Montgomery, aka "Monty." I watched these movies repeatedly, keeping Dad's comments in mind. Meanwhile, he was constantly getting up and leaving the room, only to return for a very short time, and then leave again. He never once sat and watched a movie with me all the way through.

The stories he did tell were mostly funny and concerned only a few of his experiences. In Normandy, he landed in the flooded fields around the Merderet River. Luckily for him, the water only came to his waist, not over his head. He never told us how he got wounded, but we loved to hear the story about how he terrorized a young orderly while he was in the hospital in England. Knowing that he was a paratrooper, the orderly was always pestering him for information and stories. Tired of this, one day Dad hid his trench knife under his blankets and waited for the orderly to return. When he approached his bedside, Dad let out a big "*AAAARRRGGGHHHH!*" and raised his knife in the air, pointed right at the orderly. The poor fellow ran out terrified, but quickly returned with "Sarge"—a tough, six-foot nurse who kept everyone in line and who nobody messed with. Laughing, Dad said he never tried pulling that stunt again.

In Holland, Dad worried that his troops did not have enough rations out in the field, so one time he loaded up a jeep and headed to the front lines to check on his men. He arrived to find they had just butchered a cow—"collateral damage" from the fighting, naturally—and were getting ready to cook steaks. When asked if he wanted one, he quickly replied, "Of course!" Other times, Dad told us about watching enemy tracers, and how beautiful they were as he jumped into the darkness on D-Day. He quickly changed his mind as to their beauty when he realized they were mixed in with regular rounds aimed at him with the intent to kill. He also kept a special poem in the old rolltop desk that was written by a sergeant in his regiment. It was about a deadly premonition this sergeant had about his jump into Normandy. Unfortunately, this premonition came true.

Another soldier had a premonition that he shared with Dad: in the vision, this soldier had to cross a minefield, but did not survive it. (This one also sadly came true.) Even Dad had his own premonition. Near the end of the war, after his regiment had made it through the Battle of the Bulge and the Hürtgen Forest, the 508th was placed on standby to jump into prisoner of war camps in case the Nazis began to kill prisoners. Dad always said that he just *knew* if they had made one of those jumps, it would have been his last. They loaded up three different times, but thankfully, never had to go.

Years later, when Dad was in his early eighties, Jack and I went to visit my parents. He and I had been dating for over a year, and it was time to introduce him to my family. Dad and Jack hit it off immediately. Dad felt very comfortable with Jack, who is a highly trained, experienced therapist with a specialty in treating post-traumatic stress disorder (PTSD). Soon the floodgates opened. Over the week, Dad shared many of his experiences in detail, including how and where he got wounded in Normandy. He also broke down and cried as he related the story of having to send a soldier out with a vital message when communication lines went down. This meant the soldier had to cross a minefield. The soldier most qualified to handle the job was the one who'd had that premonition that he wouldn't make it back. Dad tried to find someone else who could possibly handle the mission, but there was no one. After much soul-searching, he finally had to send the soldier out. He didn't make it, and Dad blamed himself.

He'd been holding in that guilt for over fifty years.

* * *

Before Dad passed, he asked us to donate some of the items he'd saved, like a full canopy from Market Garden and his bedroll from the Battle of the Bulge. We felt these things needed to be available for the world to see, not stuck in some box hidden away in an attic or garage. Following his wishes, these now have a permanent home at the Camp Blanding Museum in Florida, where the 508th got its start in 1942. And yes, the canopy in question was once the beloved tent of the Gurwell kids.

After his passing, we discovered several more boxes containing letters, documents, and war-related items in the basement of our family home. Mom gave these boxes and their precious contents to Jack and me to preserve. It's hard to admit, but I struggled for many years to read my parents' letters. I desperately wanted to learn more about my father and this period in both their lives, but the letters were very personal. Reading them tugged at my heart and awakened the feelings of loss I felt for my father. It would just take time. Not until my mother passed in 2016 and we took a trip to Europe to follow the wartime footsteps of the 508th, did we hunker down and finally begin the journey of discovery those boxes and all their contents were to send us on.

And what an amazing journey it has turned out to be.

As I read through the letters, examined the documents, and figured out the various historic keepsakes in our treasure trove, the full picture finally began to come into view. Those "Red Devil" glasses I grew up with? They're mentioned in a letter from Mom to Dad in August 1944. They must have been purchased in Pinehurst, North Carolina, where they lived in 1943 while Dad was in training. Mom wrote that she was unpacking them and putting them on the top shelf in the kitchen cabinet of her apartment in Portland, Oregon. No matter where we lived, that never changed: those glasses always went on the top shelf of the kitchen cabinets.

Another letter from Mom to her father mentions the Colt .45 revolver. She was surprised that he had sent that specific, special revolver for Dad to carry overseas. We also have Dad's letter to his father-in-law, expressing his gratitude for the handgun and what a wonderful weapon it was. A letter Dad sent Mom just before he jumped on D-Day was obviously written with death in mind, a "final letter" to express his enduring love in case he did not survive. Two very special letters from 1945 retrospectively recount Dad's experience in the Normandy invasion; another says he is sending her a piece of the silk that set him down in France (yes, we do have it, as we finally discovered in 2018!) and the parachute from Holland. And so it was that one by one, the letters acted as a commentary on the items in our possession, my parents' relationship, and the wartime experiences of a young parachute infantry officer and his wife, including the environment and times that they lived in.

Jack's experience in treating veterans and civilians who suffer from PTSD brought to light how many symptoms my father's letters reveal. Four days of combat in Normandy had triggered significant distress. He was shot through the muscle of the left leg on D-Day, and soldiered on for three more days before finally being evacuated to a hospital in England. He returned to his regiment for light duty on June 22. I was also surprised, because when we think of PTSD, we usually don't attribute it to veterans of World War II. Yes, my father's generation did speak of the "thousand-yard stare" or "battle fatigue" that caused them to be listed as casualties. Even my father spoke about seeing men who had lost their ability to function. One officer he witnessed started walking down the middle of the road in a skirmish, as if nothing was going on. He appeared dazed and confused—and was lucky not to be killed. Just as most do today, soldiers in World War II largely suffered the symptoms of PTSD in silence, and psychologically continued to function as the "walking wounded."

As we were sorting out the family letters, I also discovered a large olive drab green envelope separate from the rest. But it, too, was filled with letters. This packet gave us the opportunity to meet forty-eight of the wives of my father's fellow 508th officers through a unique set of letters the women wrote to each other in "Round-Robin" style to keep in touch and pass on information about the regiment and their menfolk.

The letters functioned like a group email today, only slower, as it went through the U.S. postal system. After establishing an initial list, the first correspondent wrote to the following woman on the list, who read the letter, added her own, and mailed it with the first letter to the third correspondent, and so forth. The last recipient would end up with all the letters. My mom, who was instrumental in cooking up this scheme, was third on the list. The Round Robin did not reach her again until after Victory in Europe (VE) Day; by then, it had traveled from Maine to Florida and coast to coast three times, and bore addresses from twenty-six states. The entire correspondence, spanning seventeen months, ended its journey with her. It was truly an All-American effort, all the way.[3]

Many of the forty-eight Round Robin correspondents had met each other, and often formed close ties while they were living in the little towns surrounding Camp Mackall, where their officer husbands were training for overseas combat. Along the way, original correspondents sometimes brought in friends, wives of 508th men who had met a few—but not all—of the others in the Round Robin circle. The letters express not only their pride and support for their men, but also the emotional and active support for each other that only a "band of sisters" could share. Held together by common bonds in the most difficult of times, these women knew their "sisters" could understand their experiences and emotions better than anyone else.

Jack and I caught ourselves laughing at their humorous stories, and then shedding tears as we learned about the deaths of eleven young husbands and troopers. We experienced the bravery of these young widows as they described the loss of their husbands, relying heavily on the bonds of friendship to get them through their ordeal. One such widow was Jane Creary, who shared these heartfelt words in December 1944 after the death of her husband: "Remember girls, we are paratroopers too, and we cannot give up the jump."

Only a third of the nearly 1,100 letters and two hundred documents in our possession are featured in this book. Due to its uniqueness, however, we have included all fifty Round Robin letters in excerpt or in their entirety. Our hope is that in sharing these treasures, others may find insight, hope, and encouragement for the future from the rich heritage the World War II generation has left us.

May you gain courage, faith, and strength from their stories and the example of their lives. May their voices speak out from the past and continue to inspire us to be the best of ourselves. Let us never forget them and always remember: "Never give up the jump."

# Post-Traumatic Stress Disorder and World War II Veterans

## By Jack Talley

I could not wait to meet Lt George Gurwell, an original member of the 508th Parachute Infantry Regiment, U.S. 82nd Airborne Division, and a veteran of D-Day, Operation Market Garden, and the Battle of the Bulge. It was chance that determined I would meet George, my wife Sue's father, on June 6, 2001, fifty-seven years to the day since D-Day, a day that has fascinated me ever since I learned about it as a boy. Why this should be so for a young kid growing up on a small subsistence farm in north Georgia I do not know, but television shows like *Combat!* and *The Rat Patrol* and movies like *The Longest Day*, *A Bridge Too Far*, and *Sands of Iwo Jima* made a lasting impression on me.

When I was ten, my older brother of three years would be outside learning to shoe a horse, or off making mischief with my cousins, trying to saddle up and ride grandpa's calves, and I'd be inside reading *The Rise and Fall of the Third Reich*. Years later, I reread that book and was surprised to find I'd understood enough at the time to fuel a lifelong quest to comprehend what had happened to the world in the 1930s and '40s. How did entire nations come to believe so strongly in the values of Nazism and Japanese imperialism that they executed national policies that ultimately killed seventy million people? One day in college, I was sitting on a bench reading *The Gulag Archipelago* as I waited for the dining room to open. "What class are you reading that for?" a student asked me. When I told her it was just for fun, I got the weirdest look.

Another thing I'll never know is why I chose psychology instead of history as a profession. But I do know that the biggest reason I love war heroes is because their stories give me strength, moral courage, and the best role models.

I have needed those strong role models in my professional work. In 1978, just out of college, I began working as a psychiatric assistant with adolescents in a psychiatric hospital. After completing a master's degree, and then a doctorate in 1989, I worked with school-age children in homes for abused kids, as well as a wide variety of other settings: schools, churches, hospitals, jails, and the office of my private practice. It is not an exaggeration to say that some of the things that children have told me about what adults have done to them is evil in every sense of the word.

Hearing these stories firsthand is difficult: professionals who work with traumatized people often suffer from compassion fatigue and have to take deliberate steps to prevent suffering trauma themselves. I myself turn to heroic stories from World War II because they never fail to inspire me. I have never seen tracers flying up at me as my parachute descended toward a body of water that I feared would drown me in my chute, but hearing the story of a paratrooper like George, who experienced that fear and survived gives me the strength to help wounded children.

So it is that the war veteran's story also helps the victim of child abuse find a way to heal.

I retired from school system work a few years ago, retrained as a specialist, and have been working with veterans with post-traumatic stress disorder (PTSD) since 2014. Widely (and sometimes loosely) used today, the term was not officially recognized in diagnosis until 1980. Until that time, "shell shock" or "battle fatigue" were the terms for a soldier who had ceased to function. So many battle-weary veterans witnessed the "thousand-yard stare" in their buddies or experienced it themselves. While we now better understand more about the disorder than in World War II, I can attest as a clinician that it is nevertheless still widely misunderstood or ignored today, not only in the general public, but also by the very veterans who themselves are suffering from PTSD.

The vast majority of veterans I have evaluated are surprised by the breadth and depth of PTSD symptoms. By definition, the conditions for developing combat-related PTSD occur when a soldier has experienced, witnessed, or confronted critical incidents that involved actual or threatened death, or serious injury to the soldier or others. Core symptoms of PTSD can manifest when memories trigger nightmares, intrusive thoughts, anxious emotions, and physical symptoms. Recurrent, involuntary dreams or distressing memories are major signs of the disorder, as are flashbacks, distress when cues or reminders occur, hypervigilance, startle responses, and marked physical reactions, such as racing heartbeat, sweaty palms, and shortness of breath. So the veteran constantly tries to avoid distressing memories, feelings, and cues that eventually trigger those memories and physical reactions. Racing thoughts, poor concentration, and survivors' guilt are also common.

Complicating symptoms vary widely. Most common is sleep disturbance. Patients also frequently suffer from depression, anxiety, emotional numbing, panic attacks, memory loss, flattened emotional responsiveness, lowered motivation, poor stress tolerance, and interpersonal problems. Self-medication with alcohol or other intoxicating substances is widespread. Severe cases involve impaired judgment and communication, suicidal ideation, psychotic symptoms, failure to communicate, neglect of personal hygiene, inability to perform routine daily living tasks, and grossly impaired behavior. The range of functional impairment is broad, thus requiring individual assessment.

Lieutenant Colonel Dave Grossman, a specialist in the psychology of combat, has extensively studied the reactions of healthy people in killing circumstances. A former army Ranger, paratrooper, and law enforcement trainer, Grossman persuasively argues that not only fear for oneself—but having to kill other humans in an up close and personal way—contributes significantly to the onset of PTSD.[4] In the past few years, the historical picture has been clarified concerning the training of U.S. paratroopers and the fate of the Germans they encountered on D-Day. In order to protect their positions on the night of June 6, troopers were instructed to not use firearms, but bayonets and knives whenever possible. In other words—they were told to kill the enemy in personal, hand-to-hand combat. As one green 101st trooper put it, they were to "get to the drop zone as quickly as possible. Take no prisoners because they'll slow you down."[5]

The 82nd certainly received a version of the same from their superiors, as First Sergeant Ralph Thomas of the 508th reports: "We had been ordered before we left the airport for Normandy not to take any prisoners."[6] While these were tall orders for young soldiers in their first taste of combat, the mercilessness of the enemy turned them into killers inspired by their fear and desire for revenge. As Captain William Nation, Regimental S-1, succinctly put it in a letter home, dated June 24–25, 1944: "Everything that you read about the ruthlessness they [the Germans] gave us is true and more, and I'll add that it was a long time before we could get the men to take prisoners."[7]

PTSD-causing events the troopers experienced on D-Day need not be *directly* experienced or witnessed in person according to the Department of Veterans Affairs; they can also result if the service member learns that a critical incident happened to a close friend or family member. Blocking these memories from mind is a common strategy that does not work, because memories made during a critical event are seared into the brain by the flood of neurotransmitters triggered by the fight-or-flight response. They simply will not go away. Specifically developed talk therapies like cognitive-behavioral therapies, bilateral stimulation such as eye movements, and exposure therapies all help veterans reprocess the information in their memories in ways that diminish their power over the mind and permit them to cope with the past.[8] As one veteran testified: "Just write about it or talk about it. Nothing else works."[9]

***

George gave a gift to the veterans I treat, since they appreciate hearing a story from the perspective of a veteran who fought on D-Day, and without exception, find it similar to their own experiences. George's stories certainly have the "been there, done that" quality to them that today's veterans appreciate.

I couldn't have been more pleased about the symbolism of our meeting on D-Day, and my wife Sue—at the time my fiancée—was equally happy that I would finally get to meet her father on such a significant day. A couple of months before the trip, Sue had been surprised when George stayed on the phone with me, talking about the war for an hour. This was a first. The joy of actually meeting him, however, was tempered by the stroke he had suffered four days before we arrived. Sue was very relieved to see her father by the time we got there. While he had lost the use of his right hand, his mind, speech, and legs were fine. Mom (Jeane Gurwell) had limited mobility, so Sue and I took over most of the cooking. Jeane was impressed that I could make "fluffy" scrambled eggs and wanted to know my secret. My reply of "add a little water and don't burn them" brought laughter from George and Sue that I did not understand until they explained Jeane's reputation for scorched food.

**George and Jeane, Seaside, OR, 2002.**

On that first morning of our stay, George was sitting in his usual morning spot, the breakfast nook near the kitchen bay window in order to see his "critters" in the backyard. He fed daily the squirrels, quail, and other birds, and had names for most of them. He particularly liked seeing quail and their "little ones" on their morning visits to the yard for breakfast.

I had reread Stephen Ambrose's *D-Day* and *Citizen Soldiers* before the trip. In *D-Day*, I had been struck by the actions of a 508th PIR hero named Robert Mathias, a red-haired boxing champion from Baltimore. The jump master of his stick, he had ordered his men to stand up and hook up, and was standing in the open doorway of his C-47, ready to go, when antiaircraft fire hit him right in the middle of his reserve chute and pierced his chest. Refusing medical treatment, he led his men out into Normandy's night. He was later found dead in his chute, hanging from a tree.

During our conversation with George that first night, I asked him almost casually if he knew the name Robert Mathias. George turned ashen, as if he had seen a ghost. Then he turned the tables: "How do *you* know that name?" he demanded. When I told him about Ambrose's account of Mathias's action that morning in France fifty-seven years in the past, he seemed dumbfounded. "Well," he said, "I guess there aren't any secrets anymore."

I was as surprised with George that Mathias's name held so much meaning for him as he was surprised with me that I knew the name at all. Mathias was, in fact, the *only* name of a 508th trooper I'd learned from my reading prior to the trip. As it turned out, 1st Lt. Mathias had been George's singing buddy and pal since their training days in Pinehurst, North Carolina, and Jeane and Mathias's wife, Doris, had also been close. When we visited Sue's parents in 2001, we had no idea that George had even *known* Mathias, let alone that they had been good friends. The sudden loss of such a friend is often a major factor in the long list of factors causing PTSD in combat veterans, and the death of Robert Mathias, one of the early casualties of the Normandy invasion, without a doubt had contributed to the emergence of PTSD in George.

For five nights in a row, Sue and I stayed up talking with George long into the night, amazed that after all these years, he had finally decided to share his war stories. I had come prepared with a recorder, extra tapes, and extra batteries. I used none of it, deciding it would be best just to talk with him for a while. I would try and remember as best I could and make notes with Sue's help after we finished talking.

I felt very lucky to hear George's firsthand accounts, many of which he seemed to be telling for the first time. Sue later confirmed that this was indeed the first time her father had ever sat down and shared his experiences and feelings. The whole family felt relieved, having long sensed the unspoken anguish he'd carried through the years.

It was long past time for George to get the stories off his chest.

This is not to say that talking came easy. Like most of the men who fought in World War II, George downplayed what had happened. "We just all did what we were supposed to do. I don't understand the fuss." He made more protests. "What good will talking about this do, anyway? Civilizations come and they all fall. It doesn't matter what we do— this one is going to fall too. Nobody cares about this stuff anymore."

His words struck me hard, and it was hard to argue with him. His cynicism, born of war and a life working in nuclear munitions, would be hard to defeat. I paused, took a deep breath, and answered, "It doesn't matter if it'll do any good or not. It doesn't matter if it will work or not. I believe what you did can be an inspiration to others, and future generations must be told your story. It may also help others rise above their troubles. Any person who goes to war and comes back alive is a hero to me."

"Well," he answered, "there's just no way to understand what we felt and went through if you weren't there yourself." Here George stopped, looked away, and went silent.

Sue and I sat with him, quiet for a while. Then I softly began to speak. "I've tried very hard to understand the children I work with. They have been through all sorts of hell. I'll never understand what it's like to be that girl or boy who suffered abuse, but I do know that to heal from the pain, it first takes the courage to talk about it.

"True, I have not been in combat. I have not been in the military. But I've read about World War II and tried to understand how the world could kill seventy million people ever since I was a boy. I have also tried to understand by reading books and talking with veterans about what happened during the war."

Throughout this whole speech, I tried to be as calm and persuasive as I could. "I have always thought that the veteran who withstood the test of combat is one of the best examples of how to rise over adversity in life." Then I told George, "Jesus said, 'Greater love hath no man than this, that a man lay down his life for his friends.' Men who've been in combat, even if they weren't killed, at some point have put their lives in harm's way, or 'laid down their life' for their buddy."

George began to loosen up. I think he started to like me too. When I later used the word *reppel-deppel*, he was surprised I knew it was soldier slang for a replacement depot. And I also knew the name Robert Mathias. It was enough. George decided to talk.

HARRY R. CLIFF, M. D.
DIRECTOR

DAVID W. E. BAIRD, M. D.
ASSOCIATE DIRECTOR

EMMA E. JONES, R. N.
SUPERINTENDENT

**MULTNOMAH HOSPITAL**
MARQUAM HILL
PORTLAND, OREGON

June 15, 1943

# CHAPTER I

# PRELUDE TO LOVE AND WAR

My father was born in 1920 in Jerome, Idaho, to George W. and Pearl M. Gurwell. At an early age, he moved with his family to Seaside, Oregon, where his paternal grandparents, James L. and Mable Gurwell, owned and ran a grocery store just a few blocks from the beach.

Dad, fondly called "Junior" by his father and grandparents, grew up with all the wonders that the ocean could provide, and the tides would bring in. Chasing birds over sandy beaches, playing in the waves, hunting for shells, and digging razor clams were all part of his boyhood, as was exploring rocky tide pools full of starfish, sea anemones, crabs and mussels. Fishing for all kinds of saltwater fish were favorite activities. Most of all, he loved deep-sea fishing for King salmon. As if that were not enough abundance, the sand dunes were covered in wild strawberries and the forests full of wild mushrooms. Seaside was a true cornucopia of coastal life to any young child growing up.

In first grade, my father developed a close friendship with two other Seaside characters, Bud Leonard and Dave Scoggins. So close, they were more like brothers than friends; the boys were as inseparable as *The Three Musketeers*. Dave's parents owned and operated the upscale beachfront Tides Hotel, a popular Seaside destination, and Bud hailed from a large family with several kids. It wasn't uncommon for both Dad and Dave to file through the Leonard family lunch line along with the rest of the hoard, making a sandwich with whatever Bud's mom put out on the kitchen counter.

Seaside and its environs were a boy's paradise, offering an abundance of opportunity for adventure through outdoor activities such as hunting, fishing, and pulling crab pots. One of the most memorable escapades involved a hunting trip that Dad and Bud took along the mountainous Necanicum River. Bud had borrowed a box of ammunition and a rifle belonging to Dad's father, and as luck would have it, they got the jump on a rather large black bear. Bud fired the shot and nailed the bear. But lady luck had other ideas. The bear unfortunately ended up in the river, rather than on the bank, as planned. It was so huge and heavy, no matter how hard they tried, they could not drag it out of the water. And so the river won. Wet, muddy, and tired, they hopelessly watched as their bear, caught up in the rushing water, disappeared over a waterfall. Out of sight, it continued its journey along the river and out into the Pacific Ocean. As for the boys, such experiences created a special bond that remained strong throughout childhood and well into their adult lives.

**George on the right with childhood friend, 1st Lt Julien "Bud" Leonard, USMC, November 11, 1942, Seaside, OR. Gurwell Collection.**

**George's childhood friend 1st Lt Dave Scoggins, about 1942. Dave served in the 80th Infantry Division in the Normandy and Ardennes Campaigns. Gurwell Collection.**

During adolescence, my father experienced the separation and divorce of his parents, his father's remarriage to Annebelle, or "Babe," his stepmother, and the couples' adoption of his little brother Dick. Babe was a wonderful person, and Dad felt that she was truly a mother to him. His "little" brother, who grew up to be well over six feet tall (compared to Dad's 5'7"), idolized his "big" brother, and Dad always loved him as if he were his own flesh and blood. School, running track, and working odd jobs kept Dad busy, but theatre, music, the ocean, and the wonders of nature brought him his sense of peace and enjoyment.

With the Depression in full swing, Dad worked various jobs to earn enough money to enroll in college. He assisted at the family grocery store, worked in a bakery, and even spent some time as a lumberjack. He was not afraid of hard work and appreciated the value of a strong work ethic. When it came time to go to college, he enrolled at Oregon State Agricultural College in Corvallis, Oregon, where he joined the ROTC (Reserve Officers' Training Corps) program through the School of Military Science and Tactics with the intention of serving as an U.S. Army officer. It was during his college days that he met and occasionally dated Jeane R. Slonaker, the future Mrs. Gurwell, who was at Oregon State to complete the preparatory course work for nursing school and become a registered nurse.

From a very young age, my mother called Hood River, Oregon home. She was born in Farmland, Indiana to Richard and Delpha Slonaker on September 26, 1920 (so her birth certificate said). For years we celebrated her birthday on the twenty-fifth because her mother swore the doctor got it wrong, and Jeane really did arrive on the twenty-fifth, not the twenty-sixth. Much later in life, our family agreed to go along with the birth certificate and acknowledge her birthday on the twenty-sixth, but Grandma never gave up insisting that she arrived the day before.

The Slonakers come from a long line of family farmers. Mom's parents moved to Hood River partly for its beauty: overlooking the Columbia River basin, their front porch commanded a view of the orchard with an unimpeded view of Mt. Hood, and the back overlooked the garden and Mt. Adams. But they mainly chose Hood River for the rich, volcanic soil that would enable them to create the fruit ranch of their dreams. They soon began to establish the orchard with pear, apple, and cherry trees. They also raised hogs, chickens, and turkeys, grew a large vegetable garden, and developed a grape arbor.

Grandpa loved hunting game, fishing in the Columbia River, and gathering the wild morel mushrooms that grew abundantly in the nearby woods. He became very close to the local Dalles Indian tribe and learned many of their traditions and skills. Over the years, they traded all kinds of amazing things back and forth that we treasured immensely as kids and still treasure today. I can remember many wonderful items: handwoven baskets full of Indian arrowheads, handcrafted and decorated deerskin moccasins and clothing, as well as a beautiful papoose board. The only thing that I was not too fond of was the bearskin rug, one of Grandpa's trophies, that lay on the floor in the upstairs bedroom. As a small child, I once snuck up those closed-off, very steep stairs, only to bravely reach the top and come face-to-face with that bear. You have never seen a child scurry down a set of stairs so fast! You can be sure that I never did that again!

My grandparent's first child, Robert, died in infancy three years before Mom was born, so she grew up as an only child. Being active was a big part of her life: she loved hunting and fishing with her father and developed a love for the outdoors. Her favorite activities included basketball, swimming, and riding "Peaches," her very own horse. But most of all, she loved snow skiing. Skiing was a new sport in America, and Mt. Hood was just starting to establish its ski slopes, having installed two rope tows and two chairlifts. Not to be outdone, Mom would tag along with the boys to ski the challenging trails of the still-wild slopes.

As for the more domestic arts, my grandmother succeeded in teaching her sewing, but cooking was never one of her strong suits. She did, however, share both of her parents' tremendous love of gardening. She always looked forward to springtime, so full of blossoming fruit trees and flowers of all kinds, and especially loved the wild violets that grew abundantly throughout the lawns, gardens, and orchards around Hood River. In a letter Dad wrote to Mom from North Carolina shortly after they were married, we were touched to discover a pressed violet he had sent her, knowing how much she adored them.

The Slonaker family was extremely blessed during the Great Depression, as they ran a highly successful fruit ranch and were able to employ workers, rather than having to search for work like so many others. While most people struggled to feed their families, they were not only able to survive but to thrive and continue to expand. Life was full of hard work, though. The struggle against losing crops, machine breakdowns, and the ever-pressing need to obtain machine parts, gasoline, and good help was difficult, but also richly rewarding in many ways. Grandpa oversaw everything about the orchard, supervising and hiring the seasonal help, planting new trees, and making sure all the equipment was in tip-top shape. Grandma also kept up all the books, helping in the packing house as needed, and took in sewing as a seamstress, along with performing the everyday tasks of housework and cooking. She and Grandpa together attended to their chickens, hogs, and garden. No sitting around and being idle here!

The garden was one of my mother's favorite places to help with chores—cooking, not so much. Growing up in this environment instilled a strong spirit, a "can-do" attitude, and self-reliance in my mom that always carried her through difficult times. As much as she loved gardening, her real passion was nursing; she had always wanted to become a nurse. As my sisters and I grew up, she constantly dropped hints that nursing was a great career, but try as she might, we didn't follow her into the profession.

With her degree in mind, Mom headed off to Oregon State Agricultural College in 1938, planning to become a registered nurse. Her goal was to join the U.S. Army Nurses Corps, and she was firmly committed to completing the five-year course of study needed to acquire her nursing credentials. When she first met Dad at Oregon State, they dated off and on, enjoying a shared love of dancing, but kept the relationship light. Dad remained in Corvallis to finish his chemistry degree after Mom left for nursing school in Portland, and given the distance between them, their dancing days faded away. In a letter written July 8, 1942, Dad confesses: "Believe it or not, you, Miss Slonaker, caused me more speculation than any other girl that I have met. You didn't fall into any of my classifications. As a result, I had wonderful fun trying to figure you out. No, I haven't yet, but I think that the decision is quite close. The classification? The answer is that you have one all to yourself and it is an extremely nice category."

This, of course, kept him interested.

My father kept up with Mom through mutual friends, and just before he graduated, he made a phone call that changed both their lives. He contacted the student Nurses Home and asked to speak to her, uncertain that she would even take his call. Mom kept him waiting for agonizing minutes while she hesitated and spoke to a mutual friend, but finally came on the line. This rekindled their relationship, and shortly afterwards Dad gave Mom his pin—the sign that they were "going steady." Ok, maybe the fact that he had pinned another girl in the past had something to do with Mom's initial hesitation. I'm not saying my mom was the jealous type, but to quote her exact words, she did say she was something of a "green-eyed monster."

On May 29, 1942, my father graduated with a degree in chemistry from Oregon State and was appointed and commissioned into the U.S. Army as a second lieutenant. He was called to active duty and reported on June 10, 1942 to the Commanding General for the Chemical Warfare Service Replacement Pool at Edgewood Arsenal, Maryland. On June 29, he began his studies in the Chemical Warfare Combined Basic and Troop Officers' Course. Around the same time, Dad's close friends, Dave Scoggins and Bud Leonard, also answered Uncle Sam's call. Dave, commissioned as a second lieutenant in the U.S. Army, headed to England to serve in a transportation company. Bud, commissioned as a second lieutenant in the Marine Corps, was destined for combat in the Pacific.

When Dad headed off to his duty assignment, Mom was at the train station to see him off. Over the next several months, their relationship developed through numerous letters, sharing everything about themselves and their daily lives: high points, low points, frustrations, joys, and future hopes and dreams. They encouraged each other, lifted each other up during difficult times, and laughed over silly escapades. They also wrote about why the war had to be fought.

Dad graduated from his course on August 15 and soon found himself teaching troops about chemical warfare and serving on a court-martial board. In letters to Mom, he complained that "teaching chemical warfare deals more with weather than chemistry" and signaled his dislike of "playing judge." He suggested that if there ever was an emergency, the officers of the 5th Chemical Company, where he was assigned, would be lucky if they could manage to work together long enough to solve the problem. To relieve his frustrations, he ended up regularly playing cards and drinking a fifth of Bushmills Whiskey with fellow officers. This became a main off-duty evening activity.

Clearly, it was time to put in for a transfer. I remember Dad saying when I was growing up: "If I had stayed at Edgewood Arsenal, I probably would have died an alcoholic, and the war would have been over before I got the chance to go overseas." The last thing he wanted was to be stuck stateside. Although he was never too fond of heights, he figured he had two options: go back to school to become a pilot, or look to join one of the newly formed paratroop regiments. In the end, the paratroopers won out, and he was officially assigned to the 508th PIR on October 29, 1942.

The 508th PIR was activated at Camp Blanding, Florida, on October 20, 1942 under the command of Lieutenant Colonel Roy E. Lindquist (later a full colonel). The regiment was an all-volunteer unit; every paratrooper had to make the cut physically and mentally, just as they must in today's Special Forces. Many of the volunteers were there one day and gone the next. Men who survived the cut could look forward to physically and mentally draining extensive training drills, lack of sleep, exhausting work, and specialized training directed towards molding individuals into a cohesively functioning unit. Push-ups and constant running became a way of life. This not only developed some of the best soldiers the army had to offer, but also formed strong bonds of brotherhood, like those that exist among paratroopers today.

Shortly after his arrival at Camp Blanding, Dad wrote to the *Seaside Signal*, his hometown newspaper. The undated clipping describes his training in Florida and conveys the sense of pride that he and all new paratroopers felt in belonging to an elite, all-volunteer fighting force.

> "George Gurwell Now a Paratrooper"
>
> I want to express my appreciation for the work the *Signal* is doing. The service men's column is an excellent idea and through it, I have managed to keep track of a number of my friends. After my leave last November, I flew back across the country from Portland to Jacksonville, Florida. I am now stationed at Camp Blanding with the 508th Parachute Infantry, a little south of Jacksonville.
>
> The 'Paratroops' is an excellent outfit. The men are new, but the best I have ever seen. (Tough has a new meaning for me.) We receive all types of exercise in abundance. Walking or marching is out. When paratroops travel on foot they run, and I don't mean maybe! Our trouble is, when we have time to play, we play too hard and often get hurt just fooling around. I might add, with all due respect to Marines and sailors—they have a healthy respect for paratroopers [which] they have learned in the school of hard knocks. I don't want to give anyone the idea that paratroopers aren't gentlemen, because they are, but they are taught from the bottom up to protect themselves and believe me they can!

Dad's correspondence to his soon-to-be wife gives a more humorous, yet still proud look at some of the antics he and his buddies took part in, which were equally part of the bonding experience. The instance below puts training and derring-do to a quick test, as the 508th arrives just in the nick of time to heroically avert a local disaster on their way to get a beer. The letter is dated November 24, 1942, the day before Thanksgiving.

> Dearest Nurse,
>
> Last night was quite eventful. My hut mate and a friend of his decided to go to Starke (a little town near Camp Blanding, FL) for a quick show and home. They asked me to take in the show with them. After the cinema, being thirsty from salty popcorn, we took off for the only beer parlor and bar open, something like twenty miles away. The three of us happy as larks were just chanting "seven more miles to go" when.... No—not a flat tire—we roared past a store in some small, little village.... No—not arrested. Don Hardwick (Ripstitch to me)[10] and I noticed a most peculiar type of window display

> that looked like a barbecue spit with flames and everything. Naturally we marveled at the advertising—Heck! It was the real McCoy, a fire burning away cheerily!
>
> Hal [Creary] slammed on the brakes—Ripstitch and I bailed out going miles an hour. No one knew about it then, but two minutes later, half the kids and the storekeeper knew about the fire. As usual no one did anything—so—Hal, Rip, and I pulled off our dress coats and waded into the smoke-filled store. No hoses, no nothing but a Coca-Cola machine filled with water and bottles of milk. Found a can, and after being forced out three times because of smoke—the three of us put the darned thing out.
>
> Other than feeling liked smoked herring, we didn't even dirty our dress clothes. Townspeople then appeared and proceeded to clean up and mill around the store. We three left in a hurry—here we had wasted three-quarters of an hour piddling around, and still had seven miles to go. The only trouble was, we had red-rimmed eyes and smelled a little of smoke. Don't know what we would do without a few items of interest to break the monotony.

Although Dad didn't talk much about the war, he readily shared other humorous stories about his early time at Camp Blanding. Like his letters, some of these also featured his hut mate and good friend Don Hardwick, who was several inches taller and forty to fifty pounds heavier than Dad. Don loved to pick Dad as his partner when it came to the "deep knee bend" drill, where one trooper did deep knee bends with his partner over his shoulders, and they then changed places. Obviously, it was far less strenuous for his buddy to sling Dad over his shoulders than it was for Dad to heft the Ripper.[11]

Sharing the story, Dad would just chuckle and shake his head. Other favorite tales were more serious, but still with a humorous touch, like the time he was officer in charge of a five-mile run that required the troops to wear gas masks. Dad spied a trooper from Georgia stick a wad of tobacco in his mouth just before he secured his gas mask. Figuring he would teach him a lesson, Dad ran right next to that man the whole way, assuring that he did not remove his mask even once to spit. Needless to say, the poor guy ended up looking more than a little green—and as far as anyone knows, that was one mistake he never made again!

As Dad and Mom continued to correspond throughout Dad's heavy training and Mom's rigorous nursing school schedule, they grew closer despite the physical distance between them. Christmas was always a special time for Dad, a time to be spent with family, friends, and loved ones. It was also a time for joy, hope, and peace, not the weight of what lay ahead. As he was being touched by the strains of Christmas carols and the beauty that surrounded him, his reflections became almost prophetic about the coming struggles he and the 508th would soon face. No one could have guessed how insightful this letter for a twenty-three-year-old army officer would be.

> December 14, 1942
>
> Dearest Jeane,
>
> I wandered home tonight, very slowly, there wasn't a place to go. Several of us had been down in the orderly room looking over the schedule for tomorrow. Yet, I was tired, very tired. An afternoon of really tough exercises, I hurt in every joint. Walked along slowly smoking my pipe and trying to be as comfortable as possible. Quite suddenly I realized that the moon and stars were out, you could almost reach up and touch them. I didn't know if you'd like one or not, so I didn't try. The night is very clear and cold. It is rather hard to concentrate when one is sore from one end to the other. Walking along watching the smoke from my pipe, hands in my pockets when something hit me rather hard. Passed by two very quiet hutments, in one a choir that was singing something that was just beyond the grasp of my memory, this started me thinking. The next hutment was filtering the strains of a Christmas carol. Have you ever been hit by something unseen? The Christmas carol was a blow, just as if someone had struck me in the face, only honey it wasn't my face that it bothered. With that song came a stark reality, Christmas is going to be the loneliest time in my life.
>
> It seems that killing is about all this world knows anymore. I sometimes wonder how these kids are going to forget when all this is over. How can they forget? Jeane, you want so very much to go with us, and I only want to get over there and do my part so that you won't have to go. This one, before it is all over, will be one thing that people will not want to talk about. It will make the last war look like a tea party. There is

just one thing that has worried me, that change it all brings in the mind of men. That change, like a diseased mind is so very hard to cure. Perhaps the answer lies in the clear simple beauty of the music that I hear now "Taps."

These kids that we have now will so very shortly be men. The questions they ask, their problems, their very willingness to do the things we say, it is hard to realize that as soon as five months from now, they may be bearing the brunt of opening up a new front someplace. How can we possibly teach them all the things they need to know, straighten some of them out and whip all of them into a fighting unit? Yet, they seem to know. I hate to see kids grow up in so short a time, when you stop and think of the things they are missing. War might be a glamorous game to some, but it is a "Hell" to me. This same thing has been going on for centuries. The only thing is an improvement in methods and weapons.

You my darling are a firm place in which to step on in the middle of a swamp. Someone to believe in, to help when I come back. Well honey, it is rolling around towards midnight, Good night, Darling! I miss you very much, love, George

December 17, 1942

Hello Sweet

I have been tired all over the past two days, and for the life of me I just can't seem to stay awake. It isn't like me—that I will admit. Everything has been going wrong, millions of changes, extra work that can only be done after dinner and besides that—officers' meetings two or three times per day. It makes me feel as though I were sitting in the middle of a spinning disk.

Jeane, Honey, there are just too many beautiful nights here and an overabundance of Christmas songs. The two added together make a combination that is going to floor me someday. I am human and can only stand so much (and then a little more). Honest darling, this lonely place gets on my nerves. Or is it the time of year? I wish that I knew for sure.

> No, Honey there isn't a cure for loneliness when people are apart. A drink, a good time haven't much effect. I always come home just a little disappointed. Things are never quite the same when you aren't around. You help each second of each day by just being locked up here in my heart. If you could just realize how much you help.

The special bond they built through correspondence soon led my parents to realize just how much they loved and missed each other, and as the time neared for the regiment to head overseas, they began to discuss the prospect of marriage. What would the future hold? Was marriage best now or later? Would it be fair to new wives if their husbands did not return? These questions preoccupied my parents and thousands of other young couples preparing to face an uncertain future in a time of war.

Then, in a letter on January 14, 1943, my dad popped the question: "Jean Darling, sit down in a nice chair, brace yourself, and read the following slowly. What would you say, my Dearest, if I were to ask you to marry me, provided I could get home again?"

The end of 1942 had been a busy time for Mom: classes, final exams, and training on various floors of the hospital meant that heading home for the holidays was out of the question. The heavy snow in Portland made for ideal skiing, and Mom and her classmates took to the hills around the school and hospital for some "much needed" fun. As Mom recounted in a letter to Dad, she was trying to "show a classmate how it is done," when she took a slope a little too fast and "took a flying leap onto the ice-covered road," landing flat on her back. Since no ribs were cracked, she and her roommate hit the slopes again the next day until they "disjointed" themselves completely on a "wicked trail." After they "finally collected all the pieces, sorted and rearranged them," they found "two complete persons." Kary, her roommate, had a fractured ankle, and Mom had a badly sprained knee. It was while she was recovering from this adventure, on January 26, that she received Dad's letter asking about marriage.

One of Mom's biggest issues throughout their courtship and the war was the frequency of Dad's letters. Although he wrote as often as he could, and probably more than most, if his letters didn't arrive when expected on her timetable, she had her own way of letting him know. As often as she said she understood why his letters might not arrive regularly, and promised not to complain, she routinely did.

After getting over her initial surprise, she replied to Dad's proposal the same day, but dallied with him before giving her answer.

> George darling,
>
> I'm making a speedy recovery, but I must say, the shock [of his tentative proposal] was terrific. Your letters finally came today, making up for lost time. With such inspiration, I'm bound to finish this tonight. The weather is having convulsions outside and Jeane Roselyn Slonaker is in a devilish mood, not quite ready to end your suspense just yet.

Devilish indeed, Miss Jeane Roselyn Slonaker went on to write four and half more pages before finally responding to the Big Question. "Tonight, is still white and lovely and I'm just going to have to answer your question, aren't I? Probably you know and I know what the answer would be, in spite of all the thinking we've been doing and all the thinking I've been doing today (unusual exercise). You're right! It's a big thing to decide and probably the first real big one that a person makes all by his lonesome, without the confidence of mama's apron strings. Honey, if you get home and if things can be worked out, you know darn well that I would marry you, if that's what you would like me to do."

By the end of January 1943, my parents were engaged.

Meanwhile, Jeane was subject to demanding expectations at school. Nursing students not only took classes, but rotated through all the different hospital departments, helped in the public health system, and devoted time to the children's home. The upperclassmen were additionally expected to help instruct new students. Up until 1942, students were forbidden to marry until after graduation, but with the advent of war, restrictions were relaxed, although time off was limited and marriage was in no way permitted to interfere with student responsibilities. These were the conditions my parents, like so many others, faced as they agonized over marriage: Should they wait until Mom finished school, knowing that Dad could then already be overseas? Or marry now, if Dad could secure leave, then face the consequences of putting school on hold? To make matters worse, Dad and his regiment would soon head off to Parachute School, commonly called "Jump School," at Fort Benning, Georgia. Letter-writing would be difficult and furloughs all but impossible, making communication and wedding decisions even harder. Yet despite the obstacles, my parents decided to marry as soon as circumstances allowed.

For many young couples like my parents, weddings were hastily planned and had to take place "on the fly," whenever leave was possible. Nothing was guaranteed: furloughs could be denied or canceled at the last minute. Even when leaves were granted, uncertainty reigned, including if and when the furlough began, how long it lasted, and if it left time enough to travel. Regular correspondence about plans on both sides became even more essential, yet all the more difficult. Busy schedules left little time to write, and slow, irregular, mail delivery made planning all but impossible.

Dad's letters told Mom he would soon be heading to the much anticipated "Jump School" at Fort Benning, where the 508th would undertake their five qualifying jumps and receive their coveted paratroop wings. The problem was, she had no concrete dates. For six weeks, from the end of January until the middle of February, she could only guess where he was, where she should mail her letters, and why his letters had all but ground to a halt. Moreover, this gap in communication exactly coincided with the narrow window available to plan their wedding.

A few excerpts from Mom's letters (mostly) good-humoredly illustrate the point, starting with her missive of February 1:

> George Darling,
>
> There must be a letter from you in today's mail or here's one nurse who resumes her target practice. A parachute should be a fairly easy mark. I can't resist writing any longer, although I haven't the faintest idea where to send this and whether you will ever get it. When are you going to announce your where-a-bouts? You have me expecting you to drop from a rosy cloud any moment, in spite of the new "fewer furloughs" regime we hear so much of. You know, as far as getting married goes, it would be rather necessary for you to get home. Night honey, all of my faith and courage are with you at jump school.

"Don't shoot!" Dad replied a few days later. "Not a moment to spare in the last six days."

Here's Mom's progress report:

> February 8, 1943
>
> Mother and Dad have been informed, have accepted the situation, and honey, they are really marvelous. Frankly, I think they are patting themselves on the back at the prospect of a son. Whenever you can come home, I'll take a leave of absence for as long as we can be together. Once you get here, we'll have to act fast. Oregon has a three-day wait, partly to get away from rush marriages and partly to wait for lab reports. However, it may be possible that one person could file for application and take tests, and probably military reports would be accepted, so by the time you were here, the waiting would be over. I shall

> have to do some further checking. Honey, details don't matter too much now, but we do have to plan a little and cut expenses. If we could only count on your getting a furlough and on an approximate time. As far as a diamond is concerned, will leave that up to you completely. We can always cut expenses by skipping that for the present. Oh dear, it's getting late and this must be finished to get into the mail in the morning, then pray that you will get it.

In her next letter, we find Mom hoping their families will bless the marriage and detailing the constraints of small-town life.

> February 11, 1943
>
> Mother was pouring over your picture for hours and has come to the conclusion that you are sweet and she's going to like you. Honey, what do Babe [George's stepmother] and your father think of our getting married? I would like to write but not until after you've heard from them. The war does complicate things, especially in small towns.
>
> A large wedding is out I'm afraid. Much as I have always taken it for granted that one day, I would be married in the little stone church at home, it now seems very impractical and almost out of the question. In fact, any wedding in Hood River seems almost out of the question, because it just couldn't be kept down to a small affair. Not in a town that size, where we know everyone for miles around. So, what would you think of finding a small, quiet church here in Portland, for an informal affair where our closest friends and immediate families could come? It has been good talking this over with Mother, and as she says, time counts. It really doesn't matter how we do it, the smaller the better in such times for both of us. This is the way practically all our class is planning their weddings, even those marrying med students who will be here a little longer.

While Mom was wondering where her future husband could possibly be, Dad was packing up: it was "Jump School here we come!" for the 508th. The course at Fort Benning consisted of four weeks: Stages A, B, C, and D; however, intensive training at Camp Blanding enabled the 508th to skip the physical conditioning of A Stage, so graduates could achieve the hard-earned right to the coveted airborne wings and jump boots in only three weeks. Battalions arrived consecutively, staggered by one-week intervals, starting with the 1st Battalion.

B Stage covered learning to pack parachutes, to jump and safely land from a ten-foot platform, and to assume correct body posture on free drops from a forty-foot tower while attached to a cable. C Stage centered around training on 250-foot towers to accustom trainees to jumping from a far greater height, and taught skills like "slipping" and other parachute manipulations, landing preparation, and landing techniques. D Stage was where it all came together: each man made five qualifying jumps "jumping from a perfectly good airplane," as many put it. Because they skipped A Stage, the 508th achieved the hard-earned right to wear the coveted airborne wings and jump boots in only three weeks. Dad's company, Regimental Headquarters, combined with 2nd Battalion, started Jump School on Monday, February 15, and finished their last qualifying jumps on March 5.

**Col Lindquist, with pipe in mouth, watches while one of the boys prepare for a landing. The boy with the megaphone tells and coaches them on their way down. Ft. Benning, GA, February/March 1943. Picture and caption by Captain William H. Nation, courtesy Bill C. Nation, used by permission.**

Despite this hectic and physically demanding schedule, Dad found "a moment to spare" and shared his training experiences at Fort Benning. The letters started on February 22, 1943, one week into his course.

Hello Punkin

I roll into bed just about as tired as I have ever been in my life. It isn't the physical exhaustion, so much as the mental strain. We have finished "B" stage—just like a big carnival. No men lost. Today though was the first day of "C" stage with jumps from towers. We lost one Lt with a broken leg and another man with a sprained ankle. "C" stage is run from 250 ft towers, and we don't even have to pay for the rides. I now have my boots and wings in two more weeks.

He continued two days later, describing others' broken bones and his own anticipation of the qualifying jumps.

From Ft. Benning:

Next Monday is the day—our first jump. I haven't thought about it very much, and there probably won't be much time until we are in the plane. "C" stage has taken quite a toll. A Captain yesterday—out—with a leg broken in three places. Ten other men were taken in the same day with breaks of some sort. Only three and a half days left on the towers. We jump Monday—Officers first out of the plane. I have my fingers crossed.

On March 1, 1943, Dad wrote to Mom about the private "binge" he and several other officers were planning after completing their qualifying jumps. By tradition, all officers who were also now full-fledged paratroopers joined in a "Prop Blast" party with their senior officers to celebrate just before they left Fort Benning. A letter by Captain William Nation evoked the ritual and explained the accompanying hangovers from another regiment, the 507th:

September 20, 1942

Friday night the 507th PIR had their "Prop Blast," which is an initiation more or less. We had a little ceremony and went through the procedure of getting into an imaginary plane, making the sound of the motor ourselves, standing up and hooking our glass of liquor to the anchor line, but instead of jumping out at the command "go," we were supposed to drink all the liquor in the glass. I sweated (nervously waited) the thing out because I did not know if we were required to drink it or not. I had already made up my mind that I wasn't, and so had my partner.[12]

Singing was always part of these festivities. Two 508th troopers penned the words to the now-famous "Johnny Paratrooper." Full of black humor and sung with (often drunken) bravado, the words could be all too real, as green paratroopers would soon find out. We discovered the version below, printed on the back of a regimental boxing program, dated January 11, 1943, among Dad's documents. It is the earliest copy we know of, reproduced with all original capitalization and punctuation intact.[13] The 82nd Airborne still uses the lyrics as a cadence when marching today. The song is also known as "Blood on the Risers," sung to the tune of "Battle Hymn of the Republic":

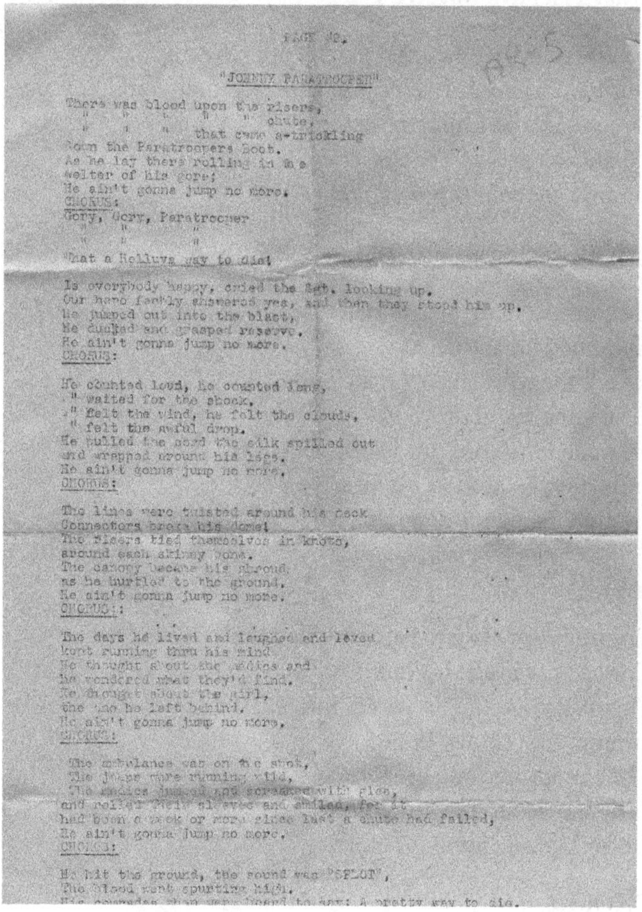

PAGE #2.

"JOHNNY PARATROOPER"

There was blood upon the risers,<br>
" " " " " chute,<br>
" " " that came a-trickling<br>
down the Paratroopers Boot.<br>
As he lay there rolling in the<br>
welter of his gore;<br>
He ain't gonna jump no more.<br>
CHORUS:<br>
Gory, Gory, Paratrooper<br>
" " "<br>
" " "<br>
What a Helluva way to die!

Is everybody happy, cried the Sgt. looking up.<br>
Our hero faintly answered yes, and then they stood him up.<br>
He jumped out into the blast,<br>
He ducked and grasped reserve.<br>
He ain't gonna jump no more.<br>
CHORUS:

He counted loud, he counted long,<br>
" waited for the shock,<br>
" felt the wind, he felt the clouds,<br>
" felt the awful drop.<br>
He pulled the cord the silk spilled out<br>
and wrapped around his legs.<br>
He ain't gonna jump no more.<br>
CHORUS:

The lines were twisted around his neck<br>
Connectors broke his dome!<br>
The risers tied themselves in knots,<br>
around each skinny bone.<br>
The canopy became his shroud<br>
as he hurtled to the ground.<br>
He ain't gonna jump no more.<br>
CHORUS:

The days he lived and laughed and loved<br>
kept running thru his mind<br>
He thought about the bodies and<br>
he wondered what they'd find.<br>
He thought about the girl,<br>
the one he left behind.<br>
He ain't gonna jump no more.<br>
CHORUS:

The ambulance was on the spot,<br>
The jeeps were running wild,<br>
The medics jumped and screamed with glee,<br>
and rolled their sleeves and smiled, for it<br>
had been a week or more since last a chute had failed,<br>
He ain't gonna jump no more.<br>
CHORUS:

He hit the ground, the sound was "SPLOT",<br>
The blood went spurting high.

**"Johnny Paratrooper," AKA "Blood on the Risers."**
**January 11, 1943. Gurwell Collection.**

Johnny Paratrooper
There was blood upon the risers,
There was blood upon the chute,
There was blood that came a-trickling
down the Paratrooper's Boot.
As he lie there in the welter of his gore;
He ain't gonna jump no more!

CHORUS:
Gory, Gory, Paratrooper
Gory, Gory, Paratrooper
Gory, Gory, Paratrooper
What a Helluva way to die!

Is everybody happy, cried the Sgt. looking up.
Our hero feebly answered yes, and then they stood him up.
He jumped out into the blast
He ducked and grasped reserve.
He ain't gonna jump no more!

CHORUS:

He counted loud, he counted long,
He waited for the shock.
He felt the wind, he felt the clouds,
He felt the awful drop.
He pulled the cord, the silk spilled out
and wrapped around his legs.
He ain't gonna jump no more!

CHORUS:

The lines were twisted around his neck
Connectors broke his dome!
The risers tied themselves in knots,
around each skinny bone.
The canopy became his shroud
as he hurtled to the ground.
He ain't gonna jump no more!

CHORUS:

The days he lived and laughed and loved

kept running through his mind.
He thought about the medics and
he wondered what they'd find.
He thought about the girl,
the one he left behind.
He ain't gonna jump no more!

CHORUS:

The ambulance was on the spot.
The jeeps were running wild.
The medics jumped and screamed with glee,
and rolled their sleeves and smiled.
For it had been a week or more
since last a chute had failed.
He ain't gonna jump no more.

CHORUS:

He hit the ground, the sound was "SPLOT",
the blood went spurting high.
His comrades then were heard to say: A pretty way to die.
They picked him up still in his chute,
and poured him from his boots.
He ain't gonna jump no more.

CHORUS:

With the end of Jump School fast approaching, Mom's next letter showed wedding plans vaguely beginning to take shape. Crystal clear, however, was her willingness, even eagerness, to dispense with convention.

> March 2, 1943
>
> Might it really be before the first of April? How perfectly wonderful! I shall be ready at a moment's notice. We will make the wedding very small and save all time possible. I would like it better that way, besides who cares about a large wedding with frills. That's all right for times of peace, but not for us. After all, marrying you is the important thing.
>
> Tomorrow I shall go on a sleuthing trip and endeavor to find out for sure about the gruesome three-day wait.... If this thing

works out, I think we can cut expenses pretty low. Really, it amounts to $5.00 for the preacher, a bunch of flowers, a license, and a little transportation. Not bad, is it? Oh, this is a riot, for once in your life you'll have to wear one of those perfectly dashing garrison hats, which you hate and which all women love. Since all of our friends are either gone, or as incarcerated with work as us, let's dispense with a reception. The others are sensibly doing the same, and I think it's a good idea.

Back at Jump School, with only one day to go, Dad elatedly wrote again:

March 4, 1943

Hello, My Dearest,

Well, we jumped today—twice. It is great fun. The first jump was with a group of officers. I was number eight. Didn't think much about the first one—but the second jump—this afternoon!! Whee! I hesitated a second on that one, and the next time I had any time to think, I was swearing to myself about the steel helmet I had on. I couldn't look up, couldn't turn, and was extremely exasperated about the whole thing. Couldn't freeze in the door—You would look too nice in wings (my wings). Tomorrow will mean two more jumps.

Once these jumps were completed, Dad became a full-fledged paratrooper. Pride and relief replace anticipation as Dad reminisces about Jump School.

March 11, 1943

...It doesn't take anything but an empty head and a desire for excitement to jump from a plane. Honey, I am very much in one piece, my only casualty being two skinned thumbs on my first jump. Thought for a moment on my third jump that I broke my leg, but it was only a bruised muscle.

Sporting his silver wings and paratrooper boots, Dad prepared to move yet again for advanced training. Their destination was Camp Mackall, the 508th's base of operations in North Carolina, where Dad arrived on March 18, 1943 as part of the forward group charged to prepare the camp for the regiment's imminent arrival. He now informed Mom of his whereabouts and described the primitive state of his surroundings before focusing on the practical problems of acquiring leave and setting a wedding date.

> March 21, 1943
>
> Surprise Dearest,
>
> We have moved again and into a brand-new camp. Nothing works in our area—poor water pressure, bare buildings and grounds that have been left by contractors literally covered with trash. We are now in North Carolina—Camp Mackall. Since arriving last Thursday, we have been trying to prepare the area for the regiment. It is really a tough job. We even worked most of the day today [a Sunday]. We rode to this camp in a motor convoy, leaving Benning at 5 AM. Breakfast at 3:45, and a prop blast party for all new officers (that is, with new wings) the night before we left. Half of the officers, including myself, started the trip in bad shape. To make everything lovely though, it rained all that first day. Stopped overnight in South Carolina and the next day was spent driving and unloading in the rain. Since then work every day. I love you and, remember, you have a date to be married. All my love, George.

After the regiment settled in, Dad was granted leave with permission to fly to Oregon on April 5, and at 3:00 p.m. on April 11, 1943, Miss Jeane R. Slonaker became Mrs. George L. Gurwell. They were married in the chapel of Our Lady of St. Stephen's Episcopal Cathedral with Dean Charles M. Guilbert reading the double ring service. Calla lilies, narcissus, and tapered candles decorated the chapel. The bride wore a beige wool traveling ensemble with brown accessories and a corsage of orchids. Her bridesmaid, Miss Betty Calmettes of Hood River, wore a frock of pink and white crepe and a corsage of pink roses.[14]

The *Seaside Signal* ran an article about the wedding and a separate interview with Dad about his duties: "All that has ever been said about the ruggedness of the life of a paratrooper is true. Men in this elite service [are] all…picked for physical and mental toughness and stamina.… Their training is rigorous in the extreme.… We have been on our feet in drill and maneuvers for 36 straight hours without sleep or rest, and the boys come back strong with a few cat naps, ready for 36 hours more. The first time we jumped was not as bad as the second because I was practically numb. But it is always a great thrill. The first jumps were made at 1200 feet and late ones at 800 feet. In action, jumps are made from 400 to 600 feet."[15]

After a very short honeymoon in Seaside at the Tides Hotel, owned by the parents of his good friend Dave Scoggins, Dad headed back to Camp Mackall for advanced training, and Mom returned to nursing school to finish her semester. "It would be great to have a nurse in the family," Dad joshed in a letter. "Who else would be able to put my broken pieces back together if I got wounded?" Although he supported Mom in her goals and wanted her to complete her degree, they also understandably wanted to spend as much time as possible together before he went to war. Mom had only one semester left before achieving her RN status. Would it be possible for her to postpone her education to join him? Or would the strict regulations at nursing school require her to remain and finish, if she ever hoped to complete her training and obtain her degree?

A letter on June 15, 1943, from the Director of Nurses, E. Katherine Sears, RN, addressed to Mom's mother, acknowledged the key question:

> My Dear Mrs. Slonaker:
>
> In reply to your letter of June sixth with regard to Jeane going to North Carolina in the month of July, I am sorry to say that we find it necessary to refuse this request.
>
> We changed our regulation about the girls marrying before finishing training...with the understanding that there would be no interruptions in their program because of the marriage. At the time of marriage, we agreed to give as much time off as possible and Jeane had 12 days of absence. To date several girls have been married and in all fairness to them and to the other students...we will need to adhere to the above regulations.
>
> I would feel sorry to see Jeane give up the course, but that is a problem that she will have to decide for herself with your help and that of her husband. War is a terrible thing and we would like to do what we can for the individual student, but I think you can understand that we must think of the whole group.
>
> Sincerely yours,
>
> E. Katherine Sears, R.N.

Given such strictness, it was very unclear whether Jeane would be readmitted to the program if she left nursing school before completing the course. Fighting her way back in looked like an uphill battle. After a lot of soul-searching and haggling with school officials, on June 14, 1943, Mom finally sent Dad the telegram he had been hoping and praying for: "Leaving this week, more news later."

The 508th was slated for deployment to Europe after they completed advanced training at Camp Mackall. Wives of officers and enlisted men alike arrived in droves from all corners of the country, moving into the camp and small, surrounding towns for a few final months with their husbands before the regiment crossed the submarine-infested Atlantic for Northern Ireland and England. The invasion of Nazi-occupied Europe lay ahead.

CHAPTER II

# PINEHURST AND CAMP MACKALL, NORTH CAROLINA

The 508th PIR assembled for advanced training under the command of the Second Airborne Brigade at Camp Mackall, North Carolina, on April 1, 1943. Built in just four months, the new, sixty-two-thousand-acre base contained a large hospital, over sixty miles of paved roads, an all-weather airfield, three five thousand-foot runways, and eventually amenities such as movie theaters and half a dozen beer gardens, but housing for married personnel was not available, and troopers bunked down in essentially tar paper shacks.

Couples cherished their time together, especially since many were newlyweds like Jeane and George, or new parents, like their friends Second Lieutenant Robert C. "Clint" Moss and his wife Helen, who had a two-month-old daughter. Never knowing when the regiment might ship overseas, wives and families sought to join the men at their new location despite its unfinished state, flooding the towns in North Carolina closest to the base—Pinehurst, Southern Pines, and Rockingham—with requests for housing.

As executive officer (XO) of Regimental Headquarters Company (HqHq), Second Lieutenant George Gurwell arrived at Camp Mackall with the advanced party on March 18, 1943. The base was raw, some of its original 1,750 buildings still under construction. Conditions were in stark contrast to Pinehurst, a quaint village and the site of a luxurious health resort that opened in 1895. Known today as the "cradle of golf," the town offered grand hotels, New England–style cottages and a spa, and featured not only golf, but polo, riding, archery, and many other recreational activities. Located about fifteen miles north of Camp Mackall, it was also close to the idyllic towns of Southern Pines, the site of the local train station, and the town of Rockingham. All provided help with the growing need for housing as Camp Mackall became a major training area for airborne units preparing to enter World War II and launch the Allied invasion of Europe. Other regiments, such as the 504th and the 505th of the 82nd Airborne Division, were already deployed in the Italian campaign.

Jeane and a number of other young wives, soon to become her friends, were lucky enough to find housing in Pinehurst in spring 1943. She and George had been married for less than a month when she got her first glimpse of the town in a letter describing George's visit to his buddy, Second Lieutenant Don "The Ripper" Hardwick, and his wife, Jerry.

> May 9, 1943 [Camp Mackall, North Carolina]
>
> My Darling, I have been in a turmoil all day today—visiting Don and Jerry in Pinehurst and trying my level best to be enjoyable company. Rather a difficult job running around with other married couples when you aren't here.... That was my first trip away from the post. How can you tell them that it hurts clear through to be a spare tire—to want to be able to enjoy things like that—but it just isn't possible when you aren't there.
>
> Looked over Pinehurst today.... The town is all curving streets—tree shaded lanes, a polo ground, country club, stables, and peculiar little stores that never seem to be open, especially on Sunday. Millions of birds and flowers with honeysuckle growing everywhere. The town is so very quiet, but Honey, it is wonderful. Jerry is going to look for a house for the four of us. By doing that all of us could...have something worthwhile and still be able to afford it. Love, George

On June 17, 1943, Jeane sent a telegram from Hood River, Oregon: "Arriving Monday 8:30 p.m. at Raleigh, Love, Jeane." Until this time, George had no idea if his new wife would be joining him or not, since joining him would mean putting her education on hold. The decision was not made lightly, but the opportunity to spend time together before George's regiment headed overseas quickly won the day. Jeane wrapped up her current semester and immediately set off for North Carolina.

During the short delay before Jeane's arrival, the Hardwicks had made separate housing plans. Jeane and George initially rented apartments F and E in Franklin Flats, above the Pinehurst Department Store. The apartments were completely furnished except for linens and silverware. According to the lease, dated July 7, 1943, rent was $50.00 a month, $38.41 for July 7 to August 1, and a $9.00 charge for one tank of Pyrofax gas. Renters additionally assumed expenses for heat, telephone, and electricity, as well as a minimum water charge.

**On the second floor is Franklin Flats, the Gurwell's first home, 2019.**

**Jack at the entrance to Franklin Flats, Pinehurst, NC, 2019.**

With housing tight and money short, Jeane and George pursued their plan to share a house with another young military couple. Sharing allowed them to save money and stretch rations as far as possible, and also provided the wives with companionship while their husbands were on base or during lengthy maneuvers. Canceled checks, check stubs, and letters from autumn 1943 tell us Jeane and George began to share Woodbine Cottage with 2nd Lt. "Clint" Moss, his wife Helen, and baby Nancy in early September. As apartments and cottages filled up, other officers and their wives settled into the historic Holly Inn, a gracious hotel which had held its first New Year's gala on December 31, 1895, at the opening of the Pinehurst Resort. A stone's throw away from Woodbine Cottage, this was the home of several of the women soon to become Jeane's close friends.[16]

**Sue at Woodbine cottage as it currently appears, Pinehurst, NC, 2019. Home of the Moss and Gurwell families during the 508th's advanced training in 1943.**

**The Holly Inn, Pinehurst, 2019. Jeane stayed here in Terry Tibbett's rooms during the Tennessee Maneuvers in 1943.**

There are no letters between George and Jeane for July and August 1943. The men were training at Camp Mackall while the wives settled in, becoming familiar with army life and getting to know each other, now a long distance from family, friends, and home. It was a time of tremendous adjustment for wives and husbands alike: many, like Jeane, were newly married and hardly had time to establish a home or even adjust to living as a couple. And like Jeane too, who was newly pregnant, many were carrying their first child or would be new mothers by Christmas, when the 508th would ship out overseas.

Among our documents is an invitation Jeane received soon after the Gurwells moved into Franklin Flats. Addressed to the officers' wives of the 508th, it announced "another delightful luncheon is to be given on Thursday, 29 July 1943" at the 508th Officers' Club at Camp Mackall. Cocktails were served at 12:30, followed by a luncheon at 1:30. The women were to RSVP by July 24. It included the names and phone numbers of the hostess in each town where the women resided: the senior hostess, Mrs. J.R. Casteel, in Southern Pines; assistant hostess, Mrs. Clyde Driggers in Pinehurst; and assistant hostess, Mrs. M.V. Peterson in Rockingham. It was a perfect way for the women to bond: later, all three hostesses would join Jeane, Helen, and others to form a band of sisters who circulated letters, Round-Robin style, to exchange information and boost morale while they nervously—sometimes agonizingly—waited for news from the front.

After thirteen weeks of small-unit and battalion-level training,[17] the toughened 508th left Camp Mackall on September 7 to participate in the U.S. Second Army's huge Tennessee maneuvers, scheduled for September 13 to November 15. Often operating as ground infantry, the regiment conducted exercises in or around Taylorsville, LaGuardo, and Unionville, then undertook a twenty-eight-mile march to assemble at the Cumberland River, where they crossed for an exercise in Gladesville before moving to Tullahoma for a night jump—the regiment's second. October 7 found the 508th bivouacked at Gallatin, where they continued exercises as aggressive, mobile ground troops for two more weeks. Praised for success on all of its tactical infantry problems, the regiment returned to Camp Mackall "weld[ed]...into a more cohesive, formidable fighting team, anxious to prove its worth in actual rather than simulated combat."[18]

* * *

Jeane's letters to George started up again on September 8, the day after the regiment left for Tennessee. By this time, they had been sharing Woodbine Cottage with the Mosses for a little over a month. Jeane was adjusting to army life—not always easily—and belonged to a circle of officers' wives, many of whom had young children. She herself was two months pregnant.

**Helen and Nancy Moss, about January 1945, Virginia. Ellen wrote RR1 and RR45. This photo was included in her last Round Robin letter. Gurwell Collection**

During the first week of George's absence, Jeane wrote newsy letters of domestic life almost daily.

> Sept. 8, 1943 [Pinehurst, Woodbine Cottage]
>
> Darling.... It's rather cozy here—a little cold, so we have a fire in the fireplace. To complete the picture, we brought Nancy [the Moss infant] in, but she isn't cooperating. The little glutton is hungry as usual.
>
> Do you know, the thought of you becoming a father seems entirely natural. But me a mother—baffling!!! Isn't it wonderful? I'm religiously taking the rest of Helen's calcium tablets and had carrots for dinner instead of spaghetti.
>
> How are conditions out there, fairly comfortable at intervals? I have a horrible vision of you sleeping with snakes (when you're lucky) and living on sandwiches, K-rations, or pork stew. By the way, we had breaded veal cutlets for dinner and I'm a heartless critter for mentioning it.
>
> Nora Thompson [wife of First Lieutenant Charles J. Thompson, Service Company] and Helen Flanders [wife of First Lieutenant Francis Flanders, F Co. ] were over this afternoon. They're living together in Nora's house in Southern Pines. Young Jerry Flanders wet his pants good and substantially, so they had to leave fairly early.

> Wilde [First Lieutenant Russell C. Wilde, H Co.] came home with Clint last night. About 10:00, they had to go back to camp to check up. Clint wasn't going to take Helen, but I called him a meanie, practically—anyway, that left yours truly minding the infant. Of course, it (the weather) stormed. I convinced myself that anyone contemplating being a mother of a Gurwell couldn't be a sissy over nothing, and it was quite time that I began to get over this "scared in the dark" business—thought real hard about you, and there was nothing to it.
>
> We had black-eyed peas and tomatoes last night for Clint. Aren't you glad you escaped? Today I thought about putting anchor lines on the house to keep it from blowing up [gastritis]. All my love, Jeane
>
> Sept 9, 1943 [Woodbine Cottage]
>
> Hello Punkin, We've just been out to Camp Mackall to the Commissary and Nancy went along. By the way, we're having fried oysters for dinner. I got my permanent pass for camp, so please come back eventually so it will get some use. We didn't have any mail today.
>
> Helen is expecting her mother and dad [the Smiths] the first of the week.... Dinner is past, it's a little after 7:00 p.m. and really a lovely evening. Guess I'll take this to the Post Office so that it will go out before eight in the morning, and then take a long walk through the park and think of nothing but you. What a lovely pastime. All my love, Jeane

Despite tensions with Helen, the following letters reveal a process of bonding between Jeane and her housemate and several other new friends. Uprooted from familiar environments and friends, fighting loneliness, and gamely enduring separation from their husbands, often for the first time, these young women were thrown upon each other for companionship and helped each other out with daily practicalities. For wives no less than husbands, the Tennessee Maneuvers served as an initiation into the demands of military life, requiring women as well as men to forgo the needs of self for the sake of the whole, shoulder responsibilities, and take the initiative in an emergency.

Sept 10, 1943 [Woodbine Cottage]

George Darling.... This is Friday evening, and Helen has a touch of the flu. We've asked Terry Tibbetts [wife of Second Lieutenant James Dean Tibbetts], Barbara Martin [wife of First Lieutenant Harold M. Martin], Marge Harvey [wife of Captain Wayne K. Harvey], and heaven knows how many other strays, over tomorrow evening. You know Helen—bridge in mind. Hope there will be enough to count me out. Wonder why I balk so at bridge with her. She's been very sweet, really, but she watches the things I do like a hawk. Don't worry, no wild horses for this cookie. Jinny Schouers [wife of Frank Schouers] was over this afternoon.[19] I minded Karen [or "Kary," the Schouerses' daughter] while she went to the grocery—that little towhead is no chore.

Helen's mother called late last night. Helen was holding the baby, so she woke me up to answer the phone, and then tagged along. Hells Fire!!! Sorry Darling—things can't always be smooth, but otherwise, all has been roses except for missing you. Today was almost cold again, Helen is calling her mother to tell her to bring some warm clothes. Her mother will come Tuesday by train and stay indefinitely.

I'm dying to get hold of some knitting needles and yarn—practice on Helen's baby, make something for Kary, and keep them all ourselves—we hope.

Helen is now talking to what I take to be a fond grandmother. Ah—now it's a fonder Papa. If you ever spoil any of our children the way Helen's parents spoil her, I'll sue for negligence. Well honey, it got dark and to cheer our little selves and keep warm, we just mixed a light, very light, little concoction. That Crème de menthe isn't so bad—promptly got ourselves hilarious over nothing. Love always, Jeane

Sept. 13, 1943 [Woodbine Cottage]

George Darling, It's kind of a blue Monday morning without you. Fall seems to have definitely arrived and last night I snuggled under two wool blankets. I worried about you being warm enough. Are you? Our first weekend without you is past. The gals left about 12:00 Saturday night. We did nothing but gab and gorge on chocolate cake and coffee. Helen and I sat up until 2:30 laughing hilariously over college days. Sunday morning, I stretched luxuriously at 8:30. Unable to sleep and missing you like the devil, I wandered into the kitchen for a big piece of chocolate cake, grabbed a magazine, and went back to bed. What a life for a 508th wife. It was cold, so I finally got up, built a fire in the fireplace. Spent the afternoon making cookies for you. Naturally Helen made most of them—one whole batch had to be thrown away (she misread the recipe). None of the others were worth a darn. Sorry, Darling, I wouldn't send them to a dog—we'll do better next time, honestly. Terry and Barbara had seen the show [weekly movie at the Pinehurst cinema], so they came over here and took care of the babies, while Helen and I went.

A pass for our birthdays—sacred image, lovely, wonderful, perfect! [Jeane and George celebrated birthdays on September 25 and 23, respectively]. Oh Honey—Helen has just decided that we three [Jeane, Helen, and Nancy] should all go out to Nashville together on account of it being hard for her to go alone, so she is asking Clint, can she come? Since the 25th is only a week and a half away, I thought Helen would be all tied up with her mother, but oh, no, not on a bet, if anyone else has anything in the wind. So, Punkin, she wants to know would the next weekend—week of the 30th—be better? More time for reservations, etc. There's something to that, perhaps. You are to get in touch with Clint and talk it over with him. All my love, Jeane

The chance to head to Nashville as a birthday present was perfect. Not so perfect was the thought of Helen and her infant joining in on the long trip out and the celebration. Yes, it would be much easier for Helen and Nancy to have Jeane's help while traveling—but that was not exactly the present that Jeane had been envisioning.

On September 12, the 508th moved to LaGuardo to commence exercises with the 12th Armored Division. An exhausted George begins the letter below on the evening of the following day, but must set it aside until the fifteenth. It is the first of his letters that Jeane received. On the thirteenth, the 1st Battalion had moved from Taylorsville by motor convoy for their first exercise in seizing and holding a bridge, while the 2nd Battalion and Regimental Headquarters—George included—followed on foot and the 3rd Battalion remained in reserve. The letterhead reads: "Tennessee Maneuvers, Somewhere in Tennessee." Under it, George wrote: "More like Nowhere in Tennessee."

> September 13, 1943 [near LaGuardo, TN]
>
> Hello, my Darling,
>
> I am honestly so tired that my writing is practically impossible to read. Last night, Sunday, was spent in moving from there to someplace else. All confusion topped off with one hour of sleep. Breakfast at 0300 hrs. this morning followed by an 18-mile march. Then after working all afternoon, I am tired, very, very tired.
>
> Sept. 15, 1943 [continued near Holloway, TN]
>
> ...I am so sorry, Honey, but there has been entirely too much to do, no rest for the wicked. The last two nights have been pretty good for sleep, coupled with movements by truck. We have fared pretty well. The first day was really rugged though, and it has taken the company the last two nights to recuperate.
>
> Can't quite figure why you haven't been receiving my letters; however, you will have by now, I am sure. On these problems [tactical exercises], my letters will probably be sketchy, but there just isn't time to write. Please though, Sweetheart, don't stop your letters. All my love, George

Back in Pinehurst, the arrival of Helen's mother, Mrs. Smith, offered Jeane a sense of relief and freedom from Helen's watchful eye. She seized the opportunity to get out and about, while Mrs. Smith kept Helen occupied. However, letters from the menfolk, eagerly anticipated and slow in arriving, still proved a source of concern. By the time they started to arrive, the women would have been waiting for nearly two weeks, wondering what and how their husbands were doing—worries that included not only their whereabouts and safety, but also whether they might be enjoying a little too much freedom out of the eyesight of their wives.

Jeane received her first letter from George on September 14, and she wrote back the same day.

Sept. 14, 1943 [Woodbine Cottage]

Honey, You are such a precious goon. Your letter has made today seem worthwhile—they always do. The 25th off, how wonderful. It would be heaven to see you again.... We cleaned the house well today, even the fireplace. It's about 5:00 p.m. and Helen is going over to Southern Pines to get her mother, due on a 6:50 train from Richmond. I felt a little woozy this morning, but it was probably mostly because we didn't go to bed so early last night. We took Barbara Martin and went over to Jinny Schouers (with the baby) for some rough bridge. Barbara wasn't feeling too sharp underneath her bright exterior, and at 2:30 today, she had a baby boy. Isn't that wonderful? Guess there will be some boys in the 508th after all.

Helen and I have been getting along famously. It's really quite amazing that two married women could live together this long without knifing each other in their sleep. If it hadn't been for you, we might not have gotten along at first. Those evenings alone with Helen and me, when everyone's nerves were on edge—somehow you always managed to smooth things over, and you were often dead tired yourself.

Terry Tibbetts has been feeling pretty well, but she's been blue and lonesome. Pinehurst is much the same, a little bit busier perhaps. It seems to be getting ready for the winter season.

Oh, oh, there goes the young Moss noise maker. Guess I'd better do something—Helen will expect her to be the image of perfection.

Well, Precious, Helen's mother seems very nice and dinner needs about four more minutes. Time to turn the chops—wish you were here to help. Terry just came by feeling plenty blue. Finished dinner, so I'm going over to cheer her up. Yours, Jeane

Jeane wrote the following letter as the regiment was about to depart to bivouac near Unionville, where they would rest for three miserable, stormy autumn days before marching twenty-eight miles, crossing the Cumberland River, and bypassing all "enemy" forces under cover of night to seize Gladesville.

September 15, 1943 [Holly Inn and Woodbine Cottage]

My Darling.... Right now, I'm sitting in a half window at Holly Inn waiting for Terry to drop in from somewhere or other. We've been writing notes to each other all morning long, but I'll be darned if I can track her down. Finally found the laundry room after miles of wandering—now I just sit and wait.

Home again, Darling. Today has been wonderful—I've been free. I'm beginning to like this idea of Helen's mother being here. It's been easier to get outside for a change—I was beginning to feel like the bird in the gilded cage.

Hello, Punkin Pie. Forgive me for not finishing this, but last evening I drove Barbara's car so Terry and I could go to see her. She's doing fine, and that boy looks like the real stuff. He's huge, and maybe not as "pretty" as Nancy, but neither is he just commonplace looking. He's cute. Then Jinny Schouers called me during dinner. She's afraid to stay in her house alone and Frank wasn't coming in [from base], so she wanted me to stay with her. Well, she's fun to be around, so I told her I'd love to. When Terry and I came home from the hospital, we stopped by the garage for a double chocolate ice cream cone, then got to Holly Inn just in time for a blackout or air-raid drill, of all things. I couldn't even call Jinny, and consequently worried to death about her. Anyway, she's great about such things and I've really enjoyed the break.

Mrs. Smith isn't feeling well— she's been in bed all day. I don't think Helen likes my being on my own these past days, although I've still managed to get dinner both times by myself, make the beds, etc. Right now, Terry and I are getting some sun on the Holly Inn lawn. I'm beginning to feel like a different person.

Helen heard from Clint again today. He said that he had seen you (Sat.) and that neither of you had any mail from us. What's the deal? That burns me up, because I've written every day, and the letters should have been there by now. All my love, Jeane

Heavily occupied with his responsibilities as Regimental Headquarters Company's executive officer, George wrote as soon and as often as possible, but the lapses between his letters and Jeane's caused her impatience and anxiety, which she both expressed and gamely laughed off amid declarations of love.

Jeane and Helen also jealously eyed the mail for each other's letters as well as their own, but sisterlike, shared their news. But when Jeane planned the trip to see George for their birthdays, sharing with Helen was not in the cards.

> September 17, 1943 [Woodbine Cottage]
>
> Darling, Clint writes letters to Helen every day and I write to you every day—sometimes I wonder if you really do love me—neither Clint nor I get letters. I'm not serious and you know it. You've been in the field, and I just like to tease you. Besides, even if you never wrote to me, I'd still know that you were the most thoughtful and considerate husband a gal ever had, and it really wouldn't matter too much, because I happen to love you drastically. Did you know?
>
> I took a bus to Southern Pines. The man put a reservation through for me. I'll leave at 10:25 on Thursday and get in at 5:25 p.m. on Friday [September 25].
>
> Mrs. Smith is interesting to talk to and makes swell biscuits. She made us a molasses cake tonight. It's good having her—but Punkin, best of all (I shouldn't tell you; it won't be a surprise), she made a cake for you and Clint which we will get off tomorrow. It's probably a bad time to send it, because you may not get it until you're in from the field.
>
> Jinny Schouers had dinner with us, and Terry came over for a little while. Terry was afraid to walk home alone, so brave me walks with her and then has to walk down the middle of the road with eyes in the back of my head to keep from being afraid myself.
>
> I'm over at Jinny's now, we're both writing letters. Frank isn't coming in and Pewellen [Jinny's maid] wouldn't stay, so here's yours truly. All my love, Jeane

George and Jeane were not alone in their oft-expressed desire for a tryst in Tennessee. In fact, dozens of wives soon started showing up in maneuver areas no less determined to relieve their loneliness, enjoy their husbands' company, and perhaps put a check on their husbands' straying behavior. Superior officers were in no way exempt from the will of strong-minded wives: during the pause at Unionville, 2nd Battalion officers Lieutenant Colonel Thomas J.B. Shanley, commanding officer; Major Shields Warren, executive officer; and Captain Chester E. Graham, commanding officer, Headquarters Company, successively all left camp to meet their wives, leaving Second Lieutenant Dean Tibbets, S-1, in charge of manning the fort.[20] With these rendezvous in mind, George wrote:

September 18, 1943 [near Unionville, Tennessee]

Darling, No, I don't want to wait until the 30th. The 25th is your birthday and that will be the day we will celebrate if at all possible. Clint isn't crazy about Helen traveling with the baby, and your traveling that far doesn't please me either—but I want to see you.

Sweetheart—this has been a long, hard week and a much harder rest period. I am losing weight and missing meals because chow hasn't been able to catch up with us. Don't worry, we are still alive, though not very happy. Miss you too much.... We marched and marched until even the generals were amazed at our speed and endurance. Mud and terrific rainstorms until I thought we would float away. Rest periods without water or proper washing facilities. It is rough, but don't worry. Too ornery to be affected. All my love, George

September 19, 1943 [Woodbine Cottage]

Oh Honey, Mrs. Smith made the cake and helped pack it—engineered the process in fact. Yours and Clint's were just alike but you're both to save the tins and send them to us if you can. If it's any bother, toss them away. We're having pot roast today with potatoes and carrots and lemon pie. When I think of the horrible things we used to feed you—For all of Mrs. Smith's modernness, we ask the blessing at each meal. It would be a panic if you and Clint were here to get stuck with it too.

Tonight will be the show, and I think that I shall take care of everyone's children and have a little time to think of you without interruptions...I'll dash this off so Mrs. Smith can mail it as they go. Always yours, Jeane

Jeane traveled to Nashville on September 24, arriving the next day to spend her birthday with George. Being together was a wonderful present in and of itself, but time sped by too quickly. George only had a one-day pass, and returned to camp on the twenty-sixth, when Jeane again boarded the train for the long, dirty trip back to Pinehurst. Passenger trains in the 1940s were mostly powered by coal-burning steam engines, leaving passengers filthy with coal dust and soot.

While Jeane wound her slow way home, George wrote the following, attempting to balance the longing incited by her absence and the desire to keep her safe, given the dangers of pregnancy and her frequent feeling of illness. Another letter expressing the same sentiments followed the next day.

> September 26, 1943 [Northern Field
> near Tullahoma, Tennessee]
>
> Hello My Darling, Only a few hours have lapsed since you have gone, but it is a severe lonely feeling that I have. At first, I wanted to have you stay over in Tullahoma [sixty-five miles southeast of Gladesville, and seventy-five miles from Nashville] for the week, but you being home in Pinehurst makes me feel a bit easier. No, I don't like being alone, hate it, but what in the world would I do if you were sick? It is better to have you safe and in good hands than here in a strange place. The regiment is restricted to Camp Area for the next five days, so it seems to be working out better all-around that you went home. All my love, George
>
> September 27, 1943
>
> My Darling, again tonight I couldn't quite see going to the club. We have a fire and I am lying here on the ground, dreaming and praying it won't be long. Tonight I wish to heaven's name that I had asked you to stay over. Gee, but I am lonely.
>
> Sweetheart, are we different, or are we old-fashioned? It isn't difficult at all for me to be true to you, to stay in my tent instead of running around. Some of these other officers think it is impossible. Tell me, is that an old-fashioned viewpoint? If it is, my Darling, I am definitely old-fashioned and proud of it.
>
> Today there are some twenty wives down here [including Terry Tibbetts] after specific orders that they were not to be

brought into the maneuvers area. I miss you, but for the life of me, I would rather have you there in Pinehurst. Five more weeks won't be too long. You are really with me all the time anyway, or did you know that? A hundred times a day I think of you and each night all the time.

Say, Angel, if Helen ever gives you a lot of trouble, and you can't or don't want to take it, move. I mean that. All my love, George

Jeane was totally unprepared for the surprise that awaited her in Pinehurst. During her absence, her friend Terry Tibbetts received word that her husband Dean (nicknamed Jimmy) had fallen ill. Terry rushed off, leaving their baby (also called Jimmy) with Mrs. Fitzgibbons, whose husband managed the Holly Inn, Terry's residence in Pinehurst.

September 27, 1943 [Holly Inn]

My Darling, Things happen so fast—I arrived in Southern Pines about 11:00 a.m., extremely dirty and more than a little hungry.... Helen came for me and I really didn't feel bad—just a little tired and stiff.... On the way home, Helen unfolded the story of Jimmy being ill out there [in Tennessee] and Terry taking off, leaving the baby here. Is he really sick and what's wrong? Mrs. Fitzgibbons couldn't find a nurse and has a nine-month-old baby herself and another due in December, so she couldn't take care of both. Terry called in route and had her [Mrs. Fitzgibbons] call me—so there went my visions of a long sleep.

Mrs. Smith was still here. I scrubbed in the shower for an hour, washed my hair, called Mrs. Fitzgibbons and told her that I would take Jimmy over.... Also, that I was going to sleep and would be over for him at 4:30. Sat 2:00, Helen woke me to find out what I thought of her going back to Richmond with her mother and the Mosses, who had dropped back by. Naturally, I urged it, so we got them packed and jammed in the car and off. Helen took everything but the dining room table—carriage, basket, suitcases, etc. Poor Mr. Smith. They were all very sweet and insisted I go up to Richmond when Terry gets back.

So monkey, here I am at 8:00 p.m. curled up luxuriously in Terry's bed, quite the Holly Inn resident. Baby Jimmy is making a stab at going to sleep and not succeeding too well. He took his 6 o'clock pabulum and bottle like a glutton and hasn't cried much at all. When I walked into the dining room, everyone wanted to know if I were Mrs. Tibbetts' nurse! The meals are nicely served and quite good. It will be interesting being here for a week and diverting.

In spite of the schedule—10:00 p.m. bottle and change, 6:00 a.m. bottle, formula, orange juice to make, diapers, etc. to wash, bath—I feel, Honey, that maybe in a minor, very minor, way I'm helping this war effort just a little. It's impossible to get good maids or nurses. And gee—I know what it meant to me to be able to see you. It's really quite peaceful here and fun not to bother with meals, shopping, etc., although I'll be running home several times a day to fix a salad or fiddle around, probably missing the kitchen.

The Tibbetts' offspring is sputtering and I hope he settles down after that 10:00 o'clock bottle. He's trying to talk now—and really, he is kind of sweet. All my love, Jeane

September 27, 1943 [Postcard, a postscript to the letter above]

Precious, You're to tell Clint that Helen wants to know all about the possibility of his coming home on a pass and that if he wants her to come out there, he's to let her know weeks in advance. It was good to be with you even for so short a time.

September 28, 1943 [Holly Inn]

Hello Honey, My days will evidently be busy for a while.... Barbara Martin is back from the hospital with her baby. Here again, Terry was going to help her out—Barbara's taking things easy—so it looks as though little Jeanie takes on another baby. I was just in to see her. It's 8:30 and Jimmy Tibbetts is sleeping. I'll feed him a little early, about 9:15—change and fix him for the night and pray he sleeps—then run down and hand Barbara's baby to her and fix him up afterwards.

Today was something like this: up at 6:00. Run up to refrigerator on 3rd floor and heat bottle. Feed, change, dress. Take up bottles, pans, etc. and put them on to boil (if you can beat everybody else). A few times out to gargle crackers and then lose them [due to morning sickness]. Breakfast—and pray that it will be retained. Back up to 3rd floor. Take off one set of dishes, etc. from the fire, make the orange juice (sterile technique). 9:15 cod liver oil and orange juice down young Tibbetts. Undress him and let him kick around while you run the bathtub full of warm H2O to make the room warm enough for his baths. (There's no heat in Holly Inn—everyone wears coats constantly.) Give him his bath. Warm his bottle. Powder and dress him. Bottle and pabulum gooked-up with one raw egg yolk. Burp him. Hope he sleeps. Change the crib. Down three stories to the basement with his clothes. Put them in to soak. Back up to 3rd floor and make the formula. Take a look to see that he hasn't smothered. Back to the basement. Scrub the clothes, rinse, hang them. Back up, dress for lunch, lunch. A few spare moments if you're lucky to whip to the post office for mail, grocery store to buy things for his formula, etc. By that time, it's about 2:00 and time for his strained vegetables and bottle. Up to 3rd floor for it. Heat it. Burp and change him. Then about a ten- to fifteen-minute sunbath in nothing [a baby nap outdoors in the carriage], at which time I can manage a little time to write a letter or knit. Then about 4:30 give him some H2O. 5:15 undress him, clean him up. Play with him a little. Cod liver oil and orange juice. 6:00 pabulum and the bottle. Fix him up for the night, try to keep him quiet, etc. while you dress for dinner.

Whip down to dinner and stop off at the fireplace afterwards by a wonderful blazing fire to thaw out at long last, until 10:00 anyway. But no, someone says Barbara Martin tried to call, and down goes your heart. So, you don't put off till tomorrow—no indeed—you find her room, quiet her squalling infant, promise you'll be down at 10:00 to help her, and that tomorrow you'll wash his diapers and clothes and give him his bath—heavens knows when. Tomorrow I was going to go home and wash my own clothing, which is soaking.

I honestly wouldn't do this right now if there were anyone at all to help, but there isn't, and someone has to take care of them. It's really not so bad. All my love, Jeane

September 29, 1943 [Tullahoma, Tennessee]

My Darling,

Last night, Hardwick and I took off, showered at Northern Field, had a beer, took a cab to the Aircraft Club in Tullahoma. A few minutes thereafter, we had collected eight officers from the regiment. Whiskey at $7.50 a quart and the table had seven or eight bottles before the evening was over. Bathtub stuff that was 2 1/2 yrs. old. Boy, was it rough. Our little group took over the club, singing until everyone else started. As the evening progressed, I grew more lonely. Everyone was dancing, but I didn't want to dance without you, so I sang, continued to drink and become more lonely. Ripper and I went home early, a little on the un-sober side but not bad. Tonight I am going to have dinner with the Tibbets, come straight back to my Pup tent, write you, and go to bed. All my love, George

Jeane felt stuck with the short end of the stick, unconvinced that Lt. Tibbetts was so "sick" that it justified Terry's hasty rush to his side, and the abandonment of her baby. She no doubt suspected that Terry just wanted to spend time with her husband. Who wouldn't? But here was good ole Jeane, back from Tennessee, three months pregnant, and literally running around caring for Terry's baby as well as for Barbara Martin and her newborn, whom Terry had also promised to help before she took off. Meanwhile, Terry was free, enjoying not only the company of her husband, but dining with Jeane's husband too!

In the end, Jeane's good nature and sense of responsibility won out over jealousy and suspicion. In this, her developing sense of solidarity with other young 508th wives, her genuine desire to contribute by "helping this war effort," and the pride of putting her rare, much-needed nursing skills to good use all contributed. In the framework of the big picture, her help may only have counted in a "minor, very minor way," but on the home front, among the newly forming band of sisters, she staunchly held the line in an emergency.

September 29, 1943 [Holly Inn]

Darling.... If Helen and Terry and all of the other 508th wives tear out here for a week—and I am left like a good girl—there's going to be war, and I mean war. You've never seen me really riled, have you? Now—you don't know what you have to look forward to. One of these days I'm going to surprise everybody, just for the novelty of it.

Margery Harvey called tonight, and we had one of those "delightful hen visits" for an hour on the party line. She and Patty Warren [wife of Major Shields Warren] were thinking of driving out there [to Tennessee] this week, but seeing as how she's due in two weeks, she logically decided against it.

Today has been lovely. I have this down to split seconds—good routine (and even started young Jim Tibbetts on his first vegetable today). I feel fine and really am sort of enjoying my stay at the Holly Inn. Frankly, catty or not, it's a damn good change from Helen, even if she's all right and can't help it. I have things worked out so that I really don't work hard at all. [Jimmy and I] both get a sunbath every afternoon, and Barbara doesn't want me doing too much for her and all of that blah, but she's one of those people that you'd like to break your neck for. She's good to talk to—optimistic, sensible, sense of humor and frank. All my love, Jeane

October 1, 1943 [Tullahoma, Tennessee]

My Darling,

I was definitely outmaneuvered yesterday and consequently wrote no letter. It will not happen again if I can possibly help it. The officers had a party last night with eighty beautiful girls (count them—eighty), entertainment, liquor and what not. No, I didn't go—mainly because the Company had a beer party out in the woods, and I stayed with them.

A big fire—plenty, but plenty, of beer, sandwiches, cheese crackers, peanuts, pickles and cigarettes. They rushed me so yesterday getting the food and beer and making preparations that I didn't have time to write or even have time to clean up.

The night before, I went out to dinner in Tullahoma with Jimmy Tibbetts and Terry along with Capt. Chester Graham and his wife Nancy. I met Ripper at the restaurant, so the two of us had a table next to the other four. I felt a little out of place anyway and they made me unbearably lonely. Besides six bottles of milk, a shrimp cocktail and French-fried potatoes, Ripper and I both had a steak that looked like half a cow.

I was uncomfortably full, but that is the first time for a long time. I came back to camp early to write but fell off to sleep.

I understand that Helen plans on going back to Richmond for a while. No matter what happens, keep the house even if we have to pay all the expenses. I am sure, though, that Clint and Helen will keep it too. It still goes, though—if you can't get along with Helen or she becomes unbearable, don't hesitate to move.

Well, Sweetheart, we are preparing for another jump come the first of next week.... It seems there will be numerous foreign commanders and our own dignitaries there. Nothing definite as yet. Keep your fingers crossed. All my love, George

October 2, 1943 [Holly Inn]

Hello Punkin, For no good reason, today is absolutely lousy and so is the world in general. I'm almost disgusted with you for letting me come back. I almost stayed out there anyway. The only thing that kept me from it was that I was afraid it would be bad for you.

I couldn't get all of the spots out of Jimmy's laundry this morning, half of it is still soaking. I let his formula pan boil dry and I broke his orange squeezer. If I don't get to do my own laundry sometime soon, I'll have to wear a barrel—haven't one thing to wear.

Don't know when to expect Terry and had a lovely letter from Helen today. I'm to find a maid (impossibility), get the house all cleaned and slicked up (still have all kinds of laundry left from her mother's visit), be in Richmond by about Wednesday, and come back with her father and mother who are driving her down. Just great, isn't it? I might consider going if I could find something to wear, scrape up the money, and accomplish everything else. Oh yes, I'm to send her shoe stamp immediately and cancel her doctor's appointment and make another for her at Southern Pines.[21]

Oh yes, Helen wrote of the bridge luncheons, dinners she was engulfed in, having a wonderful time shopping, buying loads of clothes, and that she thought she had "worked" too hard after the baby and got up too soon. Ye Gods. Sometimes I think she's the damnedest fool I've ever known. Oh Hell—everything is just all off today. I hate myself for taking it out on you, but I have to blow up somewhere.[22]

I don't mind his routine a bit, but today I mind everything. I'm sick of everybody else's babies and I'm just eating my jealous heart out because I'm not out there too. If Terry comes home tomorrow, I'll have to be alone at home [at Woodbine Cottage], but it looks as though I'll be busy enough cleaning the house.

It's quite time to get back to the laundry, then cod liver oil, orange juice, pabulum and bottles. I've broken Jimmy of the 10 o'clock bottle—rather proud of it. He is really awfully sweet and good—Dean probably won't know him when you get back. All my love, Jeane

October 3, 1943 [Holly Inn]

My Darling, Terry came today and it was so good to see her and hear about you. She was very tired naturally, but she wouldn't go to bed and leave me to do a thing, so we worked and played together, having a marvelous time talking. She made me stay here for lunch and dinner. We whipped home for a shower and now she insists I stay here tonight rather than go back to that dark, lonesome house, which I really appreciate. I've written to Helen that I'm not going to Richmond, which seems best all the way around.

Please don't blame Terry for being out there while I took care of Jimmy. It wasn't that way at all, and she has been more than appreciative. Tomorrow we're going over to Southern Pines in Barbara's car to take Jimmy to the doctor, and if she can work me in, she will.

It's good to be home and alone for a change. Finally, I'm getting the house heated. There isn't much to do really—mainly little messy Helen's room and the kitchen, where Mrs. Smith scattered things from hell to breakfast. As far as laundry goes, there's tons. Have a notion to send it out and charge it to Helen, which I shan't do. Things aren't as bad as they sound.

I probably exaggerate and as you say, no one thing is perfect in this world.

Do you honestly think it will be the first of November before you'll be home? Helen says that Clint says you'll be back in three weeks. Terry came back with the idea that it will definitely be later. Always yours, Jeane

As the night jump planned for October 5 approached, George and a group of fellow officers seized their last chance to unwind with a Saturday night on the town.

October 3, 1943 [Tullahoma, Tennessee]

My Darling,

Tonight is Sunday, and last night I let some of the fellows talk me into going with them on a spree to Chattanooga. We hobknobbed with all kinds of officers—drank brandy—and went to bed in the wee small hours. That was the last time that I ever go any place for the duration of this maneuver. It was nice to get away, but it just doesn't seem to be a relief when you aren't going to be there too.

This mail begins to worry me, I have missed a few days, but not many. Clint must have more time, because I guarantee that he doesn't love Helen one bit more than I love you. That I will state now and be very positive.

Sweetheart, it was very hard for me to watch you go back, realizing that to have you near me would only require my asking you. Honey, I just wouldn't take the chance of your getting sick with no one around. Your being safe and home meant more to me than being with you a few hours a day. So I watched my Life ride away on a train. Each day it becomes lonelier, and I wonder anew if it was wise to send you back. Sweetheart, I still manage to think, though, that it was best.

By the time this letter reaches you we will have made a second night jump. Your husband has been running all over this morning, since my letter last night was interrupted by a practice jump from the back of a truck. This regiment is driving me mad—what a mess. Somebody took my carbine. Can't seem to get to town to buy you a present. Run here, run there, until I feel like saying Go To Hell to the whole works. Have to close and thank your lucky stars I managed this much. All my love, George

October 5, 1943 [Woodbine Cottage]

Hello Honey,

It's almost 9:00 p.m. and I'm curled up in bed (finally), home at long last. Today I felt like a queen in my own castle. We went to Southern Pines. Terry is a little slow, and there wasn't time for me to see the doctor, so I'll do it later.

You're so sweet. Of course, I can get along with Helen—after all, I walked into this situation with both eyes open. I like to think that I could get along with anybody if I had to. Besides, this is a good deal, all in all. Gee, it's good to wake up with just my own day ahead. It's blessedly quiet here, and I slept beautifully. I woke up at 8:00 a.m. and feel pretty fine. All my love, Jeane

George began the following letter as Headquarters Company prepared for their night jump on October 5 at Northern Field. This was a major training exercise with the 365th Troop Carrier Group in which the entire regiment jumped in three serials from thirty-six planes, foreshadowing the events of D-Day. The pilots scattered the first serial (consisting of the 1st Battalion) over a wide area, but successfully dropped the second and third over their drop zones. Jumping in the third serial with the 2nd Battalion and HqHq, George dropped on target.

Over the next few days, he wrote in fits and starts as duties allowed, vividly describing his part in the maneuvers, and especially his experience of the jump. While he never expressed it explicitly, one cannot help but think the dangers inherent to a night jump weighed heavily on his mind. He closed his letter with a detailed, sympathetic response in total support of his wife, which looks forward to their future and guarantees his love.

October 5, 1943 [Northern Field, Tennessee]

Hello Sweetheart, this won't be very long, but it will be something at least. We jump tonight amid a profusion of orders, counter orders, and the like. Darling, letter-writing looks a little rough. These few hastily written words have been snatched more or less on the QT when I should be busy. Don't be too surprised if you don't hear for a few days. We are jumping behind the Red Force lines and mail will probably be cut off for a couple of days.

I guarantee that being away from you and not being able to send a letter will only make me miss you more. Nights are long when it is cold and you have no equipment to sleep with, no blankets, no shelter halves, no nothing. All my love, George

October 5, 1943 [Northern Field]

My Darling, Well, here we are on the ramp of the field at 1915 hrs. The third Bn [Battalion] is in line drawing their chutes and I am sitting here writing to you by means of a street-light. Received a letter from you today and it was wonderful to hear—

October 8, 1943 [continued near Gallatin, Tennessee]

Darling, that is the way this life goes. Start a line—and bang, things start to hum and no more letter. The Third Bn. took off with our Company attached. I was jump master with 12 men—13 in all—and our second night jump. We were in the air for one hour and 36 minutes before jumping—during that time I very nearly froze to death.

I had several bad moments during the flight when I actually wondered why in the world I was there—if my chute would open and the like. Upon the warning signal, though, I immediately forget such things. Went out the door with a silent prayer and thinking of you, my Darling.

Two seconds later, I felt as though someone had tried very hard to snap me in two. Sgt Kenney [Master Sergeant E. J. Kenney, HqHq] and I had a large bundle to throw out, and it caused me to have a poor body position. For the next hundred or two hundred feet down, I did nothing but become ineffectively angry—the steel helmet was all over my head, and I couldn't open my eyes or get my head back [to see if the canopy was open]. That damned thing was everywhere at once.

I did finally manage to check my canopy, and then I couldn't look down—so I gave up and simply came down. I hit the ground. Period. Went Whoof! And thought, nothing but concrete. That ground was really hard. The regiment took a lot of casualties—approximately 10 percent, which is quite high.

From then on, we were on the go night and day without sleep. Skirmishes with the enemy. Surrounded many times and really having a fine old time. We trapped an armored column and then had them turn on us. We lost three men as casualties, and I circled and captured five. The problem ended a few hours after that. Then, instead of having a rest, we moved our bivouac area twice. No rest for the wicked. There have been—

October 9, 1943 [continued near Lebanon, Tennessee]

Well Sweetheart, again too many things came up. All officers were either asleep or gone, so yours truly had to run the Company most of the day. Went into town last night for a few supplies. Came back early to finish the letter and promptly went to sleep. Couldn't hold my eyes open. The officers overslept this morning but after rushing really fast, we managed to move to another bivouac area in record time. This is turning into a marathon instead of a rest period.

Jeane—Clint and Helen are good friends, but we pay our share of things, and as such, we don't owe them a thing. As for our attitude—we will do just as much as we can, but I will be damned if I will let you take one chance [overworking while pregnant] or spend one dollar.

Remember, my Darling, you can always move if it becomes unbearable. Situations are now reversed. You need the care and watching, and Helen can do a little more. Terry and I had a talk in Tullahoma, and for her you can do as much as you like. She offered to help in any way that she could, and she means it.

Yes, we should have talked it [Jeane's departure from Tennessee] over, but I was afraid that I would weaken. If you had mentioned that you wanted to stay, it would have been difficult to tell you to go home. I am weak when it comes to having you around because I want that more than anything else.

We are getting set for the night under some of those same trees that you see. At each gust of wind, leaves flutter down, all yellows and reds. Rather hard to figure that winter is just around the corner. Christmas will be upon us before we realize it. I have already decided upon your present, and wouldn't you like to know? That is my surprise though. I want to work this that we can have as much time as possible together. Wish again that I could look into the future. Darling, I am puffed up with pride and I seem to be unable to come to Earth. It is dusk, my Darling, and I must close for now. All my love, George

October 8, 1943 [Woodbine Cottage]

Darling

...It's almost 8:00 and it looks as though the Smiths and Helen are coming tomorrow—I hope so—instead of late tonight. The house is shining, and it looks beautiful to me. All my love, Jeane

October 9, 1943 [Woodbine Cottage]

George Darling.... It's a lovely evening here, cool, a little like home—somehow peaceful, but lonesome too. It's 6 o'clock and the Smiths haven't come. I'm on the side porch, listening to the evening noises of Pinehurst and remembering when you were here.

If Helen and her family don't come now, I'm going to be riled. I fixed a chicken to roast for tomorrow, including the painful process of de-pin feathering it. It really looks pretty now, and it's all full of stuffing and the house is full of food. Frankly, I think the whole thing is all a lot of bother, because even if the Smiths would condescend to arrive when they planned, they're no doubt much too well-fed anyway.

Well, Honey—I'm darn disgusted! I feel like the devil, I want to crawl into my own bed, but here I sit under the lamp in this dim, lonesome house, waiting for them. It's getting later and later. If only I knew what to expect. I can't go to bed, unless it's back in the maid's room, and that's a dismal hole. Besides, I have to let them in. Aren't you disgusted with me? I find so much to gripe about. In about two seconds, we're going to bed in our own bed and to hell with the Smiths or anyone else.

October 10 [continued]

Such a lovely peaceful Sunday morning—everything, even the air, seems so clean and fresh, with nothing to hurry for. No, the Smiths didn't come, of course. I woke up at intervals all night long so they wouldn't be left in the cold. You don't suppose they had a wreck, do you? I'm pretty disgusted at Helen for not letting me know, after "ordering" the place be all fixed up. Oh well, small enough thing to quibble about. After all, this privacy is wonderful and I'm too lucky for words to have more. Oh Honey—a whole roast chicken for myself today! Can you imagine? Guess I'd better have somebody over. All my love, Jeane

In his next letter, we find George in a peaceful moment and a meditative, nostalgic mood. He is talking about Jeane with his tent buddy, T/5 [Technician, Fifth Grade, the equivalent of a corporal] Ellsworth Bartholomew, a veteran of the Aleutian Islands campaign, who acted as George's aide-de-camp. George and Ellsworth had become close, and when George was unable to meet Jeane at the train station, he entrusted Ellsworth to pick her up and escort her to the Officers' Club on her arrival at Camp Mackall. A somewhat older man with a romantic nature who sometimes wrote poetry at night, Ellsworth was nevertheless still single, with a cheerful, fun-loving side that made him a favorite, not only with George, but with all of his fellow troopers.

October 10, 1943 [Regimental camp area near Tullahoma, Tennessee]

My Darling,

Just about everyone else has gone to the show or is occupied in games of chance. Neither seemed inviting so I am lying here with T/5 Bartholomew writing to you.... Bart just said something that is worth repeating, "I think Lt Gurwell is one in ten-thousand in that he has found someone that suits him perfectly." Jeane, even he could see that, and I could only assure him that he was right. We had been discussing marriage these past few days....

I am not in such a hurry to go overseas anymore—find now that you are the only important thing in my life, and I can't imagine what it will be like to be a great distance away from you. Col Lindquist mentioned something tonight that may interest you: "It is quite possible that maneuvers for the 508th are more than half over." If the original eight weeks were scheduled, we would be exactly halfway through. So, Sweetheart, we may be back before November. All my love, George

October 13, 1943 [Woodbine Cottage]

Honey.... Last night about 11:30, who should waken me but Helen, via the window. Got up and let the Smith family in, including Grandma—quite a surprise. Helen had always intended to come on Tuesday, but that wasn't the way her letter goes. Needless to say, last night and today have been busy. The Smiths left by noon—Mr. Smith is likable, and Grandma was really sweet. Helen came back with all kinds of clothes, baby gifts, etc. Both she and the baby are worn out and as nervous as cats. I'll have to tone them down and get some rest behind them before Clint comes. Nancy is growing, but she has colic.

We just asked Patty Warren and Margie Harvey over for dinner tomorrow night. Helen should be rested by then. Margie hasn't gone to the hospital yet, but may over the weekend.

It's amazing how certain wives like to tear around and make their husbands think they slave. Anyway, it's almost good to have Helen back for diversion. My gosh, I'm becoming a first-class cat—what has happened to me? All our love, Jeane

While blurred responsibilities and job duties sometimes led to frustration, the band of sisters worked through their differences, mastered challenges, and learned skills and ways to adapt that helped them forge strong bonds of friendship that would last for many years.

October 15, 1943 [Woodbine Cottage]

Honey, I hope I make a better and calmer Mother than Helen. May as well say it as think it. She's doing better, though.... The only thing that bothers me occasionally is that supercilious attitude of hers, and I have one to match it, I guess. So, things are really quite smooth with nothing to "cat" about.

Yesterday I made bread, actually. First attempt, and I think I could use some practice. Helen is eating it beautifully, though, and it looks pretty good—only it just wasn't quite like Mother used to make.

Patty and Margie came over for dinner last night and stayed rather late. We had one of those wonderful gabfests on everything and (almost everyone) in general. I like Patty Warren—get a bang out of talking to her. I wasn't so sure at first, but she's right on the ground and pretty solid oak. Besides, she has a good sense of humor and tries to impress no one. I love you Darling with all my heart. Always, Jeane

While men had their own training and drills, women and civilians had theirs. When air raid drills sounded the alarm, families turned out all lights that could be seen from the outside and moved to a safe area in the home during the "blackout." In this next letter, Jeane was in the middle of writing to George when an air raid siren sounded. She followed the procedure, bringing along the letter, and managed to keep writing. Now three months pregnant, she adopted the habit of signing her letters from the baby, too.

October 16, 1943 [Woodbine Cottage]

Darling... Good heavens—10:15 on a Saturday night, and we rushed into the little hall and closed all the doors and here we are, wrapped up in blankets, feeding Nancy, etc. We were thinking we were being so smart during an air raid, and now it doesn't sound like a blackout. Probably our house is on fire or something equally brilliant.

Nora Thompson and Helen Flanders dropped by today. Nora's looking absolutely wonderful; she's looking for Tommy home early again, sometimes I almost wish you were a rigger.[23]

I've been feeling pretty good, but lonesome for you. Barbara, Terry, and I ventured up to the drug store this afternoon and indulged in cherry ice cream with pineapple goop all over it. Honestly though, Jr. has really been subsiding on a beautifully balanced diet, except for that—and anyway, it sounds worse than it was.

Helen and I had been building up to a good blow-out, but we sat down and talked ourselves around it this morning, so I guess we're set for another month or so. Attributed it to missing both of you and lots of little things, besides conflicting personalities, strong wills, and what have you. Soooo—you won't have to live in Franklin Flats [rather than sharing the house] when you come home. No kidding, Honey—it's smooth here, and some day, a most wonderful day, after this war is over, everyone will live by themselves and be happy—we hope.

Helen has decided to stay home tonight. She doesn't care about seeing Sonja Henie in *Wintertime*, so I'll probably keep a date and go with Terry and Barbara. All our love, Jeane

Writing during stolen moments from "behind the lines" on a recon exercise, George expressed his love amidst thoughts of death and his faith in Jeane and their future. Affirming life in the face of great uncertainty, this very private letter, tenderly addressed to a pregnant wife, seemingly expressed the hopes and fears of a whole generation upon entering World War II.

October 16, 1943 [Watertown, Tennessee]

My Darling,

I have neglected you so far this weekend. We have been busy and far from civilization but managed to get into Watertown (a small town near Lebanon) for a shower this afternoon. The rest of the time has been devoted to changing into ODs [olive drab uniform], straightening barracks bags, and trying to keep warm and dry. It is getting extremely cold out here with the last two days very bitter. Rain last night didn't help much, with a lot of my stuff getting wet. A problem [tactical exercise] starts again tomorrow. Just a few weeks left. There isn't a thing definite yet about our leaving early.

Dearest, I can only pray that the time is short. Missing you so very much has become a continual ache that is brought to mind a thousand times a day. My Darling—you mean more to me than anything else in this world. You see, Sweetheart, I depend on you just as much as you depend on me—but my Dearest, you shouldn't cry. I have learned something that really makes sense. I hadn't lived until I found someone to depend or be dependent upon. Darling, Love seems to be the thing that makes this world go round—it keeps it ticking. Without that quality, I lived a very shallow life, but it deepens and takes on more depth as your Love becomes more dear to me.

If this war should cause us to part, I will always know that this life has been worthwhile. Without you, Sweetheart, it couldn't have been that way. Being away from you is a misery, but Jeane, how much better it is to be with you, if even for a short time, than to have continued my useless wandering and waiting [to marry after the war]. We have something now that is precious—life itself, making my life complete. A promise to the future that it will be as good and better than the past. And with you at least, Sweetheart, as security that he or she will do their part.

Our job is large—but Jeane! It is the most important in this world. This war isn't important, it is those things that follow after the world is sane that are important. I have faith in you to do that job—faith that I have never had in anyone else. There are two jobs—the war in which I have a part to do, and the bigger job of the future which will be our job if heaven so permits. Should something happen—it will be your job then. Until I found you, I hadn't met anyone who, according to my standards, could do it properly. So, you see why I wanted you to stay out of this war. Yours now is a bigger and much more important job.

October 17 [continued]

Sunday. Darling—didn't finish this last night. Right now, I am on a recon party sitting way behind the lines on a rock and in blessed sunlight (warm for a change). Gee I love it. This—

Interrupted, and it is now growing cold, night is falling, and very shortly I am taking off on an advance party. Problem is starting early tomorrow morning and from then on, letter-writing will be haphazard. So, this is another poor letter, but I must close for now. Keep the chin up. Love, George

All the wives had returned from Tennessee to Pinehurst, and life had quieted down for Jeane. She and her friends listened to the radio, enjoying a peaceful evening in each other's company, unaware that on the previous day, October 18, the regiment's further participation in maneuvers was canceled, and their husbands had orders to return to Camp Mackall.

October 19, 1943 [Woodbine Cottage]

George Darling,

Just another Pinehurst evening—we've been knitting and listening to Jimmy [*sic*] Davis and the Philip Morris program [on the radio]. Helen played bridge with Barbara at Holly Inn this afternoon, so Terry and I went for a walk and sat in the park. I tried to initiate her into the delicacy of pine nuts, but she was a little leery. We're down to Fibber McGee and Molly now, and I had might as well go to bed—Well, we didn't, and now we've listened through Bob Hope and Red Skelton.[24]

It looks as though the second front will be a reality before we realize it.[25] I had almost hoped that it might not come so soon, for fear it might have an influence on the regiment's leaving [overseas]. But the sooner it is opened, the sooner it will all be over perhaps, and the sooner we can live our "dream of tomorrow."

We're getting Nancy and Helen back into shape. They both look much better and Nancy begins to look like a baby again. Helen is learning, no fooling—only sometimes you'd think for a smart girl, that she could have a little more common sense. Cat!!! What people won't say about me when I'm burning out my thousand years of punishment!

Hi Punk! It's nearly noon on Wednesday. I've been feeling much better, except for yesterday and the day before. I baked custard and washed curtains this morning and did all kinds of

> fascinating things. I'm at the grocery store now, in the midst of the pre-noon closing rush. I've been getting a bang out of watching a paratrooper lieutenant chase his year-and-a-half-old daughter around the store. They're quite a combination.
> All our love, Jeane

The 508th left Tullahoma for Camp Mackall on October 23, but their time with their families would be short. On December 18, 1943, the regiment was on its way to Camp Shanks near New York City to board the USAT *James Parker*, which lifted anchor for Northern Ireland on the morning of December 28.

George's future letters to Jeane look back on their time in Pinehurst as "a taste of heaven"—memories that help sustain him during many very dark days on the front lines. Jeane, too, clings to memories of the Camp Mackall period, especially in times of anxiety, and there were reasons aplenty to be anxious. Her husband was in a paratroop outfit, soon to be dropped behind enemy lines; she was alone and pregnant with her first child; and the likelihood of becoming a widow and single parent was very high.

CHAPTER III

# LEAVING PINEHURST: SENDING THE 508TH TO WAR, ROUND ROBIN LETTERS 1–7

December 1943 found Jeane and the other wives packing up belongings in preparation for heading back to their former lives. With Christmas just around the corner, Jeane secured a cross-country train ticket home to Hood River with a stopover in Washington D.C. to spend an evening with George's good friends, Margarite and Fred Lindauer, before the long train ride home. The shock of separation hit some wives hard on December 18 when the 508th PIR, without announcement, quietly slipped away to New York. With the men gone for the duration of the war, many of Jeane's friends gathered to commiserate at Woodbine Cottage on December 20. Doris Mathias, the wife of 1st Lt. Robert Mathias, one of George's friends and singing buddies, seemed to need extra encouragement.

Later that day, Jeane described events to George, addressing her letter to his APO number (Army Post Office), unsure of the unit's location.

> December 20, 1943 [Woodbine Cottage]
>
> Beth Pollom [First Lieutenant Lester Pollom, Hq2] and all the gals have been hanging around over here—Doris Mathias has been getting a bolstering up today—quite the long-eared society. Helen insisted that I spend Christmas with her in Richmond—very kind, but I couldn't stop anywhere but in Washington D.C.

With final goodbyes said, on December 21, 1943, Jeane began a seven-day train ride to Oregon; she would not be "home for Christmas," but would arrive in time to ring in the New Year. The letters Jeane wrote during her trip give a glimpse into the experience of the many others who were likewise traveling over the holidays on a grimy, lonely, wartime cross-country train.

> December 21, 1943 [Train to Washington D.C.]
>
> It's 10:36 p.m. and I'm tucked cozily in a lower berth on the way to Washington D.C.
>
> Today was a busy day, we had quite a little refund on gas, fuel, and rent, so I have lots of money and you aren't to worry about us. We'll stay with Marguerite and Fred tomorrow night, probably, before going on.
>
> Helen brought me over to meet her father. They left about 8:30 and that was kind of a hard good-bye too. Doris Mathias mailed the last letter [to George] from Washington D.C. She left at 4:30 this morning.

During her pregnancy, Jeane referred to herself and her unborn child as "us" when writing to George. Not knowing if the baby would be a boy or a girl, she used "Jr." when sharing updates. For Jeane and many other wives, children, born and unborn, were a great comfort, as if they'd managed to keep part of their husbands with them.

**Jeane pregnant with George Richard Gurwell, circa March 1944, Hood River, OR. Gurwell Collection.**

> December 22, 1943 [Washington D.C.]
>
> My Darling,
>
> ...Tomorrow we will leave on a 1:15 train to Chicago—to arrive about 8:00 Friday morning. Jr. is doing nicely and getting his exercise it seems—There is no fear if we live each moment fully and right, with no regrets for past trivial mistakes or imaginative queries of the unknown future—Quiet time to say my prayers and sleep. I am back to saying my prayers on my knees every night—Do you think you can get used to that in the future? All our love Darling, Jeane

With not much else to do but observe the people and country around her, Jeane spent much of the train ride home writing letters. Read in retrospect today, her letters to George give us a glimpse into a Christmas past, and the feelings shared by many travelers in December 1943.

> December 23 and 24, 1943
> [Pittsburgh, Pennsylvania to Chicago]
>
> It's a quarter of 12 p.m. and I am again cozily tucked in a lower berth just outside of Pittsburg. A couple of hours ago "yours truly" was a grimy, bedraggled, and slightly stupefied part of a train mob—they suddenly yanked us off in Pittsburg. Some nice agent took an interest in that ticket and got me a berth—I had tried and tried—so you see, there is a Santa Claus.

Red Cap [a train station porter] got me a nicer seat, and a policeman said he'd be glad to mail your letter. He wished me Merry Christmas. A girl's suitcase came open spilling intimate clothing, and kind paratroopers flocked to her rescue. Snow and sleet are hitting the windows. A guiding angel is looking out for me. In Chicago, the connecting train was five hours late, but I planned on this and still made my connection. My train leaves at 5:30 this evening.

9:00 pm. We're all pretty grimy. Snow and sleet are banging on the windows, and I can only wonder about now. The window is filled with coal soot and loose snow has sifted in on top of it.

December 24 and 25, 1943 [Going across the Great Plains]

Hello Again Sweetheart,

A real relief to be settled in on the right train for the last lap, though I have a terrible desire to get out and make those wheels turn in the opposite direction. I had to turn off the light for a while and watch the countryside with the Christmas trees and lights in the windows—Homes of average people like us—Christmas Eve in America. It's a wonderful thing—I have too many jumbled thoughts and feelings to write more now. I'd rather turn out the light and think of you—maybe somehow it will get to you tonight.

December 25 [continued]

Hello Sweetheart.... So, this is Christmas day across these broad Nebraska plains, broad blue sky and frozen winter plains. Our car contains mostly service men and three Navy Waves.[26] Everyone seems to feel the peace of the day, even though there is sadness on certain faces, perhaps because they can't be with those they love on this day of days. Yet its meaning and importance is felt. Yes, it's all strangely peaceful and quiet. It's about 1:00 p.m. I slept late and haven't been very sick this morning [from morning sickness].

Mostly today I can only be grateful for the time we had together and all that it has brought. For you and your child to be—above all—for your extreme patience and understanding, love and faith, and for the fact that one child was born so long ago to make all living complete, and to give us all the hope in the world and beyond.

We are riding into the sunset, the glorious kind that one sees out here—It's 5:30 p.m. mountain time and missing you is almost unbearable. Not just because of the day, Sweetheart—it's that overwhelming feeling that I can't let you go. But I didn't voice it then and shouldn't now. We have made fair time and we should be in Cheyenne about 10:00 tonight. The land is still vast and still out here, but lonely without you.

At North Platte there was a special canteen for all in the services—The fellows came back loaded with home-made cake, popcorn balls, doughnuts, fruit, sandwiches, Christmas cards and a present too. The young Lt. across the aisle gave me an apple. Everyone is most kind to everyone. We had turkey for dinner. The food isn't bad, but it all sticks a little.

Letters may get lost, and we only have about four and a half months left to think of names for Jr., or is it Beth? You will think of names, won't you honey? Always yours, Jeane

North Platte, Nebraska and nearby towns fed and nurtured over six million GIs in their locally funded canteen from December 17, 1941 to April 1, 1946. At times a thousand men a day were served during their fifteen-minute stop. GIs often found a surprise in the popcorn balls: the young women of nearby Tryon High School slipped in their addresses on a small slip of paper. As local accounts have it, at least one GI returned to marry his pen pal. The canteen was not just open on Christmas Day but every day of the war, and is one of the largely unheralded victories on the home front.[27]

As Jeane's train neared her destination, she begins to recognize the signals that she is close to the place she calls home, but she is also farther away from the husband she loves.

December 26, 1943 [Idaho]

Darling,

It's rather bumpy and we're in mountains, real mountains again, near Pocatello. Everything's covered with snow, but the sun is shining from a very blue sky. It's good to feel the bigness of the West again with its strength and quiet, but it'll never be the same without you. There's the feeling of courage and strength from these high old mountains—but I know that never again will it matter where we are as long as we're together.

The mountains and I will be waiting for you regardless of time or circumstances. If you only could feel again the freshness and purpose in the sun and snow and blue sky.Tomorrow morning early—Home! Surely there will be a letter from you. The porter has been treating me like his chief pet—guess I'd better get going. Perhaps Darling, I'd better mail this as is, and see what I can do about some food again. All our love, Jeane

December 26, 1943 [Idaho]

Darling,

With dinner successfully downed and the handouts from some amusing young naval cadets who do nothing but raid the Christmas canteens in route, yours truly is faring nicely. I really don't know why I keep trying to write because censors will voice their code.[28] They don't say all they should, yet just scribbling your name on the envelope helps.

We just left Boise and its almost six o'clock. I've been talking to a little private (who's mighty homesick and awfully nice) about people in various parts of the country and how they accept the men in service in these small towns. It shouldn't be surprising to you or me, but it is a little after some of the things we saw.[29] Lots of people though, in lots of places are really backing all of you and doing all they can to show it. Believe that Darling, and I only hope that someone did as much for you and will again—

I got off the train for the few minutes we were in Boise—that cool mountain air, those peaks, were reassuring and steadying. I remembered that once you said I was a part of you—and I felt that too—that we are a part of each other and we can never be separate again. That's the kind of love I have for you that can never die, never be destroyed—

There's a young Army Doctor's wife in my car who's going to Portland to meet her husband—He's been in Alaska for six months. Now that she is closer and only has to wait till morning, her impatience and restlessness is showing more and more. Excitement and the long wait—One day, you will be home and I shall feel all of that and more. I remember going down to you in June, it will be an even greater thing next time.

I've been talking this little Pfc [private first class] out of the glooms, got started about "it's the person that counts, not his rank or uniform." Got him happy and laughing, talking about his Dad and Mother—from there we really got wound up in an interesting conversation. Poor kid, he's so darn glad to be getting home in the morning. He was so interested in knowing all about your branch. Oh, I'm quite the little matron, and very proud of it, Honey. Everyone has been perfectly swell. I like it this way, because the fellows have been around without making one pass. Certainly, not that I would ever give them any indication to. I like it to be obvious that I'm quite in love with my husband—

The little Pfc in an elated mood because he'll be home tomorrow has gone back to shave and pretty himself up for the occasion. He'll probably come back all one bloody mass, the way this first-class jitney hits the curves. The train people have my admiration.

One of the naval air cadets is a cocky, good-natured young fellow. I get a bang of him generally, but I'd get awfully tired of having that around for any time at all. Everyone's getting excited about the trip nearing its end—restless, all but me—I feel rather calm, glad in a way. Very glad. Should be home about 5:30 a.m. Right now, it seems like a dream to think of being home in the morning. I can only think of seeing if there is word from you—

Why can I talk to just any of these service men, telling them the things they need to hear, helping them along? And yet these many days I can't write anything to you that makes sense or is worthwhile—the brave, "courage giving" sort of thing. Missing you, all our love always, Jeane

Jeane finally arrived home on December 27, 1943. She had said goodbye to her husband, traveled across the country, and spent Christmas with strangers on the train, but the hardest part was just beginning: time apart, not knowing what the future would hold.

George was eagerly waiting in Northern Ireland for word from his wife when a letter dated December 31, 1943, arrived on January 20, 1944. "First Letter," he wrote on the envelope. The others, written earlier on the trip west came as a group on January 27. From the beginning, inadequate addresses, troop movement, and difficulty with mail delivery made communication yet another difficulty of the war.

> December 31, 1943 [Hood River, Oregon]
>
> Dear George,
>
> I will never, never get over you not having my letters when you needed them most. I wrote every day and more constantly while on the train. They were all air mailed and it hurt so much because I didn't know—Eventually they may get to you, but sweetheart, they may not because like an idiotic fool I left off the company and 508th Prcht. Inf. [Parachute Infantry]. It is so hard now to know where to begin—you will tell me if and when you do receive our mail won't you?
>
> Please don't worry about me. I arrived home safe and sound at 5:30 on the morning of Dec. 27, but tired, numb, and looking for word from you. Coming home was like being wrapped in a big soft blanket, but nothing will ever be right without you. You made the past year the happiest of my life.
>
> Your letters (two) have meant the world to me because they said what I felt and wanted to know. Have to mail this, Dad is going to town—I'll start another one. All our love, Jeane

For Jeane, George's early war letters during his short stay from Camp Shanks were prized possessions. The next leg of their journey landed them in Northern Ireland, much closer to involvement in the war.

> 21 December 43 [Camp Shanks, New York]
>
> My Darling,
>
> I have been too numb to write the last two nights, the only thing that really eased my feelings was a long night of work.

Just think—it will soon be Christmas, a rather hollow day for me, but that seems to be the breaks of this war game.

Music that we have heard together is unbearable. Jeane, this being without you is going to cease forever when this war is over. The months together in North Carolina have been a taste of heaven itself. If something should happen to me as the months roll by—Please remember one thing—I have had a complete life, even though it may have been short. Ours has been a wonderful married life—The best there is. I love you Jeane, with all my heart and soul.

My mail may be ragged—but it will be through no fault of my own. Keep writing every day. Keep your chin up and God Bless You and Keep You until this is all over. All my Love, George

Christmas Day [1943]

My Darling Wife,

These days since parting been hell. No letters have come and I have done nothing but worry. I am fine except for that unappeased ache inside that comes from missing you with every fiber in me. It seems almost impossible that I could miss anyone that much. Still, when your whole life is not with you, there is just one thing to expect: a black void of loneliness.

There is one comforting thought, though—we had those heavenly months together with as near a home as anyone in our shoes could expect. Sweetheart—I do nothing but thank God for each of the hours we had together.

Oh yes! Send me the list of names that you like and those we marked. A name [for the baby] must be provided. Keep me posted in every little detail. The news will be like crumbs of bread to a starving man. I need them now more than ever before.

I have one thing that I thank God for each day—Your Love and Ours. My Christmas this year has been more complete than any before, even though we were apart. You have made it that way for me. Merry Christmas Sweetheart, and a Happy New Year. All my love forever, George

One of Captain Hal Creary's men in H Co., Sergeant James Murphy, woke up on December 28 to find many men in his group seasick, but was surprised to see the *James Parker* was still dockside. The power of suggestion! Later that day, the ship set sail for Northern Ireland.[30] While the regiment was crossing the Atlantic, George wrote several letters to Jeane. Dated from December 30, 1943 to January 12, 1944, they could not be mailed until January 23, when the shipped reached Northern Ireland.

> 30 December 1943
>
> My Darling,
>
> There isn't anything else a man could ask for in this world. You as my wife and a family on the way. It has been my good fortune to know a very full and complete life. Thank you, My Dearest, for a complete life. Only one Person knows the outcome and He will do as He sees fit. Clint had a letter from Helen: So I found out that you were on your way home. That relieved my mind. Try to write every day and I will do the same.
>
> [Undated letter, post marked January 12, 1944, Cromore/ Portstewart, Northern Ireland]
>
> Hello Sweetheart,
>
> Those v-mail letters may be just the thing, but they usually run out of space at just the wrong time. Missing you hurts more than I could ever express. There is one consolation, that each day passing by brings me one day nearer to that Heaven with you. Those six wonderful months together added at least a million new discoveries in you that made me a million more times as glad that we have the eleventh of each month to celebrate together. I am beyond a doubt in my mind the most fortunate person in the world to have you to Love.
>
> Jeane my darling, never forget that I am always with you even if you can't see me, or I can't kiss away any tears. I pray for your safety and health each night. You and Ours are the most important things in my life. You will receive cabled money frequently.
>
> My thoughts are a little troubled about what we will do later—after the war. That battle will probably be much tougher than

the one before us now. Not you and I—but exactly what we will do. Work has never been hard for me. I want so many lovely things for you. Growing up has always been a mystery to me. One test for sure was the ability to have a happy home and support it. You, my Darling, are a wonderful person and my choice that night on the porch of the nurse's home was the wisest that I have ever made.

Didn't write yesterday because of duty.

[Letter continued] So Hello again. Last night the band played for our evening meal. Those old haunting, lovely tunes keep reminding me of all we are missing. If I ever forget those small things that mean so much—will you tell me Honey? People always take things for granted.

This child of ours and those to come should be the best. Yes pride, a pride developed from observation. Jeane Darling, it is a little strange, isn't it, to realize that we will before long be a mother and father. Sometimes it stops me—that thought. Raising children is no haphazard job. You will make a wonderful mother. It is going to be a thrill for me to send you your first Mother's Day Gift. I would do anything to change all this and be with you—but duty now takes first above everything else.

I am in a dream today—it is going to be wonderful to get into those arms again. To see the eyes and person that I love so much. There are so many things to remember that will always be a part of me.

That first day when you arrived at Pinehurst, I wasn't asleep. Excitement wouldn't let me. It was hard to realize that you were there with me. I had been angry because I couldn't find you before—but my darling, when you stepped in—the world was suddenly a place to live in again. That time together…[will be] a balm in these lonely days ahead. I pray each night that I am given the chance to show you how much it meant to me.

I want you to visit my folks in Seaside. Talk to Ann and Alex. [George's aunt and uncle]. Ann would make an excellent nurse for you, and I want the best. Tell Babe [George's stepmother],

Daddy, and Dick that everything is fine. Don't listen to my grandparents—they will make our child their favorite and try to spoil you. They both have taken to you and almost think as much of you as I do. Take Babe and Daddy into your confidence—if something happens to me, you will be the only one informed and I want you to tell them.

After a long silence, I am going to try to write to my mother [Pearl Milne]. Your address will go to her and possibly she will write to you. She has been very difficult for me to write to, and it is likely my fault. Something comes between us. It is difficult to put my finger on it and I am trying again to break through.[31] How are Mom and Dad Slonaker? Wish that I could be around to help out.

I still can't believe that this is finally it. At times I am afraid—I have so much to lose now. There is only one answer—faith in Him above. It still does not seem possible though. Please don't forget about the insurance for both you and the baby.

[Letter continued] Hello Darling, Now we are somewhere just off the British Isles. I am going to try to reach Dave [Scoggins, 80th Division], but still can't figure out how to do it. Quite an argument tonight. Yes, wives and girlfriends was the subject. Boy, do I burn at some of these phony ideas. Love—especially mine—is very dear to me, and time doesn't make a damn bit of difference. That beautiful white folder [marriage certificate] is the finest thing in the world. Whew! Do I burn. I am a jealous cuss too—more bad faults. Have you heard from Terry [Tibbetts] or any of the other wives? Some of them will make excellent friends for years to come.

Already I am ready to come home. Overseas before you came along was the one thing to strive for. Now is the event that will soon bring the final result, good or bad. I am apprehensive just like so many others, but whatever happens—it will be for you, our family and our home. There is something worth fighting for, but in the scramble, you will always be in my mind and your name on my lips. Remember when I get back—you and I are going to take in dances, fishing, hunting, picnics and everything else we haven't done. We have a job together of showing people how to raise children the right way. It will be a pleasure growing old together with our children.

News these days looks good. It may not be as long as I had expected.[32] Keep your fingers crossed. It doesn't seem possible even after maneuvers [rigorous training in Northern Ireland] that I could miss you so very much. Days without you are just periods of light and nights alone are miserably lonely, distinguished only by the difference that I can't see as well. All my love, George

Once hard training resumed in Northern Ireland, George was extremely busy: he was the regimental chemical warfare officer, both the executive officer and the supply officer for HqHq Co., and the leader of the regimental bazooka platoon (twelve anti-tank teams), which would be employed wherever needed on D-Day. He also had the responsibility of censoring enlisted men's mail. While officers censored their own mail, it was subject to spot-check by other officials. The letter below had been opened, resealed, and bore an examiner's stamp.

24 January 1944 [Cromore/Portstewart, Northern Ireland]

Hello Sweetheart

...It was in my mind to write more, but there was too much of the men's mail to censor. Haven't had your ring off yet except for that one time in South Carolina during the maneuvers when I almost lost it. It would break my heart to have to take it off. It is really a consoling golden band. Your Panda is with me too—I am protected. Panda's ears, arms, and legs though are becoming just a wee bit worn [a small charm from Jeane's bracelet].

Jeane did not begin receiving George's letters until the end of January. Now knowing his whereabouts, she settled down and began writing intensely. Nearly six weeks after the regiment left North Carolina, the reality of separation has set in in earnest.

January 29, 1944 [Hood River, Oregon]

My Dearest George, How good it is to have your first letter since those written on board. People here are finally getting into this war effort. The tremendous amount of war bonds

> sold to civilians and corporations is hard to believe. The strike situation is much better at the moment.[33] Certainly, public opinion seems to be changing and the American people want to back all of you. Have courage, my Darling. We will need you back to make our present efforts and sacrifice worthwhile, but most of all I need you back.
>
> February 7, 1944 [Hood River, Oregon]
>
> ...[When we were in Pinehurst] I can see you coming home tired in dirty fatigues, and you looked wonderful. It always brought a catch to my throat, and I always wished that time, the house had been ours alone....

Once the women had left Pinehurst and disbursed across the entire United States, their thoughts turned to their absent husbands and the coming dangers of combat, but also to the many friendships that had sprung up among them while their husbands were in training. Having developed an indispensable support system, the wives had found it difficult to say goodbye to each other, and many had promised to write. A few, Jeane prominent among them, went further and hatched a plan to cast a mutual lifeline in the form of a round-robin, written by each and read by all, as way to keep up their courage and keep up-to-date on family and regimental news from the front.[34]

Military units today have Family Readiness Groups for support, but the 508th wives had to look to each other. The Round Robin (RR) was the brainchild of five friends who had formed a band of sisters at Pinehurst: Helen Moss, Beth Pollom, Jeane Gurwell, Doris Mathias, and Bonnie Hetland. Rather than write separately to each other, they would each write a letter and pass it on to the next woman. She, in turn, would add her letter to the growing group, and send it on its way, and so forth. By the end of the war, forty-eight wives had contributed fifty letters.

The letters beautifully served their purpose for the correspondents during the war, and provide a rare and very personal look at the home front for us today, as if we were gazing through a living room window, lit by the lamp of a bygone time. Even the various stationeries on which the letters are written speak of another time—yet the vivid emotions and experiences they convey are very much of today.

Helen Moss, whose family shared the Pinehurst cottage with Jeane and George, initiated the Round Robin in Virginia with a letter on Camp Mackall letterhead, demonstrating her skills at reading between the lines and gleaning information in spite of the censors. Wife of 2nd Lt. Robert C. Moss, H Co.[35], she added explicit instructions on how it is to be forwarded, dispatching her missive nearly halfway across the country to her friend Beth in Missouri.

Helen Moss, Richmond, Virginia [RR 1]

January 15, 1944

Dear Beth [Pollom],

Since no one will start the "Round Robin"—meaning namely you— I guess I will, cause I'd like to hear from everyone in the regiment that we knew and there are so many to write to—so here goes! Anyone you want to add, or the others want to, go ahead.

The news I have is that they [the regiment] left about Dec 28th or 29th, because I last got a letter from Clint written on that day, and it was censored by the Army base, whereas the ones I got before weren't. We should hear in another week or so, from what I understand from other sources.

I think I've dropped a line to most of the ones on this list as to the rest of the news concerning me. The most wonderful baby in the world, to me, anyway, is Nancy. (Here's to yours, Barbara and Bonnie.) I'll let you know when she increases her vocabulary. She knows the fundamentals now and at only five months. Beat that!

Well, I'll close now, but with another word. This is like a chain letter—n'est-ce pas [isn't it], Beth. You add your postscript and information and send it on to the next one in line after you. Also, if you want to add any addresses, please do—all of us would like to have them anyway. How about Terry [Tibbets]? Hope this works out. Do I usually foil things? Helen

1. Mrs. R.C. Moss, 203 S Boulevard, Richmond, VA

2. Mrs. L.W. Pollom, 600 W 69 St., Kanas City, MO

3. Mrs. Geo. L. Gurwell, Davidson Hill, Hood River, OR c/o R. L. Slonaker

4. Mrs. R.P. Mathias, 609 Winner Ave., Baltimore, MD

5. Mrs. E.C. Hetland, Hillsdale, OR c/o Hillsdale P.O.

[This is the only list that was preserved. Other wives were added, as the letters attest, but the expanded list is not in the Gurwell Collection.]

Full of optimism, Beth Pollom quickly responded, addressing the Round Robin as instructed, to Jeane, all the way in Oregon. Beth was married to 1st Lt. Lester Pollom, Hq2.

Beth Pollom, Kanas City, Missouri [RR 2]

January 19, 1944

Dear Jeane,

Well, the Round Robin is finally started, and Helen had to do it in the end. How are you feeling? How about your long trip home? Am anxious to hear all about that journey!

You probably have word by now that our "lovers" have landed in the British Iles [*sic*]. To me it is a great relief to know they are safe and that far along on their long journey. Sold my car after getting home, so now am "on my uppers" (more gas for the paratroopers)![36] Have a job in a defense plant—Pratt-Whitney Aircraft Corp. Can't say I'm thrilled beyond words with it, but the pay is good, have a car ride to and from work, and it's only about four miles from where I live.[37]

Jeane, if you have any sound suggestions for "our baby" please add them, anything to make this more interesting and keep it barreling along. Yvonne Hetland, how are you and Gloria, and did you get home safely? And how many days were you girls on the road? Drop me a line soon. Terry Tibbetts, darn it—you owe me a letter, and right now too. That goes for you also, Anne Havens.

I guess we are all a lot happier girls since our husbands have reached their destination. Now if the war could only end without them having to see combat, that would be the answer to our prayers. The 501st left Camp Mackall on the 1st of Jan. for Point of Embarkation [the harbor where the ship left for its destination]. They didn't lose any time. I also heard by the grapevine that the 507th, which proceeded us, landed in Ireland a few days before our outfit. Does anyone know any

Camp Mackall "latrine rumors"?[38] I'm missing the army gossip these days. Love, Beth

Jeane Gurwell, whom the reader will recognize as the wife of 1st Lt. George Gurwell, HqHq surprisingly received the Round Robin just two days after Beth mailed it. She opened the circle up by suggesting a host of additional correspondents and, in the name of efficiency, she also deviated from Helen's mailing instructions by forwarding the Round Robin to another 508th "paratrooper girl" now living in Oregon whom she never met, rather than to Doris Mathias, a good friend in Maryland. All the women Jeane proposed as potential correspondents eventually would contribute to the Round Robin.

Jeane Gurwell, Hood River, Oregon [RR 3]

January 21, 1944

Hello Everybody—

Beth and Helen, I am so glad that you have this started, especially as from now on it's going to mean more to all of us [since the men are overseas]. It came today, good speed. Beth, may I make one little suggestion first? How about sending this in a more geographical order—for instance, Doris Mathias' name is after mine, but I'm going to send it to Bonnie Hetland next because she's so close. This will save time, and it does take time to cross the county a time or two. Perhaps we should pick up everyone on the west coast before it works over to Barbara, Terry, Doris, Helen, etc.?

Isn't it wonderful to hear from our precious men? I am feeling fine. This country life is the real thing for pregnancy. The trip out was smooth but tiresome, Beth. Generally uneventful and not too interesting. But surprise. There is a good chance of twins!! Imagine! Wonder how Jean Mendez [Lieutenant Colonel Louis Mendez, commanding officer (CO), Third Battalion] is getting along. Has anyone written?

Beth, you're a good girl for doing defense work. I am proud of you. Underneath all, guess we aren't kidding ourselves—this new invasion is going to be plenty tough. But evidently the airborne group will be plenty big, and that sounds good. Besides, when we expect it to be tough, we will also be more prepared. Just ask commentator Gurwell anything—it all comes from listening to some twelve news casts daily, Elmer Peterson from London weekly, reading two papers a day and arguing with Dad nightly on the woes of the world. It's a panic—This is a fair warning! Don't get in the same rut.

I'm on the tail of a good 511th rumor, but undoubtably by the time I could get any news, the war will be over. I hear that the 506th in England is divided into three separate camps by battalion. Bonny Hetland—this is an odd introduction, but good nevertheless to know that you are so close. We must get together—will you be living in Hillsdale, and what is your impression of what you have seen of Oregon?

Helen, did I detect a note of "braggery" (is that a word?) in the description of your daughter's accomplishments? Don't blame you—It's getting to the point where I go gaga over any baby picture and talk to myself while pricing baby cribs. May I suggest that everyone have a baby—then have some more.

Life here in the country is quiet, surprisingly peaceful. The sun is catching the ice on the lower glacier of Mt. Hood right now. Snow in the valley is gone for the present, and underneath the leaves that we heap on the violet bed there are a few blossoms. They're lovely in mid-winter, but snow will come again before Spring to put them to sleep again.

"Willie" our little black cocker spaniel is quite a charm—much more spoiled than I ever thought of being, but at times he seems much more accomplished too. Dad gave him a bath (in the bathtub) and he loved every bit of it. Then I combed and brushed him, and what did you think happened to our perfectly trained pooch? He went calling, through the mud, on a little girl friend up the road, having snuck out. No moral(s)! Soap is evidently not the thing to send overseas.

By the way, Jerry Hardwick is in California with Don's family and loving it—she sent a card, but I expect a letter soon.

My bedroom has acquired a little blue baby bed—a friend insisted that I use it—and I'm very thrilled. It's still a little incredible to bring a baby bed into one's old room. Barbara [Martin], this is a late chance to apologize for not having written. How is that handsome son? Perhaps that 511th news will come to rest before mailing this tomorrow. Many wives, many Hood River girls, are coming back to the valley since so many men are now reaching or leaving POEs [Points of Embarkation]. Do you find it the same? Love to everyone. This is going to be great fun—With Love, Jeane

When Jeane slipped her newsy letter in the packet and sent the Round Robin on to Bonnie Hetland, (married to Capt. Eugene Hetland. E Co.) in Oregon, all of the 508th wives were either still blissfully naive as to the real dangers their husbands would run in the war, or gamely keeping their chins up and trying to be chipper. None could ever have imagined that their husbands would participate in the spearhead of the largest air/sea invasion force of all time or that the end of the war would leave eleven of the forty-eight Round Robin correspondents as widows, including three of the friends Bonnie mentions in her letter.

Bonnie Hetland, California, [RR 4]

February 3, 1944

Hello all you war widows,

By now I expect you all feel like widows. I know I do, but letters help a lot, don't they? My folks forwarded letters from you gals to me here in California. I'm visiting Gene's folks and will be here until the first of March. I really like California and hope that after the war we can make our home here. It's so nice and warm, Gloria even takes her sunbaths in the "nude."

This is a little past news but thought you might not have heard it. Received a letter from Bernie Shankey [wife of First Lieutenant Joseph Shankey, Hq3], who said the 508th was stationed at Camp Shanks before they left the U.S. It was just twenty minutes from her home. She said they left there the night of Dec. 28.

Marge Harvey [wife of Captain Wayne Harvey, HqHq] lives here in Beverly Hills and we went to lunch one afternoon and call each other every time we get letters from our husbands. It's swell to have someone to compare notes with.

Did you know that Anne Klein [married to Captain James C. Klein, Medical Detachment] had her baby? It was a little boy—did I say little? He weighed 8 lbs. at birth. I think it's wonderful she named him John James. I'll add her name and address to the list because I know she'd love to be in on this chain letter.

Gloria is my whole life now. She is getting so big that I bet you girls would not recognize her. Today she said "dada" for the first time. I know she does not understand what she is saying, but I'm happy pretending it's "Daddy." Good for you, Beth, for getting a defense job. I wish I were free. I'd be in there doing my bit too. I mean it—I think it's swell. Jeane, I'll certainly write you when I get to Oregon. Maybe if it's not too far we can get together. Helen, I'd love to see that baby of yours. I never did see her you know, but I bet she's cute and don't they grow fast though? Dottie [wife of First Lieutenant John A. Quaid], I never did get around to writing you, and I suppose you've been busy too. Did you and Nancy make the trip ok?

Well girls, this letter is a swell way of keeping in touch. I can hardly wait for it to come back to me again. It's so much fun to read all the letters at once. Love, Bonnie and Gloria

Continuing Jeane's proposal both to widen the circle and mail the Round Robin to nearby correspondents, Bonnie sent the package to her friend Dottie (wife of 1st Lt. John A. Quaid, H. Co.). The letters arrived quickly to Dottie's California address, but the Round Robin continued a detour of sorts that took it further from Doris Mathias, one of the friends who dreamed the Round Robin up and number four on the original list.

Dottie Quaid, Sacramento, California [RR 5]

February 10, 1944

Greetings Everyone,

It seems a bit strange to be writing a letter and know it's going to so many people in so many different places, but it's a grand idea and I hope it continues. Like Beth I am back in the old routine life of a working gal. Really have a good job with the State Division of Highways and like the work. However, the great struggle right now is to pull myself from bed each morning at 6:30 when the moon and stars are still out.[39] It just doesn't seem natural. I am also one of those people that dash madly for the bus every day. If you can get there, you're all set as the packed throng enfolds you like a mother hen. However, you are frequently passed up, as the bus is already full to overflowing, in which case you just wait and hope the next one can squeeze you in. Some kind, fatherly gentleman seems to know half the neighborhood out here, so he frequently secures a ride for all of us with some passing "A" card.[40]

I am living with another girl whose husband is overseas. It's working out grand. Her husband was in a lodge here in Sacramento and they are well acquainted, so I am meeting lots of new people. Also, quite surprised to find a number of girls I used to know still living here. It all helps pass the time. Jack writes such interesting letters from Ireland that I wish I could see it too. I am glad they are there, because the fellows in the South Pacific write back such awful letters. Have been waiting to receive some Irish linens, but as yet they haven't arrived.

Ann, I was so glad to hear that you have a little boy. You now have an ideal family. Bonnie, I'm sorry I've been so slow, but I promise a letter real soon. As for Helen, I write you anyhow, so won't get into details here. I am anxiously waiting to hear news of Jeane's family to be. It shouldn't be long now.

Don't suppose I can add any news of the activities in Ireland that you don't all know already. Their training program seems to be about the same as it was in the States. Was surprised to learn that it doesn't get light over there until around nine o'clock.[41] The novelty of the situation seems to be wearing off, although I understand some of the fellows will be making a trip to Belfast some weekend. They've probably been over there and back. It takes a good two weeks to get a letter from over there.

Will bring this little epistle to a close for this time and hope to hear from all of you again. Ann, you're the next on the list, so will forward the letter to you. Best Regards to All, Dottie Quaid

With a month's delay in getting the packet of letters, Anne Klein suggested a speedier turn around once the letters were received. She continued with letter number six, adding yet more suggestions for streamlining the increasingly bulky package and expediting its course. Anne's husband, Capt. James C. Klein, was a regimental surgeon in the Medical Detachment.

Anne Klein, Lufkin, Texas [RR 6]

March 14, 1944

Dear 508 Gals,

I think the suggestions of sending letters to the next nearest point and not holding them for longer than a week a fine beginning for a set of rules. It seems to me that as the packet grows larger that it would simplify things if we used larger sheets and fewer of them. Also, why not add our full names, as sometimes a first name is difficult to place.

Seems forever since the boys left. Jim complains he receives so little of my mail whereas I write daily. He visited Belfast one weekend—sent me some Irish linen with beautiful crochet on it which he originally described as "embroidery or stuff," so I had no idea what I was getting before it arrived. He also mentioned doing some work in a nearby hospital, so evidently the sick call is not too large, we hope. Seems as if they are comparatively safe in Northern Ireland—I wish they could stay there but be home soon.

Sue Anne, Jack (born Jan. 14) and I are very happily settled in Lufkin at the above address. We have a rather precious house which has many features with which I am just delighted. I must admit that with the children, keeping house and the social activities of a rather small town, I manage to keep more than busy. It gives me little time to worry much and I am comparatively happy. We live just a block from the Doctor's parents, which makes it mighty nice for us. I know many people here, so the disappointment of not finding a house in Dallas, where we had originally planned to live, was really for the best.

I hear occasionally from other girls in the regiment. Yesterday I had the pleasant surprise of receiving a call from Lois Elder, wife of one of our chaplains [Captain James Elder]; she is visiting her sister here for a few weeks, and we hope to get together to exchange notes on what each hears from the 508th. I was also surprised to learn that the Elders have a son born last November.

I am so glad that we are keeping in contact with each other and hope the Round Robin will be continued by each girl. I shall add a few names.

Best wishes to each of you. Sincerely yours, Anne, Mrs. James C. Klein

P.S. I took the liberty to start a new list in the order in which they came to me and then added the others in some geographical order.

The Round Robin letters next traveled to the Midwest, where it reached Barbara Martin in Illinois. Her husband, 1st Lt. Harold M. Martin, served in Hq2 and F Co.[42]

Barbara Martin, Robinson, Illinois [RR 7]

March 22, 1944

Hi Everyone,

Now that it's started, this Round Robin looks as if it'll be a success, doesn't it? I'd like to suggest that we limit the number of names, too, or it'll break us up paying postage. [The postage on the final Round Robin envelope was thirty-nine cents.]

I manage to keep plenty busy—am at home with my folks. Mother's been ordered by the doctor to stay in bed and rest so I'm chief cook and bottle washer. Since I love the responsibility of the house and baby tending, I wonder why in the world I think I want three children, as busy as one keeps me! Of course, if I'd get to bed earlier and get up earlier, I could accomplish more, but there are about five or six of my old gang of girls home, too, so we have eightsomes and foursomes of bridge about twice a week. With spring coming on, it will mean bicycling, roller skating, bowling, and Sunday hikes. A small town really has its advantages, because we're all within walking distance of each other so manage to keep from getting too terribly lonesome for our hubbies.

Was glad to hear about you, Jeane, because I've wondered about you so much—you never did answer your half of my joint letter to you and Helen, you know. My "handsome" son

> is fine, thank you, and looks more like his Daddy every day. Hardly seems possible that he's six months old already! Did you know that Pauline Paddock rented your house after you and Helen left?[43] I got the nicest, newsiest letter from her. She said Bill had only gotten to eat her cooking three days before the 11th (or was he in the 17th?) left for Tennessee and points unknown, so she was going to stay in Pinehurst till April. She said the Holly Inn had quit giving army rates Feb. 14th and now had a menu choice of four deserts. Grr! It makes me want to tear out my hair—or preferably Richard Tufts' [the grandson of Pinehurst's original owner]. They gladly accommodated the army in the summer when the money wasn't rolling in, but now that the four hundred regulars are drifting back, and Pinehurst can make more money off them—why, to H--- with the army! I wish those hotel guests had to eat K rations for the duration! Durned if I couldn't turn communist pert [very] easily. Ha!
>
> What's happened to you, Terry? Pen gone dry? You owe me a letter, you know. I know I was slow to answer your first one but promise to do better next time. Are you still with your in-laws? How's Jimmie and what new things is he doing. C'mon, you'll have to answer this Round Robin and get it on its way in a week, so why not dash me off a private note on the side. I do want to hear all about ya and how you're standing Deane's absence.
>
> Guess I don't have any Irish news that would be new to anyone. I'm still thankful the boys went that way instead of the Pacific! Well, 'tis time to feed my young 'un—
>
> Best wishes to all—Barbara Martin

As the paratrooper girls settled into their new roles as mothers and home front support for their husbands and each other, optimism still ran high. News from the men spoke of adventures in Ireland and England—foreign lands, yes, but safe, friendly ones. Wives commonly wrote of eagerly awaiting treasures and trinkets: fine Irish linen, lace, silver spoons and baby cups, and charms for bracelets. Because their men were elite paratroopers, wives believed victory would be theirs and they would all come marching home, and much of the country expected the war to be won, at latest, by Christmas 1944.

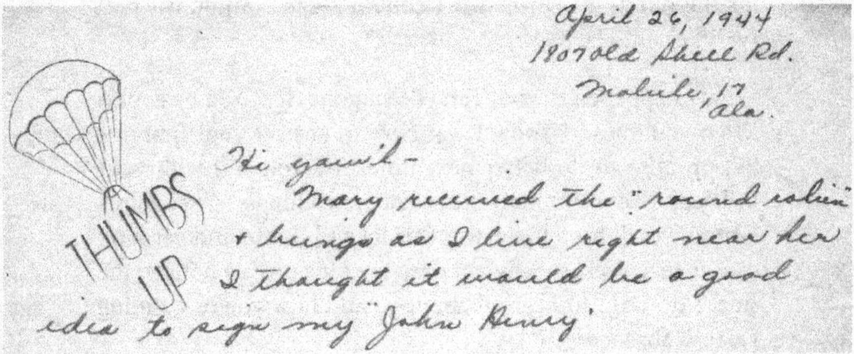
THUMBS UP

April 26, 1944
1807 Old Shell Rd.
Mobile, 17, Ala.

Hi yawl -

Mary received the "round robin" + brings as I live right near her I thought it would be a good idea to sign my "John Henry"

## CHAPTER IV

# PREINVASION JITTERS: THE 508TH IN NORTHERN IRELAND AND ENGLAND, ROUND ROBIN LETTERS 8–14

On January 8, 1944, the 508th arrived on the shores of Northern Ireland at Portstewart near Belfast. Crossing the Atlantic, the troops played cards, argued about omens of German submarines, and worried about the fate of men in lower berths during torpedo attacks. The trip included a toast of champagne smuggled aboard to celebrate the New Year. Unlike the 507th PIR, the 508th was not billeted in hotels and private homes, with the exception of a few lucky officers, like George, who found accommodation in town. The regiment—nearly 2,500 men—was otherwise housed at Camp Cromore in approximately two hundred Quonset huts.

"The main road from the gate went through the regimental area with other roads branching off to the left. The first road [was] to Regimental Headquarters, then the battalions branched off from there."[44] Rather than flushing toilets, the men used a latrine featuring "honey buckets" with toilet seats cut out from a board. The huts were heated with one small coal heater, which proved no match for the persistent damp, cold, and fog of Northern Ireland. Recalling his time there in a later letter, George described it as "cold and so black at night that a person could get lost in the Company street."

The 82nd Airborne's major accomplishment in Northern Ireland was the integration of the inexperienced 508th and its sister regiment, the green 507th, into the division. Training was tough and demanding, as the morning report[45] for January 20, 1944 attests: "Night march, 10 and 7/10th miles in 3 hours." On January 23, four senior enlisted combat veterans from the 505th were attached for a few days to George's company to brief the green paratroopers on what to expect in combat. With two combat jumps to their credit in Sicily and Italy, the 505th was the only combat-tested American paratrooper unit to drop into Normandy on D-Day.

George's letters to Jeane shared a taste of Northern Ireland, but also were concerned with the anxiety of battle and thoughts ever present in the minds of men about to undergo their first trial by combat. Sharing his feelings with his wife was a comfort to George; it seems to have grounded him and given him some sense of peace.

> 1 February 1944
> [Camp Cromore/Portstewart, Northern Ireland]
>
> We have many worried feelings these days. Sweating a little and wondering, but just imagine what the Germans are feeling. Waiting for action after coming this close is not good. I wonder what my feelings will be on the day. You will be in my heart and mind, your name on my lips. The Person above is kind—it will be His decision from the time we leave the plane. Faith is a wonderful thing. He alone knows the answer.
>
> 7 February 1944 [Cromore/Portstewart, Northern Ireland]
>
> Tom, the Irish boy [about age thirteen, who ran errands for pocket money], is over again tonight. He brought us tea and cake. I am lying in bed with Tom sitting by the fire, speculating as it were on how I can find things to write about each day. Had to tell him to wait until he had a wife and then he would understand. Tom is such a smart lad—someday he will be a cracker jack of a man. If something should happen to me, remember mine has been a full and complete life.
>
> 8 February 1944 [Cromore/Portstewart, Northern Ireland]
>
> Today has been a hectic day again, wanted to start your letter a dozen times, but I have been censoring mail until it seemed as though it should never end. Thank you for your faith in me, it won't go wrong. Tracy [2nd Lt. David J. Tracey, HqHq] and Davis [1st Lt. Donald A. Davis, HqHq] are in a hot argument about tactics. [46] Me—I am sitting in bed trying to concentrate. Tom brought tea and cakes again, and he is in the

middle just listening. Got a letter from my Dad. They are rare, he hates to write.

13 February 1944 [Cromore/Portstewart, Northern Ireland]

One of the few days I could sleep late. Tom came bounding in at noon to tell me that I had better hurry if I wanted to eat. With a little prodding from Tom, I managed to crawl out of bed. Made it to camp and chow. Arrived home again to find Tom dolefully sitting in front of a cold fireplace. There followed a session of fire-building [Tom had the skills of a British Boy Scout] and much discussion about nursing, educational systems, chemistry, language, history, and allied subjects. Quite a lad, he brings us tea every night. Tom washed windows while I wandered downtown and ate a lovely high tea….

I am again writing with Tom parked in front of the fireplace watching me very curiously. Here it comes—he couldn't figure how I could write you so often. Explained to him the best way possible that he would know in due time. There are some things you just can't explain. Love, George

George received plenty of moral support from his stepmother, Babe, who wrote him at least forty-nine times during the war, and also corresponded with his good friends Bud Leonard and Dave Scoggins. A loving person and quite the personality, she also had an unrivaled sense of humor, as revealed in the letters below, sent to George at Portstewart.

March 2, 1944 [From Babe, Seaside, Oregon]

George,

Did you hear the story about the soldier who wore all his medals at his wedding? Well, the girl was asking him what each of them was for, so he proceeded to tell her he had gotten the largest one for gunnery. She said, "Well, the Dr. told me once that I had gunnery, but I never got a medal for it. You must have had it terribly bad.

The country girl went to visit her city cousin. The city gal was going to show her around, and said she would take her to a dance. The girl did not like dances, but they decided to go just to see. The country girl asked what she should do if anyone

> asked her to dance. The other girl said, "Do just as I do and say just what I say." A fellow came up and asked the city girl to dance and she said, "Thank you, but I am contemplating matrimony and would rather sit." Pretty soon he came back and asked the country gal, so she says, "I'm sorry, thank you, but I'm constipated on macaroni and would rather s---."
>
> Don't worry about Jeane and the baby coming, she will have the best care. Loads of love and kisses, Babe.
>
> March 9, 1944 [From Babe, Seaside, Oregon]
>
> Had a cute letter from Bud Leonard the other day. Everyone that read it said that he never wrote to his folks like that, but I just told them that they probably never wrote to him like I did. I always tell him a lot of bull just like I do Dave. I took it for them to read and they sure got a big kick out of it, said that they didn't know Bud could be so witty. I sent him one of those cow pictures and he said the body was familiar, but he couldn't say so much for the face. He said that a lizard had been bothering him for three weeks but when it took a look at the picture, it ran 30 feet up a cocoa nut tree [sic]. Said from the gals he had seen down there, I could be his pin-up girl for 1944 and the rest of the time he was there. Loads of love and kisses, Babe

The 508th and other elements of the 82nd Airborne soon moved to central England, where there was more room for training and proximity to airfields for practice jumps. On March 11, 1944, the division moved to Nottingham, where the 508th was housed in tents in Wollaton Park. At the heart of the extensive park was Wollaton Hall, an opulent sixteenth-century English residence most American paratroopers described as a castle. Unable to find private housing, George lived in a large tent with several other officers.

The regiment now began training in earnest. In compliance with censorship rules, George's letters contain few details about training, but historical accounts described days full of drills, exercises, maneuvers, war games, and tactical problems: "Day to day field problems were conducted to keep the guys sharp. They ranged from map reading exercises, to simple cardiovascular exercises like long route marches or cross country runs. Time on the Range was also important. The training covered varying purposes, from lessons in disabling a tank to joint Infantry/Armored tactics in combat. Each man was also to dig a defensive position and allow a tank to drive directly over their head."[47]

Below, George reflected on the hectic pace, but also described a moment of peace and inner quiet brought on by his admiration for his friend Ellsworth Bartholomew's character, as revealed in a letter George had read during his censorship duties.

> 22 March 1944 [Nottingham, England]
>
> This is not like those days in Pinehurst. I have been working night and day. Suspect that at times I have had the combat jitters, but I have been combating them with a good little dose of common sense. Fear will be with us as we go along—anyone saying anything to the contrary is a liar. I often realize that an officer's pay is not in excess of what he earns. Psychology and reasoning are very peculiar things, and the study becomes more interesting as the days go by.
>
> Your loving husband, George
>
> 23 March 1944 [Nottingham, England]
>
> Honey, I have lost the jitters I have had the last few weeks. It is only a peaceful feeling inside of me as the night sounds of camp come drifting to my ears. A frequent laugh comes from the tents—an occasional expression as a group of men comes back from town. The rumble of a bus, the drone of a plane. This is a country to enjoy if times were different. "Intermezzo" seems to fill the air—our music darling. [The theme from Intermezzo, A Love Story, starring Leslie Howard and Ingrid Bergman.]
>
> ...Read a letter of one of the men today, Bartholomew to be exact. Am quite sure the letter finished the breakup [between Bartholomew and his girlfriend] and made me think again. It was a beautiful letter. Something that really shows the things that each American has inherited—something basic that is often forgotten, but is always there. That basic difference that makes an American the best person in the world. All my love, George

April 3 morning reports from HqHq show the company bivouacked in hangers at Barkston Heath Airfield for a practice jump code-named "Operation Sidecar." According to Captain Robert Abraham's entry for April 5, "planes failed to locate drop zone, landed at 0400—20 members of the company jumped [out of 164]. Entrucked at 1350 for Wollaton Park—arrived 1530. Weather—cloudy, rain, cold. Moral [sic] Excellent."

We speculate that since so few in the company jumped, this performance may have something to do with the Commanding Officer of HqHq (and regimental demolitions officer) Captain Robert Abraham's transfer to the division as a liaison officer. Captain James C. Driggers was assigned to Regimental Demolitions Officer and HqHq CO on April 10. While all were to jump, many did not and with good reason. General Gavin recorded 10 percent casualties among those who jumped, and stated that because of bad weather, "planes scattered everywhere. Landed all over the U.K."[48]

Meanwhile, George tried to keep it light in letters to Jeane, even when griping: "Between worries at school, company problems, gas [chemical weapons] worries, and the prospects of being a father, I should have a beautiful shock of grey hair," he wrote on April 14, 1944. That said, he certainly did have cause for griping: in addition to training, as executive officer of HqHq Co., he was responsible for carrying out the company commander's orders and completing mountains of paperwork. He was also training a section of twelve anti-tank rocket (bazooka) teams, assisted with the company supply chain, and taught classes in chemical warfare as the 508th expert in the field. Topics included anything chemical related to munitions: colored mortar rounds for signaling, phosphorus rounds for attacking and illumination at night, training to detect poison gas attacks, and using incendiary devices, smoke-making devices, and flamethrowers. To top it off, he complained, he even had to follow classes on "stuff I already know."

Troopers being troopers, the 508th nevertheless found (or stole) the time to court English roses and devour fish and chips, thus proving the saying "oversexed and over here," while escaping a steady diet of spam and brussels sprouts.[49] The Heart and Hand and The Jolly Higgler pubs were enlisted men's favorites, while officers favored The Admiral Rodney.[50] Not to be deterred from a drink, some men—including the poetic T/5 Bartholomew—even managed to turn botched training jumps into hilarious misadventures ending up in a pub.

As Sgt. Harold F. Gerkin of Regimental Headquarters recalled it, he, Bartholomew, and First Lieutenant Donald J. Johnson, the platoon leader of the First Battalion demolition section, jumped prematurely on a nighttime dry run, thinking it was the real deal, and they'd reached their drop zone in Normandy. When the rest of the plane load landed back at the airport, an emergency report was issued, and search planes set out to comb the English countryside.

Meanwhile, discerning the sounds of English issuing from the nearest farmhouse, the combat-ready troopers holed up for the night in a haystack, then hitched a ride on an army truck to London the next morning, figuring they could catch a flight back to base. Unable to resist the opportunity to toast their exploit first in a handy London pub, they were still clinking glasses at closing time. Rushing into the street, they caught a passing bus, but Sergeant Gerkin had time only to grab onto the rail at the back, whereupon his backpack blew open and his parachute unfolded, billowing out behind him as the bus sped down the street. As legend has it, the driver felt the drag, looked the rearview mirror and halted, incredulous. And that was how three Red Devils accomplished a first in English history by stopping a London bus with a parachute![51]

* * *

While the 508th was training in England, the Round Robin continued to circulate in Illinois, when Barbara Martin sent it on to Terry Tibbetts in Chicago, who had just changed addresses. A good friend of Jeane's, Terry was married to 2nd Lt. James D. Tibbets. His job was as the S-1 (personnel specialist) in Hq2.

> Terry Tibbetts, Chicago, Illinois [RR 8]
>
> April 6, 1944
>
> Dear Girls,
>
> I'm sorry to have held up the proceedings, but due to the change in my address the delivery of the Round Robin was delayed.
>
> I'm afraid I have to ask you girls to forgive my letter if it isn't a very long one, because I have a good case of the grippe [flu], and Jimmy has got a good cold. I don't know whether I got it from him, or he got it from me, but between us we're doing our best to shake it off. My baby is a big boy now. He'll be a year old this month. He certainly is full of tricks, but he's very good if I do say so myself.
>
> By now I imagine you girls know our hubbies are in England. My husband sent me some beautiful ash trays from Belfast, Ireland, which appeared to have been part of some family silver someone was forced to dispose of. Like you, Anne, while our men were in Ireland, Deane complained of not receiving mail. I'm hanging on tightly to a four-leaf clover Deane tucked

into one of his letters from Ireland, and I'm also holding on tight to a wish for a safe early homecoming for all of them.

This Round Robin is a real inspiration, and I enjoyed every one of the letters so very much. So, until the next time with all the best to everyone.

I am sincerely, Terry Mrs. James D. Tibbets Jr.

The Round Robin circulated steadily, despite the fact that so many correspondents had moved or were just about to move as it reached their mailbox, as was the case for the next contributor and Illinois resident, Lauren Dress (wife of Capt. Hillman C. Dress, Hq3). One of the few Round Robin correspondents without children, Lauren wrote an upbeat letter about her upcoming move, office work, and outings with women friends.

Lauren Dress, Canton, Illinois [RR 9]

April 11, 1944

Hello Everyone:

The mail man must have felt a little vicious when he left this in my mailbox as he tore the envelope and one letter (it happened to be the list you had made, Anne). I have made a new list to replace it and have also added a few names and checked the ones who have had the letter.

I have been staying with Hillman's brother and his family. (I didn't use his nickname, Hymie, as some of the girls who don't know him might think there was a German spy in their husband's midst.)[52] However, I am moving the last of this week into an apartment that has me thrilled to pieces. We were all getting a little cramped for space since they have three little boys and expect another (yes, another boy) soon. I had quite a bit of furniture but had to rustle up a stove and refrigerator, no easy job these days. It has been fun getting all of the things together again and making plans for the new home. It is going to be pretty quiet and lonesome as a whole though, but I can always borrow one of the little boys. Little Hymie [Hillman's nephew] has already announced his intentions of living with me.

I am working in the freight office of a short line railroad through here. It is nice work and time goes much faster than before I started working. It is the first time in my life I have ever wanted time to go fast. If there was only some way of starting and stopping time at one's own desire. I shouldn't over-complain. So many of the girls around here are in the same boat. We all get together regularly and have a bridge game, go and fool around, or just sit and talk. I find myself busy every minute. Like Barbara Martin (I don't believe I knew her), I find a small town has its advantages.

I have nothing new to offer from England way. Hymie has been sending me copies of the newspapers (my hobby), and several books and pictures for our scrap book. There is another package on the way he tells me, and naturally I'm anxious to see what it has.

If this letter reaches Madelon Miriam [*sic*] or if someone else has her address, I wish they would send it to me. A girl in town asks me for it all the time, and I haven't been able to get it. She is an old school friend of hers.

I'm writing this on company time, but feel it is time well-spent. Keep up the good work, girls, and the best to all of you.

Sincerely, Lauren Dress

Now in full swing, the Round Robin flew south to Arkansas to Mary Skipton, married to 2nd Lt. Roy K. Skipton, in B Co. Like Lauren and so many other regimental wives, Mary was pregnant and felt as if she was "filling the time" until the menfolk returned.

Mary Skipton, Little Rock, Arkansas [RR 10]

April 24, 1944

Dear Girls,

It is so interesting to hear what all of you are doing to fill the time until the 508th is back and we can again return to normal living.

For myself, I am keeping fairly busy at the Quartermaster's Camp, Joseph T. Robinson. The camp is seven miles out of town, but I have a ride to and from work which helps a great deal. We enrolled because we heard that the course was largely about the mental outlook of soldiers returning from war. So far, it has been about child psychology. Of course, I hope to be able to use that too someday, but at present the other would be of more interest.

The Irish linen got around to me too. Skip sent me a beautiful cloth and napkins. There seems to be a lull in activities in England now (I hope it continues). Skip spoke of making a trip to London and of finding most of the buildings supposed to be of interest to tourists are still standing—and still of interest.

We had a little ceremony at the office today. Civilian Employees who have been with the War Department for six months were awarded some kind of service ribbon, rather like a good-conduct ribbon in the army. Quite an honor, or so the Colonel said. When I get one, I am going to hang on to it, so when Skip gets back with his little overseas ribbons, I can dust mine off and bring it forth. I doubt very much if he will be properly impressed.

Incidentally, I hear the WACs are getting tropical worsted uniforms.[53] That isn't a military secret, but a big improvement. It is too bad that the enlisted men don't fare as well.

I notice that the letter didn't get to Nancy Graham while it was on the west coast. I don't have her address, but I am sure she would enjoy it, if some of you do have it. It is now past one, and time for all good little girls to be at work. Best of luck to all of you.

Sincerely, Mary

Making a bit of a detour for a newly added member of the band of sisters living in the South, the Round Robin reached Edith "Sis" Tomlinson, the wife of 2nd Lt. Lynn C. Tomlinson, D Co. Due to give birth at any time, she wrote from Mobile, Alabama, on stationary imprinted with a parachute and the words "THUMBS UP" under the open canopy.

Edith "Sis" Tomlinson, Mobile, Alabama [RR 11]

April 26, 1944

Hi Yaw'l,

Mary [Williams] received the "Round Robin," and being that I live right near her, I thought it would be a grand idea to sign my "John Henry." It is really nice to know what everyone is doing. As I sit here, I'm in waiting: Jr. was supposed to make his (or her) entrance April 24. Of course, I'm impatient, but don't guess you can rush such things. And of course, Tommy's sweating it out—so he states in his letters.

Mrs. Joe Gillespie (Naomi) had a baby girl, Mary Kathleen. She's as thrilled as I think I'd be (if it'll ever come). She says the baby looks like Joe, which helps a lot.

No news from this part. Tommie sent clippings of the practice jump where Churchill reviewed. I thought maybe the 508 had jumped, but Mary tells me different. Looked good to see paratroopers in their jumpsuits though.

Glad to know everyone is fine. From the looks of things, Mary will have her baby before me. Gosh! I'm impatient. Maybe tomorrow.

Regards to all, Sis Tomlinson

* * *

Jeane, Hellen Moss, Terry Tibbets, and other Round Robin writers who were especially close at Pinehurst also exchanged personal letters. Any information they received was quickly passed on. Below, Jeane updated George on news Helen had reported about her husband Clint, and queried him about rumors.

April 16, 1944, Hood River

There was a letter from Helen catching me up on most of the regimental news and what's going on in England. What's this about Col Eckman having a command of his own now? Don't quite understand this 30-man section business. [George was made platoon leader of the regimental bazooka section, a dangerous duty he did not tell Jeane about until the 508th was on occupation duty in Germany.] Stupidly enough, there are lots of things in this world that I don't understand though. Helen said that Clint had made two jumps [during training in England]. I had wondered so much about you, especially when the wind is high, and the weather is stormy. I only hope that you are safe inside somewhere.

Always your loving wife, Jeane

In mentioning a specific personnel move, Jeane had slipped up and broken censorship rules. George reminded her, gently but firmly, to keep letters confined to personal affairs in a way that reassured her while keeping George himself out of trouble with the censors.

2 May 1944, Nottingham, England

Yes, Col. Ekman does have a regiment of his own. [He had replaced James Gavin as the CO of the 505th PIR]. I usually don't mention a thing about the army in my letters, Honey—I like to forget all about it when I write. Just like a chameleon, my letters are my time, and the army can't prevent me from Hoping, Praying, and Dreaming. I don't ever mean to exclude you on anything, but Jeane, my troubles and worries are not to bother that pretty head of yours.

George genuinely wanted to forget about army affairs: his next letter to Jeane confessed the strain of being an officer and platoon leader, and shared his struggles privately with her as he would with no one else.

22 April 1944, Nottingham, England

...This war takes more than hard work. The mental strain is terrific—my job more often of late is building morale. Not a job to receive thanks, but a job that is essential to the men. I get things from both ends—orders from above and complaints from the men. Often this tension puts me in a bad mood. Writing, My Darling, is perhaps the hardest thing of all. Everything seems to be going wrong at times. Jeane, at times like that I may miss a day of writing to you—but there is one thing to remember. There isn't another girl in the world that I care about—I was born that way. You are always with me here in my heart. I must close. More work to do and then some sleep, if I can keep from worrying about you. I don't want medals, but a job is a job and I have men under my care. Had a dream last night that we had a boy.

Love and kisses, George

On the same day that George wrote the above, Jeane wrote to him, pondering a question that many on the home front expressed about the Nazi regime's brutality and assertions of superiority.

April 22, 1944, Hood River, Oregon

It's incomprehensible to me that a group of women and men could allow themselves to be so stupidly duped that they could resort to such a manner of living. Supremacy can't be obtained in that way. They can't beat God and nature. Yet all of this you know. Americans aren't perfect of course; we don't pretend to be and we're glad that we all are Americans. Love, Jeane

* * *

While Jeane was writing to George on April 22, Sis Tomlinson passed the now-bulging package to the cheerful and enterprising Mary Williams, the wife of 1st Lt. Gene H. Williams on the Hq3 pathfinder team. A little over a month after Mary replied, she gave birth to twin boys on June 8, 1944, just two days after D-Day.[54]

Mary Williams, Mobile, Alabama [RR 12]

April 27, 1944

Dear "508ers,"

Gosh, I've never been so thrilled in all my life as I was yesterday when all ten of your letters rolled in! Boy, they really have come from far and near!!

I have a few "latrine rumors" as Beth calls them, but I'm not too sure of their validity. They came from my cousin, a member of the 515th, which was up at Mackall, but he might have been handing me quite a line. Anyhow—he says that our dear ole Camp Mackall is being evacuated and turned into a *German prison camp*!! All of the paratroop outfits have moved out and only the air corps remains. The 13th Airborne is supposed to go on maneuvers in California and the 11th and the 17th left quite a while ago. Does anyone know whether this is true or not? Kinda hate to see it happen, don't you? I've grown rather found of the ole place!

Guess Helen and Beth are beginning to wonder what happened to their "brainchild." So—here's what I did. I wrote all ten of you girls a postcard yesterday so you'd know where the "Round Robin" is and will be.

Letters from England are really coming in *good*! In fact, several have taken only *five* days to get from him to me. Also—the other day I received a package sent from Ireland. It had beautiful silver antiques in it plus a spoon for the baby. Was I thrilled!

Speaking of the baby, I have only a couple more months to go, thank goodness! Y'all should see me—I look like "Mrs. Five-by-Five" instead of "Mrs. G.H.W. 0-821."

Ann, sending this on over to you. Doris [Daly], as I understand, you and I are "in the same boat"! Congratulations on Jack getting "I" Company [becoming company commander]. Can't wait for this letter to get back, but guess it'll be about *next year*!

Just, Mary Williams

The Round Robin was now moving more quickly than ever. Also pregnant, Doris Daly quickly received it in New Jersey, wrote, and expedited it on its way just four days after Mary had mailed it. Doris's husband, 1st Lt. John "Jack" Daly, initially assigned to Hq3, had recently been promoted to commander of I Co.

Doris Daly, Newark, New Jersey [RR 13]

May 1, 1944

Hello 508 Gals,

Heard a few weeks ago about this Round Robin and think it's a wonderful idea. Good work Helen, for starting it rolling. We often talked about something like this before we left Southern Pines, but like everything else, time drifted on.

So glad you sent it on to me, Mary Williams, but it went past Mary Casteel in W. Va. so I'll send it back to her, so she can continue it geographically and we won't waste any more time. I'm sure, Mary, you will have several more names to add on.

I hear so often from Jack, in fact practically every day, because I'm so near New York. Some have come in four days, believe it or not! Of course, that's airmail, but we are well satisfied with that swell service. Now that "D" Day is nearing, I know all you girls are as anxious and nervous as I am but what else can we do but pray and hope for the very best for all our boys?[55]

I, too, like so many of you girls, received a lovely package from Northern Ireland. Mine consisted of beautiful Irish linen, a darling silver baby cup, and baby spoon for our little Jr. or Miss. Only 2 1/2 months to go now but I do wish it was all over. Also in my package were some lovely pearls and some English currency, my lucky pieces now. From England, I'm now patiently awaiting a package Jack wrote about. I [already] received a lovely lace doily that Jack received at a reception of some kind from the Lord Mayor of someplace. (Very definite, ha ha. Military secret I guess, so don't ask where.)

I'm living with my sister, brother-in-law, two little nieces and my little sister. There's never a dull moment, which I'm thankful for, because with so many here it makes time fly. That's just what I want with Jack away and then the baby coming soon. Ok, yes, I'm—blossoming beautifully now, just like everything else at Springtime, ha ha.

Sincerely, Doris Daly

When the Round Robin caught up with Mary Casteel in West Virginia around mid-May, she enthusiastically added more names to the roster and supplied the missing address for one of the "girls" already on the list. Married to Maj. James R. Casteel, HqHq, Regimental S-4 (logistics and supply), Mary declared her full intent to catch up in the baby department, and raise a whole batch of little paratroopers once her husband got home.

Mary Casteel, Morgantown, West Virginia [RR 14]

May 11, 1944

Dear "508 Sisters":

Really girls, I had more fun reading all your letters. It was truly like a continued story, and I could hardly wait to get to each letter. It's great to know what you're doing and that you're all hearing from your husbands regularly.

Honestly, all you girls with babies and those of you who are anticipating the "blessed event" actually make me feel like a back number. We'll try anyhow. The Casteels may be slow—but, just wait till the boys come home! Jimmie and I will show you—we'll raise ourselves a whole Army of Paratroopers. Ha! Ha! No kidding tho, I do think it's swell that you have your babies and it helps to pass time away, which might become heavy after a while.

I've been staying with Mother and Dad since I came back. I went to work at one of our banks in January, and worked till a week ago when I "quituated"—just wasn't satisfied, or rather the job wasn't what I thought it was going to be. I slipped home to help my mother, as she isn't very well, and believe me, we are in house-cleaning up to our necks. The weather is perfect for cleaning, too. Help is practically unobtainable now, and we've been doing the work ourselves.

I hear from Jimmie so often I wonder how he can ever find time to write so frequently. He surely has been "ole faithful." I have received some gorgeous Irish table linen and napkins, all from Ireland. Saturday, I received two of the most beautiful Nottingham lace tablecloths I have ever seen. Honestly, I'm just as proud of everything as I can be. The way Jimmie goes in for table linen and lace, I have a hunch he's kinda planning on eating again when he comes home. Ha! Ha!

I was really surprised when I found my husband's picture in the paper—along with Maj Holmes, Col Harrison, Maj Warren [all 508th battalion commanders or future commanders], the Lord Mayor of Nottingham, and the Sherriff of Nottingham taken at the Civic Hall, following the banquet given by the town so American officers might become acquainted with local dignitaries. No doubt most of you girls saw the same picture in some of your papers.[56]

I've been keeping in contact with several of the girls and hear from them often. That means so very much. I would be happy to hear from any of you girls that have time to write. It always seemed that we were one grand happy family, and our relationship has been so much closer than any other regiment I have ever seen. I like it that way, don't you? I am adding the names of some of the girls whose addresses I have here. I'm sure they'll enjoy the Round Robin too. Someone asked about Nancy Graham on the west coast—I'm giving you her address too.

Girls, I must hurry along. I'll be anxiously awaiting the return of the Round Robin and more fun, huh? Best o' luck to you all.

Sincerely, Mary Mrs. James R. Casteel

* * *

Jeane gave birth on May 8, 1944. George received the big telegram he had so eagerly been waiting for on May 10, responding with a brief letter on that date.

I LOVE YOU DARLING GEORGE RICHARD IS
WONDERFUL LIKE YOU DARK HAIR WELL BUILT
PHYSICALLY ADORABLE YOURS

JEANE GURWELL

George replied:

10 May 1944 [Nottingham, England]

Jeane there isn't much worry anymore, let this war come on. Just can't contain myself for the news about you both. How much did he weigh and what color are his hair and eyes?

George's initial exuberance was soon diminished when he learned by a letter from Babe and from Jeane's mother that Jeane had hemorrhaged after the birth. She was in the hospital recovering. The timing was dramatic: Adding to the stress of being a new father, he learned of Jeane's recovery from life-threatening hemorrhaging at the same time he was preparing to spearhead the assault against Nazi Germany! A long, heartfelt letter to Jeane ensued on May 28, 1944, followed by three more letters on May 29, 30, and 31. George's letters to his wife were written behind the closed fences surrounding Saltby Airfield, where the 508th was sealed in to ensure security immediately prior to the upcoming invasion of Europe.

**George Gurwell in Nottingham, England, circa April 1944. Gurwell Collection.**

28 May 1944 [Saltby Airfield, England]

Hello My Very Dearest Darling,

Had to stop in the middle of my work—even if it isn't done. Yes, it has been quite a gap in my letters—Jeane, that gap couldn't be helped. Should be working now, but there is a limit to even my peace of mind—I just can't go on without first writing to you.

Jeane—I Love You so very much. There is something that I want you to know. You are the first person that I have really loved. This last year has been a taste of heaven that I never expected to find. There is still beauty in this crazy world—there is patience and understanding in my heart. Jeane, I want you to always keep me in mind as long as I am alive, and even after you have my heart. Words won't give the proper expression to my feelings.

Yes, Sweetheart, I have been working night and day for the past week. The Captain ordered me to take some time off last Wednesday. Dave Scoggins and Verne came down, and for one night we old cronies relaxed together. Three from Seaside, Oregon. We were at Verne's camp and I proceeded to get very drunk. Felt pretty low Thursday morning, but felt completely relaxed and tired to the point of exhaustion. Work piled up until it wasn't even worthwhile. Besides, I became so damned homesick. That has been on my back for the past six or seven days. No pity, Darling, because that keeps my mind occupied. It doesn't pay to think too much.

Jeane, this is a bad subject to bring up, but these things are important. Our Son and You are my only Worry. If something should happen to me, you will receive just about everything I have of value. It won't be much, between $10,000 and $15,000. I want you to finish that nursing training. My wish as well is that you will marry again. Our son will then be in your care and in better hands I could ever have found.

You will decide what is best for him. There are a few things that he will ever need to remember. To be as wonderful as his mother. Treat everyone as you would have them treat you or anyone that you love. Be honest with everyone—a difficult thing to do—especially when things go wrong, but a person (our son) will have the world by the tail if he can do it. Honesty is something that a person takes a beating on, but it always pays in the long run. There isn't much else in Life except a proper Trust in God and a Love of nature, which has a religion not taught by any bible. You will know of the invasion very soon after it starts. Radio, newspapers, Newsweek, etc. will go wild.

Jeane, you have a depth of understanding, faith and Honesty that you have never before realized yourself. What you decide will be the best. Decide for yourself Darling—you will always have my backing. Your love, trust and faith are too strong to

> ever shake because that knowledge alone keeps you a Husband that can never be untrue. I might date, but it hasn't and never will be love. I haven't stepped out of line, and I never shall while I have you.
>
> People are always human, and I often think that "Jeane would never know" but there is something within me that says no. I have to live with myself and I love Faith in a person. There is something in my make-up that can't quite go for the statement used by most: "I love my wife, but She is a long way away." No names, but this is straight from the shoulder [a boxing term meaning as direct as possible]. I don't think much of that kind of person. I warned you before we were married that it would be for a lifetime and after. Those are even more my feelings now. It is difficult to put my feeling on paper in black and white. My Darling, I have a tremendous yearning to see Our Son. Must admit that I think you're a just a little prejudiced—but who isn't?
>
> Well, I have to close for now. Don't worry about me. Keep that lovely chin up. I love you so very much, Always, Your loving husband, George

With the invasion just days away, the 508th made an impression on the assistant division commander, Brigadier General James Gavin, who commented in his diary that the regiment "looks as good as any new outfit that I have ever seen. If they cannot do it, it cannot be done by green troops." [57] Gavin had cause to be worried about green troops. Intelligence reports showing German troop movements as of April 1944 into 82nd Airborne drop zones areas necessitated changes to invasion plans.

As late as May 29, 1944, British Air Chief Marshal Sir Trafford Leigh-Mallory wrote to the Supreme Allied Commander, General Dwight Eisenhower, warning that the new German troop dispositions could inflict 50 to 70 percent casualties on the U.S. airborne forces on the first day. Eisenhower determined that the airborne mission was so critical, however, that the risk had to be run.[58] Gavin's diary for May 25 reads: "Either this 82nd Division job will be the most glorious and spectacular episode in our history, or it will be another Little Big Horn. There is no way to tell now but we are going in and they will, I am certain, do a hell of a good job. It is regrettable that so many of them have to get lost, but it is a tough business and they all figure that parachutists have nine lives."[59]

There is no doubt whatsoever that last-minute changes in drop zones and assault targets raised anxiety among lower-ranking officers as well, causing an incredible amount of stress and overwork, like that described in some of George's letters of May 1944. George had no illusions whatsoever about the dangerousness of the mission. Just before he boarded a C-47 from Serial 21, 50th Troop Carrier Squadron, 314th Troop Carrier Group on the evening of June 5[60], he penned two short notes intended as goodbye letters in case he died in combat: one addressed to his stepmother, father, and brother, the other a last note to Jeane.

> [Saltby Airfield, England]
>
> [To Babe, Daddy, and Dick] Your letter of the 19th telling me about Jeane caught me when I couldn't wire and had very little time to write. I am glad that you did tell me. For several days there really didn't seem to be much purpose to anything. Since then I have had a letter from Jeane and another from you with the wonderful news that she is getting along okay. Once again there is reason in the world. Tell Ann thank you from the bottom of my heart for the help.
>
> It is for people such as you that we are going to give these Germans HELL!! Our better ideals are so very clear now. Keep those chins up. If something happens—mine has been a Wonderful life because of all of you. Thanks again for a wonderful upbringing and a wonderful life. Your loving son, George.
>
> [Saltby Airfield, England]
>
> 5 June 1944
>
> Jeane—Take such very good care of yourself and Our Son. Gee! I am anxious to hold the two of you in my arms. It is surprising how full my life can be with just the two of you. We have been very busy Darling—too busy to write at times, but Jeane—I write every chance I have. Be sure and kiss George Richard for me. Please now, Darling—Don't exert yourself. Keep that adorable chin up and do what the doctors say.
>
> I am in God's care, Sweet One—so no matter what happens—it will be as he deems best. I am sending you the only ribbon I wear—A European Theatre of Operations Ribbon. Jeane, I love you with all my heart and soul and I always will. All my Love Sweetheart—Always! Your Adoring Husband—George

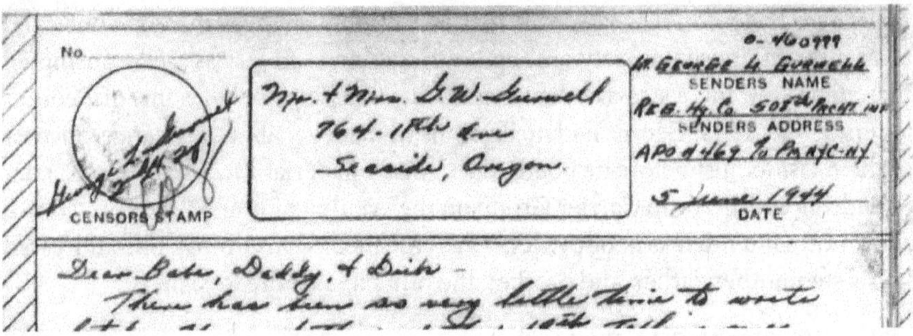

No.

0-460999

Lt George L Gurwell
SENDERS NAME

Reg. Hq. Co. 508th Prcht Inf
SENDERS ADDRESS

APO #469 % PM NYC-NY

5 June 1944
DATE

Mr. + Mrs. G. W. Gurwell
764 - 17th Ave
Seaside, Oregon.

CENSORS STAMP

Dear Bate, Daddy, + Dick -
There has been so very little time to write

# CHAPTER V

# D-DAY AND THE BATTLE FOR NORMANDY

The Normandy invasion on D-Day was the largest seaborne assault in history. There were five invasion beaches (together sixty miles long) with airborne support on the flanks or extreme ends of the beaches for this huge amphibious and airborne assault code named "Operation Overlord." Just over 156,000 Allied troops landed by air or by sea on June 6, and the arrival of more troops and equipment continued for months. The invasion primarily consisted of troops from the U.S., Britain, and Canada, but troops from other Allied countries were also involved.

The scale of the invasion is difficult to comprehend. There were thirteen thousand American paratroopers from six parachute infantry regiments (PIRs) supporting the right flank of the invasion near the French town of Sainte-Mère-Église—not including nearly four thousand glider-borne troops. The 832 transport planes were enough to get the American paratroopers into France in one lift, *without shuttling aircraft*. The 508th was one of those six PIRs, with just over two thousand officers and enlisted men. Of just over 150 officers of the

508th that landed in Normandy, forty-five of their wives participated in the Round Robin letter. One of those officers was 2nd Lt. George L. Gurwell.

While packing his weapons and infantry equipment before D-Day, George found room in his 150 pounds of gear for two good luck charms. George wore one of Jeane's charms, a panda, along with a locket with Jeane's picture on the same chain as his dog tags. He also kept the Bible Jeane's mother gave him over his heart. After two years of preparation, George jumped into the Normandy night at two in the morning. Jeane and the rest of the world quickly heard of the long-awaited invasion.

With the news of D-Day, the lives of the paratrooper families would never be the same. In the next few letters written from Jeane to George, she shared with him the thoughts and feelings that were sweeping over her. Mostly they longed for the type of speedy information that today we take for granted. Surely, her friends from Pinehurst were experiencing the same emotions.

> June 7, 1944 [Hood River, Oregon]
>
> My Dearest Darling,
>
> Words won't come very well because there are no words to convey even a small part of what we feel. When you read this, I don't know perhaps many things will look different to you, but that is to be expected my Darling. Wherever you are, however, you feel, please remember that my love for you will never change. When the first flash came announcing "D" Day, I was the only one awake and heard it through Ann's window. For a minute I couldn't call Babe's name, but I had felt it coming. Now I know how men feel when their wife is having a baby: how they suffer and imagine it all, pray, and feel helpless. I constantly pray that the path will be bright through all the days ahead.
>
> Your Loving Wife, Jeane
>
> June 20, 1944 [Hood River, Oregon]
>
> My Darling,
>
> Your letter written May 28th came and these tumbled emotions won't go down on paper. No honey, not really so tumbled, just a part of this love for you: I love you for valuing honesty so highly. We just always have that between us; it can be no other way. As far as unfaithfulness: right is right and wrong

is wrong. Surely, they can't love their wives, or they couldn't hurt them so completely, for the wives *will* know and they fool no one but themselves. You can't know how much your faithfulness means to me, yet strangely enough if you should slip, I wouldn't want you to stay away because of it. I can't help my love for you, but it's built on all that you are. And My Darling, don't ever request my marrying again.

I constantly pray that God will see us through this nightmare that must end soon. Thank you, George for the letter and all you remember to tell me. Must confess, honey, I'm jealous of those dates, but glad for you. You married a stinker.

Good Night Angel, Jeane and "Butch"

George was wounded in action on June 6. As soon as he possibly could, he wrote Jeane to inform her that a telegram was coming from the government. He wanted his letter to arrive before the official telegram to lower Jeane's anxiety. Telegrams from the War Department were dreaded by the families of troops overseas, as the news could mean their loved one was seriously wounded, severely wounded, missing in action, or killed in action. A telegram arriving at a house flying a blue service star was greeted with dread. To soften the blow, George wrote as soon as possible, and yes, his letter arrived before the dreaded telegram.

16 June 1944 [93rd General Hospital, England]

As you know by now, I have been into France. The particulars—are sealed up inside, parts I can tell you later, but parts—well, they are better forgotten.

I suppose the war department will send word that I have been wounded. Hope to heavens now that this letter arrives first. It was just a scratch. A bullet through the muscle of my left leg. Just enough to slow me down and nothing more. I am back in England now and a problem for the poor nurses. My ornery streak is coming out and they have their hands full. Am getting the best of care—too much so because I am itching to get out. The surprise is going to be that bullet. I have some other trinkets for you which I will send later. Never despair wonderful one, because no news is always good news. Keep that lovely chin up, sweetheart.

Your adoring husband, George

On June 29th Jeane wrote George about receiving the dreaded telegram from the war department informing her of his injury.

> REGRET TO INFORM YOU YOUR HUSBAND SECOND LIEUTENANT GEORGE L GURWELL WAS SERIOUSLY WOUNDED IN ACTION NINE JUNE IN FRANCE LETTER CONTAINING PRESENT MAIL ADDRESS FOLLOWS= [*sic*] [Major General James A.] ULIO THE ADJUTANT GENERAL.

Jeane thanked George in her quick reply for getting a letter to her before the anxiety-provoking telegram, informing her of his non-life-threatening injury.

> June 29, 1944 [Hood River, Oregon]
>
> My Darling George,
>
> Your address still isn't open for cables and still there is nothing that I can do. Darling, I love you so hopelessly. There is relief in knowing where you are, and the general situation, yet my Darling, you can't expect me to not be concerned about you. You're my very reason for living, but more than anything else, I want you happy, well and home.
>
> Sweetheart, how can you know how much your thoughtfulness meant in writing your letter before the official Government notification? The man at the telegraph office drove out this morning with the telegram from the war office. Naturally, it wasn't too cheerful and all too brief for those at home who love you so. You see, it said you were "seriously wounded" June 9th.[61] My Darling, how are you "really" feeling? The telegram said that a letter containing your present mail address would follow. Are these reaching you so terribly late? I want to know every little detail about you so badly. How long for recovery and then what will they do with you and where? You must guess how much I want you here to recover and recuperate.
>
> By the way, George Honey, Margarite and Fred [friends from Oregon that now live in Washington, D.C.] wrote a letter saying that they were sending the baby a bond. Beth Pollom

made him the sweetest bib imaginable, and Barbara Martin sent the cunningest sun suit, but you'll be home in time to see him wear that [wishful thinking]. Beth and Barbara have been sweating out the invasion like everyone else.

Your adoring wife, Jeane

The letter from the War Department followed, confirming the telegram's information and giving George's address.

Wives, relatives, and fellow citizens were anxiously waiting out the invasion and what the consequences would be to their loved ones on far-off French battlefields. Odds for death and disfigurement were way too high for the invasion forces, especially the paratroopers. George's stepmother, Babe, was also anxious to hear from him when she penned these words and hinted at Jeane's racked nerves.

June 27, 1944 [Seaside, Oregon]

I can't understand why you haven't gotten word sooner that Jeane was better [from postpartum complications], as I wrote you every day before coming up here to Hood River, and every day after I got here, but I guess the mail was held up before the invasion. Jeane called me right after we had gotten here to say that she had received word from you that you were hurt. It just made me sick, but at least we know that you aren't in the middle of it right now and probably won't be for some time. I do wish you would write and let us know how bad it is, but whatever you do take it easy and don't worry Jeane too much. She took it pretty good, but I told her if she needed me that I was sure that I could come back, she is a strange girl, and is hard to really understand at times, but her Mother says that I have done her more good than anyone else that they know could. She can't do anything to help her at times and said that she might have to send for me again. God bless, Lots of love and kisses, Babe

Babe's letter gives us a more unfiltered account of how Jeane was challenged by the stress of separation, uncertainty of war, and struggles of being a new wife and mother. She was facing very good odds that she would be rearing her child alone. Two factors worked to keep Jeane in the dark: George did not want to cause her undue worry, and censorship regulations. Nearly a year later, he gave his firsthand account of those early days of June '44.

Our excitement was almost without end when we read George's letters from Chartres, France, dated May 15 and 16, 1945, written after Victory in Europe.[62] For the children of WWII veterans to get an account of their parent's experience in writing is beyond belief for people of our generation. When censorship was relaxed after Germany's defeat, George wrote to Jeane about what he experienced on D-Day. Not until then did he finally reveal that he had been in charge of a bazooka platoon, a main defense against enemy tanks.

> 15 May 1945 [Chartres, France]
>
> Hello My Adorable One,
>
> The planes were loaded, and we took off around ten at night [should be midnight]. Crossed the channel and then we were over France with flak and tracers flying around. Jumped at about 0215 and landed in waist deep water in a flooded area near St. Mere Eglise—very wet, very scared, and a little mixed up as to exactly where I was. Managed to collect three men from our Company. Not one equipment bundle that was dropped was found. Four were on the plane. So, you had a husband—wet, cold, and very green wading around in the water in France that first morning in France.
>
> That Sweetheart was how I managed to ruin your pictures. They were in my wallet. Oh! An interesting sidelight. It took two other men plus my own efforts to get me into the plane. When I jumped, the opening shock tore a musette bag and a dispatch case right off me. Loops were torn right out of my belt, and a heavy harness was snapped right in two. Funny though, I didn't even notice it at the time. Bet that I really looked a sight—but no one would tell me. Still intact in France and about two hours until the beach head troops were due to land about ten miles away. More in the next issue.
>
> [Next letter continued the D-Day story]
>
> 16 May 1945
>
> Back to France on the sixth of June. With four others and myself, I worked my way over toward high ground. Just before we reached it, a battalion of another unit jumped right over

the top of us. The first officer I ran into was a friend of mine from the same class at Oregon State. The high ground proved to be a railroad. We set up a defense while I consulted a map and determined where we were and which way to go. By that time, the better part of two companies of 507 started to go by, and we acted as point for them. Moved down the railroad and about that time flares started up all over the sky out at the beach. It was one of the most beautiful displays that I have ever seen. Tracers were all around too, and several fire fights were banging away around us. Really quite amazing. Later that morning, I broke away from the two companies—they were just getting mixed up anyway. Just after that, I saw my first Jerry plane—a F.W. 190 [Focke-Wulf 190, a German fighter] going like a devil was right on its tail and headed for Germany.[63] Right after that we all hit the dirt when some Jerry opened on us with a burp gun blasting bullets all around us. Exchanged a few shots and then moved on.

By this time, it was light out, and we stopped with another small unit. Very shortly after that I found our headquarters or at least a part of it. Terribly short of everything, I took a few trips around to pick up equipment [including his platoon's anti-tank bazookas and rockets]. On returning from about the third trip in the early afternoon, I found our group pinned down around about four farmhouses. Took one of my two bazookas (two out of twelve) and moved up. One of my men blew half of the side of a house away, and with a couple of others I moved up into one of the buildings. Firing out of the stone door, some Jerry cut loose with a burp gun from a window that I wasn't watching. That tagged me through the leg. I stumbled backward instead of forward and watched bout thirty bullets kick up dust right alongside of me. I got mad—thought I had been hit by a rock fragment. Continued to fire, and soon after that the Jerries came out. Supposed to be five, but fourteen came piling out with their hands up. Two were already dead in the yard outside.[64] I could hardly walk, so back to the medics to find out that a bullet had gone right through my left upper leg.

Late that afternoon, we pulled back to another of the fields lined with those damned hedgerows and took a terrific pounding from Jerry artillery. Mined a bridge that evening just before dark. Spent the first night freezing to death and having the living day lights shelled out of us. Had a platoon the next day and managed to move in support of two others despite my leg which just wouldn't work. Finally had to go back to the aid station again. Sneaked away late that afternoon and headed at a very slow walk for the unit. Caught them at Chef-du-Pont [a walk of about two miles].

**The La Fière bridge over the Merderet River, Normandy, France. George landed near here and was wounded near here on D-Day.**

**508th Memorial Wall, near Hill 30, Chef du Pont, Normandy, June 5, 2018.**

Spent two more days there doing regular duties and finally Doc Klein sent me back because I couldn't get around enough. Had outguessed him two days then, but he finally caught me. Back to the beach and shots and a trip on the L.S.T. [Landing Ship, Tank] to a Hospital ship and then to England. Think we landed in Portland. By bus to one hospital—then by train to Central England, by train and a General Hospital.

So, you see My Darling—in and out just like that. Foolish enough to get myself tagged. Normandy passed like that with many new and not so nice experiences that I still can't talk about and I don't want to.[65]

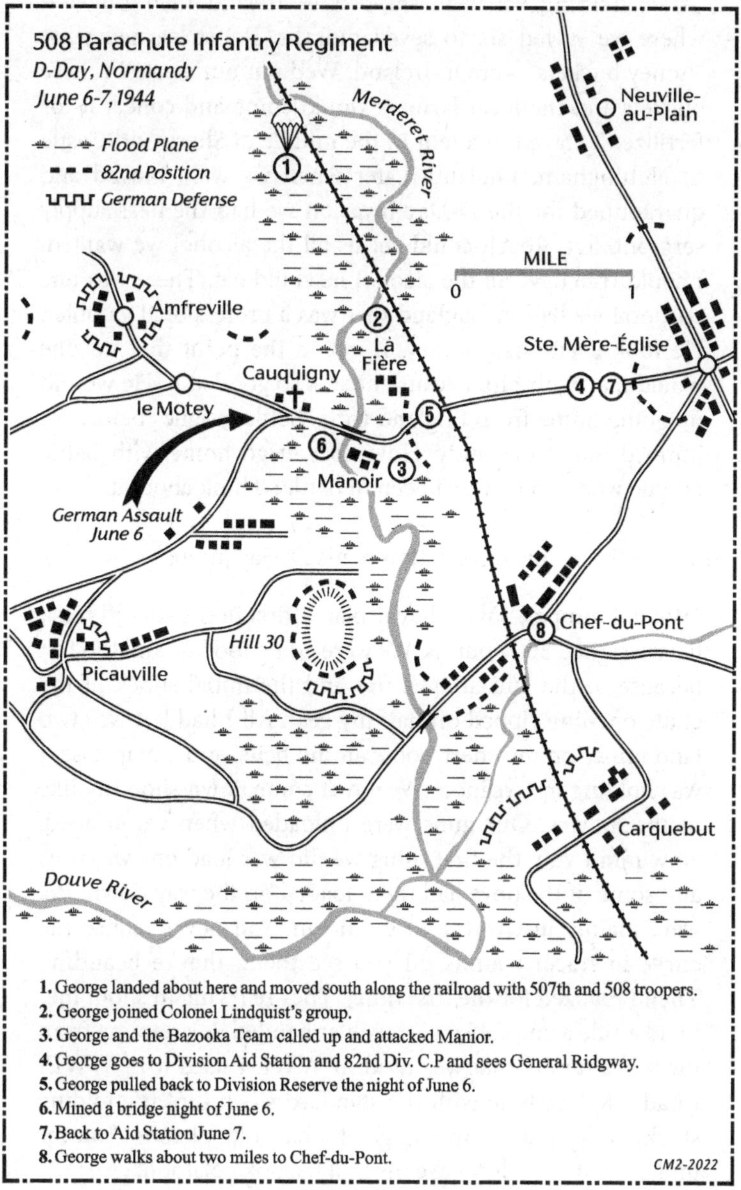
508 Parachute Infantry Regiment
D-Day, Normandy
June 6-7, 1944
Flood Plane
82nd Position
German Defense
Merderet River
Neuville-au-Plain
MILE
0
1
Amfreville
Là Fière
Ste. Mère-Église
Cauquigny
le Motey
Manoir
German Assault June 6
Hill 30
Chef-du-Pont
Picauville
Carquebut
Douve River
1. George landed about here and moved south along the railroad with 507th and 508 troopers.
2. George joined Colonel Lindquist's group.
3. George and the Bazooka Team called up and attacked Manior.
4. George goes to Division Aid Station and 82nd Div. C.P and sees General Ridgway.
5. George pulled back to Division Reserve the night of June 6.
6. Mined a bridge night of June 6.
7. Back to Aid Station June 7.
8. George walks about two miles to Chef-du-Pont.
CM2-2022

**Lt Gurwell's estimated movements on June 6-7, 1944. Map purchased by authors.**

True to his words, George did not talk about Normandy at any length until he did with us fifty-seven years later. In 2001, George set the scene by talking about the preinvasion training in Great Britain.

> "After training we were shipped to Ireland then England where we stayed six to seven months. I first learned what "honey buckets" were in Ireland. We'd put our waste in these buckets and the local farmers would come and collect it for fertilizer. I stayed in a tent in the middle of Sherwood Castle in Nottingham, England. Later when we were moved and quarantined for the D-Day invasion we had the best supply sergeant. Sgt. Roach could get us all the alcohol we wanted. I couldn't believe all the alcohol he could get. There was one corporal we had in England that was a professional gambler. He took everyone's money. It got to the point that no one would play with him because he was so good at it. He wound up going home from England with "battle fatigue" before we jumped into Normandy. How do you go home with battle fatigue when you haven't been in battle? Think about it."

George continued his recollection of his D-Day jump:

> "When I jumped out of that airplane [first in the stick] I must have weighed 300 pounds. We were going too low and too fast because of the anti-aircraft fire and the initial shock of the chute opening ripped off half my gear. All I had left was two land mines on my chest, some ammo belts, and a map case. I was holding my weapon. We didn't come down shooting like in the movies. Our guns were unloaded when we jumped. Now mind you, the first thing we did was load our weapons and some of the boys had them loaded on the way down. We were mainly just trying to get down. You never realize the curve in tracer rounds till you see them; they're beautiful. Then I realized for the first time, 'They're trying to shoot me.' I had a side arm, a .45 Colt revolver handed down to me from my wife's family that was used in WWI. I used it in WWII. I had a M1 carbine with the standard stock [not the folding stock]. They put me in charge of a bazooka platoon. I never understood why they gave me that bazooka platoon.

**Colt revolver used in the U.S.-Siberia campaign in WWI by Jeane's uncle, Myron Slonaker. George jumped with it into Normandy and Holland. Gurwell Collection.**

"When we landed, we were scattered all around. Some of our division just took terrible losses landing in the Merderet River. They were so overloaded they just went right down when they landed in the water. I landed in a flooded field near Sainte-Mère-Église in waist-high water. I had no idea how deep that water was when I was looking at it before I landed. That was a scary feeling. The water got deeper at times while we were trying to make it to some high ground near railroad tracks. You didn't have to tell us when they hit that beach with the preinvasion bombardment. It was the biggest Fourth of July show you ever saw. I never went to firework displays after that. I'll never forget the sound of those big shells coming over. They sounded like freight trains.

"When the sun came up, what I remember seeing was poppies, just like in the poem, 'in Flanders's fields where poppies grow [blow].' [66]We were right there in France where all that happened. That morning I shared a foxhole with General Ridgeway: he probably doesn't remember it, but I do. His radio man called out to send a message and we started drawing 88 millimeter fire. We all went for cover. We didn't call out on the radio unless we were in foxholes after that.[67]

"That morning we cut off a unit of Germans on bicycles coming back from the beach, and they had had it [shakes his head and stares off briefly]. [68] We hadn't had a chance to eat lunch and were eating in the middle of all kinds of Germans and horses, all dead. We were eating lunch, and these boys from the beach were coming by saying, 'How can you eat with all those dead bodies around?' They were throwing up and

> everything. We laughed; it was just the first time we'd had a chance to eat lunch. We did all kinds of things. They issued us French money to buy our way back to the lines if we were captured. I know one major that made a lot of money 'collecting" those francs, converting them to dollars, and sending the money home.'"

In the process of sharing a funny story, George also talked about being wounded on D-Day.

> "Later that first day, I stepped out from around a building, and a German shot me with a Schmeisser [9 mm automatic machine pistol]. The name of the town started with a *C*, but I forgot the name; it was a weird name.[69] He hit me in the upper part of the leg with the first round, and it knocked me back, probably saving my life, as the other rounds did not hit me. I was so mad they sent me back, I could move, but I had a limp. They sent me back to the landing beach [Utah], then to a hospital ship, then back to England. I was lucky; I did not have to fight through those hedgerows. I rejoined the outfit when they came back to England to get ready for the next jump [into Holland]."

After landing on June 6, the 508th stayed in battle until July 7, when they moved back to base camp in England. Instead of being pulled off the line after the ground forces caught up, the 82nd engaged in five major battles for Normandy. "[General] Bradley found that his conventional infantrymen lacked aggressiveness, especially in the close fighting dictated by the bocage, and he was chary of releasing troopers that, though bloodied, had proved capable of offensive maneuver in restricted terrain."[70]

The 508th started the battle for Normandy with 2,055 men and officers. Only fifty-eight officers and 780 enlisted men were available for action at the end of July 4. The rest were either missing, captured, wounded, or killed in action.[71] The September 2015 *Devils Digest*[72] reported the Normandy casualty figures broken down by category.

| | |
|---|---|
| KIA | 307 |
| Died of wounds | 26 |
| Died of injuries | 3 |
| WIA | 487 |
| MIA/POW | 165 |

Guy LoFaro wrote about the terrible arithmetic of the 82nd Division as a whole. Of the 3,077 men that were injured or wounded in action (WIA), 2,056 were able to quickly return to duty after they recovered, such as 2nd Lt. Gurwell. The ranks of second lieutenant in the division (65 percent casualty rate) and first lieutenant (71 percent casualty rate) were particularly hazardous jobs in Normandy.[73]

Going through the Gurwell collection was, at times, very emotional for us. One of those times was discovering and holding in our hands the memorial service program for the men of the 508th who were lost in Normandy, dated 29 July 1944 in Nottingham, England. After songs and poetry, Col. Lindquist eulogized the boys lost along the way:

> *Today we memorialize our comrades of the regiment who died in Normandy, France during the participation by this regiment in the invasion of the continent. Their names and their deeds will never be forgotten by we who returned nor by those who follow us. In paying the highest price, their own lives, they have pointed the way for us to follow and have given us a timeless challenge. It remains for us now to keep faith with them and maintain a devotion to duty and a loyalty to the ideals of America that will worthily match their sacrifice.*
>
> *COLONEL LINDQUIST*

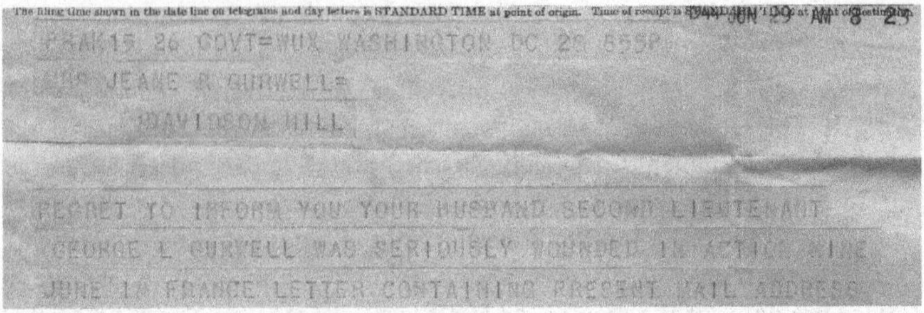
The filing time shown in the date line on telegrams and day letters is STANDARD TIME at point of origin. Time of receipt is STANDARD TIME at point of destination.
1944 JUN 29 AM 8 25

AK15 26 GOVT=WUX WASHINGTON DC 28 555P
JEANE R GURWELL=
DAVIDSON HILL

REGRET TO INFORM YOU YOUR HUSBAND SECOND LIEUTENANT
GEORGE L GURWELL WAS SERIOUSLY WOUNDED IN ACTION NINE
JUNE IN FRANCE LETTER CONTAINING PRESENT MAIL ADDRESS

# CHAPTER VI

# MEN LIKE THAT NEVER DIE, ROUND ROBIN LETTERS 15–25

As George returned to light duty in England on June 22, 1944, we pick up the narrative of the Round Robin letters written in mid-June of that year—but prior to the women having detailed reports about the invasion. At first they displayed a naïve optimism that disappeared as the letters travel around the country and the scope of the losses in Normandy was realized. The tone of the women's letters soon became much more serious as the campaign in Europe progressed.

Ruth Beaver wrote the fifteenth letter in the Round Robin. She was married to 1st Lt. Neal W. Beaver, who was assigned to the mortar platoon, Hq3, on June 6. She later learned that he was wounded in action on that first day of the invasion.

Ruth Beaver, Grand Rapids, Michigan [RR 15]

June 14, 1944,

Hi! Everybody!

> It certainly was wonderful to receive all these “swell letters.” Must be Ginnie Bridgewater [wife of Capt. Erle Bridgewater, Hq3] didn't have time to write so she sent them on to me as there was no letter with the others from her.
>
> I manage to keep busy myself with little Neal Wayne (born April 9th). He certainly is a precious little rascal and looks just like “Daddy Beaver” Ha! It's a great comfort to have a baby to keep your mind busy at a time like this, with the “invasion” taking place. All I can say girls is that nothing can happen to our “508” if we keep praying. And besides they're too good!
>
> Neal sent me his photograph, he had it taken in England. Really swell of him and he looks so fat. Must be “lonely life” is agreeing with him. Ha! Oh! Well let's hope it won't be too long before all “our darlings” come home and then wouldn't it be fun to have one of “our ole 508 parties” like old times.
>
> There really isn't much I can say except that I'd give the world to see all of you girls again and I sincerely hope you're all fine and not worrying too much. So, until the next time— “Best Wishes” to each of you.
>
> Ruthie Beaver

Next is the story of the Hardwicks. Jerry Hardwick and her husband Don were close friends with Jeane and George, and the two women wrote to each other often. Jeane mentioned Jerry in a letter written to George on February 13, 1944.

> Hood River, Oregon
>
> Jerry Hardwick wrote another sweet letter, she loves Don's family. Has been in Selma, California with one of Don's sisters on a farm and she thinks the little pigs were beautiful. Can't you see the grin on her freckled pan and that lanky figure chasing the little pigs around? Good old Jerry.

Don, 1st Lt. Hardwick, lead the demolitions platoon, HqHq. He became good friends with George from the beginning of training in Camp Blanding. George nicknamed him “Ripstitch” (an unruly, wild, reckless person). Ripstitch eventually became “the Ripper”—his war time nickname. Jerry penned her Round Robin letter after D-Day, but before the extent of the true losses were known.

> Jerry Hardwick, Jacksonville, Florida [RR 16]
>
> July 3, 1944,
>
> Dear Girls:
>
> I was pleasantly surprised when I opened a big envelope and all these letters fell out—letters from quite a few of the girls that I have been wondering what happened to. Some of you I haven't met, but I want you to know, I like you, will be glad of the chance to become well acquainted with you. I was also surprised to find that one of the girls on the list lives right here in Jacksonville, and we are meeting uptown for lunch today.
>
> All of you will know by now that our Boys have landed safely in France, and you, as well as I, are on pins and needles at the present. Let's just keep right on praying and keep our fingers crossed, and one of these happy days our hubbies will be back home with us.
>
> Ruth Beaver, I'm glad to hear that your little Neal is so nice. By the way, you owe me a letter, and I'd very much like to hear from you, so make with the pen. A lot of you may have heard by now that Jeane Gurwell had a lovely boy, and I'm anxiously awaiting another letter from her that will give the latest details. I see that the Round Robin hasn't gotten around to Elanor Thompson [RR 22] yet, and some of you will be glad to know she has a perfectly beautiful son too and is quite thrilled about it.
>
> I lead a normal, quiet life. I am employed with the War Finance Committee, and since this is the State Headquarters, and we promote the sale of bonds, we are very busy during the Fifth War Loan. I went out to California right after Don left to become acquainted with his people, and I like them very, very much. I stayed out there for two and a half months and returned here to begin work right away.

Since Mrs. Dowling lives here in Jacksonville, I'm mailing this on to her. I hope the Round Robin speeds up so I will get it again.

Best of luck girls until I hear from you again. Keep your faithful chins up!

Love, Jerry Hardwick

Ferne Dowling wrote next. Her husband, Capt. James A. Dowling, was the commanding officer of Service Company (headquarters support staff), but was transferred prior to Normandy. In addition, word had not yet reached the wives that the 508th along with the parent division, the 82nd, had been pulled off the front lines (July 7) and sent back to England on July 11, 1944.

Ferne Dowling, Jacksonville, Florida [RR 17]

July 10, 1944,

Hello Everyone,

Was I ever more surprised when Mrs. Hardwick called me, first to learn that another 508er lived in Jacksonville, and also to hear a Round Robin awaited me—was I excited. Oh boy and how!

Let me spread the news about Mary Williams, on June 8th she presented the world with two fine baby boys! Isn't that wonderful? They were born five minutes apart, if I remember correctly, the first is Gene H. Jr., and the second is John T. Now can't you imagine Mary with twins? She has what I want, if only I could, which looks like I can't, so I don't guess I will—of all bad luck, that's mine.

Well girls I must tell you, I've only had one letter from Jimmy, but it made me very happy, I guess I have no right to be so lucky and happy when the rest of you must worry as I did till I got his letter—anyway, he was not in the invasion. I only know this new work he's been transferred into since arriving overseas is the cause, but I don't know what his work is. Regardless of where he is, my prayers still and shall continue to go out for all our swell fellows, and may God soon send them all home to us.

Mary Williams tells me that Phyl Hoffman, Ann Klein, Mary McDuffie, and Barbara Martin have all heard from their husbands. [All RR wives except Mary McDuffie, wife of First Lieutenant James H. McDuffie, I Co., who was WIA June 29. He did not return to the 508th]. Martin was wounded in the left arm and is back in England. I pass that bit along as I'm sure all of you won't know this but will be glad to hear it.... Also, Gene Williams has written too and is alright. Don't you know how happy Mary is with her babies and news of Gene.

After reading the many letters and seeing that most everyone is working besides having children, I feel quite out of the picture—up until now (I'm on a visit back in dear old Rockingham, N.C., with people we met and have become close friends with.) I was my own boss, working about the house and in the yards—going to the beach ever so often, even making a trip to the hospital one month, gossiping over the back fence, trying to keep in touch with the few girls I had addresses of—you can readily see how lazy I am. I have our phone listed and if at any time any one of you ever pass thru please call, and if possible, I'd be glad to have you stop over for a while—just my mother and my self.

Would you like a brief rumor on Mackall—at present all glider units have been moved, there are still some parachute troops here, mostly 13th Airborne, part of the 541st and 542nd are here but the rumor has it they are rapidly being sent out in small groups as replacements. There is also a German prison camp situated there too. Some say the camp will be cleaned out and forgotten, while still another rumor has it that it is to become even a larger [Airborne Base] than ever before, with the gliders and all being brought back—I guess any guess will do—[Camp Mackall continues as a special forces training center as of 2022].

I'm adding a few more addresses, and I want to thank Mary Casteel for adding mine.

Sincerely, Ferne Dowling

Next is the story of Clyde and Dot Driggers. Capt. James Clyde Driggers was the company commander for Hq3 until he was made the commanding officer [CO] of HqHq as of April 10, 1944. One of our surprises while reading the Regimental Morning Reports was that Capt. Robert Abraham was relieved as CO of HqHq and made the liaison officer to the 82nd division six weeks before D-Day. After Driggers was injured on June 6, Abraham was again moved back to CO. Driggers was Lt Gurwell's commanding officer on D-Day.

Dot Driggers wrote:

> Dot Driggers, Madison, Florida [RR 18]
>
> July 16, 1944,
>
> Well girls—
>
> I've wanted to write each one of you since D-Day to tell you that I was thinking about us all. I think if I had been a rich woman, I'd have wired everybody. It was a rough day, wasn't it? Clyde was wounded and is back in England at the present time. Hear Lt. Merriam didn't go because of injuries, Capt Bridgewater had the mumps, and that Capt Bell got sick over in France. I know of none but these. Oh, yes Reba Holmes writes that Ott was in France and ok.
>
> The reason Ginnie Bridgewater just sent the letters on was because she was busy having a boy. I just envy all you girls with babies and especially Mary with twins. Guess I'll just have to do something about this baby business one day after the war.
>
> Right now, I'm working for the Dept. of Agriculture here in Madison, Florida. The work is hard, but interesting—however you know about us Southerners—we just don't get in a hurry!
>
> I'm so glad about this Round Robin letter. It will take a long time for it to get around again, but I do believe it will be worth the waiting. Let's all hurry it up so I can get it again soon huh? I don't have much time to write letters but would love to get news of you all.
>
> I've just got to tell you that I too, got some Irish linen and some English silver. Boy isn't it fun? <u>But</u> I'd give all of that there is in the world just to see Clyde right now.
>
> The best to you all, Dot Driggers.[74]

Some in the 508th did not see eye to eye with Captain Driggers. George had this to say, "We didn't like Capt. Driggers, he was so by the book, he wouldn't even use his head. The book was his head." Pfc. Joe Hamm, HqHq, wrote the following to his wife, Mrs. Hamm on June 29, 1944:

> "You mentioned Capt. Snow in your last letter—he's now a Company Commander in the 1st Bn. and Lt Tracey is our Commo. We got Capt. Abe [Robert Abraham] back as CO a few days after the jumps as Capt Driggers has an arm shot up so everyone's happy again. We miss Capt Snow, but Lt Tracey and Capt Abe will see that these eggheads around here give us a fair deal."[75]

The next letter added to the Round Robin was written by Helen Bell. Her husband, Capt. Alton L. Bell, was the executive officer, Hq3, on D-Day.

> Helen Bell, Colora, Maryland [RR 19]
>
> July 23, 1944,
>
> Dear Girls,
>
> Each letter has been so thoroughly enjoyed. I have been thinking so much of each one and then when so many letters came all at once, it was so grand. I can add no news to that of Dot Quaid's other than to say Alton's last letter came from England [The sad news of the casualty rate had not yet reached the network.]
>
> Baby news is of particular interest here, as our little girl is now six months old. Baby Sue arrived January 18, 1944 and has been a fine healthy child.
>
> We are living with my parents out in the country. My brother is also home too, working on the farm. As Mother underwent a major medical operation the first part of June, found plenty to keep me busy with the responsibilities of the house and baby—But like you know too, it helps so much to keep busy.
>
> I have already done some canning and the preparing of food for freezing at the cold storage plant. Nevertheless, I find myself recalling memories of last summer and thinking of the reunion we will have with all these babies.

With very best wishes to all, Sincerely Helen

Mrs. Alton L. Bell

[Enclosed picture] Sue Ann Bell, daughter of Capt. and Mrs. Alton Bell

Born January 18,1944. Picture taken July 4. Age 5 1/2 months

**Sue Ann Bell, picture included in RR #19. Gurwell Collection.**

Next in line to write her Round Robin letter was Doris Mathias. Her husband, First Lieutenant Robert Mathias, was assigned to E Company. In the next letter, Jeane Gurwell wrote to George on January 21, 1944, demonstrating how the friends kept in touch:

> I have written to Terry [Tibbetts] and I'm waiting for an answer. Helen [Moss] has written several times, there was a card from Jerry [Hardwick] from California with Don's family which I answered and an exchange with Doris Mathias. Everyone seems to be fine. Don't look too charming for those English girls.

1st Lt. Robert Mathias, E Co., holds a special place for us in our hearts. We were moved to tears when we read Doris's letter for the first time in 2018. The significance of the letter in our hands was hard to grasp. The Round Robin letters filled in some missing information about why George seemed shocked when we knew the name and story about Robert Mathias back in 2001. George still held the pain of losing a close friend. In a million years, we could have never guessed that we would discover a letter from Doris Mathias telling of how proud she was of her husband's heroic actions on D-Day. She included an article and picture of 1st Lt. Mathias from a Baltimore paper. With strength and courage, Doris shared the sad news of her husband Robert with her band of sisters.

**1st Lt Robert Mathias, E Company, 508th, was KIA on June 6, 1944. This picture was taken as part of a one-page photo compilation of all 139 officers of the 508th at Camp Mackall, NC in 1943. Copy courtesy of Ruth and Neal Beaver via Jack Williams. Individual portraits displayed on 508pir.org.**

Doris Mathias, Baltimore, Maryland [RR 20]

August 15, 1944,

Dear Gals,

What a simply superb idea of Helen Moss! One can't quite say how very much it did for me—arriving at a time when letters won't come.

I am enclosing a clipping that will speak for itself. Needless to say, it just seems too unbelievable. Perhaps the full realization will not be dealt until the other men return. May the Powers That Be send many back.

The awards are coming in—the Purple Heart, the Presidential Citation and a letter from Henry L. Stimson, Secretary of

> War. It looks personal. Perhaps it's due to the fact that the Washington Post carried a story about a 508 private who killed six Nazis and was made a corporal. The story stated the private was under the command of Lt R.P. Mathias. Also, many letters and telegrams from people I've never met. They help so much. As one man wrote, "his rugged features belied the gentle nature." Another said, "No man can do greater." Of course, I'm proud. We all are.
>
> Sarsfield, my cocker spaniel, is complaining of the heat. Am inclined to give him a GI haircut. He has beautiful ankles, but no bark so far. He's only six months, tho.
>
> We are forming a War Widows' Club here in Baltimore. Since our men gave their lives, we feel it is our duty to see that this country isn't in too much of a mess after all this is over. At least, that's our aim. Also, to help the newcomers over the jumps. It will keep us busy and that is the only salvation now—to keep busy.
>
> Any information concerning my Bob would be a grand help, if you all hear anything. As usual the wife hears last.
>
> Dotty Quaid's husband was reported missing and then killed the 23rd, I hear. Also Lt. Donald Johnson [Lt Johnson was a witness on George's power of attorney documents] was killed June 7th and Captain Wayne Harvey, June 6th. It sounds like a very small percentage. Was reading where some paratroopers had dropped on an anti-invasion German maneuver. I'm wondering if it could have been the 508th. The story said naturally the Germans in that particular region were prepared. One hears such stories, tho.
>
> Please send me any scraps of information, and I'll do the same. Good luck to all,
>
> Sincerely, Doris Mathias

Doris's hope for a "small percentage" was sadly wrong, as ten of the forty-eight husbands of the Round Robin wives were KIA in Normandy and one more was KIA in Holland. By the end of the war, nineteen of the remaining thirty-seven men were WIA.

Next to write was Harriett Peterson, who was married to Capt. Melvin V. Peterson. He was the CO of the Regimental Band and adjutant [assistant] to Col. Lindquist.

> Harriett Peterson, Minneapolis, Minnesota [RR 21]
>
> August 18, 1944,
>
> Hello Girls,
>
> I've been walking around in a dream of memories since I received all of your nice letters this AM. My only suggestion is for each girl to insert her first name on the list. I recall most of your faces, but the first names stump me. Oh yes, on the second trip around why don't we all add a snapshot of ourselves and family to the letter? I'm not sure girls, but I don't think any of the 508th participated in this new invasion of Southern France. [This is correct, the 508th did not participate in Operation Dragoon].
>
> Mel, Capt. Kenneth Johnson, and 2nd Lt. R.C. Moss went to Glasgow, Scotland on a final day leave last month. My poor Honey had such a good time the first two days he was sick for the last three days of his leave!
>
> Captain Edward King who was CO of Special Service Co. was killed on June 11. His brother asked me to try to get some details about it, have any of you heard from your husbands about Capt King?
>
> My time is completely filled with "Army" as I can make it. I've organized a Paratrooper's Wives Club of Minneapolis. [The WWII equivalent of what is currently known as a Family Readiness Group]. We have twenty-one members if any of you are interested in starting such a club, if you write to me, I'll be glad to give you any suggestions you want. There is one girl besides myself, whose husband is in the 508, Corporal Thomas Clevenger [F Co.] Also Capt. K. L. Johnson's [Ken Johnson, Service Co.] mother lives six blocks from me so the three of us have chatty (not Catty) time together.
>
> I've also joined the "Army and Navy Officers Wives Club" work two days a week styling hair in a nice salon. Miss Marsha

Jean Peterson is now sixteen months old, blonde, blue eyes, and looks like her daddy (or is it just our imaginations girls that make us all think that?)

My Mother and Dad are back from Calif. and are living with me. Mother is going to visit Doris Mathias next month. Maybe some of you remember my mother. She has red hair and attended several parties in Blanding and Fort Benning. She sends her regards to all of you.

My deepest sympathy to all of you girls who have the supreme loss to suffer from this war. I know only of Doris Mathias but there are others of you that I haven't heard about yet.

I'd love to have personal letters from all of you. Good night, chin up, chin up, girls of the 508.

Harriett (Mrs. Melvin V. Peterson)

Eleanor Thompson was married to 1st Lt. Charles J. Thompson. He was in Service Company, serving as the assistant parachute packing officer. The sad news about Normandy casualties began to trickle in, but an overly optimistic outlook prevailed.

Eleanor Thompson, Montevideo, Minnesota [RR 22]

August 22, 1944,

Dear Girls,

I too, was pleasantly surprised when my sister walked in and handed me this huge envelope. I was in the midst of bathing Little Tommy, but I couldn't wait to open it, so as Jerry Hardwick said, they spilled all over the floor.

My life out here on the farm isn't exciting, but it sure keeps me busy. This time of the year especially. My brother drives the children for the school district, so while the weather is nice it's my job, so he can finish his fall work. Tommy is growing so fast and is a lot of work, but he is so much fun especially now. He just turned 7 months today. He was born the 22nd of Jan. at the Moore County Hospital at Pinehurst. He weighed seven pounds and had black hair, which is still hard for me to believe because I always knew I'd have a little tow head. I was pleased as punch that it was a boy. That same evening Mom brought me my first letter from Tommy, and I could have walked out of that hospital. I felt on top of the world. Helen Flanders stayed with me from the time the boys left until the middle of February. Her and little Jerry helped me through the rough spots. I don't think I'd have fared so well without her. Sad part of it is her husband Capt Flanders is now missing.

I also heard that Lt Bodak [First Lieutenant Michael Bodak] was or is missing and Captain Hal Creary. My heart goes out to each and every one of you girls who have to stand the supreme loss. I too pray all the boys will come back to us. We're all mighty proud and mighty happy that we belong to the "508."

Congratulations, girls I must say the 508 has increased considerably since we were together, and I know you'll all feel pretty proud when their Daddys see them the first time. I think about it and get "duck bumps" all over and my stomach feels as if its full of butterflies. That day can't be far off now. Things are shaping up beautifully.

Tommy did not jump in the invasion. If I would have known that before, just think of the worry wrinkles I wouldn't have now. Thankful can't express how glad I was to hear that news. I hear quite regularly and in his last letter said that he had been to London and there sure was lots to see. He was in a truck accident once, but only received some bruises and a black eye. Kinda embarrassing. I must mention that I'm receiving a package, I just can't wait until it arrives. He said it was something he had made for me. In the next installment I'll tell you what it is. I hope it's something I can show off, even if it isn't, I think I'll be tempted to. I've enjoyed the Round Robin immensely and I'm sending it to Mrs. Frank Novak which is the closest. Here's hoping it'll be around again soon.

Sincerely Eleanor, Mrs. Charles J. Thompson.

I think it's a good idea to enclose snapshots.

The twenty-third RR letter was written by Doris Novak. Her husband, Capt. Frank. J. Novak, was company commander of G Co. when he jumped into

Normandy. Naïve optimism continued among the wives even as Doris wrote about Frank's significant wounds.

> Doris Novak, Baltimore, Maryland [RR 23]
>
> August 31, 1944,
>
> Dear Girls—
>
> Certainly is fun reading letters from everyone and am so anxious for them to get around again. I have just arrived back from Pierre, SD, with my sister and was working at the Air Base there, but her husband was sent to school, so we are all home again, much to my mother's delight and have been enjoying myself as much as possible.
>
> Frank was wounded on the Fourth of July, a shell exploded above his head and his head was hurt, but not so badly. The thing that caused him the most trouble was his back. A piece of shell lodged in his back and was pressing against his spine. Up to now it hasn't bothered him since he came from the hospital, as they didn't take it out but this morning in his letter, he says it hurts when he breathes, and it will have to come out. However, considers himself lucky.
>
> Isn't it wonderful that the end is in sight? Dottie Driggers in your letter you were expecting Clyde, and I know how happy you must have been.
>
> Can't help it, but envious of you girls with babies and think it is wonderful to have them in times like these.
>
> There is one air base here in Lincoln, and lots of newcomers, therefore there is quite a lot to occupy one's time. Also have been trying to improve my bridge a bit.
>
> Terry Tibbetts would like to hear how you and young Jimmy are getting along.
>
> Can't think of much more news of interest. Oh yes! I also have had some lovely gifts, the last one was a sterling tea set and tray. I could hardly wait until each piece arrived and certainly

am proud of it. Perhaps by the time this reaches everyone the war will be over and we can really look forward to something.

Good Luck!

Sincerely, Doris Novak

Madelon Merriam's letter gave insight into women in the workforce during the war. Long hours were expected and given. She was married to 1st Lt. Armon L. Merriam, who was assigned to Service Company during the Normandy campaign as the motor transportation officer.

Madelon Merriam, Shaker Heights, Ohio [RR 24]

September 9, 1944

Dear Gals,

Have often longed to write each of you and every wife I ever knew but somehow or other am never able to give into my good intentions. Ever since I had to leave Armie, I have kept myself just as busy as I possibly could. When I first got home way last Christmas time the doctor wouldn't let me work for a while, so I just helped out at the USO, Red Cross, and China Relief. I also took a short trip to Chicago to see my mother. The first of February, tho I started job hunting and believe me I looked into everything that I had even been remotely concerned about. If you ever need a job, just come to Cleveland, as the impression I got was that everyone could use you and it was just up to you to pick the spot you wanted. Well, I ended up at Standard Oil of Ohio and have been a faithful employee for just about seven months now. I work in the control Laboratory making all kinds of physical and chemical tests on all different gasolines and oils. I sort of feel as if I am doing a little bit for the war effort right now, we are turning out 100 octane aviation fuel as fast as we can. Most of our gasoline goes entirely to army and navy sources without a drop being used in the States. Every time I see the tank cars, and boats loading up I get a thrill and when I am on the night shift and hear the truck convoys go out, it sounds like Southern Pines maneuver times.

We work shift work; one week of 7:30 AM to 4 PM—one of 7 AM to 3 PM—one of 11PM to 7 AM—and one 3PM to 11 PM. Every month we shift over and put in fifty-six hours one week instead of the usual forty-eight and we get a different day off. Right now, Friday is my day to howl! Having Sundays off only once in seven months makes me feel like a positive heathen, but "production" must go on!

If my poor chem teacher who almost flunked me could only see me now! We really had some excitement the other day as one of our big tanks caught on fire and there were several explosions and a roaring blaze for several hours. (No, I didn't do it). I felt as if my number was up for sure, but I'm hale and hearty yet!

As Dot Driggers told you already, Armie did not jump in the invasion. However, my heart was in my mouth when she said "due to injuries" as that was a new one on me!! All he told me was that he was withheld at the last minute and that he had tried to do his damndest about getting his orders changed. He said that he was unable to tell me the reason for it and I sort of gathered that it had something to do with his position. However, that is water under the bridge now as the minute the outfit got back to England, he got himself transferred into a line company (C Co. to be exact) and will be in on the next jump wherever it may be.

My presents include some lovely silver bracelets and a coin bracelet, some English ladies' riding spurs and a very stunning crop. He wants to get the English boots too but knowing what the prices must be in leather goods over there, I sort of stopped that idea. Bless his old jump boots! Right now, I am in the midst of wrapping up all his Xmas packages and I bet I'm having more fun out of it than he will have opening them all!

Jean Thomas and I get together weekly and have just about daily telephone conversations. It is wonderful to be together in Cleveland and we have really sweat this thing out together. I have visited Reba Holms [RR 47] and young Rod and she has also come up to Cleveland to see me. That plus all the letters to Phyl Hoffman, Jeanette Foley, Reba, Selma Abbott, [all RR writers] and many others keeps me pretty well informed on the outfit. At present, I'm writing to many of the boys there and trying to get a weekly letter off to Jr. Hughes [Second Lieutenant Charles R. Hughes, C Co.] who is in a German prison camp. If you have ever tried to write a letter with absolutely no mention of the war whatsoever, you have a fair idea of what it is like! He was captured on D-Day and I know how he must be wondering about his friends. So, I mentioned them all in such a way as the Germans would think that they were all my little boys! Now I'm afraid the Nazis will think that I'd make a good German house frau on the production angle! And me without a baby! Oh well, our day will come, please God.

My heart really aches for so many of you and I wish that there were words to express how I feel. I found this article that I know will be of interest to you all and I'm quoting from it. "Battle dress of the 82nd Airborne impeded no movement. There never was a group of men who went forward so steadily, so small a group, and so relentless an advance. Combat troops of the 82nd and 101st held inner lines for two days and one night against German reinforcements that vainly tried to reach our larger forces and push them back from the beach heads before their organization was complete. In the original plan the paratroopers were to be relieved as soon as they had established contact with their main forces. However, their misfortune was that they were too good. For 33 days they spearheaded our advances, thinned by casualties and worn by exhaustion, these few thousand immortals punched holes in the enemy lines that sealed the Cherbourg Peninsula. For the military record, the 82nd Airborne Division liberated the first town on French soil, St. Mere Eglise."

All I can say is that men like that never die and will never be forgotten.

The very best to you all and many happy landings! Puzzie

Mrs. A. L. Merriam Jr

PS. Hurry so I'll find out whether or not Sis Tomlinson has had her baby yet! Bernie take good care of Gloria now! Jean Thomas, Iris and I thought and spoke of you so often to Anne

> Klein while Iris visited Greater Cleveland. Mary Casteel—My thoughts are often with you and thanks to Reba I keep track of you and give my best even though I don't write. Don't you worry, we'll have our babies yet!

The news of the tragic number of KIAs and WIAs reached the band of sisters with Mrs. Shankey's letter. Her husband, 1st Lt. Joseph Shankey, Hq3 (supply and logistics) was captured on D-Day.

> Bernadette Shankey, Wappingers Falls, New York [RR 25]
>
> September 20, 1944,
>
> Hello, hello, hello,
>
> Golly I was so-o-o excited to receive this round-robin this AM!!! I've been having a gay old-time shooing Pat (our offspring) out from under my feet so I could read snatches. Time for her nap finally rolled around though, when I could light up a "cig" and read every word of them. The boys were sent to Camp Shanks in Orangeburg, NY just five miles from my hometown, so I saw Joe every night [before boarding the ship for Northern Ireland]. They left Shanks on Dec. 28 about 5:30 pm and Joe wrote that they had a very good crossing. Sgt Knowles, who was sent back to the states because of injuries sustained while in Ireland brought me a letter from Joe (uncensored). In it, Joe said they were billeted in Port Stewart [*sic*] in Ireland and later in Nottingham Park in England. Lt. Nello Caponera [G Company] was sent back with injuries too and on his visits to me has given me some news which I shall pass on.
>
> The 505, 507, and 508 comprised the 82nd Airborne Division; Colonel Ekman was made CO of the 505 and was killed in action[76] [this is in error, he lived through the war]; Lt. Malcom Brannen (Hq3) killed the first German general [Lt. Gen. Wilhelm Falley] in the invasion; Gene Williams was killed soon after the twins arrived. Lt Caponera cried over this as Gene took Caponera's place in the regiment when Cappy was sent back here. Cappy can't jump anymore but is down in Parachute Training School at Benning and seems well posted on 508 news since he hears from most all the boys. Chaplain

Maternowski (Cath) was killed, Hymie Dress injured [shot through the thigh], Jimmie Castell received the Bronze medal for meritorious service in the field of combat. Doris Daly received a telegram telling her that Jack was killed on July 4. Her baby, an eight-pound boy was born on August 29th. She is going to name him John Joseph after Jack. I also heard Capt. Harvey was killed and Creary and Bodak are missing.

I received a telegram July 25 saying that Joe was listed as missing since June 6. Then on Sept 10 (two days before our second anniversary) I received a telegram saying that Joe was killed on July 1 [date his status changed from MIA to KIA, not his date of death]. I shan't be reconciled wholly to it until I hear from or speak to the person or persons who saw it happen. Jimmy Castell wrote me that Joe was dropped ten miles south of Cherbourg, and was 3rd BN's supply officer so if any of you gals have guys you think would have been near him, would you ask about it for me?

In looking over the mailing list I find there are so many girls I never knew personally, and I know many will wonder who I am, so here are a few facts. Doris Daly and I paled [*sic*] around together all the time, shared a house way out in the woods in Pinehurst near Nancy Driggers. My Baby girl, Patricia Marie, was born in Moore County Hospital, Pinehurst, on June 10, a year ago. When the boys went on maneuvers in Tennessee, Doris went to Wisconsin and later to Tennessee, so I lived with Bonnie Hetland then. I don't know whether that will help out or not!

Now for my contributions to the baby news! Pat (15 months old) is a miniature "Diablo" [battle cry for the 508th Red Devils]. She's much too smart for me, jabbers very confidently to me by the hour and I sit bewildered as I haven't the smallest idea what she's talking about!!! She just has enough hair for a buttercup curl and many people take her for a boy. So now when someone says, "Oh what a cute fellow, what's his name?" I just answer, "Pat"! I'll enclose a little picture (ahem!) [it is 8.5 x 11 inches] and if you look closely, you can see a bow on top of her hair. I stuck it there with some scotch tape! When she's naughty I just stick her in a corner and give her my

"How to Raise an Obedient Baby in No Easy Lessons" to read. Simple. I was in training in Bellevue Hospital, New York City, when I left to be married. Have just a year and five months to finish so expect to go back next year this time and complete my training.

**Patricia Marie Shankey, February 18, 1944, age eight months, Wappingers Falls, NY. Little Patricia never got to know her Dad. 1st Lt. Joseph Shankey (Hq3) was killed on June 7, 1944 in Normandy. This 8.5 by 11-inch photo was included in RR#25 by Bernie Shankey. Gurwell Collection.**

Well Golly I better sign off and get this Round Robin on its way to Phyl Hoffman. So long gals and best of luck! Regards,

Bernadette (Bernie) and Pat Shankey

PS. Just received a list of 508 casualties from Cappy, given to him by Mary Williams via Col. Mendez.

Killed in action: Capt. Breen, Capt. Maternowski, Capt. Harvey, George Miles, Jack Daly, Jampetero, [Fred E.] Gillespie, D.J. Johnson, Quaid, Shankey, Shavitch, Simonds, Smith, Abbott, Hamilton, Mathias, Snee, Lehman, Cook, Bell? [Bell survived] Stull, plus all the boys in the pathfinder group except Lt Pollett.

Missing: Creary, Bodak, Flanders, Hughes

> Injured: Snow, Driggers, Tutwiler, MacAtamany, Gurwell, McDuffy, Martin, Dress, Grabbe
>
> PSS. Am going down to see MacAtamany tomorrow in Halloran Gen. Hospital, Staten Island, NY. He was with Joe when he was killed. Bernie Shankey

There are errors in the above lists typical of word of mouth during the fog of war. George Miles lived through the war. Many more of the pathfinders survived than just Lloyd L. Polette. [Polette was KIA in 1945 in Belgium.] Victor Grabbe was not only wounded, but was also a KIA in Normandy. These errors are examples of rumors born out of extreme dread and worry.

Michael Bodak was wounded severely and sent back to the States. Joe Shankey was captured on D-Day and killed in action on June 7. After Bernie Shankey's letter, the reality and cruelty of the war was made plain to the women of the 508th.

In addition to the update on Shankey's death, the worst possible news came to three of our previous Round Robin letter writers as well—Dottie Quaid, Mary Williams, and Doris Daly. John Quaid was declared missing on June 9 and declared KIA on June 23, 1944 when his remains were located.[77] Lt. Ralph DeWeese wrote that, "Lt. Quaid had raided a pill box and the Germans had surrendered and were coming out with their hands up. The fourth came out firing a scmizer and killed him. You could never trust the Jerries."[78]

Gene Williams was killed in action, June 20, 1944, in the assault on Hill 131, near the end of the 508th's involvement in the Normandy campaign. Lt. Williams was KIA three days prior to the arrival of Mary's telegram in France announcing the birth of the twins. The word of the twins' birth in conjunction with Williams's death was a terrible blow for the men of the 508th. [79]

Doris Daly also wrote in the Round Robin prior to getting the dreaded telegram from the War Department that her husband was also KIA. 1st Lt. John J. "Jack" Daly was killed in action July 4, 1944 in the assault on Hill 95, just days before the 508th was pulled off the line in the Normandy campaign. First Lieutenant Malcolm Brannen recounted Doris writing to him after Normandy. "Later while we were at Nottingham preparing for another mission, his wife, Doris wrote me and asked me if he really was dead—or could he possibly have been captured. I hated the answer that I had to send to her—He was actually dead and there was no chance that he was a POW."[80]

Doris Daly, Bernie Shankey, and Mary Williams now faced parenthood without their husbands. The list of children that would never meet or have memories of their fathers was sorrowfully growing. The eleven officers that were KIA from the Round Robin group were survived by seven fatherless children by the war's end. From this time on, the tone of the Round Robin letters became substantially more serious as letters from husbands grew few and far between, and some of the "widows" in the band of sisters became true war widows indeed.

gh

**WAR DEPARTMENT**
**THE ADJUTANT GENERAL'S OFFICE**
**WASHINGTON 25, D. C.**

IN REPLY REFER TO:
Gurwell, George L. 0-460999
PC-N ETO 107

IO-33

27 June 1944.

Mrs. Jeane R. Gurwell,
Davidson Hill,
Hood River, Oregon.

Dear Mrs. Gurwell:

I am sorry it was necessary to send my recent telegram, which this letter is confirming.

Your husband, Second Lieutenant George L. Gurwell, was seriously wounded in Action on 9 June 1944, in France.

Theater Commanders are instructed to submit to the War Department periodic reports of progress and accordingly you will be kept informed of his progress promptly as these reports are received. However, as I am sure you realize, such reports must of necessity be brief and therefore will contain information on his condition or progress, but will not include information concerning the nature of wounds in the case of wounded personnel.

I can assure you that our hospitalized soldiers serving overseas are receiving the very best medical care and attention and it is hoped that a favorable report in his case will be received in the near future.

Knowing your desire to have a letter reach him as soon as possible, you should use the following temporary address until a change of address is furnished by him or by this office and so advise all interested relatives and friends who might also want to write him:

2nd. Lieut. George L. Gurwell, 0-460999 (Hosp.),
Central Postal Directory,
APO 640, c/o Postmaster,
New York, New York.

Sincerely yours,

J A Ulio

J. A. ULIO
Major General,
The Adjutant General.

1 Incl.

## CHAPTER VII

# GHOSTS, MEMORIES, AND A HORRIBLE LONELINESS

The 82nd and 101st Airborne Divisions were pulled out of Normandy in mid-July 1944, and returned to England to rest, refit, and replace casualties. With the exception of the veterans of Italy and Africa in the 505th PIR, D-Day was the "baptism of fire" for all U.S. airborne troops in Normandy on June 6. Code-named "Operation Neptune," the assault phase of Operation Overlord was a success, but the price was very high. In the 508th, only 939 of the 2,055 troopers who jumped on June 6 returned from Normandy with the regiment.[81] The survivors of both divisions—six parachute regiments, two glider regiments, and support battalions—formed the battled-hardened backbones of the units that returned to England to train and incorporate incoming officers and men. There were plenty of replacements to train; the American airborne operations on D-Day were a near disaster, nearly comparable to the Omaha Beach landings.[82]

Oral accounts, veterans' memoirs, and regimental and divisional histories all testify to the many rivalries between the "All Americans" ( 82nd Division) and the "Screaming Eagles" (101st Division). When we interviewed George on June 6, 2001, he was still poking fun at the 101st: "What's that Eagle screaming for? Help me, 82nd! Help me!" Shenanigans and downright brawls between paratroopers on leave or out for a night on the town in England abounded. According to the troopers, the local women were starved for male attention, and there was ample opportunity to give it to them, since their men were all off fighting in the war. U.S. servicemen, and especially paratroopers, who earned fifty "extra" dollars a month, hazardous duty pay, for "jumping out of a perfectly good airplane," were, as the saying goes, "overpaid, oversexed, and over here."

Venereal disease rates soared: George made a note in one of his lieutenant's books to remind the men going on leave to "take rubbers."[83]

What most sources do not mention, however, is the trauma of first-time combat—the terror, chaos, and surging adrenaline of coming under fire and shooting to kill—and the grief of losing many friends in battle.[84] The 508th had trained together since its inception in October 1942. By D-Day, its members had been living and working side by side for nearly two years. Officers and men knew each other well and had forged a cohesive, close-knit unit where many had made close personal ties. All paratroopers were proud to belong to an elite, all-volunteer brotherhood; each man, irrespective of rank, was trained to lead and perform all assignments to maximize the odds of completing their mission and the odds of survival for a maximum number of men. All of this, George told us—the long-shared training, personal friendships, unit pride, special skills, fighting style, and operational techniques required to survive behind enemy lines—caused paratroop units to bond more closely than others.[85]

George was discharged from the 93rd General Hospital on June 22, returned to regimental base camp in Nottingham three weeks before the rest of the regiment, and was assigned to light duty while continuing to recuperate. Base camp was staffed by Special Services Company, which included mail services, personnel, and other administrative functions such as morning reports and payroll. George was assigned to the latter until he resumed his usual duties on July 26.[86] During this time, the wounded streamed back to Nottingham with good news of battles won, but horrible news of the cost. As the names of the killed and missing in action became known, survivor's guilt set in, and many men like George, who had suffered non-life-threatening injuries, struggled with why they had survived while friends paid the ultimate sacrifice. The 508th had more men killed in action in Normandy than in all the rest of the war combined.

By the time the last remnants of the regiment arrived in Nottingham on July 15, George had acquired a whole congregation of ghosts. Among the missing were Hal Creary, Ellsworth Bartholomew, Donald Johnson, Robert Mathias, Gene Williams, and more, all of whom died in Normandy. As a couple, George and Jeane were friendly with the Williams and Mathias families; and individual soldiers like Bartholomew and Johnson had been personal friends of George.

While censorship regulations prohibited the mention of specific names, other signs in George's letters show he was deeply impacted by these losses. "As you know by now, I have been into France. The particulars—are sealed up inside, parts I can tell you later, but parts—well, they are better forgotten," he had written haltingly on June 16, in the second of the two letters sent to Jeane from the hospital. Adding to his grief, emotional distress, and physical exhaustion was the arrival of the distressing letters that his step-mother and mother-in-law had written in mid to late May that described his wife's long hospitalization and continuing medical struggles after the birth of their son. Like a rogue wave at sea, everything hit George at once.

Throughout his time in England, he often expressed the inability to write, and his correspondence dramatically declined.[87] He did not write again until July 11, when his wife had been driven near mad with worry. Unlike soldiers termed "non-battle casualties," George was still able to fulfill his duties, but the letters he did manage to write presented a compelling case that he was experiencing symptoms of "mild" PTSD, including insomnia, alcohol abuse, depression, and nightmares. After a silence of over three weeks, his first letter from Nottingham attempted to reassure Jeane of his love and was the first to venture to put into words a deeply disturbing "peculiar mood" and a feeling of loneliness that no amount of hard work had been able to dispel.

> 11 July 1944 [Nottingham, England]
>
> My Darling, I have been missing you so terribly lately and yet I just couldn't write. There just seems to be turmoil in this poor, addled brain and turmoil isn't much to write about. This lonely husband of yours has been working very hard since being released from the hospital.... I shall write much more often now.... I am trying to lose this peculiar mood I am in.
>
> 20 July 1944 [Nottingham, England]
>
> Yes, there's been another long delay in writing—it isn't because of you Jeane, there is something inside that just doesn't seem to want to work out. Can't seem to find a thing to write about. There is such a hunger in my heart for you and our son. I miss you two so terribly. Days come and go and there's not a bit of difference unless a letter comes from you....
>
> Jeane Darling, there is something wrong with me inside. Nothing serious, but I can't quite put my finger on it. Perhaps it is just being completely tired out—working too hard and being so lonely for you Punkin that I can't see straight. I do have a leave coming, five whole days, but Jeane, I don't know what to do with it. There is just one thing to do without you and that is to get drunk to ease that pain in my heart. I can't seem to write a decent letter to save my soul. I can't ever be myself again until I am with you.

After George resumed his regular duties as regimental gas officer and company executive officer on July 26, he began to write more frequently, but his letters nevertheless continued to express what seemed to them both an incomprehensible loss of his old self, setting up a dialogue of impossibility and necessity. On the one hand, he guiltily apologized for not writing, and struggled to get a grip on his thoughts and emotions by describing his state to Jeane; on the other, she repeatedly counseled him to buck up and leave his memories behind.

> July 31, 1944 [Seaside, Oregon]
>
> Have you lost that bad mood that you had? Forget all that you see and do it at the end of each day.
>
> 2 August 1944 [Nottingham, England]
>
> Yes, My Dearest One—I haven't been writing. Jeane—I have been feeling fine but there is a lump inside. Couldn't write a darn letter for the life of me. There have been so many nasty things to try and forget.

Both George and Jeane were only twenty-three at the time of these exchanges, and both had recently undergone significant trauma: George had narrowly escaped drowning in the Merderet River, been wounded by enemy fire, survived several firefights, endured bone-jarring German artillery bombardments, and was mourning the death of numerous friends. Jeane had undergone a life-threatening hemorrhage in childbirth, been bedridden in the hospital for nearly a month, had heard about D-Day just three days after her release, and was worried sick about her wounded, oddly inarticulate husband. She was now juggling the duties of new motherhood with reapplying to school, finding a new apartment, and moving to Portland to complete her nursing degree—pressures and practicalities she kept from George. Meanwhile, she acted as his pillar of strength and fretted that all-too-available foreign women might be the reason for his all-too-infrequent letters.

In 1944, no one in either the military or medical professions had as yet fully fathomed the horrible, long-term effects of war on the human psyche. Jeane's correspondence is a case in point: despite her training as a nurse, she found George's inability to write, and especially his conviction that something was "terribly wrong" with him, as incomprehensible and deeply unsettling as he did. Near the end of July, George's loss of his bearings, and the feeling he had lost his old peacetime self were further heightened symbolically and factually by the loss of his wallet, where he had carried his photographs of Jeane. He also sorely "misses" his son, now ten weeks old. The fact that he had never met his son—nor even saw a photograph—made his absence all the more acute.

2 August, continued [Nottingham, England],

Three of us just returned from a blessed five-day leave [July 26–30]. We went to Scotland and proceeded to get very drunk every night. No, my precious darling, that didn't help. I hope and pray this all will end soon. There just isn't a thing this side of Hood River for me—English WACs included. This adoring husband of yours has been so blue lately. Lost all my snapshots of you a while back plus a keepsake bullet and a number of other things. Please send me more pictures.

This thing inside of me needs someone to talk to—you, Sweetheart, are the only one. Ghosts, memories, and a horrible loneliness make me sick inside.

Well Sweetheart, the sun is setting again on another day. A day wasted because you are not here. Sweetheart I love you with all my heart.

August 4, 1944 [Seaside, Oregon]

My Darling George,

It's been hard, bitterly hard for you, hasn't it? Yes, try now to forget—that is forget enough to take the edge off. Guess we would all be better off if we didn't think about solutions that only time can bring—or brood about unpleasantness, especially when it seems as though it will never end. There was a card from Helen [Moss] yesterday. She said you had gone back to the company and that you, Clint, and Snow spent Clint's birthday celebrating. It's good to hear something about you even though it can't be firsthand. Guess she was hearing from Clint right up to the 12th. We all check up, you know.

8 August 1944 [Nottingham, England]

Here I am again—Sweetheart, you are never forgotten. My letters are a little slow, but I am getting back to normal again. I have been almost sick for the last four days. This stomach of mine just doesn't seem to want to settle down. Much better

> today though. Days are just not right without you and nights are pure torture. I recall so vividly a walk of ours in the moonlight through the woods opposite the Holly Inn and down toward the church. Such lovely memories.
>
> ...I am mighty proud of Hood River for that bond drive.[88] Pretty good I should think when some of these civilians can't even go to work every day. Some of these Boys would like to be there in some of those strike areas for just one day. There might be a few accidents, but I am afraid that some people would forget some of these petty differences. I could just see some of the men going on strike in France or refusing to move up. What a laugh. They only give their lives—not a few work hours.[89] A little bitter my Darling, that's all. Pray Darling our separation won't be too much longer. Jeane I am going quietly mad....
>
> The Ripper and I are prosecution and assistant respectively on a court martial board.[90] How I hate that type of work. Everyone is probably a little peeved at me for not writing, but Sweetheart, just explain that letters from me only come when I feel like writing, and something has been wrong. I think about them all every day, but there just isn't much to say.
> Love, George

Many of George's letters from Nottingham pled with Jeane to send photos of herself, and repeatedly invoked beautiful moments they shared in the past. In doing so, George was spontaneously establishing a "safe place" to go to in his mind when he felt distressed, a habit that PTSD therapy now seeks to develop and reinforce. The idea is to help patients recall a favorite experience in place of obsessively trying to block intrusive, traumatic thoughts and feelings. As expressed in his letter of August 8 and elsewhere, George's safe place was at home with Jeane during their blessed time in Pinehurst. At other times, his longing was such that he personified or idealized safety in the very person of Jeane herself. Her photograph became George's sole means of returning to, or conjuring up, a familiar and far better alternate physical reality that permitted him momentarily to escape the war.

In creating a safe place through letters, George showed great natural resilience to the depression and self-destructive thoughts that accompany PTSD, yet he could not shake the conviction that something was injured. Meanwhile, his repeated refrain that something was "deeply wrong" inside, and the lapses between his letters caused Jeane great anxiety. Her very fertile imagination took over while she waited for news, and she was plagued with worries that made her despair of ever figuring out what her husband needed to hear from her. The doubt that she could fulfill his needs also caused her to poke fun at herself in a nervous, self-deprecating way, as her suspicions heightened that he may be dallying with other women. The irregularity of mail delivery from abroad only increased her tension: his letters, at best, took a week to ten days to arrive, while Jeane's letters to him often took even longer.

> August 16, 1944 [Hood River, Oregon]
>
> Got your letter written August 8. What's this about a tummy ache? You just can't have that! Is it tension, etc.? One thing Honey, especially with strain and nervousness, drinking doesn't help as much as it seems to at the time—Uh Huh—W.C.T.U. [Women's Christian Temperance Union] Gurwell—anyway it's a fact that most of us can't realize. You are too good a guy to drown yourself in your own sorrows. Butch is trying to crawl. It's a panic. He does more than the Tibbett's or Moss' baby at that age.
>
> August 12, 1944 [Hood River, Oregon]
>
> It's kind of hard to write when there is no mail from you. When something is troubling you and I can't know about it then it's as though it's coming between us. Yes Honey, maybe still trying to make those mountains out of mole hills—or realizing that I could have made you happier if an inferiority complex hadn't gotten in the way, or if I hadn't been so slow to awaken.
>
> Well, you're the only one who could do it. You realize that by now you got either a slow or hesitant "on the beam" cookie for a wife, don't you? How about scribbling down our rating and sending it by the nearest carrier pigeon? Might be nice to know also just what's eating you. Maybe I don't understand completely.
>
> All that you've undergone and face—maybe I understand better than you think. Of course, it isn't easy and of course it's hell—it's no bed of roses here either, nor is it easier to have you away over there going through all that you are and missing

you every bit as much as you miss me. How do you know it isn't more?

Darling, I want to understand, and I'll try—don't know how you've managed to take all that you have, but you did it where others couldn't. Please try to toss the strain off. We need each other—but the day will come and then we'll build from where we left off or begin again if you like. All that matters is that nothing comes between you and me. Write and say that my imagination is off on a tangent if you like, but we cheerfully admit that you married a worry wart (where you are concerned). I love you too much now Darling and can't help it.

Of course, you're working hard. Most of the fellows overseas or in combat are, I believe, and of course it's more than just hard work. Now you'll say she doesn't understand. But you know what, Honey, in spite of things, we do pretty much the things that we want to do first. When you can't write to me because of something within you, I wonder "Why?" and when one tries to find a reason for things that are unknown, some pretty fantastic ideas may present themselves. For heaven's sake don't get the wrong slant to whatever I'm scribbling—but George Honey, I'd like the answer and I'd like to think that you would like to work it out with me.

Yes, we're on the peck, aren't we? Not finding fault, just going crackpot worrying over you and things—it's late! The books and War Department say that when in this frame of mind, reread it in the morning so you'll tear it up, so I'll hurry and put this in an envelope and seal it, so it'll go off—and see what happens—if anything. Whew—sick sarcasm—(watch me repent tomorrow). Anyway, I love you more than anything Lt. George L. Gurwell—O46099—There hasn't been any sarcasm until tonight—and there isn't any more. It's just that I am going crazy Darling—I love you so.

It's practically time to get up—drop a line sometime before your son turns twenty-one. You may consider this a timely and perhaps slightly sarcastic rebuff, only I love you more and more.

Your wiltingly waiting wondering wife, Jeane

August 13, 1944 [Hood River, Oregon]

Sweetheart,

Repenting I am for last night's letter since finally one came today from you. Patience was wearing a little thin—not with you entirely—things here sometimes too. Honey, I'm so darn grateful for your letter today and so glad you are all right. I wish I could take that lump away from inside of you and help you forget the things you want to forget. Of course, you are sick inside. You're too fine and complete for all of it not to bother you. I can only write a letter, for a while yet, and I can't know how to write what you need. Please Darling, don't brood or worry over things that seem to have no answer, one gets nowhere. There's lots I would like to know about what you're doing and have done, but you know what you can and want to tell me. Mostly we want to know if you still love us, I guess.

15 August 1944 [Nottingham, England]

There doesn't seem to be a darned thing to do but wait for this war to end. I am so terribly lonely. Jeane, I just can't seem to write any more—nothing of interest is going on. Still in the Company Punkin, but on detached Services with a job that is terribly monotonous. The work leaves me ready to bite myself each night, and not a word of thanks or anything from this so-called regiment. There have been times recently when I have seriously considered asking for a transfer. It just doesn't seem the same anymore. No time to do anything. Nothing—absolutely nothing interesting without working in the company. Tired—yes darling, all of the time. That leave wasn't long enough

I am in a horrific mood. I badly need pictures of our son. Something to pep up this failing spirit of mine. Once this war is over, no one will get me in the army again.

August 18, 1944 [Hood River, Oregon]

Why don't you ask Eisenhower when you can come home? Tell him your wife wants to know.

August 20, 1944 [Hood River, Oregon]

How can time drag and speed all at the same time as it is doing? Oh Darling, I pray that somehow it will be over before too much longer and that you will be back with us; that we shall be able to help you forget the hopelessness, the things that you have known, and help build the life that you deserve. I guess we'll never be able to quite make up for it all. You know that I am desperately proud of you and proud that you are a paratrooper. You're recognized as the "elite" completely these days. "I am proud of you" seems such a small drop of the praise that I feel. Just hope you know, Sweetheart.

21 August 1944 [Nottingham, England]

Two letters from you—well, we will skip those, and one Saturday that was so wonderful. Silly, I didn't mean any affair with anyone else on that "wrong slant." Do I find it hard to be faithful? No Jeane, that is the least of my worries. I have not touched anyone yet, and it will be many years before I would. That Jeane is something that most cannot say—yes, officers included. I go out with this English WAC once in a while, but a show is the only thing. There isn't a thing more for me. No family—no son to occupy my time. Nothing that I love.

About pictures of you and our son: If I had gone in again [to the front] without a picture, you would have had a crazy husband on your hands. In July I lost my wallet, pictures and everything. I have been lost until today—the pictures arrived, and they are grand. You look so good. So that is our son hmm. That is my first look at him. He looks so very good to me.

The piece of silk was cut from the chute that set me down in France. The Ribbon is a German Iron Cross and there are some German Ration Stamps (yes, they have them too). Good night for now, Your Adoring Husband, George

**The fragment of George's D-Day parachute as described in his letter of August 21, 1944. Jeane did not receive the letter until September 6, just thirteen days before George's second combat mission, when the 508th jumped into Holland in Operation Market-Garden. Gurwell Collection.**

August 21, 1944 [Hood River, Oregon]

The Aug 11th letter came today. Happy anniversary.[91] Labor strikes are much less prevalent. The government doesn't wait long to step in anymore, and they [the strikers] are learning that it's either work or fight. You've probably heard that a few doves [pacifists] immediately reported to their draft boards without benefit of exemption. Yes, we could do better, but we can never do enough for the price you've paid. We're bitter with you over the things that are wrong, but don't be too bitter Sweetheart, for the vast majority sees things more clearly. People are looking to you who return from action for a better peace. You will help name it and we all will work toward it. Certain principles can never die or be buried long. Remember standing before the Capital in Washington, D.C.? I shall always remember and hear you say, "There's the heart of the country." And a great country it is, even with its faults. Love, Jeane

The photographs of Jeane and baby "Butch" seemingly worked their magic on George. His relief was palatable in late August as he penned a series of letters in rapid succession while the regiment was ramping up for the operation in Holland. Although George could not have known the details about the upcoming mission, the increased activity and scuttlebutt surely made him aware that something big was about to happen.

22 August 1944 [Nottingham, England]

Still pouring over my pictures, I feel so much better since they arrived. Two letters today, the 10th and 13th. Wonderful letters that mean so much. Nothing here in England. War news sounds good and we are having terrible weather. That is the limit of my feeling toward both. I expect to be back in the Company soon. This extra work is about over, thank God. Tell Mother and Dad Hello.

23 August 1944 [Nottingham, England]

Darling, it's a good thing your letter of the 13th arrived before these last two on the 11th and 12th. Yes Punkin, that letter of the 12th was a little on the sarcastic side. As it was though, I could only laugh because I was happy again. We still can't talk about France even if I wanted to—which I don't.

It isn't true that I can do what is uppermost in my mind, and "it isn't writing to you." I just can't write when there is only bitterness in my mind. I want to write all of the time because letters from You are the only things that make this life bearable. [How] I wish that by not writing it was possible to do other [things]. Besides, nothing ever happens to me but work and more work. More so this last month, because due to losing my wallet, I have had exactly 20 dollars to spend.

Now for that letter of the 12th. Carrier pigeons are very slow—even more so than my letters. My Wonderful Wife, if I could explain what was "eating me" I would, but even I don't know. The pictures were something that relaxed this poor tense brain almost 100%. Jeane, do you know what it's like to be so miserable that you are numb? In one of my last letters, I told you something of the people over here. Anyone can have a woman that wants one—no one will know. There is nothing for me here—not even so much as a home or friends that aren't in the army. I almost have to go out once in a while to keep from going mad. This girl knows that I am married and that

I have a son. When I married you Jeane, I gave up willingly other girls. I won't have them because I don't want to—not because they aren't there to be had. That my Dear is more than most officers and men can say—From the top down.[92] Now, My Wonderful One—what is your rating? You are as close to perfect as anyone can be.... Your adoring Husband, George

24 August 1944 [Nottingham, England]

Tonight has been a terrible affair. Rain just before 4 o'clock, a nasty angry feeling all over. Then to top everything we had a very silly officers' school. Long and very disinteresting until I could have screamed. Now, a dramatized program of France that fairly drips. I am growing very rapidly into a mood for getting gloriously drunk. This waiting on the sidelines is enough to cause a person to wonder. Sweetheart, what a case this husband of yours is tonight. There is good music on the radio, but just try to hear it here in the club. So damned many new officers that they get underfoot. Sorry punkin, but there is a nasty mood that I am in this evening. You did ask for it though—don't feel like writing.

My heart just isn't over here, Jeane. I love you so very much. News is very good, yet we get no encouragement whatsoever. Time seems to be standing still. Yes, I am tired of trying. Just a normal humdrum life seems the only thing worthwhile.

August 25, 1944 [Portland, Oregon]

George my darling, I want you to come home to something alive, to a wife who can make you forget and who isn't afraid of all the little or big things ahead. For when you walked away from the car that night in Mackall [to go overseas] my heart walked with you. I don't have to close my eyes to see you. Your shoulders were so straight. I hadn't wanted to watch, but I couldn't turn away. Bring it back soon Darling.

You married a goon child honey, one that doesn't catch on very fast.

September 6, 1944 [Portland, Oregon]

The D-Day chute came today. When you ripped out that part of the chute, what were you thinking about? Did you really have time to get it? There's much to know and wonder about.

September 7, 1944, [Portland, Oregon]

Got four letters today dated August 22, 23, 24, and 27. Golly, you wrote almost every day and I am a nitwit. You've been better sending gifts than anyone can ask. As for the dime-a-dozen women abroad or here, we are quite well aware of their frequency. Supply and demand perhaps? After all no one sells what no one wants to buy. Yes indeedy.

September 13, 1944, [Portland, Oregon]

How is that handsome husband of mine? You have me wondering you know, what with no letters for a spell again. Not a mood is it Honey? Hope you are remembering some of those evenings before the fire in Pinehurst? Next time they will be ours alone.

September 14, 1944 [Portland, Oregon]

Your letters get more lop-eared each day from reading them. Honestly now Spook, if this becomes another month of no letters without combat for an excuse, then don't hold this cookie responsible for the results.

11 September 1944 [Nottingham, England]

You have a very ashamed husband; it has been a long time between letters. [To be exact, 15 days; the regiment is gearing up for the Holland campaign.] I will do better, I promise. Work piled up on me. I have been working night and day for the past week. Jeane Darling, your letters have been coming through. Thank you, they have been a God send. Sweetheart, this heart of mine is so very heavy. You will never know how very much I need you. Hope with all my heart that this mess is over soon. Love, George

Despite a heavy training schedule, George managed to write just before the 508th took off for Operation Market Garden on September 17, 1944. Although he could not intimate that a mission was imminent, he enclosed some precious documents for safe keeping in his final letter to Jeane.

> 14 and 16 September 1944 [Nottingham, England]
>
> I am the new trial judge advocate (prosecution) for court martials. I hate that work. Enjoying a quiet house while everyone else is out on leave. No birthday present—will explain sometime.[93] Stopped a moment ago to reread a poem that I am going to enclose. Brings back memories of France.
>
> Thank your city for me. That bond drive really is grand. Believe me, I've been telling some of these East Coast people about it. I am sending you a few orders I want you to keep for me. Just a matter of record. Time for more work for this First Lieutenant.[94]
>
> Your loving husband, George.

This letter enclosed a very descriptive poem that was found in the effects of a sergeant who was killed in action in Normandy. We think that George sent this poem to Jeane as a way of sharing the horrors of combat while staying within censorship rules and satisfying his own reluctance to tell his wife about his personal fears and war experiences. Later, when Sue was just a curious little girl, this poem became her father's way of sharing—and not sharing—old fears and lingering grief with her as well.

Sue recalls: "This poem held a lot of significance throughout Dad's life. I remember the special drawer where he always kept it while I was growing up, and the faraway look in his eyes when he would catch me sneaking a peek at it. It was one of a few very precious items that Dad eventually insisted be placed into a safety deposit box. I don't remember him ever mentioning who wrote it, but as I got older, he did share the history of the poem and how it was the author's premonition of his own death. Reading it always touched me deeply and gave me a tiny insight into my father and the sacrifices of the war."

> **JOURNEY INTO DARKNESS**
> On soaring wings our transports ride
> Below, one lightless countryside;
> A thin, cold moon; light clouds; dark sky.
> Tonight we live, we fight—and Die.

The planes roar on. Not far ahead,
Bursts of flak, flame flowers spread.
Our plane is rocking, rising, falling
Scant miles to go…Seconds crawling.

Ack-Ack behind, drop zone near—and now
"Stand in the Door," Ready, we're there…
"GO!" We're out, we're coming down.
Planes goodbye; here comes the ground.

We're down and armed.
The enemy is everywhere…
And in the sky, our transports gone into the night.
We are alone, and now the fight.

Staccato, as machine guns bark,
Rifles cracking in the dark—
"Forward—double—hit the ground"
The night, a holocaust of sound.

A figure rises—charges—my rifle
Swings, now right, now left, now up a trifle,
My finger closes gently on the trigger,
I see Death touch him, Death's icy finger.

A sudden flash of flaming Hell,
A blast of death, a bursting shell—
The roar of more, as raining down
They bracket every inch of ground.

"Crouch down! Dig in! Dig in!"
I hear myself screaming o'er the din.
The firing round and round me dies
Beneath those deathly flaming skies.

A flash of pain across my back,
Splintering shrapnel's bloody track
Warmly trickling down my thigh—
A black-red puddle where I lie,

And to the left, the front, the fight—
One light flickers, stabbing white.

The shells, Praise God, have ceased to fall;
I see those stabbing lights, that's all.

Snaking forward, here they come…
Rushing, firing as they run—
And in my hands, my rifle's hot,
Aim and fire—"Get that dark blot."

But what's the use? I'm alone;
No holding fire but my own.
They know I cannot hold them long,
They come more boldly, coming strong.

Now the end, the time to die;
My five grenades are ready.
I lie so I can throw them, one by one
When they come too close to gun.

Now they're here, and I throw.
Three men die by this last blow.
Two are they who came tonight—
The third, I know, is I.

For I am weak, my aim is slow—
My blood and strength, together flow,
One second now, and then, and then—
This is it; this is the end.

The poem was typed, and George had penned a note at the end to Jeane "Darling, this poem was written by a Sergeant in one of our line companies before he went into Normandy. It might not read too well, but it was so much like the events. Very real to those of us who came back. Yes, Jeane—He was killed over there." In the course of writing this book, we discovered that "Journey into Darkness" was written in England on the eve of D-Day by Sgt. James H. Ellifrit, Company C. Records show he was killed in battle on June 7, 1944. [95]

The official stance of the 82nd Airborne on mortality rates in World War II is best expressed in a memo by General Matthew B. Ridgway: "The losses are part of the inevitable price of war in human life."[96] At foxhole level, the threat of mortal danger every living moment left no time to mourn, or often even to pause, when death found your buddy. Losses were deeply felt and just as deeply repressed. Paratroopers had a phrase they used when they heard they'd lost a friend. To sum up their feelings of anger, grief, loss, and disgust, they simply said, "Too bad," and went about their assignments. As Command Sergeant Major "Rock" Merritt told us in 2018, "too bad" had the connotation of "a waste." It was the most serious of statements, to be used exclusively when a soldier had been seriously maimed or killed—but never if he would recover.[97]

**Kenneth "Rock" Merritt was a corporal on D-Day and rose to the rank of Honorary Command Sergeant Major of the Army. Pictured here with Sue Talley's M1, Ft Walton Beach, FL.**

In letters, veteran interviews, and other sources, we would sadly encounter that phrase again: "Too bad."

CHAPTER VIII

# OPERATION MARKET GARDEN: THE JUMP INTO HOLLAND

On September 17, 1944, the largest airborne operation in history—and the first to be executed in daylight—took place in Holland. Two American divisions, the 82nd and the 101st; the British 1st Airborne Division; and later, the 1st Independent Polish Parachute Brigade, participated in Market, the air assault phase of Operation Market Garden, which was the attempt to cross the Lower Rhine at Arnhem and end the war early by going through "Germany's back door." Conditions were bright and clear as the immense sky train of 2,024 planes and gliders took to the sky from twenty-four airfields, escorted by nearly a thousand Allied fighter and fighter-bomber aircraft. Departures began at 9:45 a.m. and continued steadily for hours.

Carried in 132 C-47s from the 441st Troop Carrier Group, the 1st and 2nd Battalions of the 508th took off in that order from RAF Langar Airfield, followed by the 3rd Battalion, which departed from RAF Fulbeck Airfield. Regimental Headquarters flew out of Langar.[98] All were headed for Drop Zone "T" north of Groesbeek, with orders to "seize, organize, and hold key terrain features in sector of responsibility, be prepared to seize Wall River crossing at

Nijmegen on Division order and prevent all hostile movement south of line Hatert–Klooster."[99]

The drop was accurate and highly successful: the men assembled quickly, with good recovery of their color-coded equipment bundles and 95 percent of the regiment accounted for.[100] The HqHq Morning Report of September 30, 1944 reflected that George's company shared in this success: "17 Sept 44. Woke Co up at 0600hr. Enplaned at 1030 hr. Took off at 1100 hr. Flew over England, Channel and Holland. Encountered flak near the DZ. Dropped at 1330 hr. No opposition on the field. Co. assembled at 1500 hr. All equipment salvaged." As George later summed it up, "The jump into Holland went fairly easy. It was during the day, and we only took what we needed. My chute blew a panel, and I threw it away. I later picked up another one."[101]

After the initial assault, the 508th was assigned to protect the division's right flank near—and at times, over—the German border to the east of Nijmegen. The regiment withstood several attacks by German forces, which quickly rallied, acted decisively, and nearly penetrated American lines. "The fight along the division perimeter [was] a near-run thing. The 505th and 508th held despite being everywhere outnumbered and outgunned because of the toughness, tenacity, initiative, and leadership of the troopers, noncommissioned officers, and officers at all levels."[102]

In fierce fighting south of Arnhem and north of positions assigned to the 101st, the 82nd seized and held the bridges over the Maas-Waal Canal and the Maas River, as well as the highway and rail bridges over the Waal at Nijmegen, but the British XXX Corps was slow to advance over "Hell's Highway," the narrow, sixty-five-mile corridor through central Holland leading north into Germany. Stalling just past the Nijmegen Bridge, XXX Corps failed to reach its objective at Arnhem, the notorious "bridge too far," where the British 1st Airborne was surrounded and fighting in desperate straits.[103]

**Nijmegen bridge, objective of the 82nd Airborne in Operation Market Garden, 2018.**

Like many U.S. veterans of the Holland mission, George had a special feeling for the Dutch, a feeling that was almost inevitably tied to intense resentment of the British, who had failed to push their armor aggressively up the highway and over the bridges the U.S. airborne had taken and held at tremendous cost. "I can't tell you how much we loved the Dutch people," he told us in 2001. "We could have almost shot the British. Their own men [the British 1st Airborne] were getting blown away just up the road and they [the British XXX Corps] stopped to brew tea. We'd begun taking volunteers to go up and relieve those boys [in Arnhem] when we got the order to pull out. You can't believe how angry we were."

George and his fellow paratroopers were fortunate indeed not to suffer the fate of the other paratroopers at Arnhem. The failure of XXX Corps to achieve its objective resulted in catastrophe: the destruction of 80 percent of the British 1st Airborne, the decimation of the Polish Parachute Brigade, and the division of Holland into two parts, one liberated, the other occupied, over a long, brutal winter known as the *Hongerwinter*. The western part of the country under Nazi control suffered terrible starvation and upward of twenty-two thousand deaths as the Germans extracted retribution for a Dutch railroad strike and Dutch cooperation with the Allies. It also meant a protracted stay in Holland for airborne troops.[104]

With the bulk of the battle—and hence their initial mission—complete, the 82nd Airborne, under the control of the British Second Army, was tasked with holding a static defense, therefore becoming the new front line. Responsible for a perimeter of more than twenty-five miles, the 82nd remained in defensive positions for over two months. George dug in with the 508th on "the Island," a five-kilometer area near Bemmel, bordered by the Lower Rhine to the north and the Waal River to the south, where troops endured conditions reminiscent of World War I trench warfare, including frequent artillery fire.

George's cow story is repeated here with more detail. "At this point I was at HqHq Co. as a supply officer," he recounted. "I also was the company executive officer and the chemical weapons officer. We finally got a food drop [K rations], and I wanted to be sure this one group up front had something to eat. We got in a jeep and were taking all kinds of fire moving up to the line. When we got there, our group had slaughtered a cow and were cooking steaks! You better believe I got me a steak too!"[105]

The 82nd Airborne remained in Holland for fifty-seven days, from September 17 through November 11, 1944. George's correspondence contained no description of the jump or initial fighting: planning, training, and the assault presented neither time nor place to write. This resulted in a month-long gap, between September 9 and October 8, 1944, in his letters to Jeane.

As much as she tried to keep a stiff upper lip, her need for frequent information and letters got the best of her as she wrote her next letter.

> September 26, 1944 [Portland, Oregon]
>
> My Darling,
>
> How are you Sweetheart, and where are you tonight? If there isn't word soon from you, I shan't have a mind to lose. You remember my violent imagination, don't you? Well, it finds you in all kinds of predicaments. I'm OK on the outside Honey, but inside, this war is making hamburger of yours truly.
>
> Almost a month since your last letter again—so much has been happening in the world. The immensity of all the airborne divisions must have experienced leaves me speechless. There is nothing I can say because it demands so much to be said. Can't help that old worrying business that's always there, inside—silly, isn't it, when things are going to come out OK. With all my love and faith, Your adoring wife, Jeane

Jeane, too, was writing under stress. She had just moved to Portland to finish her nursing degree and was now juggling the duties of new motherhood and the necessities of study and frequent travel. Knowing that George was in combat, she worried constantly about the infrequency of his letters, fearing the worst. Wanting desperately to keep the feeling of connection between them, she plead for him to share his thoughts and feelings, promised to try to understand, wanting desperately not to be shut out.

> September 29, 1944 [Portland, Oregon]
>
> The past war news, especially of the invasion of Holland, leaves us stripped, speechless, because it hits so hard. Yes, we who are left here know something of what it means to all of you. We picture much, live part of it all inside with you, yet I expect you to reeducate me. When you're back, I want to occupy the same spot in your life that I have. Don't leave me out of too much. I want you to be happy and to think that it was worth it perhaps. But perhaps then it never can be.... We can't have all of you by sharing those experiences now—but we don't care how you come home—just come. Please believe, Sweetheart, awfully strongly in that wonderful day ahead when we can erase the past—the parts we want to.

Trying another technique, Jeane attempted to raise George's spirits by sharing one of her escapades at the hospital. A truly Jeane endeavor!

> October 6, 1944 [Portland, Oregon]
>
> Last week, in that typical manner you must remember, your brilliant wife burned the OB [Obstetrics] Department's last aluminum formula pan so badly that the smell could be smelled for miles. Not only did the bottom fall out, but it burned completely up on the grate. How's that for conservation? (We got another one.) Does that remind you of some of those meals down South? Too bad it wasn't full of black-eyed peas.[106]

George's first letter from Holland and many that follow were written from a foxhole in a defensive position north of Nijmegen. The Germans had stopped the main Allied assault short of the bridge at Arnhem and were firing on George's position as he wrote between the shell bursts, drawing ink up from a bottle with a fountain pen.

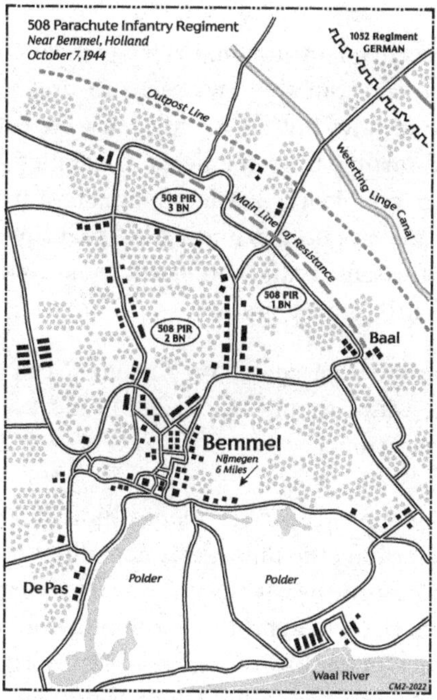


**Map of front line near Bemmel, Holland October, 7, 1944. Map purchased by authors.**

8 October 1944 [Foxhole near Nijmegen, Holland]

So My Darling, You must have just about given up all hope of hearing from me. Jeane—there has been no time to write this past week or so. I have been on the go continually until at times I felt like saying—To Hell with everything!!! Today, though, things slacked up a little and this lonely husband of yours took advantage of it. Washed and cleaned up thoroughly—in a foxhole, too (home). Now with a few minutes more grace, I should be able to at last drop a few lines to you. Shells are whistling and moaning overhead from both sides and occasionally one drops close. Have to keep one ear peeled for those. The Germans are very resentful of our presence for some reason.

Jeane, your letters have been coming in beautifully and I thank God for that. Need a lift like that all the time. Those color pictures arrived today: they were good, and I promptly devoured them. I want to get home so very badly (there went a close one).

The war seems to go on and on. Each day makes it that much nearer to the end, but the days seem to drag. We are faring pretty good now, but for a while we were eating mainly potatoes and turnips from the fields. Cigarettes were scarce, but now there are plenty. Ran into a bunch of fruit orchards recently and we have been eating apples, pears, plums, grapes, and more of the same until I can hardly look fresh fruit in the face. WHOOMP (quite close).

I hope to heaven that soon—very soon—I can spend time with you the way I should (Close one) (and yet another). I miss you so very much.

George was under the necessity to silence himself; even if he were emotionally capable of describing the nitty-gritty actualities of combat, army regulations obliged him to censor nearly the entirety of his experience. One of the most traumatic events occurred shortly before he wrote this first letter from Holland, when four men under his command—Pfc. George Hartman, and Pvt.s Richard H. Thomas, Martin Jones, and Clyde Fisher—were killed by a single artillery blast on October 1, 1944. Not until June 2001 did George ever speak about the horror and the overwhelming sense of responsibility he felt for them even then, fifty-seven years later, when he called it "one of the worst days of my life. He said," "I knew something happened to my men, and I had to go check. Their foxhole took a direct hit, and all four of them were just gone. It was awful. I wish I had never looked, but I had to. They were my men, and I knew something had happened."[107]

Hearing George's account made us later reflect on what it must have taken for him to write that first letter to Jeane on October 8, so soon after the event. Yet he picked up his pen even as artillery shells were bursting around his foxhole. He continued his letter the next day, injecting a few light notes in the attempt to reassure her he was fine.

> 9 October 1944 [Foxhole near Nijmegen]
>
> See Punkin—More things to do and the darkness very early. So, My Precious, it is another day with more shells whistling around. Sometimes I think that everyone would get tired and stop, but they go on night and day. Hold your breath and cross your fingers and maybe I will be able to finish this letter before lunch. Another long, cold day.
>
> So far, I have seen a few windmills and quite a few wooden shoes, but there has always been somebody in both, so I couldn't get them [for souvenirs]. I must close, almost time for chow. When you don't hear from me you will know that I am OK. Just busy as a little bee. By the way, I have a mustache now.
>
> Your adoring husband, George
>
> 11 October 1944 [Foxhole near Nijmegen]
>
> Hello there Adorable,
>
> How is the most Wonderful wife in the world today? Yes, Punkin, Our Anniversary again. Rather nice here today but heavy rain yesterday and most of the night. I am almost completely dried out and just succeeded in bailing out my foxhole. Rather a strange business this bailing out a foxhole!
>
> Right now, I am alternating between eating a pear, smoking an English cigarette and writing to you, Punkin. Confusing to say the best. Will probably begin with the pear pretty soon.

Jeane, you would most certainly have had a good laugh at me last night. Wet to the skin, crawling into my little hole in the ground and piling blankets all over me to try and dry out. Water then proceeded to leak through the sides of my foxhole. The German shelter half over the top did a fine job. Woke up about three in the morning very wet where I had been sitting. Too mad to do much of anything but wad a blanket up and slip it under me. Went back to sleep then for a couple of hours. Just think, Punkin, usually in bed (or semblance thereof) by eight o'clock each night, just like a chicken.

12 October 1944 [letter continues]

Sweetheart, a lively night. That German artillery is enough to take years from your lifetime in short order. Too close, my Darling, for comfort. No rain last night, so no bailing necessary. How is that Lovely Wife of mine today? Remember—don't work too hard. Haven't had any mail for the past few days so I imagine that between the hospital and our son, you are pretty busy. The men have plenty of time to write, but us poor officers always seem to have something to do.

I get very lonely over here as the war seems to be won, but Germany just doesn't want to give up. Will probably take a good fight clear into Berlin. I am most amazed at the Germans. I did so want to spend this Christmas at home. Darling—almost a year now since we left the States.

Jeane—I must close for now. More work to do before night comes. So Adorable One—All My Love Always—Your Adoring Husband.

13 October 1944 [Foxhole near Nijmegen]

Received two letters from you just before dark last night. Jeane—they startled me very much. Written on the 26th and the 29th of September—and Punkin, they didn't sound like you.

Sweetheart—you will always have my love. There is no one to take your place. I have a job over here though, Jeane, and it must of necessity take preference over both you and our son at times. I write every chance I get, and this morning I skipped breakfast so that I might write again.

There is only one thought in my mind over here, and that is to get back to you. But we are fighting a war. Anything can happen, and it will always be that way. Never let this war prey on your mind—because if I am going to come back, the Lord above will take care of me. Faith, My Dearest One, is the greatest thing in this world. He alone makes the decisions. I take every precaution that I can, but precautions are such a small thing. Adorable one—you are never left out. You are always with me Darling. All My Love Punkin—always. Your Adoring Husband—George

George's letter of September 14 announcing his promotion to First Lieutenant did not reach Jeane until nearly a month later. When it did, she celebrated the news on stationary with an orchid motif. Later, George would always buy orchid corsages for Jeane and his daughters on Easter Sunday.

October, 13 1944 [Portland, Oregon]

My Darling,

An orchid to you with the deepest Congratulations and a big, big, big, kiss. I'm oh so glad, mostly because you are well, and yes, awfully proud, even if your promotion isn't too big of a surprise. Somehow, I knew you would get it soon. I was proud enough anyway though—this finds your family bubbling over and even little George R. laughed and giggled. He wanted to eat your order sheet (but he didn't). It was such a happy surprise that I couldn't gripe because a letter wasn't there also. The papers are in your 201 file, though I still get them out to show off.[108] It was good to see the names of the other fellows and catch up. (Poor Clint, huh?) [Clint Moss was not promoted.]

October 15, 1944 [Portland, Oregon]

Got home about 10:30 pm and fooled around, hoping that Uncle Cleatus [Jeane's uncle] would get back from Hood River with those letters of yours. Oh Darling, he didn't let me down—he did come, and it was a wonderful, wonderful letter written from a foxhole in Holland, with the sand, even. It brought you so near that I could see it all.

You know surely, my Darling, that I understand why you can't write, though griping is to be taken for granted. It's good to hear something of Holland and the people. How about a pair of wooden shoes? Good old Ripper, tell him hello—or is it safe to write something like that these days? The sand is peculiar, isn't it? Not like what one would find on the beach at Seaside.

As the men settled in, holding a static defense line, George wrote a "domestic" letter describing his latest activity: foxhole renovations.

15 October 1944 [Foxhole near Nijmegen]

Hello Darling,

It is too dark to see exactly what I am saying, but I have something new: music in my foxhole. Tapped in on a radio belonging to the British. German equipment, and from an American in Holland. Pretty good my Darling. Had to light a match—lost my place. Really something, music in a foxhole. Darling—It is just too dark.

16 October 1944 [Foxhole near Nijmegen]

Still music Sweetheart—this was a German sound-powered telephone system, but now it is an American broadcasting device. It rained almost all last night, a very quiet night in general. Lots of sleep and plenty of love for you, Punkin.

Strange isn't it—no cold or sickness while we are out like this. You will probably have to put a tent in the backyard for me for the first few months. Houses seem to be just something we see as we pass by.

Mail has been very scarce. Nothing much of anything except a package of cigarettes each day. Rough at times, but I am usually too busy to think about it until I crawl into my foxhole at night. Due for another little excursion today—running down some German chemical munitions.[109]

There is the prettiest little bird playing around not over 15 ft. away. Saucy little thing, not any bigger than a minute. It is very cold here now. I don't notice it much—really shouldn't with four layers of clothing on. Heaven help me if I ever fall down. Probably roll around and won't be able to get up.

Every time I think of music in foxholes, I have to laugh. Pretty darned soft. Felt hungry a minute ago, so just reached into a little niche in my foxhole, and got an apple. Central heating and hot running water is all that we lack. "Blue Danube" is playing now. Darling, here I ran out of ink and time, so Sweetheart I Love You Adorable One.[110]

22 October 1944 [Foxhole near Nijmegen]

Everything has been very wet and muddy over here. Things just won't stay dry, including yours truly. Spent all day today cleaning guns, boots, etc., trying to dry out after almost continual rain. A cold rain at that. Had quite a little shelling last night. Some too darned close. This artillery is not very good stuff. Can't do much about it but hope and pray.

We are dug in beside some farmhouses out in the orchard. The farmer is beside me saying something in Dutch. A boy here looks enough like my brother Dick to be his twin. He spent quite a while this afternoon watching me take apart and clean a German rifle. Very curious and very interested. No pretty girls except two. About two years old, but very pretty, even if they are just about as dirty as pigs.

Just think Punkin—going to bed at six-thirty. Not bad is it. Had to get up several times during the night though. Darkness comes pretty early here. Again, there are things to do before darkness—so Jeane Darling, I have to close for now.

With letters arriving inconsistently and not always in order of the date written, Jeane's earlier letter of October 11 finally reached George's muddy foxhole. Her cryptic remark stating "that by now you must have heard about Bud" elicited a feeling of dread. Never giving any real explanation, it left George a little confused and a bit anxious about his friend's fate.

24 October 1944 [Foxhole near Nijmegen]

It seems almost impossible to write during the day. There are many things to do, so I have a little light in my foxhole now besides the music. (Working on inside plumbing next.)

So—you have a mental picture of me sitting on the step entrance to my foxhole with the deep, wide part just in front of me. A tent pitched over the whole thing, and a heavy German box filled with dirt over the top of the hole and under the tent. (Box is to stop shrapnel.) Then part of the hole is dug or hollowed out under about two feet of good solid clay. I am sitting on my step with the tablet on my knee—tent all buttoned up, and my head leaning against the box. Earphones around my neck—half listening to music and the other half trained on the artillery, mortar, and small arms fire going off.

Nothing wrong physically but your letter of the 11th arrived today. You said something about Bud. I haven't heard a thing from him or about him. I am a little apprehensive now even though you didn't say very much. I hope against hope that what I fear isn't true. Bud, Dave and I were more like brothers than anything else.

It is quite cold today and without rain, thank goodness. Oh yes, I have about four or five inches of straw on the bottom of my foxhole. So there, My Darling, you have a picture of my home. Not very grand, but it is all handmade. Rather a difficult job too, in this clay.

This so-called picture that I am sending was taken just a little before we left England.[111] [T/5 George A.] Fredrick, [*sic*] one of the men, took it and someone at the base camp had it developed. The one on the left is that lonely husband of yours. The laughter is due to the fight to pull me out of the orderly room. Ripper and two others ganged up on me. Quite a tussle. (Camera shy.) Darling—it is a quarter after eight, past my bedtime. Love, George

P.S. Clint and I were talking today about all the good times back at Pinehurst. Some memories.

When the spate of letters George had been writing was slow to reach Portland, Jeane felt resentful of her luckier friends, but tried to hold her tongue and blamed it all on work.

October 24, 1944 [Portland, Oregon]

A couple of recent letters from Jerry Hardwick and Helen Moss mentioned having several letters from Don and Clint from Holland. So, yours truly is close to going on the peck about her *one*, even if you always did do more work for that regiment than both of them together. It's a wonderful regiment, though. You should all be so proud to be a part of it—but you've all made it that way.

With a second Christmas apart from Jeane fast approaching, George's spirits entered an all-time low. Full of jumbled thoughts and feelings, he mailed his second bronze jump star home to Jeane, writing "Still in Holland" under the date of his letter.

29 October 1944 [Near Nijmegen]

Hello My Precious Darling,

Received a letter from you today and Sweetheart, I really needed it. My morale has been pretty darned low. It is cold and wet here and it is a big problem to keep warm and dry. Besides, I miss you so much it isn't even funny. Here it is, almost Christmas, and all I want is to be with you.

Jeane—how are things going at home? I have never in my life been so tired of anything as I am of this being away from you. Can't quite imagine what it is going to be like when this mess is over, and our lives will be our own.

Say Precious One, thanks for the plug about the promotion. You must be my most ardent admirer and just a little prejudiced. Now admit it. I certainly am happy about it myself, but mainly because I can send you more money. Rank has never meant much to me because my respect for people doesn't correspond to the rank they carry. You know me though—never a really good army man, and never will be. Just a civilian in uniform.

I am sending you another little bronze jump star [signifying his second combat jump] in this envelope. It goes on the left-hand side as you wear it, or on the right as you hold the wings in your hand looking at it. Here is a picture showing you where the star should go. A jeweler can drill the hole and solder it on for you.

**George's diagram for placing battle stars on jump wings after jumping into Holland. Gurwell Collection.**

The heather is a little something that I pulled up just after I landed in Holland. The flag is a reserve that I jammed in as a reserve supply. We wear them on the right shoulder and sew them on just before we jump in combat.[112]

October 29, 1944 [Portland, Oregon]

How are you, sweet? I regret any and all griping about lack of letters. You have an ardent promise that I'll try to be better. Where are you and how are you? There's oh so much that we want to know. I pray that someway, somehow, much of it will let up soon; that you will come back before much longer—to rest, peace, and all that you want so much.

31 October 1944 [Foxhole near Nijmegen]

My Dearest Wife,

I have a souvenir paper [*Paraglide*] put out by Division to send to you. It tells a little of what we have done. Makes a pretty nice keepsake. It will go into the mail as soon as I can find some stamps.[113]

Well, My Darling—time is dragging along and soon another month will be here, November already. Not much longer until we have been gone a year. A year, Jeane, that has seen many changes for me. From a lifetime in the States and then Ireland, England, Scotland, Wales, France, Holland, and Germany, all in a very brief span. I have realized with each different country and the different people just how lucky I really am. America has the good points of all combined with very few of the bad, I have the best wife in the world, and we have a son. A person in his right mind couldn't ask for anything more.

Your love, My Darling, and a faith that has never deserted me, has pulled me through some pretty tough spots. Time is a funny thing—sometimes going so very fast like in Pinehurst, and sometimes so very slowly as it is doing now. Each day seems so very long, and yet the months slip by.

Jeane—do you know something that has always tickled me? Those shopping tours in Pinehurst. I really enjoyed them even if I did have to carry the packages. What a disappointment to come home and find that you were downtown or someplace else. Used to mope around the house just wishing you would hurry—or try to think of some way to appear nonchalant and disinterested, while inside I just couldn't wait. Something you didn't know, isn't it? You have been the best wife in the world to me. I have known so much happiness since we have been together.

Jeane's next letter came with an apology as she tried to assure George that she understood that writing was not always possible. She continued to drive herself, interning on a rotating schedule at the hospital, as she finished her nursing degree and tended to her baby on her limited off hours.

November 2, 1944 [Portland, Oregon]

Our Dearest Darling,

No letters for a couple of days—I've wanted to, but was too tried to write. Things seem to have piled up lately with long hard hours of work, but none of it matters because there were three whole wonderful letters from you, written from that Holland foxhole—Oct. 8, 11, 13. They were such *good* letters Darling, and I'm so proud of your morale and spirit in the face of all that has been so tough, all those things that you miss and lack.

Now, finally, for those precious letters—let's start with the first. Most of all, my conscience bothers me terribly and I'm more than humble for any griping about you not writing when it was impossible to do so. Yes, Sweetheart I do understand—in spite of the stinky tone that creeps in at times, always needing and asking for your love, getting sometimes a little too tense and tired, and then not being the wife you deserve—but will watch it. What a poor soldier and an impossible 1st Lt I would make. The shells that were so close. You know about tenseness and loneliness and more.

What a sight you must be, bailing out a foxhole and with a mustache. I can just see your disgruntled soul. Was it more of a job growing or dismantling the soup strainer? Glad it's dismantled, you might get bugs in it. Seems a shame that when you're in your little foxhole, safe from the women, you can't be safe from the shells too.

The last letter held the cross. What a lovely, lovely thing, so intricate. Wonder what the craftsman dreamed of while making it? Made in Italy [We do not have it], found in Holland, now here. Not so long ago, you held it in your hand and dreamed your dreams. Somehow, I could see you turning it over, smiling a little to yourself. I proudly showed it to everyone at the hospital. They raved and exclaimed over it.

Now your letter—the last one dated Oct. 13—startled me in turn, George Darling. Please go on reprimanding me and snapping me on my feet when I need it. You married kind of a childish girl, didn't you? But she'll try harder to grow up—to get rid of old tendencies to doubt and that little green-eyed jealously monster. Sometimes I get tired, lonesome for you and wonder about the things I see and hear that I don't understand, or maybe it's a strained moment that begs for reassurances. Funny how we all gripe and think ours a sad lot, when it's never half as bad as it could be.

November 8, 1944 [letter continued]

George, Sweet, if we don't hear that you're out of Holland soon, I'm going to start sending you vitamin pills—can't have malnutrition over there. You'd probably give them away to the kids and teach them how to shoot marbles.

It's late, George Darling, 1:30 a.m. We're pretty lucky and thankful to have a warm bed, peace and quiet to sleep here, with no shells banging around too close. A little too quiet without you though....

November 24, 1944 [Portland, Oregon]

Surely no one could be as happy as I am right now, because there were three letters from you tonight—three wonderful, wonderful letters. So, you're still living with the turnips in Holland. Precious Punkin, no plush beds or steam heat yet for a while. The picture of you and Don Hardwick looked awfully good. It was in the first letter I opened and I squealed like a puppy to see it. Brought you several thousand miles closer, and a nice warm feeling all round my heart. You're good enough to eat, sweet. Don looked good too (all corn-fed for a hard winter, you can tell him).

From the sound of that foxhole, we have evidently all sent you the wrong things— starched, dotted-Swiss curtains or a nice wall hanging might have been more appropriate. Or oh, of course, a toilet seat cover with a big embroidered rose on it.

This letter of the 29th sounds as though your morale was taking a drop. What's the matter, besides this stinky war-making business? I know well enough, Darling.

It's such fun finding the little things you tuck away in your letters. The heather satisfies an old, old curiosity to really see the heather that blooms there. The flag is like the ones we see in the news pictures at times, but it's the first real one I've seen or held. Two little bronze stars now, for the wings. The next visit to town, I should get them on. I'm awfully proud of them, George Honey.

**George's Ike Jacket decorated with awards he had earned by the end of the war. Notice the jump stars are attached differently than in his diagram. Gurwell Collection.**

> Your last letter was full of the same memories that I remember so often, ones that I've wondered if you remember. You had me howling out loud, too. Darling, you're a pickle for waiting this long to tell me that you cared if I weren't home when you arrived those days at Pinehurst. Yes, you did have me fooled, and yes, you did worry me to death by seeming nonchalant and disinterested. Better not do that anymore, because I'm not very bright among other things, and it really cools me quick.
>
> It's late Darling, just keep praying that it can all end soon, that we can be together. With all my love always—Jeane

Unbeknownst to Jeane when she wrote this letter, George had not been "living with the turnips" for over two weeks. The entire 82nd Airborne Division had been pulled out of Holland on November 11, 1944 and transferred to France. The men had to march twenty-two miles with all their gear to Oss, Holland, where they met up with British lorries [transportation trucks] that transported them to Camp Sissonne. Two weeks after their arrival, the Memorial Service of November 25, 1944 was held in nearby Reims.[114] We again end our chapter with a service for the fallen, this time for the dead of the Holland campaign. We challenge anyone to read the following with dry eyes.

> For the second time in the history of the regiment we have returned from combat with thinned ranks—with files left blank by those who joined the lengthening line of 508th heroes who have made the supreme sacrifice.

Although these recent members of the regiment who were lost in Holland are physically absent, they will always be present in ranks in spirit along with those we lost in Normandy. They have left with the regiment more than a name to be carried on the honor roll. They served, fought, and died gallantly and fearlessly, and their history-making deeds and accomplishments will serve as an inspiration to us all, whenever and wherever future operations confront us.

This morning as we hear the names read, we silently salute them. In the days to come, whether in combat, garrison or civilian life, we will honor them for the heroes that they are, and always remember the obligation that is now ours to keep faith with them as they have kept faith with us. We will keep that faith.

ROY E. LINDQUIST

Colonel, Infantry

*Phyl Hoffman*

September 27, 1944
23 Redington Street
Swampscott, Massachusetts

Dear 508 Girls:

# CHAPTER IX

# SEEMS LIKE A BAD DREAM, ROUND ROBIN LETTERS 26–32

While the 508th was fighting in Holland, the Round Robin journeyed around the home front among an ever-widening circle of correspondents. Many expressed similar feelings to Jeane's—loneliness and flagging morale, fits of jealousy, and the determination to forge ahead to build a life for their budding families despite their husbands' absence. According to all reports, the women found the camaraderie of the band of sisters a solace, and often a source of valued, hard-to-come-by information in a grueling, uncertain time.

* * *

Phyl Hoffman received the now-considerable packet of letters in late September when news of regimental losses in France was still trickling in and the first reports from Holland were hot off the presses. Her husband, 1st Lt. Herbert Hoffman, was the S-1 (personnel) for Hq1 during the Normandy campaign.

Phyl Hoffman, Swampscott, Massachusetts [RR 26]

September 27, 1944

Dear 508 Girls,

What a thrill it was to receive all these lovely letters! I do wish I could see every one of you and have a long chat. I feel so isolated away up here in New England. My Herbie seems to have been the only one to join the paratroops from these parts! If any of you know any troopers' wives from around here, please let me know—I would like to meet them.

All you girls seem to be keeping yourselves pretty busy. The 508 men are a brave and gallant group of soldiers—and so are their wives. You are wonderful—so faithful and brave. Right now, I want to express my deepest sympathy to you girls who have lost your husbands. I have cried about each one. It just doesn't seem possible that we were all so very happy such a short time ago and now all this sadness is around us.

My Herb came safely through the Invasion of France, but now I am "sweating" out this latest jump in Holland. The fighting has been terrific—I'm living in constant fear, just like the rest of you.

I guess I've kept up with the 508 news pretty well as I correspond with Madelon ["Puzz"] Merriam, Mary Williams, Selma Abbott, Edna Taylor, Doris Daly, Mary Casteel, Rosemary and Jeanette Foley. I'm living at home with Mother and Dad. Work for the War Manpower Commission—am secretary to the Head man for the Northeastern Mass. Area. Very interesting work and it keeps me busy six days a week.

I live by the ocean, so have had a wonderful summer, spending weekends and other spare time on the beach. Quite a few of my married girlfriends are home as their husbands are away too, so we all get together and comfort each other. We go in town (Boston) frequently to the theatre. The Fall season has started and there are lots of good plays on at present. We took in a few Operas in the Spring, and sometimes just go in for cocktails and dinner. I've been intending to go to the Officers' Wives Club but have never got around to it. During the summer, we went bicycling and golfing a great deal. Soon the skiing season will be in full swing. But—I want my Herbie! Nothing can take a husband's place. I try to keep busy, but it is just like going in circles—I'm still lonesome and will continue to be!

I miss you 508 wives very much, too—such good friends you all are—other people just don't understand how we feel! I hope we can meet again someday.

I'm going to close this letter now by saying: The very best of luck to all of you from that "Damn Yankee." Phyl [Technically, Phyl was only a "Yankee." A "Damn Yankee" is a Northerner who comes to the South and stays.]

Sent from Massachusetts, Phyl's letter took almost two weeks to reach Edna Taylor, who was living with her sister in Memphis. Her husband, Capt. Royal R. Taylor, was the last of the four commanding officers of B Co. on D-Day.

Edna Taylor, Memphis Tennessee [RR 27]

October 9, 1944

Dear Girls,

What a pleasant surprise to find twenty-six letters from the 508 wives. I started reading and could not stop until I had finished. It seems almost as if we have had a get-together. I particularly enjoyed the pictures of the babies.

I haven't been doing anything exciting since the boys left, but I have kept busy. In February my sister came to Georgia to visit and I came home with her and have been in Memphis since. I live with my sister, her husband, my niece (19) and my nephew (13). I have been going to school, getting some "book larnin." Hope to go to work soon and do my bit. There is another war wife living near me. We have become good friends and get together occasionally and go to church on Sundays.

Girls, I ran across a good book the other day, *We Jumped to Fight*, by Colonel Edson D. Raff.[115] I'm putting a copy in one of my Christmas boxes for Royal. Don't know if he will have time for books or not. [116]

My "morale" is a little low right now. Haven't heard from Roy in quite a while. I'm sure there is a good reason, as he has always been so good about writing. He was very fortunate in France; his only injury was a broken bone in his foot. He has been awarded the Purple Heart. I extend my sympathy to you girls who have lost your husbands. It still seems like a bad dream.

They have a Paratrooper Club here, but somehow, I haven't joined yet. I understand they have about 100 members. I want to join right away, bet it would be lots of fun. There isn't any news, so I will say goodbye for now. Best wishes to everyone.

Sincerely, Edna Taylor

The Round Robin started to circulate in the South for a while, traveling first from Edna in Memphis to Rosemary Guillot in Texarkana. Rosemary's husband, 1st Lt. Gerald P. Guillot, served in Hq1.

Rosemary Guillot, Texarkana, Texas [RR 28]

October 15, 1944

Dear Girls,

When the Round Robin got to me, I was so thrilled. It felt just like I had had a little visit or talk with all of you out at the old 508 Club while waiting for our dear husbands. When I look back, it seems that I spent half my time sitting in that club. But I'm not kicking myself. How I would like to be doing the same thing right now.

Like all of you, I am waiting for news, from Holland. My last letter from Gerry was written Oct. 4. It seems that some of the letters are being held somewhere though, or maybe they were sunk. I feel lucky so far that my "hubby" has come through okay, and my heart goes out to those whose husbands have been taken to a better place. I hope and pray that this time there will be practically no casualties. I think maybe the jump was a lot more successful than the other one.

Gerry Jr. came Feb. 24, and of course I am so very thankful that I have had him through all this period of worry. I am taking a few courses at our Junior College, and so I am really busy. I like to keep my mind occupied, though it makes the days go faster.

I surely would like to hear about your latest news from Holland. SOOO please keep me posted.

I enjoyed everything in your letters about the Normandy Invasion, and wish I had something to add. Lots of luck to all our dear 508ers. I feel so close to most of the wives and men.

Love to all, Rosemary

**Rosemary Guillot and Jerry Guillot, Jr., Round Robin # 28. Gurwell Collection.**

A Texan from Waco, Evelyn Milam, the wife of Capt. Robert L. Milam, wrote in late October when the Round Robin arrived in her mailbox from Rosemary Guillot. By this time, the regiment had been in Holland for a month and ten days, and was still hunkered down in the cold and wet, slogging it out on the line.

Evelyn U. Milam, Waco, Texas [RR 29]

October 27, 1944

Dear Girls,

It was indeed a pleasure when I came home and found all these wonderful letters which Rosemary had sent. I learned many interesting things and extend my heartfelt sympathy to all you girls who have lost your loved ones.

Bob was injured on the 13th of April on a regular night training jump. He broke his left ankle in two places and had to stay in the hospital three months. He returned to duty once, and his ankle was too weak, so they put him back in the hospital. He missed jumping on D-Day, which really broke his heart. I live with my father and sister. We have a duplex house. I stayed at home about two months after the boys went overseas, and then started work in February as a receptionist and P.B.X. operator [Private Bank Exchange, switchboard operator] for the construction company that is building the General Tire & Rubber Company here in Waco. I enjoy my work very much. Guess I will continue when the plant opens, unless our boys come home before then. I do hope and pray it won't be long.

Rosemary, you certainly do have a fine-looking son. Most of you girls are so lucky to have little miniatures of your husbands. I know they mean a lot to you these trying days.

If any of you girls come down Texas way, call me up. I'd love seeing you. Even if I don't know all of you personally, news of the 508th is always interesting. May God bless and keep every one of you, and fill each need our boys might have over there. I'll be anxiously awaiting the return of the Round Robin.

Sincerely, Evelyn

The Round Robin traveled next from central Texas all the way up to northeastern Ohio to reach Betty Hager, the wife of 1st Lt. Ernest J. Hager. He had served with George in HqHq on D-Day.

Betty Hager, Burton, Ohio [RR 30]

November 5, 1944

Dear Girls,

Last Monday was really a lucky day for me; besides getting a letter from my "better half," I also received these wonderful letters. I was thrilled beyond words and couldn't get to them fast enough. They've been re-read several times, and I enjoyed them more than a novel.

May I extend my deepest sympathy to those of you who have lost your husbands; your brave letters were very inspiring, and we all admire you for the courage and bravery you are showing.

My latest letter from Ernie was dated October 12, and as far as I know they're still in Holland. He came through this invasion all right but was slightly wounded in France. He was shot through the ear and was awarded the Purple Heart. That was too close for comfort! He has sent several souvenirs, his helmet with four bullet holes in it, a German compass, a German belt (which belonged to the one who shot him), and [he has] a swastika armband and a Luger pistol he can't send. I've also had gifts from England, some silver and linen from Ireland. The baby has a silver spoon from England, a ring from Scotland, and a dress from Ireland.

Anita [the Hager's baby] and I have been living with my parents but hope to find an apartment in Cleveland. A small town is wonderful in summer, but so isolated in winter; it's one of the coldest, snowiest points in Ohio. Besides helping to keep the house running, I have been sewing (working on my hope chest) and reading a good deal. Even then it's been lonesome, but are there any of us who haven't been lonesome this past year? I recently joined the Northeast Ohio Officers Wives Association and had the good fortune to meet Jean Thomas there. I understand "Puzz" Merriam belongs to the Association also, but she wasn't at that meeting; I hope to see her at the one next Sunday. I didn't realize any 508ers lived here. I didn't know a great many of you girls very well and am so sorry I missed the companionship. I didn't drive at the time, but finally learned.

My Anita is almost 16 months old now and—here it is again!—looks exactly like her Daddy. I'd be lost without her. We have a lot of fun now, though she's so active that I'm after her 24 hours a day. Her health is good except that she throws up easily and once she starts will throw up every meal for a week or more. I'm going to have her x-rayed to see if I can find the cause of it. She gets car-sick too. We flew to Detroit and back this summer to see Ernie's people and had a grand trip; flying agreed with both of us, but I know I'll never be a Paratrooper!

Winter finally seems to be here; it snowed today for the first time this fall. The month of October was beautiful—Indian summer, much warmer than other years. I really must close now with the hopes that all of you are well and are hearing good news from overseas. If my prayers—and yours too, I know—are answered, this ghastly war will be over soon and our loved ones back with us once more.

Best of luck to you all, and let's keep this traveling. And let's send more pictures; those enclosed were precious.

Lots of love, Betty Hager

**Anita Hagar, 14 months, RR#30 Gurwell Collection.**

Betty sent the Round Robin on to another Ohio resident, Jeanne Thomas, who wrote a very newsy letter from Cleveland, including a surprising story about her husband, Maj. David E. Thomas, the regimental surgeon, who had managed to escape his German captors after he was taken POW in Normandy.

Jeanne Thomas, Cleveland, Ohio [RR 31]

November 13, 1944

Dear Girls,

Written words are usually so empty, but I do want to express my sincere sympathy to all the 508 women who have paid for this cause with the person dearest to them. I was very happy to be included in the Round Robin and will make every effort to contribute news to its eager readers.

The first thing to straighten out is about Bill Ekman. He is intact and has done very well. [Bernadette Shankey's letter of September 20, 1944 erroneously reported that Colonel Ekman had been killed in action.] I have heard from those in the know that he makes a fine CO 505 and won a Silver Star for himself. His wife Iris and two children visited me for several weeks this past summer, and due to that I am kept well posted on Bill.

From other letters you can tell that Betty Hager, Puz Merriam, and I represent the 508ers in Cleveland. We all belong to the Off. Wives Assoc. and have met a 503 and a 505 wife, so you can well imagine the gab fests.

I could go on and on about my husband. To refresh your memory, he is David Thomas, Regt. Surgeon. Well, France seemed to be the arena for him. After a bumpy landing and setting up a First Aid Station and moving due to repeated burnings, he was captured. An enlisted medic was with him, and they were put to work in a German station of some kind. Now this is just the way I got it and I quote, "after several days of this, I took off." How he accomplished the feat, I'll never know until his return, but he reached American lines after days and nights of anguish (although he won't admit it). In fact, all the medics did so well that they are established not only as good M.D.s but fine soldiers.[117]

For my routine—I'm living with my mother who takes over my two children so well that I'm free to do Red Cross Nurses' Circle work two day a week. I've been assigned to Charity Hospital where Dave spent two busy years. It is rather like old home week.

Our children are thriving under all the attention, although Nancy fell and put a gash over one eye. This happened late at night, so it was dressed with all intentions to have a doctor see it the following morning. This was done, [but] too much time had passed. They can't throw in a stitch after six hours. After having spent most of my life eating Medicine for breakfast [as a doctor's wife, I missed] the one thing that would have prevented my daughter from having a scar. So, gals—a stitch in time as the saying goes.

As far as I know the men are still in Holland. I await more news.

Sincerely, Jeanne R. Thomas

On November 14, one day following Jeanne's letter, the 508th finally arrived in Sissonne, France after an exhausting three-day journey by foot and by truck. Anne Havens, wife of 2nd Lt. Robert N. Havens, added her news to the Round Robin almost a week after the regiment arrived, but neither she, nor her correspondents, were yet aware that the survivors of the Holland mission were now safe at base camp.

Anne Havens, Harrisonburg, Virginia [RR 32]

November 20, 1944

Dearest All,

I received the "Round Robin" and who could have asked for more on a dreary Monday morning! How wonderful all the letters were!! I have just completed reading them and even opened the envelope to see if by chance there might be another. Had planned to accomplish lots today, but after receiving the letters, I dismissed the accomplishments and sat down to read.

I feel as if I should apply for a commentator's job, for I know so much news. I knew only a few of the 508 wives in Pinehurst shortly before the boys left for overseas but feel that now I'm truly a part of the family after today's gift.

We have had many days of anxiety, haven't we? Surely, they can't number many more. I personally want to extend my heartfelt sympathy to each of you who have lost your darlings. You are indeed brave ones. We must keep our chins up and hearts warm for their homecoming and may it be soon.

It is ever so grand to hear from Bob and know that all is well. I hear often, but usually get the letters in groups. My last letter was dated Oct. 19. He told me they had a good jump this time in the Netherlands; Jerry wasn't exactly waiting for them as he was in Normandy. This was a daylight jump and they encountered a great deal of flak over the drop zone. They are truly a great outfit, and we are proud of every one of them. Our one aim and wish is to have them home and pulling together we shall accomplish this. Words somehow just seem so meaningless, but my heart too aches for many of you through these long months.

Puzzie [Merriam], Bob wrote me about the article that you sent your husband on the 82nd and 101st from the NY Times. As Bob put it, "a friend of mine received it from his wife." Beth [Pollom], I have proved to be a very poor correspondent, but you must forgive me. You are perhaps the [only] one who knew we were expecting a little "stranger" in our family. I will admit she helps to no end to shorten the worrying time about our husbands, and nursing is a 24-hour job. We are lucky to have these little ones to occupy our time. The enclosed pictures are precious, and I can't let this package go on without a snap of my little dumpling. Aren't we the proud mamas? I "ditto" the suggestion of enclosing snaps of each of us in the next round of letters. Perhaps we'll recall faces that we couldn't pin names on before. Truly Beth, I'm going to write you soon, even perhaps before this gets to you.

Some of you experienced Ma's "tell me if I'll ever have 30 minutes leisure time again in my life." It's great to hear of all the babies, and couldn't we have some baby show with all of them. Their Daddies are ever so eager to return to see them.

It seems that I can't stop writing after all the grand news, and yet I realize someone else must have space to get another letter in the envelope. I've forgotten to say lots of things, I know, nevertheless, I'm sure I've tried enough for this time.

Do wish I could find some 508 wives living near me. If anyone knows of any living near Harrisburg, Virginia, do let me know. If ever any of you are going through, please call and stay overnight with me. I am living with my single sister (older) for the winter. We see movies and play bridge for entertainment. I seem to be the best [nanny] I can find, so I stay at home pretty close.

Merry Xmas and a Happy New Year to all. May we see our beloveds soon. Our ceaseless prayers surely shall be answered.

Cheerio!! Anne

**Elizabeth C. Havens, six weeks old, Round Robin # 32 Gurwell Collection.**

At this point in the war, the band of sisters was resolutely keeping their chins up, finding strength in the love of their of precious young children; support in their families, old friends, colleagues at recent jobs; and, of course, the special bond they felt with each other as "508th paratrooper girls." Protected from the realities of war by distance and the censorship of news and letters from the front, they could hardly conceive of the horrors their husbands had endured, or even that they often went without food or shelter. Later, the adamant silence the survivors maintained largely shielded their wives from ever knowing the most horrific and terrifying wartime experiences: combat veterans wanted nothing more than to forget the deeds they had witnessed and were constrained to commit themselves. As the saying went, and as George himself told us when he finally opened up nearly sixty years after the war, you "could never understand it unless you were there."

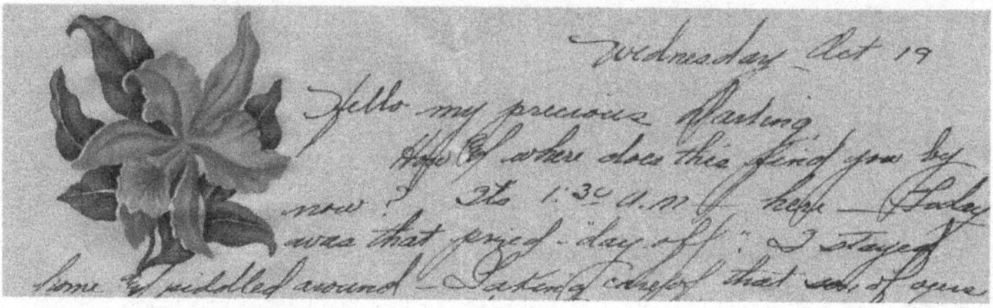


# CHAPTER X

# DREADED DOWNTIME

When the 508th arrived in France on November 14, 1944, the exhausted troopers bedded down at an old French army barracks at Sissonne, surprised to discover themselves in the heart of Champagne country. George's relief at finally leaving Holland was short-lived, however, when two letters from Babe, dated September 27 and October 28, finally caught up with him at base camp with bad news.

> September 27, 1944 [Seaside, Oregon]
>
> I have something I have hated to tell you, Darling, but guess it is best to let you know. Bud Leonard was killed in action July 28th. His folks got the first word about a week ago—and the confirmation came yesterday. Everyone around is plenty broken up over it. But keep your chin up, Honey. Things like this are bound to happen even in everyday life. God bless you, Darling. All our love and kisses, Babe

October 28, 1944 [Seaside, Oregon]

Adah & Tiny Leonard have gone to California for the winter. They sure took it hard over Bud. Ben Young wrote them that he had seen Bud's grave over there—So they knew there was no hope whatsoever of a mistake. There was another Lt Leonard in his outfit, and they had hopes there had been a mistake.

**1st Lt Julian E. Leonard was killed in action on Guam, July 28, 1944. He was in the Second Battalion of the 4th Marine Regiment, the "Magnificent Bastards," formerly the 4th Marine Raider Battalion. Gurwell Collection.**

The blow of Bud's death initiated an onslaught of depression for George, and the routine of camp became a "dreaded downtime" filled with thoughts of newly acquired ghosts. The day after he arrived at camp, he wrote a letter to Jeane in despair of ever finding "a reason for anything," and especially for why some survive while others are senselessly killed.

15 November 1944 [Sissonne, France]

Very few letters from my folks these days and it is bad news. Heard about Bud!—Seems impossible. There is such a senseless waste of life to war. Sickening. At times, there doesn't seem to be a reason for anything. Life is so cheap that living seems unreal. So many times, those shells falling all around could have been deflected just a little and that would have been all. I could have staggered forward instead of backward in France and caught ten or fifteen more in the space of a few seconds. [George was wounded on D-Day, receiving one round in his left leg.]

* * *

As the regiment settled into their new base camp, the constant grind of training and night tactical problems began anew. Yet the possibility of a looming combat mission was nowhere in sight: with the vast Allied army deployed on the German border, what need could arise for paratrooper units now that Germany was all but defeated? Any sane person could see that all available resources should be used for defense, not offense, especially with the Soviet army bearing down from the East.

Nevertheless, George's duties as the executive officer afforded him time of his own, during which he struggled to overcome his grief and sense of loss by partaking of his "medicine" and writing regularly to Jeane.

17 November 1944 [Sissonne]

Now, isn't this better? Letters coming much more frequently. More time of my own Darling—at least for a while. Yes, safe and sound at a base camp in France. Maybe not safe, because in the closet is medicine—15 bottles of Champagne, 5 bottles of Benedictine and 16 bottles of Cognac (very Potent). Don't mind though, because that's about all there is to do. Drinking champagne right now and faintly in the distance a radio is playing "Jeane with the Light Brown Hair." A song that I associated with you when I used to take you to dances at college. Sweetheart, your picture is standing right alongside of me. The big picture that I carry in my footlocker.

**Jeane Gurwell, circa late 1944, Portland, OR. Gurwell Collection.**

> Punkin—have I forgotten to tell you so far that I love you, Sweetheart, love you with all my heart and soul. There can never be another you. "Blue Rain" is coming softly over the radio—making me a little on the blue side. Getting so that I can't take good music. Haven't had any mail for several days now, but the service over here is lousy.
>
> There may be passes soon, but nothing definite about a furlough or leave. I have a pair of wooden shoes here, but when I can send them is another thing. Have some more surprises for you if things just work out.
>
> Haven't heard from anyone but you, my Darling, for such a long time. (Except a letter from Babe with bad news.) Think that everyone else has forgotten about me. Really doesn't matter though. You, Jeane, are the one who counts.

George was far from alone in his uneasiness and increasing reliance on the all-too available "medicine." Maj. Gen. Gavin's diary shows that the division's commanding general was well aware of the widespread low morale—a problem further exacerbated by the lack of a rotation policy and an acute awareness that survivors' luck, especially among the division's original members, was running out.

18 November 1944 [Sissonne]

The four-jump people [from the 505th PIR] are sweating out any more jumps, feeling that they have used up about all of their luck. I understand exactly how they feel. I feel the same way myself. They have always done a fine job but now their ranks are thinning, many of them are banged up from combat and hardly fit mentally or physically for further parachute operations, yet they have no other prospects. It hardly seems right, there should be some way out other than being killed or wounded. There is no other now. Someday there is going to be a hell of a mess when complete units refuse to jump in combat again. There should be some relief for them or promise of relief.[118]

With time on his hands and nothing to do but think and drink, the arrival of Thanksgiving deepened George's depression. Feeling trapped and alone, he swung from expressions of anguish to numbed indifference.

23 November 1944 [Sissonne]

How is that wonderful wife of mine tonight? Yes Jeane, Thanksgiving even way over here. A good dinner today and the day off. That makes a long day for us over here. This base camp life is so darned lonely. Drinking is just about the sum total of our play. Yes Darling, I have been making quite a project out of the Champagne and beer around here. Jeane—I am so very, very homesick for you and our son. Nothing really seems important anymore except to get home. Front lines seem good compared to this life with time on your hands. Darling—we have so much to be thankful for, but——.

27 November 1944 [letter continued]

So Darling—can't understand what is wrong. I just can't seem to write, even though every fiber of me longs for you. Unhappy—Jeane—I have never been so unhappy before in my life. The same old things are starting again—training and there isn't a particle of interest left in my heart for anything but you and our son. I am hurting more than I ever have before. Homesick, lonely and so blue that I don't know what to do. Seems to me now that this war will never end. I really am bad. We aren't getting any leave this time and my Darling, I am tired clean down to the depths of my soul. Let's hope that it is only the after effects of those many days at the front—this indifferent feeling. Just doesn't seem like me to not give a dang about anything, including the men.

I have some more things for you, but as yet I can't send them. No packages until our A.P.O. [Army Post Office address] arrives at our new camp. Perfumes, a linen from Holland—nick knacks and really quite a conglomeration. The paper [*Paraglide*] that I mentioned in another letter about our Holland jump, is on the way.[119]

Christmas appears now to be just another lonely, lonely day. Maybe someday things will be different. Must close for now, Sweetheart. Another day tomorrow of work. Don't work too hard Adorable One. Keep that chin up. I love you with all my heart and soul—always.

Meanwhile, bored and restless troopers drunk on cheap champagne were reacting hostilely to the restrictions of "civilization," as General Gavin's diary describes.

28 November 1944 [Sissonne]

Friday night in Reims the troops of the division raised so much hell that at the request of Gen Thrasher, all of our troops were restricted.[120] The trouble seems to center on three things. There is no way to get a girl of easy virtue, all houses are off limits and guarded, food cannot be bought in town anywhere, champagne can be bought by the bottle anywhere, anytime. At present the situation is well in hand.

Delighted to have received George's first letter from camp, Jeane wrote anew, encouraging George and telling him that she now knows he is safe in France.

November 28, 1944 [Portland, Oregon]

How is that wonderful man of ours, and incidentally the best officer in the whole darn army. You can't fool me sweetheart, I know you are. Your letter of Nov. 15th came today from France. You're dead tired and low, of course. Let's hope this

> finds that things are seeming a little better, for so they will be in time.
>
> The folks have certainly been wonderful. Mother feels progressively worse because she never gets a letter finished to you but wants to all the time. Dad's jump pants that you sent him are the envy of the Valley. You should see him strut his stuff and hear him brag about his son-in-law, who can absolutely do anything and everything in this world. See, I'm not prejudiced—it runs in the family.

When a letter from Jeane's mother, Delpha Slonaker, finally reached George in France, it seemed that keeping Jeane occupied with less time to worry was working out. But it also revealed that Jeane had been hiding things from George, too—namely, her shaky health.

> November 14, 1944 [Hood River, Oregon]
>
> George, how wonderful it will be when you are with us again. I know our prayers have kept you with us.
>
> We miss Jeane and the baby so terribly much—and I do hope you feel as we have felt, that it was better for her to go back to finish at the hospital. The Dr. thought it much better to keep her from worrying too much over you. In other words, to get her mind on something at hand. She had been terribly despondent since she was so sick [after the baby was born]. She looks so much better now, although she gets awfully tired, but she is more like the old Jeane.

George continued to write to Jeane about his loneliness, disturbed sleep, and feeling blue—all symptoms consistent with PTSD. What he did not tell Jeane was that he had received an additional assignment that was sure to increase his collection of ghosts. "Special order #8, 17 Nov 44," reads: "1st Lt George Gurwell is hereby placed on special duty with the Regimental Supply Officer for the purpose of processing casualty effects." In other words, George is now in charge of shipping the personal effects of the dead to be processed—including the effects of some of his own friends—and of forwarding the belongings of men wounded in action.[121]

29 November 1944 [Sissonne]

Today has been a little better. Received a letter from you dated Nov. 4. Had a picture of our son in it. Gee, Punkin, it was swell. Now Pie Face, how about one of you? Pretty Please! Haven't any good pictures of you to carry with me except in the locket. The others were ruined in France, and then I lost all of them. Mail has been pretty bad here too. Nothing seems to be getting through.

Can't get over being so darned lonely and blue that nothing else really matters. Haven't been out of camp yet. There isn't a place to go. Nights really are rough. Makes it even worse when you are restless and need a rest to get away from this army life.

Home certainly sounds good. I have a little junk [to send home as gifts]. Mostly linen, but some of it will go [be thrown away] if you don't like it. Wish to high heaven that I could send it soon. At least my Darling—you know that I have something for you even if it doesn't arrive for Christmas. Have some things for Dick, both of our folks and just about everyone. Oh, yes, a pair of wooden shoes too. Gee! I was certainly bow-legged for a while when I tried to carry it all back from Holland [when the regiment marched twenty-two miles from Nijmegen to Oss to entruck for France].

As Christmas approached and George's thoughts consistently turned to home, he sent a letter to Jeane's parents on the same day that he wrote to her, reassuring them he was safe and expressing his love and longing for his wife.

29 November 1944 [Sissonne]

Just a few lines to let you know that this wandering son of yours is once more in a place with time to write. Hope the two of you haven't been worrying. No news from me is always good news [No news is better than the dreaded telegrams from the War Department].

Another chapter is over now, and still no bad results. Two combat jumps and I seriously hope that we don't have anymore. Flack was very heavy this time, but the ground was soft. Holland was nice—reminded me of home. There were plenty of fruit trees and we really nipped a bumper crop from German hands. Added three more countries to my list this time—Germany, Holland and Belgium. Beginning to feel like a traveler—against my will though, because there is just one thought in my mind—to get home and stay there. Miss Jeane and the baby so much that I can hardly see straight. She seems to be getting along all right at the hospital. I am certainly glad of that. It gives her something to occupy her mind.

Time drags horribly here in France. We're living in the middle of nowhere. Cognac and champagne seems to be about all there is to do. There is a chance that I will be able to visit Paris before long. That should be something in itself. No leave this time though, and I am just about as tired as I have ever been. Days seem endless about now, but then why shouldn't they, it has been almost a year since I saw Jeane. Loneliness is a peculiar thing—it grows and grows until it seems to overpower you.

Jeane's next letter showed that she was suffering from her own brand of blues.

December 3, 1944 [Portland]

On the home front life goes the same way. It seems just as good as it can be without you—only, frankly, that makes it not much [good]. Oh, who are we to kick—to have you back is worth it and things can't always be smooth as ice. Time has passed slowly, as it's seemed to you and me. The time will be less until we shall be together again—until you can rest, know real food and a bed at night.

On December 1, 1944, George did indeed go to Paris. A letter of introduction from Lt. Col. Thomas J. B. Shanley states George and his two companions, Staff Sgt. Wallace Roach and Sgt. Andrew Loewi, have been sent for "the purpose of obtaining equipment and merchandise, to include liquors, for the establishing of a 'sergeants club.' All possible consideration should be given their requests." Their travel orders were signed "Command of Major General Gavin."[122]

It did not take the regiment long to put George's purchases from Paris to use. Clubs were set up and parties planned to occupy the men during down time. Self-medicating with alcohol for sheer boredom ramped up even further.

In his next letter to Jeane, George was so blue that his trip to Paris sounded like a bore.[123]

> 4 December 1944 [Sissonne]
>
> Well Jeane—I have been to Paris—on business, though. Didn't have much time to do anything but business.
>
> "I'll Be Seeing You" just came on the air—as if I wasn't blue enough already. Jeane, my Darling—there is just one thought ever present in my mind—to get home to you. For the first time in my life, I have had enough before a job is finished. There is no desire in my heart to go on. I care for no part of my work—it is just something to fill in time and there isn't a care about whether I get anything done or not. Working now is just force of habit. Tired? Yes, Punkin, I am very tired—not physically but mentally. So, Honey, you have the first real change in me. Can't help it Sweetheart, that may be just because of no time off since this last deal. Am trying to snap myself out of it, but I have had no success as yet. Maybe though, Darling, I will be able to do it.

As Christmas neared and the war dragged on, drowning his sorrow at the bar proved to be less than an effective strategy for George to fight the symptoms of PTSD.

> 9 December 1944 [Sissonne]
>
> Hello my Adorable Darling, I feel pretty bad this morning—Officers party last night. Danced twice and didn't enjoy it. Just can't do a thing anymore, Darling, unless you are with me. Proceeded to get very drunk—led the orchestra (which I shouldn't have), served drinks from behind the bar (definitely the wrong thing), and had a good time, so they tell me. Had to do something though, because there was no woman there that I even considered dancing with.
>
> So far, only one picture has arrived. Mail has been very bad lately. A letter arrived yesterday dated the 14th of November. There is usually a lapse of about five days between mail. There, you have the situation over here. Nothing to do except shows [movies]—no place to go—no nothing. We have had

no indication of a leave and Darling, this Husband of yours is doing just as little as possible. Suppose to be working now, but there isn't an ounce of ambition in my soul.

Here it is almost Christmas and Punkin, I haven't sent you a thing. Will love do, until I can send this box that I packed? Won't be there for Christmas, but Jeane you have all of my love. That, Darling, will always be yours.

11 December 1944 [Sissonne]

Today was another anniversary of ours. It hasn't been such a terrible day—rather nice, even though it was cold. Spent almost all day out in the field—listening though, instead of teaching. Didn't learn much that I didn't know—not bragging, either. Rather a wasted day, as so many have been so far. How much better it would have been to be with you. Moody, and so darned Homesick.

Time is coming very close now when yours truly will be able to wear two overseas stripes—almost a year now, Jeane. Time drags by so very slowly over here and yet the regiment tries so very hard to make you work all of the time. Just finished up a few minutes ago—and here it is after ten o'clock, time for bed—and yet, you fight against it until you are dead tired the next morning.

Jeane then wrote a steadying letter to George, tying the depression he feels after Holland to his symptoms after the Normandy campaign.

December 12, 1944 [Portland, Oregon]

It's late, Sweetheart, but days aren't complete without a letter to you and this is my time alone for you, even so far away. Everyone is asleep, the house is quiet except for an east wind that rattles the windows occasionally.

Today there was another letter from you to make my heart fairly sing—though you sound low all right. Cheer up, Darling—it's mostly reaction from the front—now is the time when all the past weariness sinks in—just as it did after France. That's just the way it goes. Sometimes after a hard day,

I come home that way too. Remember how much we love you and how proud we are too.

Today was this week's day off, with little accomplished really. Had part of a physical check-up at the hospital this morning. Ruthie Hartley [a nursing student] has been on leave and stopped on her way back to Bremerton. She was engaged to Gene (can't remember his last name) of the 506th, now reported missing from Holland. Taking it pretty well, considering.

George's kid brother named Dick fired off a letter. While he may or may not have been attempting to lift George's spirits, he was certainly delighted to keep his hero up on eighth-grade shenanigans.

December 16, 1944 [Seaside, Oregon]

Dear George,

Well, we got some letters from you. We were glad to get them too. You ought to be in my grade at school, how we sure have fun. I didn't have anything to do with it, but one of the kids put glue in one of the seats at school the other day just as we were going in another class. It was Jack Ryan, so the teacher came right in after him and grabbed him by the ear and took him up to Mr. Babcock. He sure got the devil and got expelled from Science class.

Fed up with the tedium, George complained he would rather be at the front. Little did he know that his wish was about to come true.

10 December 1944 [Sissonne]

Still, only one picture has arrived. The others are somewhere in between. Have been very anxious to get them, but that doesn't help a bit. Patience is a wonderful thing. Just finished buying another Christmas present for you. Just wait—because I am not going to tell you. Not very nice, but I think it will get there for Christmas. The box will beyond a doubt be way after Christmas, but that just shows you what a thoughtless husband you have. I might at least have sent it earlier.

Say, my Darling—don't you think that you had better start teaching that son of ours that he can crawl forward too, instead of backwards. Just think, he feeds himself. It would be wonderful to get a look at him. So—he has a temper already—well, it took me years of hard work to overcome mine, so there is hope. It flared up the other day for the first time in a long time. This solitary existence with no place to go is bad. Wish we were on the front again. At least there are things to do up there. Soldiers are never satisfied—that is a forgone conclusion. Hard to realize, Sweetheart, that I am on my third year of army life.

Training is starting here with a vengeance—that, on top of no leave, makes everyone so very happy. Oh well, war can't last forever. I have been trying to straighten out the collection of junk that I call "My Stuff." Didn't realize that I had collected so much trash. Hate to part with any of it, and that makes the job just that much more difficult. [The "stuff" George had been amassing since his enlistment, along with wartime documents and other items mailed home to Jeane, now constitute the Gurwell Collection.]

It's a gray Sunday. There is a definite bite to the air. No leaves left on the trees—Christmas is just around the corner and then another brand spanking new year. Wonder what it will bring for me? Which reminds me—I am getting old. Feel at least fifty each morning as I roll out of bed. Parachuting has that effect on you. [George and Jeane both are twenty-four at this time.]

Well, my Adorable Darling—time to clean up my room again. Then chow, listening to the radio and bed. So goes another day so far away from you.

13 December 1944 [Sissonne]

Punkin—there hasn't been a thing going on of any interest. Training takes up most of the time. It is just as well since there is still no plan to go. A few more months of this life, and I could develop a beautiful case of psychoneurosis or something.

By the time he wrote the above, George had been on constant duty since August 1944. Fighting loneliness and alienation, he wrote to Jeane a second time on December 13, recalling the past in a V-mail that takes him back to his "safe place" at Pinehurst. Doing so, he instinctively used a strategy now known to be effective against PTSD. The technique works best if the sufferer can call on all the senses to recall the sights, tastes, sounds, bodily sensations, and smells of a safe place in the past.

> 13 December 1944 [V-mail, Sissonne]
>
> Bob Hope is on the air right now. That is the limit of our entertainment, except for shows. These radio programs make me homesick. They are good, but there are so many memories. Pinehurst was such fun. Those nights at home and our theatre excursions—at least once a week.

By mid-December, widespread problems of morale reached such a height that an airborne officer committed suicide, a tragedy which, in turn, only heightened restiveness within the ranks, as General Gavin noted from Sissonne in his diary of December 14: "Everyone has been encouraged to take some time off, particularly after Bud Milner, [*sic*] C/S [Chief of Staff] of the 101 committed suicide. The troubles with young officers are on the increase. I have four cases to be tried by general [court martial] now.[124]

At the end of his tether, George wrote to Jeane. Wishing he knew when "home would be the next stop," he again expressed his preference for the front.

> 14 December 1944 [Sissonne, Thursday]
>
> Received an old letter from you today—November the sixth. Evidently that one caught a rowboat. There was another picture though—and well worth the waiting for. Two more, my Darling—patience is a wonderful virtue.
>
> This husband of yours is extremely low tonight. Nothing seems to be going right. Maybe it is just my lack of ambition. Have several lectures to give in a division school tomorrow. Just don't feel up to it though. A night problem and then work through it that night. Time off Saturday morning, but what's the use because there isn't a thing to do but sit around. It isn't any wonder that my cigarette smoking has increased. Feel like getting gloriously drunk, but that wouldn't do either, because there is much to be done tomorrow. Need to get away from

> this army life, even a day would help. Have started talking to myself, and that is bad.
>
> Words have suddenly failed me—just too darned blue, lonely and miserable. This is a great life—give me the front lines anytime. Tomorrow will probably be different, and I will undoubtedly feel almost human again. There always have to be complaints—that is army life. Wouldn't be half bad though, if I could just know for sure that at a certain date "Home" would be the next stop.

Unfortunately for George, he was about to get what he asked for—the "next stop" would not be "home" but the Battle of the Bulge.

8/3/44

Dearest---

I know it is oweful but I can not think of your first name so please excuse me. You see by the picture that Hal is missing in action. Have you heard any thing from your husband? I hope you have and that he is ok and you will keep on hearing from him. I got a letter from Jerry Hardwia-k and she has heard from Don .He is ok. She said

## CHAPTER XI

# WE CANNOT GIVE UP THE JUMP, ROUND ROBIN LETTERS 33–36

While battles roared on through Holland and into Belgium, deadly news about Normandy began to trickle back home. Many 508th families were living in great uncertainty, unsure if their loved ones were even alive; for others, the unthinkable had happened—although some still denied it. Testifying to this atmosphere of dread and hope against hope, a growing number of especially touching messages from Gold Star wives added their weight to the envelope of Round Robin letters, once so cheerful and brave, as it zigzagged its way across the country.

As the Round Robin circulated, several of the women who had befriended each other at Pinehurst also wrote individually to one another. These letters shared more intimate content, seeking information and advice about their husbands that they had otherwise failed to obtain.

One of the most striking of these is the August 3, 1944 letter from Jane Creary, who wrote to Jeane desperately seeking information on her husband, Capt. Hal Creary, Commanding Officer of H Co., who had been classified as missing in action since early in the Normandy invasion. Unlike most letters in our collection, this one is not handwritten, but neatly typed. Attached with mild glue at the top of the page were a picture of Hal and the newspaper article reporting him missing in action.

> August 3, 1944 [Atlanta, Georgia]
>
> Dearest __________, I know it is awful, but I cannot think of your first name, so please excuse me. You see by the picture

that Hal is missing in action. Have you heard anything from your husband? I hope you have and that he is ok, and you will keep on hearing from him. I got a letter from Jerry Hardwick and she has heard from Don. He is ok. She said she got a letter from Carol Bodak and Mike is also missing. I feel like Hal is a prisoner of war or with the French underground, and we will hear better news soon. If you are hearing from your husband, I wish you would ask him if he knows anything about Hal. I do not know if he could tell you if he did know anything. Let me hear from you soon.

Lots of love, Jane

P.S. Do you have a boy or a girl? You would not know me now, for I only weigh 120 pounds.

On August 8, Jeane followed up on Jane's distraught letter by inquiring whether George had any news about Hal, although she certainly knew it was against regulations to pass it on, even if he could help out. "Jerry Hardwick wrote to say that Don had just cabled her from England and that the whole outfit must be there. Yesterday there was a letter from Jane Creary. She believes that Hal must be a prisoner and asked me to ask you if you could tell her anything. While we're on the subject—if you break down and tell me anything that you can about what goes on over there, I shan't repeat it or pass it on to the girls we know if you would rather that it not be repeated." Two weeks later, George replied as expected that he really could not be of help. "As far as the letter from Mrs. Creary: nothing much I can say," he wrote on August 22. "Just hope and pray. Things like that are hard to believe—but true. It hasn't been easy."

What George cannot say, but certainly knew by early August, was that Capt. Hal Creary had been killed on June 7, 1944 in an incident near Picauville on the outskirts of Sainte-Mère-Église.[125] The incident also took the life of Capt. Francis Flanders (CO, F Co) and 1st Lt. Joseph Shankey (Hq3, S-4), both of whom were married to women who contributed to the Round Robin. All three had been captured and were being transported in a German convoy when the vehicles were strafed by American P-47 fighter-bombers. The Germans dove for the ditches, but held their rifles on the prisoners, forbidding them to take cover. Approximately thirty to forty men were killed in the attack, and over eighty were wounded. Among this latter group was 1st Lt. Michael Bodak (Hq3), who was hit by three .50 caliber bullets from the planes. He survived the war, but never walked again.[126]

Four months after writing to Jeane, Jane Creary informed the band of sisters that she had indeed received the dreaded news, enclosing with her own letter a copy of Hal's last letter home and a news article with his photograph that reported he had been killed in action. While her previous typewritten letter was very legible, in medium dark ink, by the time she wrote in December, the print was so light it was barely visible. One can only imagine she had worn out her ribbon from all the letters she had typed, seeking information about Hal.

Jane's letter notably illustrates how the unity created by the Round Robin served to buoy up individual contributors, and is even more remarkable in its acknowledgment of shared grief and the expression of renewed "group spirit" in the face of adversity.

**Capt Hal Creary, (Co H) KIA in Normandy, officially listed, July 1, 1944, the date his status changed from MIA to KIA. He died on June 7th after being captured. This picture was taken as part of a one-page photo compilation of all 139 officers of the 508th at Camp Mackall, NC in 1943. Copy courtesy of Ruth and Neal Beaver via Jack Williams. Individual portraits displayed on 508pir.org.**

Jane Creary, Atlanta, Georgia [RR 33]

5 December 1944

Dear 508 Paratrooper girls,

You all can imagine what a happy surprise I had when I opened the huge envelope and thirty-two letters were inside. I enjoyed each and every one.

Enclosed is a picture of my little ole sweet husband, who I am sure most of you know about by now. I still hardly believe he is gone. My heart goes out to all of you girls who have lost your husbands, for I know what you have been through and what you are still going through. A lot of us are in the same boat, but remember girls, we are paratroopers too, and we cannot give up the jump.

After I received the sad news about Hal, I took a trip to his home in Memphis, and then to my home in Kentucky. I am now keeping myself busy in my office. I have reservations for December 19 to go to Memphis to spend the Christmas holidays with Mother and Pop Creary. However, I am not dreaming of a White Christmas.

Girls, this is a small world. After all the time I was in North Carolina., I did not meet Selma Abbott until I came back to Atlanta. Selma saw Hal's picture in the paper and called me up and we have become great friends. We go out to dinner and movies together often and have helped each other out a lot in our sad moments. I will send this letter to Selma (Mrs. Edgar R. Abbott) since she is here in Atlanta. She will send it on to Helen Flanders.

If anyone knows Mrs. Bobby Mitchell's (Betty) address, please add it on. I know she lives in Augusta, Georgia, but I do not know her street address. Same, Jane Creary

P.S. How about a letter from you, Ruth Beaver [RR 15], telling me all about yourself and little Neal Beaver Jr.

P.S. Enclosed is a copy of my Hal's last letter

From: Hal Creary

3 June 44, Folkingham Airfield, England

Dear Wife, Mother, Father and Brother,

Please do not think I am lazy for not writing a long letter to each of you because I am not. I have worked [harder] and longer the past two weeks than ever before in my life. I am trying to save my life and others' lives by doing everything I can to make this coming jump a success. I am sure it will be, whether I live to see the finish or not.

Somehow, or for some reason, I am not scared. I have known for two weeks where we are going, how many troops we have, have seen aerial photos of the actual ground I hope to land on and set up a defensive position in. I know what and where enemy troops are in the area, who commands them, their morale, age of men, and everything anyone could want to know. We know we are going on a dangerous mission, but things are in our favor. I have not lived in our regular camp for over a week now. We are living at an airport. Our planes are a few hundred yards away.

If I should not return to camp with my outfit after this mission, this letter will be mailed. If I do, you will never see it. Even though I may not return, I could be a prisoner of war and may return later, so don't give up hope until you receive official notice from the War Department. Their notice is official and none until then. I am enclosing the names and addresses of some of our officers. Write to them and get information about me after the war. I have underscored the ones that should know more about me than the rest.

All of you have made my life the happiest it could ever be if I lived to be a hundred years old. I love you all for that.

James, you and Jane have a hard job. Take good care of Mother and Pop.

I am proud of what I have done to make the world a better place to live and worship. All of you please feel that way and don't be sad. I will see you all again, I am sure. May God bless every one of you and may you all have a long and everlasting life.

All my love to the best wife a boy ever had, the sweetest Mother in the world, and the best Father and brother in the world.

Hal

The next letter in the Round Robin testifies to Jane Creary's renewed friendship with her friend Selma, who followed up Jane's letter with the news that her husband, 1st Lt. Edgar R. Abbott, had also been killed in Normandy, June 17, 1944. She included a picture of her husband, clipped from a local paper.

**1st Lt Edgar R. Abbott (Hq1), KIA in Normandy, June 7,1944. This picture was taken as part of a one-page photo compilation of all 139 officers of the 508th at Camp Mackall, NC in 1943. Copy courtesy of Ruth and Neal Beaver via Jack Williams. Individual portraits displayed on 508pir.org.**

Selma Abbott, Atlanta, Georgia [RR 34]

December 12, 1944

Dear Girls,

Jane Creary called the day she received the Round Robin, and we were both thrilled to hear from so many of you girls. I am dropping in my note before sending it on its way to Helen Flanders.

I suppose all of you know by now about Ed's death. Like you Bernie Shankey [RR 25], I would not accept it until a letter came from Chaplain Elder saying he had personal information concerning Ed, but due to censorship regulations he was not permitted to give it to me now. He told me that he recovered Ed's body and buried him himself, which is a great consolation to me. I am so grateful for having known Ed the time I did and having his love for even that short while. Every memory is a pleasant one.[127]

You can imagine how thrilled I was to find another 508 wife here, and Jane has been a great help to me in my low moments. We have been each other's strength ever since we got together in Atlanta, and I am to stop over a night in Memphis with her. Then I am going on and spend the Holidays with mother and dad Abbott in Missouri. I hope to see Beth Pollom [RR 2] while in Kanas City.

I read that some of you girls have cocker spaniels. I have a black one, and she has been a very devoted companion.

If any of you come through Atlanta, please give me a ring. I would like to hear from you again soon. I will close for now wishing you a Merry Christmas and a Happy New Year.

Sincerely, Selma Abbott

A letter from Helen Flanders, wife of Capt. Francis E. Flanders, immediately followed those by Jane and Selma. She, too, had received the news that her husband had been killed. Her letter, written while she still was struggling to believe he was yet alive, was a brave attempt to keep her sense of humor and concentrate on the positive things she and her friends shared: children, pets, and the coming Christmas holidays. Helen includes a one-by-one-inch picture of herself and her son, Jerry.

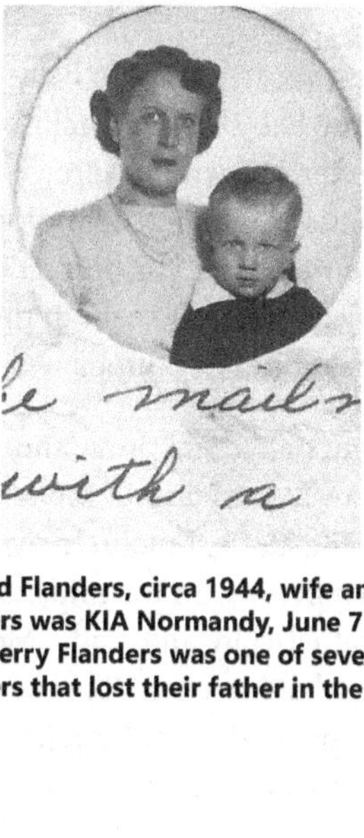


**Helen and Francis Gerald Flanders, circa 1944, wife and son of Capt. Francis E Flanders Co F. Capt Flanders was KIA Normandy, June 7 1944. Helen attached this picture to RR #35. Little Jerry Flanders was one of seven children in represented in the Round Robin letters that lost their father in the war. Gurwell Collection.**

Helen Flanders, Brooklyn, New York [RR 35]

December 19, 1944

Dear "508ers,"

At last, the mailman on my route can breathe a sigh of relief as he approaches my mailbox. You see, I heard about the Round Robin sometime in March and I've been haunting him ever since. The day the long-awaited for envelope arrived I wasn't home!! Can't you picture his exasperation! I have met a very small percentage of you girls, but somehow, I feel as though I know each one of you after reading your letters.

Officially, Fran is still listed as missing in action since June 6th. Three weeks ago, I received a letter from Carol Bodak. She told me, upon my own request, that Fran had been with Mike Bodak and Hal Creary and that he was killed on D-Day. Although such a possibility had entered my mind, the actuality of it came as a terrific shock. I know Lt. Bodak must be positive about it, yet I must admit that I still find myself thinking perhaps it isn't so. If anyone has any information concerning Fran, I would appreciate having them write to me. I'm sorry to say that I don't have any news to contribute in regard to the boys.

My next best bet is a contribution to baby news. He's a pretty big boy, but he is my baby. I have enclosed a small photo of Francis Gerald (better known as "Jerry") and myself. [Jerry was one of the infants Jeane took care of in Pinehurst.] Jerry will be 3 years old in January. His biggest interest just now is Santa and his reindeer. He can't seem to figure out how Santa will drive his reindeer on the rooftops.

Here's a little incident that might prove amusing to you. Several weeks ago, Jerry awakened me complaining of a "tummy ache." Naturally, being alone, I pictured everything that could possibly happen, happening. In the midst of my worries, Jerry looked up at me pathetically and said, "Mommy put a band-aid on it." This was what I needed. It broke the tension. Just so I don't leave you suspended in mid-air, Jerry after a day in bed recovered without any ill effects.

After the holidays I'm planning to meet Doris Daly and Bernie Shanky in New York City. We're planning to make a day of it. Draw your own conclusions as to what our favorite subject of conversations will be—our offspring. [All three are recent widows.]

I'm planning to go back to nursing very shortly. Just where, I'm not sure, although Brooklyn is entirely out of the question. Finding a suitable nursery or making arrangements for someone to take care of Jerry will be the deciding factor.

I really can't think of anything more to write about, except I wish you all a Very Merry Christmas and a Happy New Year. May this coming year bring you all happiness. I pray that this war will be over soon. God Bless you all.

Sincerely, Helen

Jeanette Foley, wife of 1st Lt. John P. Foley, A Co., rounded off the momentous year of 1944 with a newsy missive penned in the midst of the holidays. Her "chins up" letter illustrates the adaptation of a young wife to the disruptions and displacements of war and the bonds and relationships available to her in her husband's absence. Despite its difficulty, the life Jeanette described is likely as good as life could be for a paratrooper's wife as 1944 reached its end: above all, she knew her husband was still alive.

Jeanette Foley, Brooklyn, New York [RR 36]

December 27, 1944

Dear girls,

The Round Robin reached me on Christmas Eve, and I haven't had a chance to finish reading all the letters until tonight, what with all the rush of the holidays. I think it is a wonderful idea and I feel flattered to be included. I didn't realize how few of the 508 wives I did know until I read all those nice letters, but then my stay at Camp Mackall was very short, much too short.

Another thing I didn't realize was just how many of our boys have made the supreme sacrifice. I feel very lucky indeed that my John is still safe and sound. My deepest sympathy to all of you who have lost your husbands.

I don't really know any news from the boys right now. The last letter I had was written Dec. 3 from France. About all I know is that the base camp is in France now instead of England. John writes that except for the fact that he isn't having to dodge bullets right now, he would much prefer being back in Holland to the present set-up. He has been Special Services officer since going to France and the job seems to keep him busy. He sent me a copy of the Para-Glide from Holland, which probably all of the boys who made that jump sent home. It gave a very good description of the jump and the battles that followed. Of course, I was proud of all of them, and especially 1st Platoon, A Company.

About a month ago I had a visit from a Cpl. Smith who was with John from Blanding up until he was wounded in Normandy and sent back to the States. He told me most of the things I have wanted to know all this time about the Invasion. Wish I could tell you everything he told me, but it would take up too much space. He spent the whole day here and we talked of nothing but the 508.

Seems Marion Farrell and I are the only 508ers in this "neck of the woods." I am adding your name to the list, Marion. Am surely going to try to get in touch with you the very next time I am in Philly. Jean Snee sent me your address and phone number, also the bad news about little Bonnie [who has polio]. Surely hope she is well on the road to recovery by this time.

I have been living with the Yankees now for five months. Came up from Atlanta the first of August to be near John's family. My young trooper and I have a small but adequate apartment here and like it fine. Of course, I take constant ribbing about my Southern accent, but I don't really mind—I just spread it a litter thicker and give them a good treat.

Our son and heir is almost ten months old. He has had croup for a couple of nights now and it scares me half to death. My four years of nursing doesn't seem to help at all when it comes to having my own sick.

I will be looking forward to getting the Round Robin on the next go-round. In the meantime, best of luck to all of you and much better days in 1945.

Sincerely, Jeanette

**John Foley, Jr., six months old, September 11, 1944.**

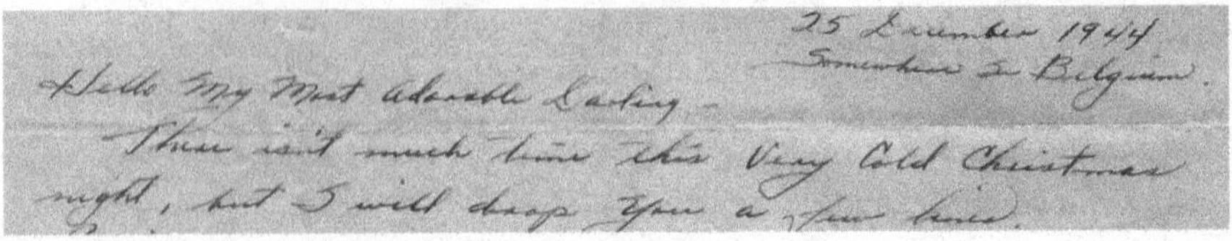
25 December 1944
Somewhere in Belgium.
Hello My Most adorable Darling—
There isn't much time this Very Cold Christmas night, but I will drop You a few lines.

CHAPTER XII

# THE ARDENNES CAMPAIGN: JUMPING FROM A TRUCK INTO THE BATTLE OF THE BULGE

Finally relieved from fifty-seven days of frontline duty in Holland, the 508th had lingering hopes of early victory and an old-fashioned Christmas back home. As the regiment settled down in Sissonne with the grind of training and tactical problems, another combat mission was nowhere in sight: transportation was in such short supply that replacements and even mail were held up at their old base camp in Nottingham; arms and ammo had all been turned in; and the regiment was in no way equipped to take on another engagement. Soldiers were going off on furloughs to Paris, and the 82nd was preparing for a football game on New Year's Eve against the 101st.[128]

What need could arise for paratrooper units in Germany? The vast Allied army of over six hundred thousand troops was now deployed on the German border, the Soviet army was bearing down from the East, and the Wehrmacht was all but defeated. Any sane person could see that the enemy must marshal all its resources for defense.

Clearly, Hitler was not sane. At 10:00 p.m. on December 17, the 508th was alerted to depart for the Belgian front. The German army had launched an aggressive counterattack through the rugged, thickly forested terrain of the Ardennes. Surprising everyone from Eisenhower on down, heavily armored

German forces had crossed the western border of Germany and moved into southeast Belgium, rapidly causing a bulge in the thinly defended Allied line. Eisenhower had but one option: to call up his only reserve—the 82nd and 101st Airborne, seventeen thousand of the army's best.

So unexpected was the attack that Maj. Gen. Matthew Ridgway, the XVIII Airborne Corps commander, and Maj. Gen. Maxwell Taylor, commander of the 101st Airborne, were away at the time of the alert.[129]Maj. Gen. James Gavin was made acting corps commander and put in charge of deployment. Positioned first on the road, the 82nd was trucked in double haste to Werbomont, just southwest of St. Vith, the critical road junction the Germans planned to use to make it all the way to Antwerp and split the allied armies. The aggressive armored assault of December 16 had overwhelmed the inexperienced 106th Infantry Division, causing approximately eight thousand troops to lay down their arms, and now threatened to envelop elements of the 28th Infantry Division and the 7th Armored Division. Close behind the 82nd, the 101st Airborne was assigned the vital southern hub of Bastogne, where they famously engaged in vicious battle and were soon outnumbered and surrounded.

Hastily equipped with the little on hand, the 508th left Sissonne at 9:00 a.m. on December 18. "We made our third combat jump out of the back of trucks when they sent us to St. Vith to hold open an escape route in the line for the units that got overrun," George recalled in 2001. "I have never seen the army move so fast. We were completely reoutfitted in less than a day. Some of us didn't even have usable boots. We passed through Bastogne where the 101st would be surrounded. We always had it out for those guys and wanted to beat them at everything. The 101st was 'the Hundred and Worst,' and the All-Americans were 'the All-Alcoholics.' The units in the quiet sectors such as the 106th at St. Vith were supposed to be where it was safe…now were running out of there like the Germans were right on their tails. The men looked so scared—their heads were just straight down. We made fun of the 106th for that, we called them 'the hungry and sick.' The funniest thing I ever saw was a truck full of Red Cross Doughnut girls[130] sandwiched between two tanks waving cheerfully at the troops while the convoy withdrew".

By December 23, the 508th was maintaining an escape route open over the Salm River, preventing portions of the above units from being surrounded. This action saved one hundred tanks and fifteen thousand American soldiers to fight another day, despite the largest group surrender of about eight thousand U.S. troops to the Germans.[131] Much is made of the mass surrender, but not enough credit is given to the defenders of St. Vith for delaying the Nazi tide. The German army's timetable was in disarray as the major armored thrust of the entire Battle of the Bulge was disrupted. [132]

The main offensive thrust towards the Meuse River was assigned to the 6th Panzer Army, elements of which were the 12th SS Panzer Division and the1st SS Panzer Division. Home to Kampfgruppe Peiper, infamous for massacring nearly a hundred American troops near Malmedy, the 1st SS Panzer alone had over a hundred Mark IV and Panther tanks, along with forty-three of the giant Tiger tanks.[133] "Belgium was the first place I saw a Tiger tank," George recalled. "I was in charge of a bazooka platoon that we farmed out to where it was needed. Only a lucky shot with a bazooka would knock out a Tiger tank. We mostly tried to avoid those if we could—they would target an individual soldier with that 88 millimeter gun on the tank."

In addition to wrecking the German timetable, the northern defenses brought fifteen thousand men and a hundred tanks into the 82nd Airborne Division's perimeter, which were put to good use by General Ridgway.[134]

* * *

On December 24, British Field Marshal Bernard Montgomery, who commanded all forces on the northern shoulder of the bulge, "told Ridgeway that the XVIII Airborne Corps 'could now withdraw with honor to itself and its units.'" Montgomery had decided it was time to "'sort out the battlefield and tidy up the lines. After all, gentlemen,'" he remarked, "'you can't win a big victory without a tidy show.'"[135]

After sacrificing so much blood so late in the war, 82nd paratroopers were furious. They had accomplished their mission, helping the other American units hold a U-shaped line around the town of St. Vith, then moving west to Thier-du-Mont Ridge at great cost of life, and now, they were ordered to withdraw! Moreover, the order came from Montgomery, the overly cautious *British* commander, who had already disastrously failed the airborne in Holland. Like every other 82nd trooper in the Bulge, George emphatically emphasized withdrawal was *not* defeat as he told us in 2001: "It's the only place the 82nd retreated. It was a tactical retreat because we were sticking out like a sore thumb.

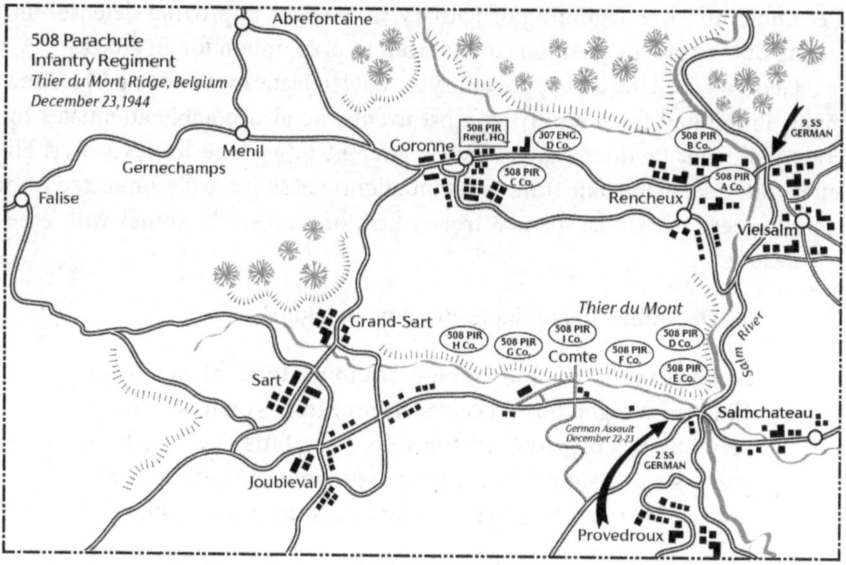


**Bulge Map December 23, 1944, professionally made for the authors.**

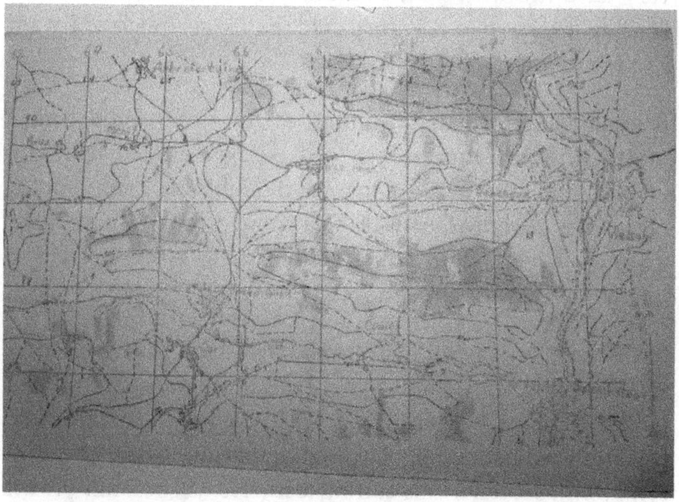

**Hurriedly made, crude, mimeographed strip maps of Belgium, used by the 508th in the battle. Notice Vielsalm on the far right and the dark center area is Their-du-Mont Ridge similar to the previous modern map. Gurwell Collection.**

On Christmas Day, HqHq found itself digging into defensive positions near Haute-Bodeux, several miles to the west of the original lines, and as William G. Lord II reports in his book about the history of the 508th, "[t]here would be no more withdrawals, no more surrounded American units.... The end of

December and the beginning of January were spent improving defenses and feeling out the enemy positions to the front in preparation for an attack."[136]

George seized the first opportunity to write to Jeane on a freezing Christmas night. Prohibited from reporting most events, he also notably attenuates the gravity of what he does express in the attempt to assuage Jeane's worry. His letters often seem to come from a distant, nightmarish place disconnected from reality, where the landscape is a frozen hell, or conversely, shines with ethereal beauty.

> 25 December 1944 [Haute-Bodeux, Belgium]
>
> Somewhere in Belgium—There isn't much time this very cold Christmas night, but I received a letter from you today and it certainly brightened Christmas up. Very little sleep lately—going strong, sometimes fifty to sixty hours. Am very tired, but I did manage to get about four hours sleep last night.
>
> There is a let-down feeling inside—mostly from the fact that today is a day to be near you, my Darling, and I have to be so very far away. Miss you, Punkin, like everything. I am fine Darling, except that it is very cold. Eating as much as I want and warm tonight for a change.
>
> It is almost 9:00 p.m. My mind seems to be wandering—mostly to you, Jeane, and our son. A few scattered shells are falling, momentarily stopping my thoughts, as I run a quick analysis as to how far away. The mind works in a peculiar manner. When I am tired, any interruptions to my train of thought make me very annoyed.
>
> Sweetheart, the [new] mattress and bed stand sound wonderful. Those things are up to you, Punkin. Pretty soon, we will have a good start on furniture. That is good, Adorable One, because I hate shopping. Crowds bother me [another PTSD symptom]. So, our son is cutting teeth. He will be a full-grown lad if I don't get home before long—reminding me that my disposition today has been like a grouchy old man. Lost a filling from a tooth that left jagged edges—my tongue is really getting sore. Like son, like father.

> Letters will probably be scarce, at least for a while. Sorry Darling, but it can't be helped. Keep that chin up, Darling, and remember—if I don't write, it isn't because I don't want to.

George's letter-writing time was cut short when elements of the 9th SS, including the19th Grenadier Division, attacked the Third Battalion of the 508th near Erria from December 26 to 28. The Germans overran the 508th defensive line, but the troopers held firm, staying in their holes and firing on the Germans in seemingly all directions. The German assault made it to Erria, but was soon driven back by E Company, held in reserve to respond to such a breakthrough. Three elite German divisions were decimated and the 508th held Erria.[137] The paratroopers went on the offensive after this action and never looked back.

While the 508th engaged in bitter fighting near Erria, Jeane attended to nursing duties, working on Christmas day. She kept her attitude positive in the encouraging letter below, written soon after the holiday.

> December 27, 1944 [Portland, Oregon]
>
> George Darling, It's a stormy night, and somehow I can't write about Christmas here, not the Santa Claus and sleigh bell version. We do realize what's going on over there and something of what it seems to you. Yet the true meaning of Christmas is all the hope and faith it gives us, isn't it? Go on believing as you do. We can buckle down harder here, and we will.
>
> We understand that mail has been lost, perhaps yours and mine, but they can't stop all of it. Remember we shall go on writing and loving you always. We are fine—your son is steadily becoming the example of all you have given him and are fighting for. He's into everything, but terribly sweet.
>
> Today is the first day at Doernbecher [a children's hospital]. It's good working with the kids. We are happy to have steam heat and good equipment—humble over what those Army nurses are accomplishing under different circumstances. Spent time playing with Ricky this evening (were a pair of morons) and dreamed about you over the dishes, which didn't speed the process. Good night and keep that wonderful faith of yours burning bright!

* * *

30 December 1944 [Near Haute-Bodeux]

Hello my Adorable One, You probably have guessed that we are back in again. Not much rest between, and no leave whatsoever. It is cold here and snow has started to fall again, but we do have a house to sleep in.

Buzz bombs pass over us all the time. [V-1 cruise missiles headed for the greater Antwerp area of Belgium and Holland].[138] They sound just about like a Model T putting across the sky. That is about all the new things we have seen. More tired of the front than in Holland and very ready to come home. Just think, a year overseas has come and gone.

Mail has been very slow. I still have just two pictures. Received a letter from you late last night dated December 11, also a V-mail from Babe dated the same. Received two papers today, one from Hood River and one from Seaside. Those are the first for a very long time.

Still in the best of health, Sweetheart. We have some air-corps, fur-lined pants and a kapok-lined jacket with a fur hood that really keeps us warm.[139] Leather gloves and overshoes complete the picture.[140]

Everyone owes me mail. I have managed to catch up on my letter-writing. Can't promise though how long that will last. Am still writing a V– (interrupted by a close one, had to step out and see what had happened) mail just about every time I write an airmail. There are so very many things ahead for that son of ours to learn. Hope and pray to God that I have a chance to help. Well Jeane, war is the same—and most stories are not pleasant, even if we could write about them. Keep that chin up, my Darling. Take care of yourselves for me.

Your Loving Husband, George

Buzz bombs and Tiger tanks were not the only new enemy weapon the Germans employed in the Bulge: jet fighter-bombers, the ME-262, were also introduced. George attested: "It was in Belgium that we heard and saw a jet aircraft for the first time. Believe me, we were all just trying to figure out what it could be. One came over every day for a while and dropped some bombs, but didn't hit anything. We saw our planes try to box it in. Suddenly, the box would still be there, but that jet had just taken off and was gone. At another place I looked into a downed German plane, and all that was left of the pilot was his dog tags. I wondered if his mother knew. With the weapons they had and how they fought, I figured we were lucky to win that war."

Jeane wrote her last letter of 1944 on December 30th, the same day George wrote his. Up to this time, the American public had been kept in the dark about events on the Western front, but news of the winter defensive had now been announced, finally allowing Jeane to deduce George's whereabouts.

> December 30, 1944 [Portland, Oregon]
>
> Our precious Darling, At least we know where you were for the Christmas stretch. A few divisions and their locations were announced in this big defensive. It seems as though I've felt the whole thing along with you, which has made it hard to write about Christmas here.
>
> There aren't words to say what we feel, the humbleness in our hearts for this latest great piece of work that you have all done over there. Oh, what it has meant to you and to us. Our hearts and love are with you, as always.

* * *

As the war dragged on into another year, thoughts of loved ones filled George's mind more than ever. Written to his wife and in-laws, his first letters of 1945 conveyed a sense of angst and deep weariness, punctuated with glimpses of natural beauty, which further aroused his longing for home.

> 1 January 1945 [Near Haute-Bodeux]
>
> Hello Sweetheart, Here it is 1945—just another day to us, but still another date on paper. Years don't mean much except for one thing—a little older. These mornings as I get up, I am beginning to believe that this husband of yours is an old man [George is only twenty-four at this point]. It isn't hard to realize now why parachute troops are all young kids. Afraid that they are going a little beyond my class.
>
> Took a couple of long rides last night. The pines and fir trees with their coats of snow in moonlight and shadows made a wonderful picture of home years ago. Everything was so quiet

and peaceful that it was hard to believe that a war was on. All too soon though, the picture was shattered by the sharp bark of our artillery. Realization came, flooding back like sea water pounding over a sand wall. Each shadow, each tree possibly shelters an enemy gun, while snow is just a trick of nature to make the going a little rougher. Punkin—there is beauty though, even in war, as I watch the clouds or a lark cross a valley into the haze of the distance beyond.

Everything seems so useless as this new year dawns. Such a terrific waste of time and lives. Everyone is set with one desire—to push and push until there is no such place as Germany, not wasting a moment until they are completely destroyed or subdued, and we can get home. We all have just one desire—to get home as soon as possible. Most of us have been convinced for a long while that there is just one country in the world worth anything, and that is ours.

There will be many problems after this is all over. These kids are all so young and have so many hardships and requirements ahead of them. But hardships are one thing they are accustomed to. I only hope they get the chance to tackle these new problems.

Still feeling fine Jeane—just a little tired mentally. At times, things look hopeless—but that is only natural. It is bad on a person to have time to think. Letters have been pretty slow lately and that doesn't help either. Words are running out. Take good care of yourselves for me.

1 January 1945 [Near Haute-Bodeux]

Dearest Mother and Dad, Received your letter of December 14 today and was very glad. Mail has been quite slow recently with the result that news from home has been very scarce.

You will probably know, or at least guess by the time this reaches you, that we are in again. We have a name for our new home—Buzz Bomb Alley. They go over quite regularly, sounding much like a Model T putting across the sky. Otherwise, things are much the same as in Holland and Normandy. War doesn't change, it just gets on the nerves a little more each time. There wasn't much of a Christmas here. Very cold with snow on the ground. Not at all pleasant when you have to be out in it. I did manage to sing a few carols, but they just made me all the more homesick. The holidays are only for being home. It is really lonesome when you are so far away. I certainly hope that the next one is different. Mother, I hope that you and Dad had a good Christmas, and as the date shows, the very best of the New Year.

My letter-writing should have been better—but things are happening too fast for anything but a note to Jeane. Army life doesn't make a very interesting letter. Glad that you liked the card [from Holland]. Thought that you might be interested in Dutch postcards as a curio. Had some apple seeds from Holland to send, but some darned mouse in my foxhole made a meal of them one night.

The hospital was an excellent idea [to keep Jeane busy at nursing school]. I know how it is when there is nothing to do but think. My only worry was whether or not the work would be too hard. Besides, the training would be very handy in case I forget to duck sometime.

Well, the first day of 1945 is almost over. The year has a pretty poor start, but I hope that it sees us back in the States. Another year over here is a lot to ask. I keep praying for the chance to come back to Jeane and that son. Would certainly like to see him. Take care of yourselves and don't work too hard. Love, George

4 January 1945 [Near Haute-Bodeux]

Hello, my Darling, Received your letter of November 17 last night. It had the last two pictures in it. A package of apples also arrived and in pretty good condition. They are certainly a treat. Must write to Mother and Dad again and thank them. Answered a letter from them a couple of days ago—Dad seems to like that jumpsuit for hunting. It is a break that he could wear it.

Today has been extremely lonesome. Nerves are on edge and I am in one of those restless moods. Need something to occupy my mind besides this darned war. The usual swapping of tales—idle chatter and the like is very boring. Still, it is hard to concentrate. Jumpy, I guess, since it has been fairly quiet today.

Punkin—this is a miserable life—always on the alert, keeping one ear peeled for trouble. Went hunting rabbits the other day up in the hills behind our lines.[141] Darling, it looked so much like home. Fir trees and fire breaks covered with ferns. Came back quite hurriedly though when Jerry threw a big shell mighty close. I hit the ground and listened to the shrapnel buzz through the trees. It was a relief to get out.[142]

Missing you, Sweetheart, until I ache all over. Each day becomes more difficult, especially if there is a little free time. Jeane—I love you—love you with all my heart. This whole world of mine is wrapped up in the two of you. How can I possibly put down in black and white the things that take so many little odd actions to prove? Flowers I can't buy—things I can't send. So many little things that are impossible when we are in the fire. Plans that can't be worked out. There are times when I can't even write and times when I feel so darned bad that a letter is impossible. Yet, my Adorable One—there is always my faith in you and my love. Those have never failed and never will.

Jeane reported in a mid-January V-mail that she had received George's Christmas letter.

January 14, 1944 [Portland, Oregon]

What a wonderful night it is to read your Christmas letter, to have it, and to know you were safe and warm that night at least. Perhaps the pictures and Christmas boxes will eventually catch up with you. Just got back from Hood River today. You would be proud about how our son gets around for his eight months, but he is still a baby and will be for a while. They [Jeane's parents] insist that no one is going to spoil him.

The new year also brought proud news from George's cousin, Don Moss, who was serving with the 80th Infantry Division. A key division in the victory in Normandy, the 80th Infantry Division had also seen important action in Belgium, where it notably coordinated with the 4th Armored Division in the relief of the 101st Airborne at Bastogne on December 26, 1944.

5 January 1945 [Luxembourg]

Hi Cuz, Your letter arrived several days ago and as I have a few spare minutes, thought I'd attempt an answer. We've moved quite a distance lately, left France, and the present finds us in a nice set-up here in Luxembourg. We all like the place, the people are friendly and cafes well stocked, so we would just as soon stay a while.

We came across Normandy pretty fast and our Division did plenty—I think we've made a good name for ourselves. Our regiment is quite famous for Delme Ridge [France], I gather from the papers, and we're still doing more than holding our own without too many casualties.

When we were in Saint-Avold the first of December, I won a 48-hour pass to Paris on a draw and had the time of my life. I really fell in love with the place—did everything I wanted to, including a couple of champagne drunks. Saw the Folies Bergère, Moulin Rouge and really did the town.

I haven't heard too much from home—my mail isn't coming through too well, and I'm almost at the point of suspecting a conspiracy in the Post Office. I got a box the other night and began to drool as I opened it, but found it full of soap—some Christmas present! Well, Cuz—it's getting late—so I'll bring this to a close. If you ever get up this way or see any trucks around with 80 X on them, inquire as to the whereabouts of Division rear. Sorry I couldn't make Rheims. Drop me a line when you have a spare minute—or do you?

Yours—Don

Letters continued from George to Jeane:

> 6 January 1945 [near Fosse, Belgium]
>
> Have a slight headache—really no good reason except from eye strain. This reading and writing by candlelight is hard on the eyes.
>
> This husband of yours isn't happy in the least tonight. Homesick, Sweetheart, for you and that son of ours. Time seems to drag so much this time. There just doesn't seem to be an end—just go and go and then a little more. Five days leave in fourteen months is getting on my nerves. Working on the sixth month now after the last break. Oh, well—maybe after this. Still haven't given up hope.

On January 7th, the 508th retook Thier-du-Mont Ridge, ground they held at the beginning of the battle, but lost when Montgomery pulled them back, forcing them to retake it again. Mixing in with the troops at the front, General Gavin described the harsh conditions of the preceding week, recalling a too-close-for-comfort encounter with German artillery at Grand-Halleux on the Salm River, just north of Thier-du-Mont.

> 14 January 1945 [Nonceveux, Belgium]
>
> Crossing the valley from Abrefontaine [sic] was very rough until the 508 captured the west end of Thier du Mont thus denying the krauts observation. Capt Olson my aid was again hit, this time in the right leg.... The krauts threw lots of arty at us. Tree bursts. I was very lucky. The boy between Olson and myself had his leg severed just above the knee. I put a tourniquet on him and to our surprise we saved his life. Olson gave him morphine. His leg flew across the road and for a minute Olson thought that it was his.... Came close to getting shot at Grand-Halleux when I had to dive into one of our own fox holes to avoid a Schmeisser [MP40 submachine gun] that was squirting in what quick estimate led me to believe was my direction.... Conditions have been very rugged. Temperature around 18 degrees F, snow, wind. It is amazing how these lads live sometimes.

* * *

Following the battle, George wrote his first letter to Jeane from the regiment's new defensive position, expressing bone-weary tiredness, simultaneous restlessness, and a deep desire for sleep.

> 9 January 1945 [Arbrefontaine, Belgium]
>
> Managed at long last to snitch some paper, so again you will have a regular letter. Really hate to write V-mail, but at times it is that or nothing at all. Received your letter of December 14 yesterday, no time last night to write—so am answering tonight.
>
> Still sliding around over here on ice and snow, and I am really disgusted with the stuff. Very tired tonight, Punkin, and a nasty headache is pounding on my skull. Comes from reading and writing by this lamp and candlelight.
>
> Today has been a terror with a lot of unnecessary running around. How has your day been Sweetheart? If I get back, I want nothing better from life than to have you always near me. Have been feeling pretty low—time seems to be creeping by on crutches. Hard to believe though that already almost a third of a month has gone by. It is cold—dark and snowy out tonight and I am very restless. Am sending you a Belgian coin to put on your bracelet to make the countries complete.[143] That should make England, France, Holland, Belgium and Germany, or did I send one for Ireland too? That just about covers them all except for Scotland and Wales.
>
> So, Sweetheart—I must close for now and get a little sleep. Good night my Darling—pleasant dreams.

**Belgian Medal George sent home in the Battle of the Bulge.**

**Belgian Medal George sent home in the Battle of the Bulge. Gurwell Collection.**

From January 10 to January 27, 1945, George got the chance to eat and thaw out as the 508th was billeted in houses at a reserve position at Chevron, about twenty miles from the front, now at the Salm River near Vielsalm. While George took advantage of the brief respite to write to Jeane more frequently, his letters betrayed his increasing war fatigue and underlying symptoms of PTSD. Feeling old beyond his years, he attempted to describe the inexpressible, but could only reiterate his sense of loss—loss of imagination, the ability to think, and verbal fluency.

This emotional numbness and cognitive decline recalls the empty "thousand-yard stare" of the war-worn combat soldier who seems in a daze and unaware of their surroundings. This condition was evoked in a poem George copied out by hand and included with the letter below, in the hope that the "grounded parachute officer" of the poem would convey to Jeane the sentiments he felt but could not articulate. The one sentiment he could and did express, repeatedly, was his deep love of her, anchoring himself to the emotional bedrock of their relationship and hopes for the future.

> 11 January 1945 [Chevron, Belgium]
>
> Hello my Beloved—Today is our Anniversary. One year and nine months, and all I can do is write or try to write the things in my heart. Trying to tell you, my Darling, that I love you with all my heart. That package I mentioned is on its way—don't know when it will get there though.
>
> Have been working pretty hard, but again there is a lull. Should be able to get a few things done—straightening out my junk, washing a few clothes and the like. There has been very little mail for me the past few days and I should have quite a pile of it somewhere along the line. Wonder how your mail has been coming in? Those V-mail letters will probably throw

everything off. Couldn't help it because for a while V-mails were all we had.

This poor old brain is a little off tonight. Can't seem to settle down to writing. This life is so devoid of interest that only an imagination can see anything in it, and my imagination is very poor. Just too much army. I am wordless tonight—can't seem to think of a thing.

This was from a clipping in a New York paper. Well, my Darling—It is late. Happy Anniversary. I love you, Jeane, with all my heart.

The Feelings of a Grounded Parachute Officer
Sometimes when I am all alone
In the middle of the day,
I catch my breath and say a prayer
For the lads so young and gay.
I've seen the canopies of white
Unfurl above their heads,
And carry them through drifting clouds
Toward earth's uncertain bed.
It blossoms like a fresh new rose
Beneath the summer sky,
And none will ever know its thrill
Except my men and I.
My soul knows all the silent fears
That sometimes grip their hearts....
That breathless moment stepping out
As the airborne journey starts!
So, if I'm starring into space
Or blindly turn around,
The people near me can't know
My feet are off the ground....
That I am floating through the air
With all my gallant men,
Blinded to all earthbound things....
At peace with God again.
And for the safety of my men
Each night on bended knee,
I say a prayer, and hope their chutes

Will open fast and free.
—1st Lt Edward F. McKillop[144]

15 January 1945 [Chevron]

Received two letters from you tonight Jeane—dated the 28th [of December]. Sweetheart, you will never know how well timed they were. I had all but given up and time was really dragging by. Lonely Punkin, am so sick at heart that nothing seemed to help. Had to keep writing even when words seemed to stick in my throat. So it goes when everyone gets mail but me.

Have been on the go today. Took a long jeep ride that resulted in my practically freezing to death. Had on half of my clothes and still the cold managed to beat me down.

It has been a pretty rough holiday without a thing to look forward to. So, our son has had his first Christmas—I can just picture him. Say, that was really a nice present—two teeth. Looks like I am going to miss most of the really tough times of teething, walking the floor and the like. Those are things that I wanted too. Well, guess a guy can't have everything.

Our band played tonight—it made me so darned homesick. They are much the same as at Camp Mackall—only better. It was wonderful to hear them again.

16 January 1945 [Chevron]

Hello again Wonderful One—Sitting here tonight, listening to the radio. "What a Difference a Day Makes," is coming in now and, my Darling—how very true that is.[145]

Time is dragging Punkin—dragging until days never seem to end. Wish that you could have been here tonight. I walked around the house—the sun was just going down. I was up on a hill that looks right down a valley. The hills on the right and left are covered with fir trees and over all of that, a blanket of snow. The sky shaded from purple through many shades of red and finally almost orange. The valley was just starting to haze over—a quarter moon with one brilliant star was hanging in the sky. On the left, on a low hill, was a little town with one church spire. The view was breathtaking in its simple beauty. I had to stop, my Darling, it was a picture that makes or breaks a day. A moment of outstanding beauty among so many moments of strife and discontent. So—even over here—there are things of beauty.

Jeane's long-lost letters on January 16 opened George's eyes and heart and enabled him to see beauty even in the midst of death and hardship. In her next letter, she wrote (not without relish) of a mishap which had sent her to the hospital for a stay of several days. Jeane, too, had been dashing off V-mails, but at long last, enforced bed rest afforded her the time to write a proper letter.

January 16, 1945 [Portland, Oregon]

At long last, a letter and not a V-mail to the best man in the whole darn army. How are you, Darling? Last night I wrote a V-mail explaining all about how I got mixed up in the fan belt of the refrigerator trying to coax it to run. Nothing serious, Darling—just pulled the ligaments in my arm a little, bruised my hand a bit and squashed a finger. Stupid, isn't it? Just enough to rate me a nice, soft bed in the Infirmary. This morning they took yours truly to surgery to take the nail off and clean it up a bit. All uneventful except that I got sick from the gas—didn't last long though, because at lunch time I devoured a hot dog. So, you see, nothing but the life of Riley.

Perhaps before much longer you will be out of Belgium and can have a bit of the rest you so deserve. You must know, Sweetheart, that this is really three combat missions, though not all jumps perhaps. Will the old rotation rule hold good and how long will it take to reach Lt. Gurwell?[146]

Babe thinks Jr. looks more like you used to look every day (we don't call him Jr. really), except for his hair and gray-blue eyes. He crawls like mad all over the house and when he finds something solid, keeps pulling up to a standing position almost. He's a darling—never still a minute though, has more energy than a barrel of monkeys, with every bit as much mischief.

Sweetheart, it's about 10:30 p.m. and in the hospital that's past bedtime. Remember, Darling—I love you with all my heart.

20-January 1945 [Deidenberg, Belgium]

We go on fighting—more and more of the same each day. What a monotonous existence. There is only a faint, hazy recollection of life as a civilian. It has been so long, that it causes a little apprehension in my mind when I think of going back to it someday.

January 20, 1945 [Portland, Oregon]

For some strange reason, today has an unreal quality about it, seeming even emptier than usual. So it is when the Infirmary begins to get you down and you're really well. Four-wall confinement without knowing it, and the war goes on. Restless, Sweetheart. Here we sit, Punkin, with a big old hot pack on one paw, ready to go home, and if we don't make it today, the sparks are going to fly.

Darling, how are you and the cold making out? Will things be letting up a bit by the time you get this? Still, it's peculiar though, how much higher your morale sounds in combat than after a time out of it.

Well, Punkin Pie, it's 1:20, practically half a day gone and time's a wasting—a certain self-centered Surgery Resident is avoiding me. Me thinks he knows darn well I'm getting restless wanting to be discharged and am prepared to argue my way out this time for good.

George wrote the following letter while the regiment was on the move: first to corps reserve by truck, then on the 26th they moved to St. Vith with the purpose of attacking east toward Holzheim and Modendorf.

25-January 1945 [near St. Vith]

Hello my Darling—Today hasn't been much to brag about. Haven't had much to do—took a long drive through Belgium and enjoyed it very much. The scenery was beautiful. The snow makes a glorious picture even though it is cold even to look at. The trees wear their mantle of white so very well. Tall, straight, and green with their ermine coats. Valleys that stretch into the unknown as haze obscures the outer ends. Falls that drop away into such sheer walls. It is a pity that war has to come to places like this. Towns that look like tiny doll towns from the hills are in reality just the shells of towns that continually remind you that not so long ago, Jerry was here.

It has been about three days since my last letter to you. Can't help it, because conditions won't always allow a letter. Since we have been in Belgium though, I bet I have written more letters than the rest of the officers in the Company put together.

I am getting tired of listening to people and big shots rave about what a grand and glorious job we do, then sitting back and leaving us in the line with the toughest and dirtiest jobs. We have about a quarter of the equipment of regular infantry and about a tenth of their transportation. Many times, our companies are the size of their platoons. Then, to top it all off—we go in and get them out of holes and take places that they can't take. Nobody, including me, quite understands how these men keep going, but we are always there. Few people realize this and the rest give us such names as overpaid killers—uncouth—wild, and things like that.[147] We get a break, and it's always in some little place where there isn't even a [movie] theatre. Boy, they really fix our clocks. Appreciate us? Yes—by all means when there is something too difficult for others to do.

Sorry Jeane—I am about fed up, and I really didn't mean all that. The continual things we put up with get on our nerves sometimes. Or is it the news that we get from home about strikers here and strikers there. So-and-so thinking the administration is unfair because meat is rationed. An article reporting people screwing nuts and bolts are getting fifty more cents an hour. People flooding to war jobs when it looks as though some of them will have to be drafted. Gee! We love that. We watch people stand, live, eat, and sleep in the snow and cold—then watch them eat their hearts out when the girlfriend back home sends them a short little note—"Sorry, but I met the nicest man over here and you were so far away." Watch them grit their teeth, laugh, and say it doesn't matter—and I can't help them any more than they can help themselves. Thank God for you, Jeane. We watch them take hardships—no meals, frozen feet, and hours of battering by Jerry and they come up smiling.

> God knows I wish that some people over there could spend a week with us here. Then the report of a thousand-yard gain might look a little bigger, as big as it does to us.
>
> Right now, I bet that millions of Americans are saying—well, it won't be long now. We can rest up a little. Yes, probably not over a hundred thousand more casualties, and then in two months they can forget all about the men who fought and died. Sometimes I actually want to quit when I read about these attitudes—but there is that unfinished job, and all of us have an aversion to half-finished jobs.
>
> Darling, kind of wound up tonight, but all finished now. Missing you, Lovely One, until at times my heart seems ready to break.

The 82nd resumed the attack on January 28, 1945 retaking St. Vith. The 508th pushed on to the Siegfried Line near Lanzerath. Fierce fighting followed, thus destroying any hope the Germans had to stave off the Allied invasion of the Third Reich. The historical record explains George's emotional state in his letter of January 31, written on the night of one of the "toughest days," as he put it. That day, in the dark preceding a foggy, early dawn, a German Tiger tank fired on the Regimental Headquarters Company command post. Three rounds from the tank's powerful 88 caliber gun caused significant casualties, as an eyewitness account attests: "1/31 - 0700 hour assembled at road junction. Received artillery and machine gun fire from outskirts of town. Passing over our heads, it was hitting the burgomaster's house appropriated by regimental headquarters staff. Some causalities—too bad."[148]

Capt. William H. Nation was killed in the attack; Technical Sgt. Wallace J. King and Capt. Robert Abraham were wounded. According to Capt. Abraham's account, "the initial establishment of the farmhouse CP [command post] was militarily sound and by the book." However…they had unknowingly selected a site in front of the MLR [main line of resistance] rather than a convenient distance to the rear. Capt. Abraham admits "a mild departure from light or noise discipline occurred, which alerted the crew of a Tiger tank," [and remembers] "three rounds whamming into the house, temporarily interrupting [his] memory." T5 Harry Hudec (Hq Hq) found the body of Captain Nation.[149] Hudec and others helped care for Nation's remains. "Nation was a mess," he recounted. "A tank came up and blew the building. His guts were wide open. The building fell down on him. I pulled his body out and put it on a stretcher."[150]

We recently located the regimental S-3 report of January 31, 1945, showing that moving the CP up to the line also converged with a German attack, not just a random firing of a tank gun:

> At 0400, Regt'l CP opened in LANZERATH. Regt attacked at 0500. 1st Bn was in position at 0725. At 0800 Company C was attacked by elements of the 9th Pz Div estimated at 6 tanks, 1 halftrack, and 200-250 infantry. The attack came up North from RJ 010950 in 504th Prcht Inf sector. Attack advanced to 007956 where it was stopped by combined efforts of Company C, Company B, and 319 FA Bn. Tanks fired on town demolishing a building being reconnoitered for a Regt'l CP and killed the Regimental Adjutant. [Capt Nation] At 0830 enemy withdrew to RJ 010950 and were massing for resumption of attack when this intention was changed to one of departure by artillery fire directed by C Company artillery observers. Artillery knocked out one MK VI tank and scored one probably during the attack.

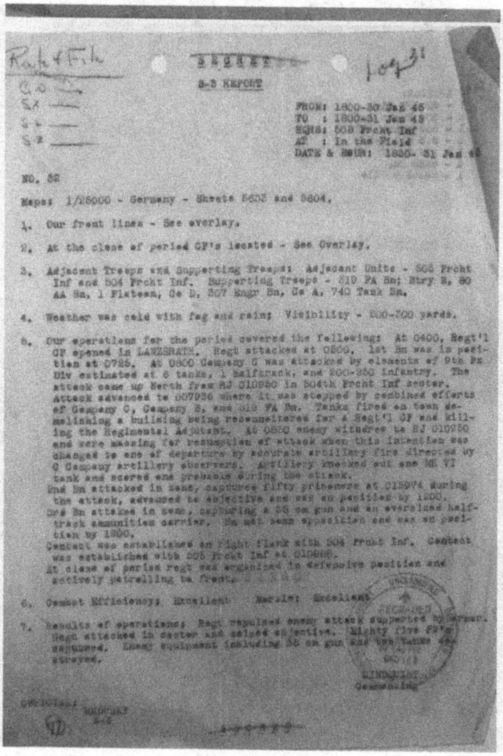

SECRET

S-3 REPORT

FROM: 1800-30 Jan 45
TO : 1800-31 Jan 45
HQRS: 508 Prcht Inf
AT : In the Field
DATE & HOUR: 1830- 31 Jan 45

NO. 86

Maps: 1/25000 - Germany - Sheets 5603 and 5604.

1. Our front lines - See overlay.

2. At the close of period CP's located - See Overlay.

3. Adjacent Troops and Supporting Troops: Adjacent Units - 505 Prcht Inf and 504 Prcht Inf. Supporting Troops - 319 FA Bn; Btry B, 80 AA Bn, 1 Platoon, Co D, 307 Engr Bn, Co A, 740 Tank Bn.

4. Weather was cold with fog and rain; Visibility - 200-300 yards.

5. Our operations for the period covered the following: At 0400, Regt'l CP opened in LANZERATH. Regt attacked at 0500. 1st Bn was in position at 0725. At 0800 Company C was attacked by elements of 9th Pz Div estimated at 6 tanks, 1 halftrack, and 200-250 infantry. The attack came up North from RJ 010950 in 504th Prcht Inf sector. Attack advanced to 007956 where it was stopped by combined efforts of Company C, Company B, and 319 FA Bn. Tanks fired on town demolishing a building being reconnoitered for a Regt'l CP and killing the Regimental Adjutant. At 0830 enemy withdrew to RJ 010950 and were massing for resumption of attack when this intention was changed to one of departure by accurate artillery fire directed by C Company artillery observers. Artillery knocked out one MK VI tank and scored one probable during the attack.
2nd Bn attacked in zone, captured fifty prisoners at 015974 during the attack, advanced to objective and was on position by 1200.
3rd Bn attacked in zone, capturing a 55 cm gun and an oversized half-track ammunition carrier. Bn met some opposition and was on position by 1200.
Contact was established on right flank with 504 Prcht Inf. Contact was established with 505 Prcht Inf at [illegible].
At close of period regt was organized in defensive position and actively patrolling to front.

6. Combat Efficiency: Excellent Morale: Excellent

7. Results of operations: Regt repulsed enemy attack supported by armor. Regt attacked in sector and seized objective. Eighty five PW's captured. Enemy equipment including 55 cm gun and two tanks destroyed.

LINDQUIST
Commanding

OFFICIAL:
[illegible]
S-3

SECRET

508th Operations Journal, Jan 31, '45, 6:30 PM, courtesy Thulai van Maanen, 2022.

As he wrote to Jeane on the night of January 31, George was in a very somber mood. The loss of Captain Nation, one of the regiment's most beloved officers, was an especially hard blow. [151] It was also especially significant for George. Nation had been with the 508th since its inception; he was an "old man," just like George, and the two had served together since 1942. Making his death all the more bitter was the fact he died so late in the war: on the day the Captain perished, lead elements of the 508th were in sight of fortifications on the Siegfried Line.

**Sue at 508th plaque, Lanzerath, Belgium, 2018.**

**The Siegfried Line near Lanzerath, Belgium, now a pasture. 2018.**

31 January 1945 [Lanzerath, Belgium]

My Darling, It has been several days since I dropped you a line. We have been very busy. Out in the snow most of the time, with not a chance to write. Have never been so uncomfortable in my life. Darling—it has been so darned cold. Snow has definitely lost its appeal for me.

Jeane—I am so very tired tonight. Just stopped long enough last night to sleep for an hour. Sweetheart—this life makes you old before your time. Haven't had word from you for some time but I have to write tonight. Need something to ease the tension and nothing works better than a letter to you.

Sweetheart—I love you so very much. During the toughest days, that love burns bright enough to change the whole day. This cookie of yours is mixed up inside tonight. It is just the fact that I am tired, though—tomorrow is another day. Soon, in just a few short hours, it will be February of 1945—another month, Jeane—and so many long days ahead.

Jeane Darling—I can hardly keep these eyes of mine open. I must get some sleep. Take care of yourself, my Adorable One.

Retrospective knowledge of what transpired after the fact can do no more than convey a limited sense of the pressure of silenced grief and fear behind George's seemingly simple statement, "Life makes you old before your time"—an observation which, without the context, could even sound banal. Such are the experiences that make up PTSD, contributing to the constant feeling of personal vulnerability that makes combat veterans so "jumpy," as George put it. Just seventeen days from the final day of combat for the 508th in World War II, George had acquired yet another ghost.[152]

After the January 31 attack, Capt. Robert Abraham was hospitalized for wounds and George took over as acting company commander of HqHq. During this time, the Red Devils assaulted the German positions at Holzheim, where the arctic cold was as deadly as the Germans, and on February 4, they were relieved by the 99th Infantry Division.

With mounting tension and weariness, George wrote to Jeane late on the eve of the regiment's temporary relief from engagement.

3 February 1945 [Lanzerath]

Hello my Darling—No word from you for quite a while—then early today, a mail call and no mail. Felt pretty bad, but Sweetheart this afternoon saved the day. Three letters from you. Gee my Darling—I was just on the verge of writing a very nasty letter. No mail, all this tension, and a variety of troubles just about got the best of me. For a while, I forgot about mail complications and the like. I would have been sorry right after it had gone, but this last mail call set everything straight.

This lonely husband of yours has been a little under the weather the last three days. A few chills and a little fever, nothing serious enough to do anything but slow me down. Just a result of K-rations [cold meals], on the go night and day, and catching a few hours' sleep out in the snow. There is more snow falling now, which should make things worse. Roads here have been a nightmare and have caused most of the complications.

Most of the information that I can't give will be in the papers and on the radio. We are still betting on the Russians and praying each day that soon this war will be over. [153] Time goes by—dragging on and on until it seems something must give. There is just war the next day and so on—indefinitely. Someday there has to be change. Tired, Sweetheart—very—very tired, such is life over here.

Feel much better tonight though. I feel a little flow of interest in things going on and the old morale is coming back to life. Just too ornery to really get sick. Well, Jeane—I must close for tonight—it is late and there is much work to do tomorrow.

4-February 1945 [Rencheux, Belgium]

This morning brought three more V-mails from you—I hate these things, but they fill in the gaps. Feel much better today—right back in shape again. Thought for a while that I would have to visit the medics—still following that old idea of medics only when they carry me in. Just don't like to be pampered.

Also on the fourth, Captain Abraham wrote to George to tell him how to handle his personal possessions. Feeling terrible about Captain Nation's death, he commented on the critical error made in placing the command post too near the front.

From: Capt Robert Abraham, 508 Prcht Inf

To: Lt George Gurwell [Rencheux, Belgium]

4 February 1945

Dear George,

At present I am in the town you visited while we were in Chevron. Remember? I'm feeling O.K. but mighty tired. They knocked me out for a couple of days and the effect hasn't worn off yet. Until I get back or until I get an address, I'd like to have you hold my mail for me. There's not much point in its chasing me around Europe. I may be gone two or three weeks, it's hard to guess at this point. Maybe sooner. I also asked Ripper to grab on to my bedding roll, sleeping bag, dispatch case, musette bag and that large mail bag full of junk I was toting around. Throw it on the truck and let Sgt Lundquist watch it for me.

I heard that Nation was killed at the same time I got my ass blown off. Too Bad. The Colonel will have a tough time getting another adjutant like him. Is [1st Lt. Charles] Yates OK? Give him a kiss for me. All I have to do here is stare at the four walls and keep them from closing in on me. None of this would have happened if we hadn't decided to put the Command Post on the Main Line of Resistance. I still maintain it's too close.

Best Wishes, Abe[154]

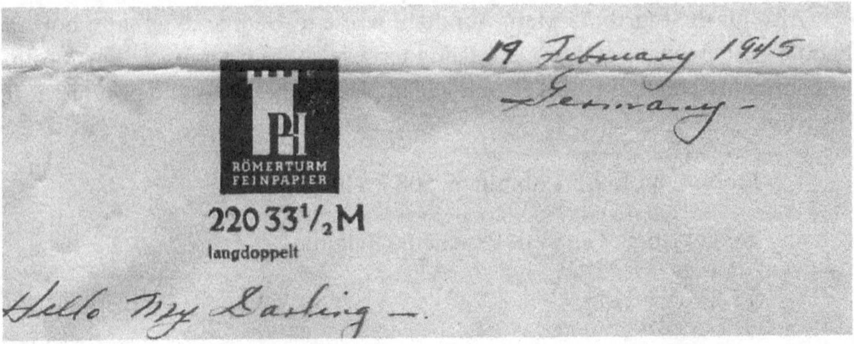
19 February 1945
Germany -
RÖMERTURM
FEINPAPIER
220 33½ M
langdoppelt
Hello My Darling —

## CHAPTER XIII

# THE ARDENNES CAMPAIGN: HORROR IN THE HÜRTGEN FOREST

After three short days of reprieve at Rencheux, the 508th was trucked southeast of Aachen to Hahn, Germany. The next day, February 8, they relieved the 507th PIR in the Hürtgen Forest, in the vicinity of Bergstein, about three miles west of the Roer River. In the fall of 1944, while the 82nd Airborne was in Holland, a continuous battle for the Hürtgen Forest area of Germany had raged with little progress on either side. The 28th Infantry Division suffered horrible losses. Of the 120,000 U.S. soldiers sent into battle, 33,000 were killed, wounded, or captured with little to show for it.[155] The snow and ice of one of the most brutal winters Germany had ever seen covered the killing fields, burying the bodies of thousands of soldiers before they could be identified and removed. Thankfully, the German defenses were weakened by the recent unsuccessful counteroffensive started in mid-December. On February 10 the First Battalion, 508th took Hill 400 in Germany, clearing the way west of the Roer River.

Germany was on her last legs.

While in broad terms, General Gavin knew the purpose of the 82nd being in the Hürtgen (to protect Monty's flank), but he, like George, questioned the use of thinly armed and clothed paratroopers to do the job of big infantry units that were clothed with winter gear, well-armed, and equipped with more than adequate transportation. Writing in his diary, also on February 10, General Gavin expressed war-weary skepticism about the 82nd Airborne's mission, "Up here the 505 and 508 have been working with V Corps to assist in capturing the dams along the Roer river. Nasty job and one that could have been done by anyone." The nasty job consisted of navigating acres of anti-personnel mines, as described in George's letters.

The General continued his entry of February 10th describing the unimaginable conditions: "The snow has melted uncovering many of the dead and decayed of the past several months on this front. The 28th Division evidently took a bad beating in this area. A discouraging sight to see. Much of their tanks, jeeps, weasels [tracked light cargo carriers], arms, etc. abandoned. Their wounded and dead left on the ground rotting. If only our statesman could spend a minute hugging the ground under mortar fire next to a three month old stiff. We just simply have to stop wars...."[156]

George's memories of the Hürtgen—among the most nightmarish of the entire war—haunted him throughout his life. Recounting his experience for the first time in 2001, he became very emotional and broke down in tears. Even late in life, he still felt morally responsible for a terrible situation he had been unable to control and remembered, triggering, intrusive, painful memories.

> "When the fighting finally cooled off in Belgium, they sent us to the Hürtgen Forest. I'm not even sure what we were doing there. What an awful place. The Germans would aim their antiaircraft guns at the tops of the trees, and the shrapnel would be awful. It was one of their little tricks. The mines were horrible there too.
>
> "There were all kinds of dead GIs and boots lying around with legs sticking out of them. I had to send a man out with a message. A corporal—can't remember his name—the best we had at getting through minefields, asked not to go, but there was no one else to send. The message had to get out. He explained he just 'had a bad feeling about this one,' and requested not to go. Even though he was a friend, there just wasn't anyone else capable, so I had to send him anyway.

> "We knew then that there were mines in the area and I told him to be careful. I later learned...a bouncing betty got away from him. [When tripped, a bouncing betty pops up waist-high before exploding, guaranteeing maximum damage.] I think about him all the time and it still hurts. [Tears, a pause, and a hug from Sue.] I felt responsible. I wish I never had to send him out, but there was nothing I could do."

* * *

By February 1945, war fatigue was also spreading in its own way on the home front, where the worried population, aware that U.S. troops had reached the German frontier, was anxiously waiting for long-delayed letters. They followed the news as best they could and wrote supportive, yet worried letters of their own. The following from Jeane's mother, Delpha, is a case in point.

> February 1, 1945 [Hood River, Oregon]
>
> Dearest Son—According to maps, newspapers and the radio, we are with you day and night. Somehow our prayers must be answered that you will be back with us before the year is over. Jeane has probably told you about hurting her hand, poor kid. These three months are the hardest for her because she has studying to do, then she worries about everything. Last week "Ricky" (did you know we are calling him that now) had a little "stomach ache," and of course she was sure he had everything in the book that a baby could have. He is the most wonderful baby that ever was and George, she worries day and night for fear something will happen to him before you get home. Babe tells me you didn't get the Christmas boxes from Jeane or us and we are just sick about it. Your letter came about a week ago and we were so glad to have the Belgium note and flag.
>
> Jeane is fine, only she gets awfully tired. Sometimes I wonder if she should have gone back to the hospital, and yet she is happier there. It keeps her busy and she says she just couldn't stand it if it wasn't for the hospital work. The thing of it is, she worries because she doesn't have time to get letters written to you as often as she wants, then she worries for fear something will happen to the baby and you won't get to see him. Really,

she is fine, but she will not be happy until you get home. She lives for you and little George. I really believe your marriage was made in heaven. Keep dodging those bullets son. All our love and prayers, Mother and Dad Slonaker

True to the description in her mother's letter, Jeane was all but played out from school, work, and caring for little Ricky. The letters below, typical of those she wrote in February, nevertheless attempted to ease George's pessimistic state of mind, emphasize her love, and strike a note of hope, looking forward to better days—the end of nurses' training, the end of the war—and George's homecoming.

February 1, 1945 [Portland, Oregon]

My Darling—I love you and thought that surely by this time you would get at least a wee little rest, while other units took over, but you're the ones who do such a big, big job. Believe, though, Sweetheart—it will come, it will, Darling.

Two letters did come from you this week—still from Belgium. You don't know what it means to have you writing when it's especially difficult for you. George Darling—along with the snow and cold, I realize you are tired now, desperately tired clean through, until you actually feel half dead and dull inside—with more than good reason. My Darling, just remember it is a normal reaction, it will change, and won't last forever. There is so little I can say against all that you've undergone that is war—just know that I understand at least in part.

Now where on earth you are getting those "Detective Story" names you tacked on yourself, I can't imagine—but if you think any Americans think of you that way, you're sniffing up the wrong tree. Don't believe any dodo who tries to tell you otherwise. Either you got it from some crank who is cranium static, or the source is unreliable. Of course, as long as there is a world, there is bound to be a wacky few, but they are a stinky little minority, that's life. I just want you to believe so badly that there is good with the bad—but you do. Love, Jeane

February 7, 1945 [Portland, Oregon]

My Precious Darling—You're absolutely the sweetest thing in this world even if we have the sweetest son possible, and you're spoiling me in a heavenly way with flattery—besides two letters in two days from cold, lonely Belgium.

Yes Darling, will try harder to get some pictures to you. This next week is mid-term week and I'm always tired these days at Doernbecher. Our resistance [to infectious diseases] is knocked to nothing when working with children—but only a couple more months of that—thank goodness.

There was a letter from Helen Moss today with not much new news of Clint, except that he is still in England getting teeth, etc. fixed. Nothing new about the kidney condition. She's still hoping he won't go back in.

George R. is a bit more daring every day about standing and stooping—always with something to hang on to of course. Tomorrow he will be nine months old—it just doesn't seem possible, does it?

It is late again, Sweetheart—which means bed now or I'll never hold out. Keep up the good work— it will come to an end one of these days and you will be back.

As another monthly "anniversary" came up on February 11, George's thoughts turned naturally to Jeane and fond memories of the past, aided by a recent letter from a college friend. Relived and shared through letters, these positive memories allowed George to abstract himself, if only momentarily, from the sweeping devastation of the once-pristine forest he had earlier described to Jeane as "a wonderful picture of home."

11 February 1945 [Hürtgen Forest, Germany]

Happy Anniversary my Adorable One—it won't be long now, and we will have our second anniversary. Time is crawling by—each day getting a little longer and bringing spring a little closer. We have been on the go this past week—haven't stopped very long in one place and there has been very little time to write. Haven't been getting any mail, so everything is about evened up.

Everyone seems to think that this old war is about over but there is still plenty of activity around here. Snow has just about all melted but in its place is a sea of mud. Rather nasty to splash around in. About five days of good sunshine would really set this area up in good shape.

Remember Caroline Wall, my next-door neighbor from Oregon State in Corvallis? Had a letter from her—she and Lowell Eddy are planning on getting married after the war. The four of us should be able to have good times together. Lowell had stopped writing—evidently, he was in on one of the recent invasions. School seems to be much the same, except for a shortage of men. They still have dances at the M.U. Building and classes seem to be going on as usual. Did seem good though to hear about Corvallis again.[157]

Mail has been very slow here. Moving around too much for it to keep up with us. Feeling fine Jeane—that one little sick spell has passed over. Lost a little weight, but that is to be expected, working night and day with one meal a day if I was lucky. Things have settled down a little now. Well, my Darling—I must close. Time for hitting the sack.

12 February 1945 [Hürtgen Forest, Germany]

Just a few lines to let you know that I am still okay. A little muddy and quite dirty, but that is to be expected. There is quite a wind and rainstorm blowing. Have been to the medics today—an irritation in one eye and there doesn't seem to be anything in it. Very annoying when I try to read or write, but other than that I am in good health.[158]

15 February 1945 [Hürtgen Forest, Germany]

Very little time for writing these past few days. On the go, busy and just generally on the move. Once again, we are in Germany. It would have been a rather beautiful place, but the towns around here are just a mass of debris. We live in one of the rooms left in town. The only other places are cellars. The mud and shattered buildings remind me of pictures from *All Quiet on the Western Front*. The only living things around besides the soldiers are birds. Not very pleasant surroundings.

Oh! Speaking of irony: there is a piano here in the house that is still intact. It plays very well. That is the only whole thing that I have seen. War is a strange thing.

Took a trip up past the front lines today for equipment. Not much luck. It was a beautiful day though, with the sun actually out and shining. Have you ever seen or dreamed of whole mountain sides of trees with the tops of all the trees blown off and about 3/4 of the limbs sheared away? We moved through miles of that today. Just imagine the hell that must have been going on as our first troops moved through. The sights that we see at times are beyond the imagination.

Got two letters as late as Feb 1. I better be getting home. No more of these fan blade episodes. Yes, Jeane, I knew about Clint [being in the hospital] and that leaves just one other besides myself who used to be around with us a lot in Pinehurst—The Ripper.[159] Slowly one by one they go out. Before long, it will be 14 months overseas and the war still isn't over, no matter what people tell you. Lead still flies over here. Picked up a vase for you today. I am going to pack it soon and send it. It is a beautiful job, at least I think so. That was all that remained from one of these houses, and I stopped someone just as they started to break it. The snow is gone and in its place is a sea of mud that has dried out quite a bit these last few days.

Sometimc during his stay in Belgium, George received an entertaining, undated letter from "Freddie," who earnestly assured him he had mailed Jeane's long-delayed Christmas box exactly as George had instructed. We have deduced that Freddie was T/5 George A. Fredrick, the eager regimental mail clerk back in Sissonne. We like to think his breathless letter, reproduced below, offered George a bit of comic relief. Freddie also joked with George about sending home the "right" package, as it has been rumored that some soldiers sent their girlfriend's package home, and caused a real ruckus.

Sunday afternoon.

Dear Sir, Just a few lines to let you know that I sent your one box to your wife, right box too, rather proud of myself the way I got your name signed on it, too, better be careful or I will be censoring my own mail (only fooling) and can get the other one sent now, if you will be sending the girls address back here.

Hope that you are making out ok, and Sgt. [Ernest S.] Hubbard says that you better be coming back here real soon and bring some weapons back, oh not that we need any, as we found enough equipment to supply half a company, guns (carbines, M-1s, and Tommy guns) but all of these were left us by a bunch of replacements who were here for a while, found over 40 blankets stored away in the supply room, helmets, and field equipment and combat boots, but when the company left, they didn't have anything at least that's what they said. Good luck and hurry back, will be waiting. Freddie

PS. If you need anything let me know, should be able to send it to you.

In the latter part of February, when Jeane finally received her special Christmas gift, she is delighted by everything, including Freddie's special touch with the packaging.

February 17, 1945 [Portland, Oregon]

George Sweetheart, the box of things is a theme in itself. Haven't quite come to earth enough to make my ravings writable. Everything came through beautifully and was really packed to travel. Whoever you had send them couldn't spell our name correctly. I got quite a bang out of that, but the wrapping was heavy, taped together—tied with parachute risers. The linens, oh the linens and the laces, each and everything is exquisite and the perfume—oh George Darling, I could sleep in it.

Relieved by the 9th Infantry Division on February 18, the 82nd Airborne entrained the next day and began the journey back to base camps in France. Like most regiments, the 508th had a fairly rough ride home in "40 & 8" boxcars [able to carry forty men or eight horses]. On arrival at Sissonne, they discovered their barracks were now an army hospital and they would be billeted in tents.

While in route to safety in France, George wrote a confessional letter telling Jeane about some of his near scrapes. Both his pen ink and paper had been "thoughtfully" furnished by the Germans.

19 February 1945 [train from Aachen, Germany to Camp Sissonne, France]

It has been several days since I sent a letter your way. Yes Jeane, on the move again—it seems as though we are always on the move. Picked up this German writing paper on the way. Peculiar stuff, but helpful. We were just about out of writing-paper, but Jerry is quite thoughtful. This ink is from a bottle I picked up in a minefield. Yes, Punkin—we manage to stay supplied, though some things do come from peculiar places.

This husband of yours is on the nervous and tired side. Can't seem to get enough sleep and that old habit of pacing the floor has returned. My old sunny disposition has gone with the snow—must be getting tired. Just a growly old bear lately. Try not to be that way, but for some reason, I just can't help it. The army is wearing me down Darling—little by little, month after month—it grows a little worse. The fact that there is a war on meets only a dull mind. Told you Sweetheart—just so very-very weary. Your letters are the only bright spots in such dull days. Yes, my Adorable One—the war is still going on. Sometimes it is hard to believe that Jerry can keep fighting. He does though—believe me.

Was rather amused at myself the other day. Kicked myself all over the countryside as a result. I went on a patrol out past our outpost lines—looking for equipment, carried a Thompson, sub-machine gun. Snipers had been and were active in the area. Searched several likely spots by sticking the "tommy gun" around the corners first. Very good security. The next day I decided to clean the gun. Guess what—there wasn't a round in the gun. I certainly would have been embarrassed if I had pulled the trigger expecting the thing to go off. Yes Jeane—I really felt foolish.

Saw minefields that were really horrific, tremendous things. Houses and whole towns with nothing left but piles of debris and ruble. Maybe there would be those rooms left that people could live in. War is amazing, there were miles and miles of thick woods with all of the trees topless, three fourths of the limbs were blown off. What a hell on earth that must have been.

After leaving the front lines in Germany on February 18, the 508th settled down in France, near Reims, once more. Worn out physically and emotionally, but finally out of combat, George now had a chance to write, but when he did, he described himself as an old, broken-down man.

> 25 February 1945 [Camp Sissonne, France]
>
> Haven't been quite as regular on letters lately. Your letters, though Darling, have been coming in very well. We have been very busy lately—moving and more moving. This poor, broken-down husband of yours is looking for a nice quiet foxhole already. Have been Company Commander these past few days. Work and more work—still no promise of any time off.
>
> The pictures of that son of ours are with me all the time and I show them to everyone. He looks so very good that I can't believe it myself. I am speechless because he looks so wonderful.
>
> Have had a good dose of 40 & 8 boxcars while coming back from Germany. Really not a pullman and quite chilly too! This last little tussle saw me lose about fifteen pounds. Down quite a bit, but that should be coming back soon.
>
> We are in tents, and my Darling—it is cold even though the days have been lovely. Take such good care of yourselves for me. Good night, Sweetheart, and pleasant dreams.

George enclosed an undated, unidentified newspaper clipping with the above clarifying that the 82nd in no way "classified our brother Airborne Division, the 101st as *amateurs*. To the best of our knowledge no such statement was ever made officially or unofficially." Despite his self-description, George still had his sense of humor.

News about conditions back home came mainly from letters, hometown newspapers, and newspaper clippings sent from family and friends. One friend, Pat Wilson, was so close she was like a second mother to George. Pat, her husband George, and daughter Patsy supported Jeane while she was finishing her nurses training in Portland. Pat wrote to George and shared her observations about the home front.

Pat Wilson to George

March 2, 1945 [Portland, Oregon]

So glad to get such a nice long letter from you. We are buying the two lots back of us, so I'll have plenty of room for the Victory Garden this year. We had wanted to get the two lots, where the old orchard is, but the woman who owns them thinks she is going to make her fortune with them. She is asking one thousand dollars for them. She said three years ago she was going to sell them in the war boom but now she is saying there will be a boom after the war, and she will sell them then. I wish her well, but they certainly are not worth that, with no sewers or streets there. Just another profiteer.

I read the little paper [the *Paraglide*] you sent from Holland, so have been able to follow you a little. I also read the *Collier's*, though at the time, I didn't know it was your outfit. Thanks for telling me about it. You will have a lot of things to tell us when you get back home.

The need to keep the war machine supplied and going meant many items were rationed. One way that the people on the home front were asked to help was to plant Victory Gardens. These gardens helped provide produce close to home and saved on transportation costs, while leaving the majority of farm-grown products available for the troops. Pat wrote again on March 7, 1945.

[Portland, Oregon]

You ask if the war has made any difference here. Not a whole lot, except Portland is overcrowded and our activities are different. As for rationing, we have never been hurt in any way. In fact, George [Pat's husband] is getting fat on it. He weighs 183 lbs., which is the most he has ever weighed always stayed at 165 before. Some people do some whining, but they would have whined even during normal times. The big difference is the radio. It's all war, at all times. I've got the news on now. It makes me wonder, what we used to hear on it. Most of the shows put on the air, are given for the armed services. In fact, they are broadcast from different army posts and its boys are hilarious audiences, especially for Bing Crosby or Bob Hope.

> Bing Crosby won all honors this year for box office popularity. He walks somewhat in Will Rogers footsteps. Not that he is like Rogers, but everybody loves him. He has the faculty of making his listeners feel he is just a close friend.
>
> As for the overcrowding—every day is like Saturday afternoon downtown. Portland is still a small town in its stores, etc. but not in the people that are here. You can stand on 5th and Morrison and see many strange and curious sights, especially the women that are working in the shipyards. Some of them are unbelievable in their overalls—so fat you can't see how they could possibly get on a ship, let alone working on it. All unemployables are employed now. For me, this is the biggest difference, that and the crowed streetcars and buses.

During February and March 1945, Jeane averaged about a letter every other day. While her later war letters are more positive and supportive than those she wrote while adjusting to life as an army wife, single mother, and nursing student, her anxieties continued to show, especially when it came to George's health.

> February 21, 1944 [Portland, Oregon]
>
> Darling you are so darn sweet, but what is this about being close to paying the medics a visit? COME ON GIVE!! Knowing you, you would go till you dropped—and we'll have none of THAT Sir!! Going to worry till you're back of course.
>
> Now about that news concerning strikes. Must hit you fellows over there between the teeth, knocks you flat. I am ashamed news about strikes or unfaithful girlfriends goes to your men and you, but that is not all the news from all the girlfriends. It balances, and honestly strikes are not what they used to be—they're coming in check. I can only say that I am so proud of you and above all love you so much.
>
> February 26, 1944 [Portland, Oregon]
>
> George precious, Your fatigue, chills, and fever worry me. You know, Sweetheart, especially when you ignore such things and keep them from us too, it makes it worse. If you don't check up with the medics, well let's see—mail might be a good penalty—Love you desperately, Jeane

February 28, 1945. [Portland, Oregon]

Darling, Another letter today and a recent V-mail at that—February 11, our day. It had the German SS tag in it—I am still filled with wonder—what a souvenir *that* is. It is so darn good to know you are feeling better, and I pray that you still do.

Of course I remember Caroline and Lowell. There are good times ahead, aren't there? Will hope they will be as happy as we are. Ricky is getting sweeter every day and mouths something like "dada" to your picture. I know you hate V-mail. I'll try to send more airmail. Your adoring wife, Jeane

***

Though George did not know it then, the 508th had seen their last day of combat in World War II on February 18, 1945. Since Christmas, the Germans had been pushed from Belgium back to their preinvasion positions and into the industrial regions of Germany. By the end of the campaign, 101 troopers of the 508th PIR had been killed in action. Other casualties totaled 398 wounded in action, 273 injured in action, 33 died of wounds, and 23 missing in action. Many of the injured were due to frostbite, trench foot, and other cold-weather afflictions, and most of the missing were prisoners of war.

In France during parades and reviews, General Gavin addressed the assembled division and awarded decorations for valor.[160] We have no record of a separate 508th memorial service. As Guy LoFaro has noted, Gavin compared the Hürtgen Forest to "'the lower levels of Dante's "Inferno," and angrily blamed the ineptitude and indifference of higher headquarters staff officers for the carnage. He also later "compared the Battle of the Hürtgen Forest to Passchendaele, the World War I battle in which the British Army lost some 240,000 soldiers.... Both were fought in seas of mud, both raged on inconclusively for several months, and both resulted in little tactical or strategic effect." To Gavin, however, "the strongest similarity" was that both had been conceived "by château generals with little conception of what they were demanding of their soldiers."[161]

When many WWII history enthusiasts discuss the Ardennes campaign, they think only of the battles around Bastogne. The 101st Airborne Division has long overshadowed the other accomplishments of American units in the campaign. Bastogne was never a major obstacle in the path of the German advance, however. Antwerp was the ultimate goal in the desperate German thrust to seize the deep water port, which was to be reached through the northern approaches.

Only determined defense in the northern sector of the Bulge blocked the Germans from reaching their objective. No lone division deserves the main credit or share of attention in the saga of the Battle of the Bulge. "Eight American Divisions were initially involved, and others soon joined in the battle. It was a joint effort and a magnificent feat of American Arms that defeated the Germans in the Ardennes and not one lone division in one small city."[162]

IN REPLY
REFER TO..............................

ADDRESS:
PUBLIC WORKS
NAVAL AIR STATION

# UNITED STATES NAVAL AIR STATION
FORT LAUDERDALE, FLORIDA

PUBLIC WORKS DEPARTMENT

20 January 1945

Dear Girls:

## CHAPTER XIV

# THE GRANDEST PEOPLE I'VE EVER KNOWN, ROUND ROBIN LETTERS 37–42

While their husbands were slogging it out in Belgium, wives back home were still learning how events in Normandy and Holland had affected their friends and were catching up on how they had been doing since they all had left Pinehurst. January 1945 found the Round Robin still in the Northeast, where Marion Farrell, married to 1st Lt. Joseph Farrell (C Co. ), wrote the first letter of the new year from New Jersey.

> Marion Farrell, Vineland, New Jersey [RR 37]
>
> January 2, 1945
>
> Dear Girls,
>
> I was very puzzled when I walked in the house and found this huge envelope bearing my name—from Jeanette Foley. Just couldn't imagine what it was, but was thrilled when I opened it and letters began falling out from girls of the 508th. I've enjoyed reading each letter and all the news items and seeing pictures of those wonderful offspring. Must say, you girls have done a bang-up job!! Yes, a bang-up job *in many ways*!! The bravery of you who have lost your husbands is truly deserving of the highest tribute. Please accept my deepest sympathy.
>
> I have been residing in Durby, Pa. (a borough of Philadelphia) since the regiment left Camp Mackall last December. Joe was

fortunate in getting home for a few hours on two nights while they were at the Point of Embarkation. One was Christmas Eve and even tho it was short, we had our Christmas while he was here, and he had the pleasure of seeing Bonnie with her toys. It was a great thrill for both of us.

Joe was wounded in the Normandy Invasion. He sent me his Purple Heart and Presidential Citation ribbon, and whenever I look at that box it makes my knees go weak. He wasn't evacuated back to England, but paid for it later by having to be hospitalized when the Regiment returned to England. He did recover alright however, and as of my latest letter he was in fine health. Since that letter was dated Nov. 21 (and that is a long time), I'm just praying with all my heart he is still safe and well. Since reading that the 82nd Division went into action in Belgium on the 19th of Dec. and was one of *three* divisions that took the "brunt" of the Nazi offensive, my heart has been in my mouth. The fighting has been so fierce in the sector they reportedly are in. He didn't jump in Holland, and I could have saved many "worry wrinkles" had I known this beforehand.

I started working in the Stock Control Office at the Philadelphia Quartermasters Depot last January, and one day while having lunch in the cafeteria, I was thrilled to hear a private from B Company, 508, give a talk on his experiences in Normandy. He had been wounded and was undergoing treatments at the Valley Forge Hospital here. I could hardly wait until he finished before dashing up to start firing questions. It was wonderful that he had recently seen Joe and knew him quite well.

I have been on the inactive list of war-workers since our little girl was stricken with infantile paralysis [polio] late in July. The disease left her paralyzed in her left hip and leg, but now I'm happy to report she is recovering due to Kenny treatments. [163] We spent some very tense moments with her and it's something I hope never to experience again. For you girls who knew her, she has definitely grown up in the past year and it's hard for me to realize when I look at her that soon she will be *four*! I'm happy to feel certain this paralysis has been licked.

She won't be left crippled. There isn't enough I can say for the Kenny treatments.

Lt. Art Snee was the first casualty I heard of in the Regiment, and when I received Jean's note my heart turned to lead. Jean was in Washington, D.C. for a few days this fall, and I called her and insisted she come to Philly and spend some time with me. She was only here a short time, but I did enjoy every second of it. I wired Dotty Delfs in New York and she came down and spent a day visiting with Jean and me.

I'm sure the trip brought Dotty good luck because she left here one night to return to N.Y., and her husband (who was wounded) walked in the door the following morning. I was so happy for her. I'll let her give you the details of Lt. Delfs' injury when the letter gets around to her.

I went up to Springfield, Mass. late this fall and had a wonderful visit with Dotty Hamlin. She has an adorable son, but I'm sending these letters directly to her, so I know she will give you *all* the details on David. He's a grand boy!! Since finding Jeanette Foley lives close to me, I'm more than anxious to see her and have a long chat.

I'm sure a lot of you remember Lt. Bill Preston [H Co.] and Sue. I heard some time ago that Bill was killed in action in September. They were with the 508th in Florida and Georgia, then Bill was transferred to another outfit shortly after we reached North Carolina. Sue has one baby and was expecting another in December. I was so sorry to hear of Bill's death.[164]

Many of you have spoken of your dogs. I have something to brag of too, although as of yet I haven't *seen* the Farrell pup. Joe acquired a dog in England, and from all reports it's his constant shadow. He calls her "Shorty" and seemingly she's quite a super-gal. I've lost count of the jumps she has to her credit, but I know he lost no time in giving her the required number to make her a full-fledged "para-pup." I'm just praying that one day soon I'll be meeting Shorty and become acquainted all over again with that wonderful husband of mine.[165]

It was wonderful hearing from all of you, and I do hope the letters will speed up and soon be around again.

My best to all of you, Marion Mrs. Joseph F. Farrell

Picking up the thread from her friend Marion, Dotty Hamlin, wife of Chief Warrant Officer Arthur N. Hamlin [Norman], wrote next from Massachusetts. She included a news article featuring a picture of herself and her son David. The article is captioned: "Children who have not met their fathers' club."

Of the forty-eight Round Robin families, no less than twenty-two children qualified as members of the club.

Dotty Hamlin, Springfield, Massachusetts [RR 38]

January 9, 1945

Dear 508 Wives,

The Round Robin letters just reached me, and my household duties took a back seat once I started reading. I simply had to continue until I had read them all. Luckily, I live with my folks. Mother took David over while I read and reread. First of all, I want to express my deepest sympathy to all you girls for the loss of your brave husbands. Your letters certainly give us fortunate ones the courage to keep smiling.

Norman's last letter was dated Dec. 16th. He is well, and like all the others, thinks the trip back home can't come too soon. He told me about their big officers' party—Champagne predominated! A good time was had by all—but as he always adds, the parties are not complete without the wives.[166]

I too have a little son to brag about. He was born Jan. 24, 1944. His name is David. He has big dark eyes and light hair. He started walking alone at nine months, and that alone keeps me on the move continually, but I love it! David has been a great comfort to me. The pictures of your little off-spring are very sweet. If the day comes when we can all get together again—what a session that would be!!

Not long ago I got a pleasant surprise. A Major Lord phoned me from Washington, D.C. He had just returned from a special mission overseas. This Major is a paratrooper, and his son is a sergeant in the 508. After completing his mission in France, he went to England to look up his boy. He arrived too late—Sergeant Lord had already left for Holland.[167]

Norman gave Major Lord all the news possible concerning his son, and he was very grateful. He offered to call me up and relay any message to me after he'd arrived in the States. I was excited—it was comforting to speak to someone who had actually spoken to and seen Norman one and a half weeks before. My husband is still in Headquarters, but he has taken up glider riding. He mentions "trips" and that's all—I guess it's another of those military secrets.

You must all remember Capt. Droge [Service Company] and his wife and little son Dennis.[168] They now live in Columbus, Ga.

It certainly has been grand hearing from you girls. I hear from Virginia Johnson frequently. I'm sure she'll love getting all these letters. I plan on writing Marion Farrell next week. We shall spend our time talking about—you know what!

I pray the Lord that he continues giving strength and courage to our boys and to their loved ones back home. I'll be anxiously awaiting the next round of letters. Best of Wishes to All,

Sincerely, Dotty Hamlin

Dotty Hamlin passed the baton to her friend in New York, Dottie Delfs. Her husband, 2nd Lt. Hamilton Delfs, E Co., had the stupendous good fortune to have survived a streamer on a qualifying jump, a wound on D-Day, and capture by the Germans.

Dottie Delfs, Mt. Vernon, New York [RR 39]

January 10, 1945

Dear 508 Girls,

I certainly have enjoyed reading your letters, since I write to just three other wives and have often wished I had more news. How true we are all one big family. All the unhappy news I've received of the boys who are gone has hurt me deeply. I know you girls have the courage your husbands had and are carrying on the best you can.

Ham almost missed jumping on D-Day. On one of his practice jumps his chute was a streamer and the reserve opened just in time to break the fall. Two injured ankles and one knee was the result. After much persuasion, he went along on D-Day and was wounded by a sniper. The outfit couldn't assemble, so they had to pull out and leave the wounded behind. They gave all their ammunition to those who could fight and just stayed there, hoping. The Germans found them and fortunately took them to their general field hospital where they received medical care. When our boys came back for them, they were gone and so were listed as dead. Thank God, I never received the telegram. From then on, they traveled along with the Jerries from hospital to hospital, constantly under fire from our troops, and were in Cherbourg when the city was liberated. Lt. Tibbetts was with him all during that time and they had many anxious moments. Terry [RR 8], he will have many experiences to tell you and they will make your hair stand on end.

Both Lt. Tibbetts and Ham were flown back to a hospital in England. Ham's injuries were so severe he was sent back to the States, and on July 19 he walked in on me. I was weak for hours—just couldn't believe it, but he looked swell to me. He is now at England General Hospital [in Atlantic City, NJ], where he will be at least eight more months, and then will be discharged as he will never have full use of his left arm again.

A first of four operations were performed Friday. He was in a great deal of pain when I arrived. However, when I left, he was drinking beer, so I 'spect he was alright. We are so lucky. Thank God many times for it all.

I stopped in Philly to see Marion Farrell and had a grand visit. Bonnie is getting along fine. I spent the afternoon playing dolls and stuff. You all should hear her sing "Don't Fence Me In." It's priceless.

I think it's a splendid idea to enclose snapshots the next time around. I know so many girls by sight, but their names have slipped my mind.

> I hear from Dotty Scudder quite often, and her Bill was killed July 6th. We received a photograph of Billy, Jr. for Christmas. Ham and I just sat down with tears in our eyes, for Bill was our closest friend and Billy is the exact image of him. I have added Dottie's name, so Jean [Snee], please send this on to her. She has been fortunate in receiving a great deal of information about Bill's death. We miss Art Snee too, Jeanie, for we always remember our weekend together.
>
> Ham has had three thirty-day leaves and has gained forty pounds from not being able to exercise, but he looks grand in spite of everything. I keep busy taking care of him, especially cooking his favorite dishes.
>
> When the Regt. went overseas, I got my furniture out of storage and found a cute little apartment thirty minutes out of N.Y.C. It was a comfort to fix it up and take care of it. I was kept busy by taking a secretarial course which I loved—did I study! Three days after I finished, Ham came home, but I managed to work a month. I'll be going back soon, as Ham can come home weekends only. It seems so unpatriotic these days to be idle when there is so much to be done. Guess I can stand a little hard work when our boys are fighting night and day with no Sundays off.
>
> Jane Creary, your husband's last letter was the most beautiful I have ever read. He must have been a grand fellow.
>
> I shall send this Round Robin to Ham at the hospital for I know he is anxious for news of his Regiment. We have many happy memories of Camp Mackall, for which we are both grateful. Sure hope you all receive good news from this latest fighting. If at any time you are in N.Y., please look us up, we live in Westchester County.
>
> Best to you all, Dottie

The Round Robin next headed all the way south to Florida to reach Jean Snee, another recent war widow. Her husband, 2nd Lt. Arthur F. Snee, had enlisted as a private in February 1941, and was already commissioned by November. Serving with F Company, he was killed in action on June 6, 1944.[169] Jean's letter is another good example of how wives kept their chins up, regardless of circumstances. While Jean turned to other "508 girls" for comfort and companionship, she also developed a social life of her own, seeking meaning in artistic expression, and was proud of her professional life, where she believed she could make a difference for the better. Her description of Arthur's death is the only account we have located to date.

> [Letterhead: United States Naval Air Station, Public Works Department, Ft. Lauderdale, Florida]
>
> Jean Snee, Fort Lauderdale, Florida [RR 40]
>
> 20 January 1945
>
> Dear Girls,
>
> The Round Robin reached me last night and I can't begin to say how very pleased I am to be on the list. I was so excited I could hardly open the envelope. And now that it has come, I can hardly wait for it to come around again.
>
> First, I would like to extend my deep sympathy to the many of you that, like myself, have lost loved ones. I hope and pray that our ranks grow no larger. They always called us such good "troopers"; lets never let them down and break that faith.
>
> To begin, a little news of myself. I am living with my parents who moved here when Art came to Blanding to join the 508. My wire came June 27, saying Arthur was killed on June 6. Since then, I've been proud to learn he drowned while trying to rescue some of his men from a similar fate. I returned to D.C., my former home, in July for a few weeks to see Art's family and hold a Memorial Service in the church where we were married three years ago in August. I had the pleasure of spending a wonderful day in Philadelphia with Marion Farrell and Dottie Delfs. I still have my bracelet we spent so long selecting, and never wear it without recalling the day.
>
> When I returned to Fort Lauderdale, I obtained an appointment as a stenographer in the Public Works Department of the local Naval Air Station and began working there August 16. It is a good feeling to know I am in a small way contributing to the day when this war will be over. I've made some

very fine friends there and through them had introductions to some people in town I've wanted to know.

I've turned to music and painting to "find myself" again and have begun a fast-growing collection of records, classical and popular. After several evenings at the home of Norman Kennedy, a prominent artist, and his wife, talks with him have encouraged me to try my hand at watercolors again.[170] Five inactive years have taken their toll, but each watercolor has shown improvement, and I am about ready to show them to Norman for his criticism. If he believes I have sufficient talent, I want to change to oils as I feel this is the better medium for me.

My social life is mostly movies or evenings with friends from the station, sometimes just talking or playing records and occasionally a Saturday night cocktail party. I have had the pleasure of meeting some very lovely Mami Beach people and spend a Sunday afternoon there about once a month, swimming and sunning on the terrace and just relaxing with Mrs. Hooker's grand "old fashioned."

I find Jacksonville and Georgia addresses in the list that I didn't know and I hope that someday we can get together for a weekend of 508 chatter. I suppose it would be unpatriotic to suggest a trip these days because of gas rationing, but anyway I want to extend an invitation to you all to come and bask in Florida's sunshine with me. Just wire what train to meet.

Dottie Delfs asked me to send this on to Dottie Scudder. I am sure, Dottie, that you won't mind if I send it on via Vee Johnson in New Orleans. By the way, Vee, I'll try to answer your letter in the next few days, so don't think I've forgotten about you.

It has been wonderful hearing from you all, even though much of the news was sad. You have been the grandest people I've ever known, and our days with the boys in Carolina, Tennessee, and Florida will not be soon forgotten.

> I haven't any names to add to the address list, but I would like to make a suggestion. That is to keep amended and up to date the list which Bernie started of those missing and dead. I, for one, am trying to keep a history of 508 happenings, and need this information to make it complete. One name I can add is that of Lt. Hal Richards [A Co.] who is now a German Prisoner of War.
>
> Good luck to all of you, and I hope the 508 returns so many families will once more be together. Love, Jean

True to her word, Dottie Delfs forwarded the Round Robin on to Virginia "Vee" Johnson in New Orleans. Her husband, Capt. Kenneth L. Johnson (Service Co.), the regimental munitions officer, was wounded on D-Day, but went on to have a long military career, retiring as a Major General.[171] Attached to Virginia's letter was a silver *V* pin—standing for "Victory," as well as her name—along with a note: "This rightfully belongs to Ken, but as long as I have it, what do you say if we use it as our 508th Mascot?"

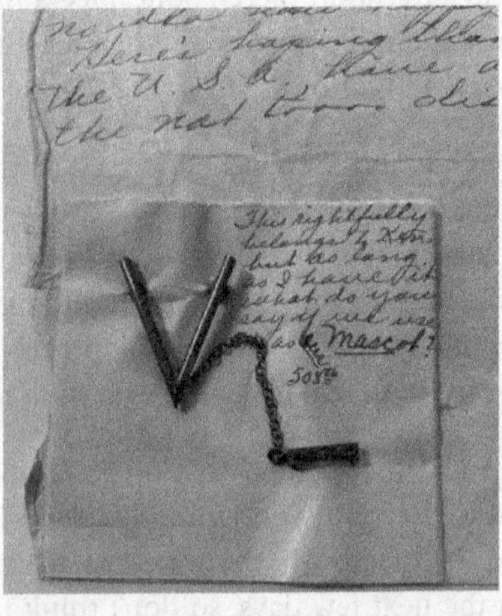

**Virginia Johnson's "V" pin attached to RR # 41. Gurwell Collection.**

Opening her letter for the first time, we were surprised and deeply touched to discover this memento, which had not been removed in seventy-five years. What clearer sign could there possibly be of the bonds between the band of sisters than the sharing of this gift, originally from her husband, as a symbol of luck and the mutual determination to keep the faith and *never give up the jump.*

Virginia Johnson, New Orleans, Louisiana [RR 41]

January 25, 1945

Greetings "troopers"—

The most exciting thing happened to me today. That's right! The "Round Robin" came my way! When I first heard about it through Harriett Peterson [RR 21] quite some time ago, I eagerly awaited it daily 'till finally I gave up. Then suddenly, out of a clear blue sky, it pops up very unexpectedly. Need I say thanks to Jean Snee! You see girls, never give up hope.

Before going any further, I would like for every one of you who have lost someone very near and dear to please accept my deepest sympathy in your bereavement. I never dreamed so many were gone. From all indications, you have all been wonderful and very brave "troopers." That's just the way they would have wanted it, so let's keep it that way, girls. I'm sure most of you have heard the old saying, "So stick to the fight when you're hardest hit—it's when things go wrong that you mustn't quit."

The pictures of Capt. Creary, Lt. Abbot, and Mathias will long live in my memory, to say nothing of the many others. It was very touching and almost unbelievable to read about them.

I also have much to be thankful for. Perhaps my Ken is just a lucky Swede. Let's hope his Swedish luck continues to hold. His last letter was dated Jan. 17. They can't come fast enough to suit me. It seems almost impossible to go on without the help of those letters, yet *He* gives us the strength and courage we so badly need when the time comes to see it through.

I have quite a number of correspondents, but there is always room for many more. Thought I had loads of news for you, but to be truthful, most of my information comes from the girls, Dot Hamlin, Marion Farrell, Harriett [Peterson], Mary Casteel and Jean Snee. Trying to get anything out of Ken is like pulling teeth. He won't talk. It wouldn't pay for this to be a woman's war.

This new year started off rather exciting for me in more ways than one. First of all, I attended the Sugar Bowl football game (Alabama vs Duke). Secondly, I met Mary Williams [RR 12] in all the mad rush. It was such a shock to both of us that when we finally realized who was who, we just sort of yelled and embraced each other. The game was underway, so we had to snap it up a bit. It was only after departure that I realized I hadn't given her my phone number or address, but with 70,000 fans (of all the Rebels I ever saw), it was impossible to locate her. Please forgive my carelessness, Mary. Seeing you was like seeing a bit of heaven—the 508th—you're the first 508er I've seen since I left N.C. over a year ago.

I too received some lovely table linen from No. 1. Also a beautiful Nottingham lace doily. Ken sent a box of souvenirs from France—a German belt buckle, coins, French perfume, hankies, and oodles of other things. Anytime any of you care to visit me, I assure you I shall insist upon showing you *all* of my cherished possessions. Seriously tho', anytime any of you visit N.O. and don't look me up, I promise you your visit shan't be complete. 'Member that girls!

Really girls, I am very envious of all of you who have had babies. I adore them. As Mary Casteel says, just wait till our husbands return, we'll show you. You bet we will, Mary!

All the snap shots of the babies were very sweet, and I enjoyed them immensely. Especially the one Bernie Shankey sent in [8.5 x 11 inches]. What's a matter Bernie, couldn't you spare a larger one! Ha! By golly, if I had something like that, I'd be proud to show her off too.

And now a little about my social life, which isn't any too interesting. I had been working steadily until recently when I became ill. My career is hair styling. Working conditions are so pleasant, and it's really amazing what one can create with a few strands of hair. I sometimes surprise myself. Ha! You girls should have seen me at the last tacky party. I was a very poor imitation of a paratrooper, but we really got our laughs.[172] O.K, who knows, someday I may be known as "Madam Johnson," the famous hairstylist. Am I being too optimistic, girls?

There's one other name I'd like to add to the address list, Jean Mendez. We correspond occasionally. Col. Mendez has been cited by Gen. Eisenhower, but I'll let Jean tell you all about his accomplishments. O.K. Jean?

I hate parting with all these wonderful letters, but all's fair in love and war. Besides I have the assurance that "Round Robin" will again be rolling my way soon—I hope.

My very best wishes to all of you. You've no idea how happy your letters have made me. Here's hoping that we may all have a very happy reunion in the not-too-distant future.

Much Love to all,

Sincerely, Virginia, Mrs. K.L. Johnson

Dorothy Scudder was another young mother whose baby belonged to the "children who have not met their fathers" club. Her husband, 2nd Lt. William S. Scudder, G Co., was killed in action in the battle for Hill 131, the 508th's last battle in Normandy. His company had come under enemy fire and retreated, but Scudder organized volunteers to return to the field under the cover of darkness to recover the dead and wounded. He was killed by sniper fire during the rescue and recovery, and posthumously received the Silver Star for exceptional bravery in action.[173]

Dorothy Scudder, Tulsa, Oklahoma [RR 42]

February 2, 1945

Dear Girls,

I can't begin to tell you how happy the Round Robin letter has made me. While I don't know a good many of you, I feel that we are old friends after reading your letters. To those you who have lost your husbands I extend my deepest sympathy. I know exactly how you feel girls, for my Bill lost his life July 3rd, and it isn't an easy fact to realize and understand. None of us will ever have an answer to "Why?" I'm sure you have asked yourself that question as many times as I.

Perhaps I have been more fortunate than some of you in learning details about what happened. Well—about six weeks ago a Lt. Jack Southall [G Company] spoke at a luncheon here and a friend of mine heard him. Since he was a paratrooper and had been in France, she took a long shot and asked him if he knew Bill. He said "Yes," that he had been with him when he lost his life. To make a long story short—I talked with him over the phone, and he gave me quite a bit of information. Lt. Southall was a replacement officer and had only been with Co. G a few days. They were near the town of La Haye-du-Puits, about eight miles from St. Lo, and the Germans were throwing in all they had. It was a terrific battle, and unfortunately, we lost several men—but the Germans lost more. Bill never knew what hit him, so if it had to be, I'm thankful for that. He is now in the Airborne Cemetery near St. Mere Eglise. Oh yes—Lt. Southall said Bill had a long goatee and mustache. Any of you who knew him will probably get a laugh out of that. I certainly did.

**2nd Lt William Scudder, KIA July 3, 1944 in Normandy. Dorothy and William Scudder, circa, Fall 1943, North Carolina. Photo courtesy of Dorothy's daughter, Lee Ann Gable Daugherty.**

Our "Little Bill" was born Feb. 7, 1944 and is practically one year old. He's really a corker. He has been saying "da da" to Bill's picture for two months. Guess I forgot to mention he's a black-eyed rascal and "looks exactly like his daddy" (seems to me I've heard that one before). Billy and I are in our own home here in Tulsa and are getting along quite well. My brother stays with us, so we don't have to be alone.

**William Blaine Scudder's first Christmas, 1944, age ten months. Picture provided by Dorothy Scudder in RR # 42. Gurwell Collection.**

> Gosh girls, you sure have some fine babies. Rosemary [Guillot, RR 28], I remember back in N.C. my husband wanted to bet with yours on whose baby would be born first. If they did bet, I guess we won, 'cause Gerry made his appearance the 24th and Billy the 7th.
>
> As to social life—that's practically nil. I go to a movie occasionally and have seen a couple of stage shows this season and that is all. If any of you have a chance to write, please do. I'd love to hear from you, so how about a letter, huh? Good luck to all of you and may this ol' war be over soon so every one of you can once again have a happy normal life.
>
> Sincerely, Dorothy Scudder
>
> P.S. I also received lovely linens, silver jewelry and baby things from Ireland. Aren't we lucky?

Fifteen days after Dorothy wrote this letter, the 508th was relieved from the front lines for the final time in the war. Is her closing remark a touch of sarcasm on the part of a young mother and recent war widow? A brave attempt to keep up her spirit? Or a genuine expression of gratitude for these mementos of her husband, sent from abroad before he was killed in action? We have often wondered about these questions. The answer we will never know, but her indominable spirit, and that of her sisters, the "508 paratrooper girls," is plain for all to see.

# CHAPTER XV

# ON STANDBY: RESCUE MISSION FOR ALLIED POWS

While the regiment was recovering from the rigors of the Ardennes Campaign back at Camp Sissonne, being in reserve also had a downside. Living with memories and ghosts, difficult at best for George, was all the harder at Sissonne, where his duties included corresponding with the wounded and processing the effects of the dead. A poignant case in point was the death of his aide and good friend Ellsworth Bartholomew, whom George mourned in the letter below, after coming across Bart's notebook while gathering his belongings. While censorship prohibited him from mentioning any names, George embedded clues in his letter to Jeane that revealed the identity of the friend he had lost.

> 5 March 1945 [Camp Sissonne, France]
>
> That old let-down in morale has taken place again. We just have too much time to dream of those we love while at Base Camp. So lonely and homesick that it is almost impossible to sit still. There, my Darling, lies the answer to gaps in letters. We try to neutralize those feelings with the one thing on hand—liquor. It just doesn't work.

A man that I knew and loved, used to keep notes for a book that he intended to write. He was the kind of person one very seldom finds. We lost him in Normandy. Found his notes today in our supply room. A mention of you caused me to remember just how clear-sighted he was. He spoke of us as a perfect couple. He remembered two things about you from meeting you for a few moments at Mackall and taking you down to the Officers Club. My Darling—he remembered what a sweet and gentle person you were, and the quiet dignity he could feel as you walked along beside him. Strange how much I have noticed those same things, and how I love them in a person.

***

When George finally received a well-deserved pass to leave the camp, it seemed to do nothing to relieve the "wound up" tension he felt.

10 March 1945 [Camp Sissonne]

Darling—this lonely husband of yours has just returned from a three-day pass in Brussels. A little time to relax and forget about the army. Sweetheart, the horrible let-down feeling that follows. Camp has never looked quite so dull and dreary and the war so far from won. This is by far the lowest ebb I have ever had. Homesick—and so are so many others.

The big city was very nice—people were pleasant and liquor was high. Managed to get very drunk one night of the three but that was all. Dates—no. Jeane—I just don't know what to do with myself when you aren't with me. Spent one whole afternoon taking a tour of the town. Ancient things, some of them dating back to the time of the Crusades and much later. Something for the eyes to see while the heart and soul are so far away.

It is great, this being an officer. You act a part day in and day out. No one gets to know just how low you feel or what you really think. The army game is a thankless thing—or am I just morbid? Could really get wound up tonight—think I shall stop before my feelings really break loose. In the end, the ultimate source of strength and courage, the glue that kept morale up at home and on the battlefield was faith in God, in country, and in good over evil.

This was certainly true of George, whose bedrock belief in God provided moral grounding even in these, the worst of times.

> 11 March 1945 [Camp Sissonne]
>
> I have an enviable faith; I know and see the good with the bad. Idealistic—yes—but this would be a very poor world without ideals, and even worse if everyone was not sure in his or her own heart that there is a God above. Something that I shall never forget—He has been close at times.

***

The extensive correspondence that kept George busy at Sissonne also included answering letters from the ill and wounded, who often feared they would not be returned to their home units after their release from the hospital. This was indeed real cause for fear, given that many regiments were seriously depleted, and units could be relocated at any time or place, leaving hospitalized soldiers stranded far from base. Men displaced from their units were not returned directly, but temporarily transferred to replacement depots—the dreaded "repple depples"—where they could be immediately reassigned to any unit that needed reinforcements. The following sample from the letters George received gives a sense of his duties and rapport with his men, and the desperation of many to return to their home outfits.

> From: Pfc. Robt. Gundlach
> [Ground Forces Reinforcement Pool]
>
> To: 1st Lt. Gurwell [Camp Sissonne]
>
> March 14, 1945
>
> Sir, I am writing a note asking for your help. I am at a replacement depot and can't get back to the outfit. Our officer said it may take a month or better for me to return. I want to get back, but quick! (I guess this depot is one of the slowest ways to return.) I'm only about seven or eight hours from your camp. If I could get permission or something, I could be back in no time. Another guy from the outfit with me, his name is Kessell [Pfc. George P. Kessell, B Co.], wants to get back as bad as I do. I hope you can do something for us. Say hello to the guys for me, and that I wish I was with them, and don't want to miss out on anything. Please Sir, try and get me back. Gundlach

We are pleased to report that Pfc. Gundlach returned to the 508th on March 31, 1945.[174] Pfc. Leo Willensky, who had been with the regiment since its inception at Fort Blanding, had a more difficult problem to solve. He had been wounded and wanted to go home. His family had lost his brother in combat, and his parents were not doing well. The possibility of losing not just one, but two or more sons in the service was an anguishing prospect for many families, and a moral and practical dilemma for the military that only worsened as the war dragged on.

> From: Pfc. Leo Willensky [242 Gen. Hosp.]
>
> To: Lt. George Gurwell [Camp Sissonne]
>
> March 12, 1945 [Postmarked 14 April 1945 ]
>
> I am feeling fine and getting along great. My foot is still in a cast from one end to the other, but that's not what I'm really trying to tell you about. I should be writing this letter to Chaplain Elder, but he's done so much for me I'm almost ashamed to come to him anymore. I guess you know what I'm getting at.
>
> Since my brother was killed, my folks haven't been getting along too well. In fact, Sir, it's a lot worse than I'd ever be able to tell you. I guess I could go to the Red Cross and try, but that's not the way I want it. I've given the Regiment the best I have in me. I never did ask for any favors till now. I'm not asking you now, I'm begging you Sir. I've got to get home. How about seeing what you can do for me. The Doctor told me if I got a chance to get home, he'd fix me up, so I could make the trip on crutches.
>
> Whatever turns out Sir—Please don't think I'm riding my brother's death so I can get home. Give my regards to Everyone and Best of Luck to you, just in case I don't get to see you before anything comes up. Yours truly, PFC Leo Willensky

According to the morning report, Pfc. Willensky left General Hospital 241 for home on June 12, 1945.

A letter of a different kind came from George's buddy and fellow officer, 1st Lt. Charles Yates, who broke his legs in several places during a catastrophic training jump on March 14, 1945, when a propeller fell off one of the planes and the crippled aircraft snagged some of the deployed chutes while men were in mid-jump. Lt Yeats was one of the lucky ones: seven troopers and four aircrew members were killed. While it was rumored that its only purpose was to entertain Marlene Dietrich, who was visiting Camp Sissonne at the time, replacements needed the training, and troopers who had last jumped in Holland needed a fresh jump to keep their jump pay intact.[175]

> From: Lt. Charles Yates [in hospital in England]
>
> To: George [Camp Sissonne]
>
> 4 June 1945
>
> Dear Georgie,
>
> Thanks for the nice letter. Sure, appreciate it and the thing you guys have done for me. I'm going to ask you to do something more for me too, Georgie. If and when they publish that Special Orders for the Purple Heart in Holland, will you send me a copy? If they give away the medals, could you send me one of those too?
>
> Here in England, it is normal. That is, raining like hell, as it has been for a month off and on. I'm at a different hospital now, waiting for a boat to take me back to the sunny shores of California.
>
> I see the kids up around Lakeview, Oregon, have new playthings: Jap balloons and such. Those incendiaries are liable to raise hell in the North Woods.[176] Well buddy, thanks again. Give Ripper a boot and steal Tracey's liquor for me [1st Lt. David J. Tracey, HqHq]. Incidentally, Davis was at this hospital [1st Lt. Donald A. Davis, demolitions]. They liked him, except he and I were always getting out of bed when we shouldn't. Broke my third cast the other day, so got a new one, the sixth.
> Yours, Charley

Another correspondent needing help was 2nd Lt. Clint Moss. The Mosses had shared a cottage with George and Jeane, and Clint's wife Helen had helped cook up the Round Robin with Jeane and other close-knit friends just before they all left Pinehurst. Plagued with kidney stones, Clint had been ill following the Holland campaign, and was now writing from the hospital to ask George for help in locating his belongings.

From: 2nd Lt. Clint Moss [in hospital in England]

To: George [Camp Sissonne]

March 17, 1945

Dear George,

Hope this finds you well and plentifully supplied with mellow champagne. I am in England, where I've been since January, enjoying the country between times when they're doctoring on me.

This morning I got a box of personal effects from the Quartermaster at APO 513. The stuff wasn't mine. Are you still handling personal effects, and do you know anything about this? The Quartermaster Officer here advised me to put in a claim for all my stuff, but I imagine it's all still back at Sissonne. Is it? I have two zippo lighters, a P51 fountain pen, and a P-38 pistol, which I'd hate to lose. If you come across them, could you hold them or send them to me?

Expect to get kicked out of here soon. March 21 completes 90 days of hospitalization for me and that's the limit. I should be moving back to the outfit.

I saw McNerney here—he went home [2nd Lt. Edward W. McNerney, Hq1, mortar forward observer, WIA 24 December 1944]. Schermerhorn is in the ward next door and doing ok [1st Lt. Roy A. Schermerhorn, E Co., WIA 4 July 1944 ]. Got any big news on your mind? Give my regards to the fellows and let me know something when you have time to write. Yours, Clint Moss

George's time as acting company commander came to an end when 1st Lt. Harold Feuerhelm was assigned to the position. The decision left George with disappointed hopes of a promotion and further burdened with additional administrative tasks.

27 March 45 [Camp Sissonne]

Darling—I have started a dozen letters this last week and completed not a one of them. So much has been going on that this husband of yours has been head over heels in work. It seems impossible we can be so darned busy in a so-called rest camp. That is good, because it keeps the mind busy, but it is hard on letter-writing. Usually, I am too tired by night to do anything but roll into bed.

This new Company Commander doesn't help matters any, since now every bit of paperwork goes through me—Gas, Supply, my own section [bazooka], Special Units Public Relations Officer, and general handy man just about covers my duties. 'Tis good though, because I love you so much that each hour without a lot of work is a misery.

It seems rather strange, but good to read about airborne landings and not be in them—a new and unusual position.[177] Our hopes and prayers go with those lads, though.

Except for the last two days, the weather has been lovely, warm with plenty of sunshine. There is an optimistic feeling in my heart for the first time. The war does look good. Can't be really happy though, until it has ended. Spring has so many wonders—new life, beauty—flowers, birds, everything has so much meaning. What a contrast to thoughts of war.

Back home, Jeane was rotating through hospital floors, specialty hospitals, and a variety of clinics that gave student nurses hands-on professional experience, including training focused on public health. Described below, her rotation at the public health V.D. clinic took place at a time venereal diseases had become a terrible problem in the States, as well as overseas.

March 28, 1945 [Portland, Oregon]

Sweetheart—how is our war-weary veteran? Can you begin to see the end? Guess it will never look that way until you see those orders for home. My heart and prayers are with you.

There is a teletype machine set up in Meir and Fredricks [a department store], where a news staff is broadcasting and posting reports about the war on the windows as they come in. Everyone stops all their business to pick them up. Everyone is concerned, and don't think they aren't. We look for the small

> details, anything that tells something about those we love. No one expects to see the war miraculously over in a day, either.
>
> Today I was at the V.D. Clinic—very interesting. A tremendous number of patients are put through. It's sad more of them can't realize what's being done for them. You should see your wife buzzing around like a bee, being kind to all the prostitutes with a smile. As for the young victory girls, I'd like to kick them in their britches, wring their necks, and find some of them decent homes.[178] The men with sense enough hang their heads and show you a lot of respect (or something). What a future, this public health work—great environment! Guess you have done quite enough in securing the world to put such things in perspective without worrying about the fate of mankind. Say Sweetie Pie, if you're still worrying about something to do post war (between kicking Jerries' teeth in)—how would you like to be a Social Worker and use some of that Psychology?

As the war dragged on, hope for its end and the chance to go home were in the minds and hearts of the men. Yet they faced another spring overseas. Easter was over and now, it too, was part of a year of holidays that had come and gone. In a small attempt at humor, Jeane mentioned that George must have had a wild Easter. An Easter with the wrong kind of Easter eggs—exploding ones! Those eggs you don't want to add to your Easter basket.

On April 4, 1945, the 508th Parachute Infantry Regiment was officially detached from the 82nd Airborne Division and moved to airfields near Chartres, France. Triggered in Washington, the verdict came from above "when the division strength was reduced to the TO&E (Table of Organization and Equipment) level, which authorized one glider regiment (the 325th) and two parachute regiments (the 504th and 505th)." [179] The separation was greeted with bitterness and dismay in the 508th, especially as it came with a new assignment, ironically dubbed "Operation Jubilant," which kept the regiment on forty-eight-hour standby jump notice.

"The plans were to send us to jump near POW camps to liberate prisoners before they were moved or killed," George told us in 2001. "We loaded and unloaded the planes three separate times, but that jump never came. On the plane, off the plane, three different times, and each time I had the awful feeling, *If we jump, I'm not coming home*. Patton got there first, so we never had to go in. I thank God that I never had to go near one of those camps. It wasn't that I was scared or that I wouldn't have jumped. I would have done my job, but I really don't believe I would have come back from that one."

As April 11 approached, George and Jeane's second wedding anniversary was much on their minds. Meanwhile, censorship prohibited the men from sending the news immediately that the regiment has been detached from the 82nd Airborne, so wives and others searching for "small details" that might revealed their loved ones' whereabouts were led astray by the news.

> 9 April 1945 [Chartres, France]
>
> A lovely Monday—have been taking a sun bath outside this here dusty old tent. Lovely Sweetheart, for just lying and dreaming of the most wonderful wife in the world. Was a little on the pink side by evening. There is plenty of time, but Darling—I can't seem to write.
>
> It is a strange world that we live in. So much loneliness, misery and devastation—and to what end. A better world—yes! What price this victory. Germany should be made to pay, but how? The effects of this war will be felt for many years to come.
>
> April 10, 1945 [Portland]
>
> Another day gone and what has it held for you? I can guess pretty well. There were pictures in the last *Life* magazine of airborne landings east of the Rhine—enough said. There have been quite a few paratroopers in Portland lately, some with campaign ribbons. Perhaps before long then, they can replace some men over there. What a big hope that is.
>
> Tomorrow, Sweetheart, will be our day. I have been unable to get anything to you, which breaks my heart. Just think, two years ago today, we were as busy as two little cranberry merchants trying to get ourselves all ready to be married. What a Day!
>
> Made a few home calls today with Mrs. Cooper, the school nurse. Went to one upstairs apartment where a twenty-four-year-old mother does a good job of caring for her shipyard-working husband and *eight* children (in seven years). Living with them for a while is a sister-in-law with *five*. The husband sleeps through the day, and what's more, they're

all clean and happy, if a bit messy. Zowie—what courage! It makes me a panty weight of a less hardy variety.

Just went through the defeating task of writing out checks for the bills and feel quite like the 100-year-old group—200 if there isn't word from you soon, and 599 if you aren't given the chance to be home soon. Darling, I love you.

11 April 1945 [Chartres]

Happy Anniversary, my Darling—two years ago today. I was the luckiest guy in the world. Jeane—a person couldn't ask for a better wife. You are everything that I have wanted. These two years have just added to my love. We have had difficult times and loneliness has not been easy—but there has always been a guiding light. Jeane—you are that guiding star. How can mere words tell you how many times you have brought me through tough spots or how many dull, dark hours you have brightened up for me. How wonderful our time together has been, Jeane—words just aren't adequate.

There are so many lovely memories. I am sitting under an apple tree, looking at the blossoms and remembering. In the tree next to me two pigeons just landed, and about 75 yards in front of me a farmer is running a plough, his young son riding and very much interested in everything. Overhead, guess what? C-47s—forcibly reminding me a war is still on. It is such a pleasant picture—green fields, fresh green leaves on all the trees, and in the distant valley a little village with trees full of white blossoms all around. The sun is sinking on another day away from you, my Darling—and yet so close.

Those beautiful days at Pinehurst come back, giving me warm feelings inside. Those days were heaven. Remember our leave in November [1943] with Margarite and Fred? Then the memories hurt a little. My having to send you home when we moved out. Since then, a parade of places and events, a few friends, and loneliness I had never known before. So, my Adorable One—I am ready to come home to you and that son of ours. So very, very ready.

***

On April 12, 1945, President Franklin Delano Roosevelt died of a cerebral hemorrhage at Warm Springs, Georgia. Vice President Harry S. Truman became commander in chief, raising questions about how the change would affect the war, and any consequences it would have on the troops.

> 14 April 1945 [Chartres]
>
> Today has been another hot spring day. Tried to continue my tan—but something always comes up to keep me moving.
>
> The President's death left us very downcast. It is such a crucial time to lose such a grand statesman. Our nation really suffered a tremendous blow yesterday. Much hard fighting and a great deal of common sense will be needed before peace is won. We have lost too many to lose the peace.

Planning and preparing for their husbands' homecoming helped the band of sisters keep their chins and morale up. Putting aside favorite canned foods, gathering household items, and storing away pretty outfits were all part of the process. We had to laugh when Jeane recalled the horrible dinners she had prepared in North Carolina. The one memory the Gurwell family would always agree on was that Jeane came up with some very "creative" meals.

> April 17, 1945 [Portland]
>
> How are you tonight? The old letter you started in Germany and finished April 4 came through today. A lovely letter Darling—except for the patrol escapade and the sub-machine gun without ammunition. That, Sweetheart, gives me chills—please, oh please, remember to always watch yourself.
>
> Today was a slack day, found a few cans of things to store away for your home coming. Shrimp, crab, baby lima beans—some new and different recipes, which I hope by some miracle will enable me to be able to concoct in a jiffy and without practice??? Still shudder, Darling, thinking of the horrible dinners you had to put up with when we were in the South. Same old things, without imagination or butter—but they were wonderful times, weren't they? There may be less butter in the country now, but by golly, we'll manage to have it for you anyway.

23 April 1945 [Chartres]

Hello Sweetheart—received three good letters from you today—one from April 9, one from the 10th and the last one written on our Anniversary. An old V-mail from Babe also came wondering in. Pretty good for an old, broken-down correspondent like myself.

Jeane—news has been on the rare side. We aren't working very hard but there always seems to be something to do. News about the war is very good. Keep your fingers crossed Punkin, and maybe this mess won't last much longer. Visited Paris again yesterday for a few hours—and believe it or not, I ran into an officer from home, one I hadn't seen before. We had quite a chat. Am trying to visit Dave Scoggins—have finally located him, and he isn't far away.

Tired, not physically—but mentally. The regiment just pulled another of those fast deals. A Company Commander that is just some new 1st Lieutenant. He doesn't rank Ripper or me and has been in the outfit since Normandy.[180] For two cents I would transfer. A hell of a lot of good this regiment does for you. This last move really hurts, and it isn't much of an incentive to do your job. My Darling, sometimes I am actually ashamed for being just a 1st Lieutenant—for all of the thanks anyone has received here, we might just as well have dug ditches all this time.

Hurt Sweetheart—this last blow left a sting. I hope that I live through everything to tell the colonel man to man. Sorry Sweetheart—it isn't often I get really burned up. It wouldn't be so bad, but this has happened so many times to those who have raised this regiment from a pup. Old officers who deserve the breaks and never get them. West Point must really be some school. It is hard to believe that so many officers haven't been there, because no one else knows anything but West Pointers. A new low-level tonight—the depths. Really though, Sweetheart, it won't last—I promise.[181]

26 April 1945 [Chartres]

A light warm rain today—reminding me so very much of the rains there at home. Well Darling—there is good news tonight. I am going on a seven-day rest tomorrow down into Southern France. Gee, Punkin, I am going to rest, swim, and generally take life easy. Seven days to forget the army. I won't forget to get you something for your bracelet. It might not be much because I am short of money. Don't worry though—there is always enough to pull me through. Trips to Paris are expensive—so Paris has seen the last of me. There is one serious trouble with this leave though—no mail for seven days. Don't know how I will get by. Your letters are such a help to this tired morale.

April 26, 1945 [Portland]

You're really on record what with three V-mails coming through today—just like Christmas, with snow of apple blossoms blowing across the road.

"Ricky" is fast asleep—he's going to sleep without a fuss, pretty much. Won't you be surprised to come home and be able to slap your son in bed without a tussle? (Let's hope you will!!!) Do you happen to know the technique that pediatricians advise for bed wetting at night? Well, among other things, the father must wake them and trot them off to the bathroom. So, prepare yourself Punkin—you might get home in time to try it on your grandchildren, who knows? It is probably possible that the war could be over by then.

Our son climbs all over Hell's half acres these days. He's learned to climb off things backwards (that wasn't such a smart thing to help him with) and consequently attempts anything. I put him on the bed turned around, and yes, our little toad simply climbed down, talking to himself a mile a minute. At not quite one year old—how do you like that?

28 April 1945 [The Riviera, France]

Give you three guesses where this husband of yours is. All right, my Beloved—the Riviera no less. An *Alice in Wonderland* place. Hot sunny days—wonderful beds with mattresses and sheets!!! Boating, swimming, bicycles, dances, bars, and the Glenn Miller Band in person. Could any fool ask for more? Walked out to the beach last night with a warm balmy breeze and a full moon—music coming faintly from the hotel, and I just couldn't take it. Wanted you here with my whole heart and soul.

How are things at the hospital and how is that son of ours, Sweetheart? I want so to see him before he is a year old, but it really doesn't look like it will turn out that way. Explain it isn't his Dad's fault—but maybe by his second birthday.

George's letters from May 1945 were written on 508th Parachute Infantry Officers' Club letterhead featuring silver jump wings and paratroopers descending from C-47s.

3 May 1945 [The Riviera]

Hello, my Darling—this leave is almost over. Seven days on the Riviera, and only drunk one night. No dates, no dances, but lots of loafing around. Went on a tour a couple of days, and oh yes—Perfume. I have seven bottles, one for each day in the week. They come in little aluminum bottles to prevent breaking, and you don't have to pay for the fancy bottle. Didn't have much money and didn't need it. Some Chanel #5, Christmas Eve, and various others that caught my fancy. Sweetheart—I hope you like them. Will get them off tomorrow.

Last night I was invited to a party—and above all things, I met an honest-to-goodness Princess. A very entertaining person. Thirty-seven though, and the rest of the women were about the same. Got myself stinkin from drinkin—so walked out about 11:00, while I could still walk. You should have seen the waiters and everyone else bow and swoop. Don't I meet some of the darnedest people! I had that folder with the pictures, and she thought that son of ours was quite something. Her own son is about ten. You would have enjoyed talking to her. Quite a name—I can't begin to spell it. Just called her "Shoo-Shoo," like everyone else.[182]

**George (third from left) sitting next to the "Princess of Ghosts" while on leave in the French Riveira, May 1945. Reverse: "To George. With all my Love and best wishes from the Princess of 'Ghosts' [--- Alphon] de France. If you look a little stiff it's only because you are so homesick." The other individuals have not been identified. May 1945. Gurwell Collection.**

The war news is really good. Maybe, my Adorable One, this will be over soon. I hope and pray anyway.

[letter continued, 4 May 1945]

Hello again my Darling—fell asleep last night, just couldn't hold my eyes open. Getting to be a softie. Do you suppose we might soon have the chance to be together again? War news looks so darned good. There are so many possible uses for us. I only hope that we get to the States before long—though they might keep us here for quite a while. No one knows and couldn't even guess.

* * *

It was official! On May 8, 1945 Victory in Europe Day was no longer a dream but a reality. A doubly good day for George and Jeane, V-E Day was also their son's first birthday.

8 May 1945 [Chartres]

Hello, my Adorable One—just think—today we received the news that the war is over for sure. And our son's first birthday too! What a day to celebrate. Jeane, I have been walking around all day light-headed. It doesn't seem possible that war can actually be over here in Europe, yet the headlines are right here in front of me. It has an unusual feeling. What and how do you feel, my Darling? No cause for wondering and worrying for a while. It is so strange not to think in terms of flak, shells, and guns.

May 9, 1945 [Portland, Oregon]

Sweetheart—can you find it within your heart to forgive the lapse in my letters? There is so much to do, and I'm always so tired. Never get to bed, never get out, never seem to accomplish anything important, and it seems they will never let you come home. Sometimes it seems I'll never be untired again. Such gloom—aren't you ashamed of me? Maybe I should go out and eat worms, suppose? Anyway, I know a little tiny bit of what you've felt—it helps to understand.

Maybe there is some let down with V-E Day having been declared, but I can't feel much until you're back, or until it's all over. Thankful though beyond words that this much is past and you're safe for a while. Yes, "Ricky" was one year old on V-E Day. He's such a little live wire, always so curious, into everything, and quite a little handful.

Oh Darling—what's this talk about transferring? Let's hope *that* brainstorm is past. I know it's tough, Sweetheart, to put up with the hypocritical side of the Army—but I knew you *meant* it when you said you wanted to come home, and *that* little trick would certainly speed it up, wouldn't it? But then, we both know that your love is with the 508th.

Can't you tell us what you *think* will happen to you now? Remember one thing—when the time comes (if it does) when you come sailing in—*Don't Surprise us*—I just can't take it Sweetheart, not now. Whenever it will be, I've got to quit and rest some first. Goodnight, Sweetheart.

10 May 1945 [Chartres]

The last two days have been rather hectic. Managed to get on the stinko side the night before last. Had to do a little celebrating. Last night I was on M.P. duty in town keeping a weathered

> eye on the second day of celebrating. A very busy night and didn't get to bed until the wee hours of the morning. It is still difficult to realize that the war is over in Europe. Pinch me Darling—so I will know it isn't all a dream.
>
> No one knows a thing about what is in store—what we will do, when, where, or how. Everyone expects to be the first one home, and all are waiting with anxiety for the famous point plan to be put out.[183] There I have no idea how my chances are. If the chance comes though, Jeane—I am getting out. Very soon now, I will have been in three years and overseas a year and a half. There isn't the least desire in me to travel anymore. I have just one place in this world, and that is with you. If the South Pacific is in the stars, I will go, but protesting inside. Hard to believe, but this husband of yours has managed to keep his skin through half the war. Many times, I wouldn't have given much for my chances.
>
> Jeane—just think, there is a good chance that I will actually see that son of ours before his next birthday. There is suddenly so much more to look forward to.
>
> 19 May 1945 [Chartres]
>
> How is the most wonderful wife in this old world tonight? I am spending a quiet Saturday night here in camp. Didn't have a chance to see Dave Scoggins. The rain didn't hold off long enough. Maybe next weekend. These last few days have brought the first real storms for about two months, but really made up for it. We had a river running through our tent and the whole camp is a sea of mud.

While the end of the war in Europe left George feeling buoyant and a little strange at the prospect of actually soon returning home, his words of caution rang true: there were many uses yet for the 508th, and no one knew a thing about what was in store—what they would do, when, where, or how.

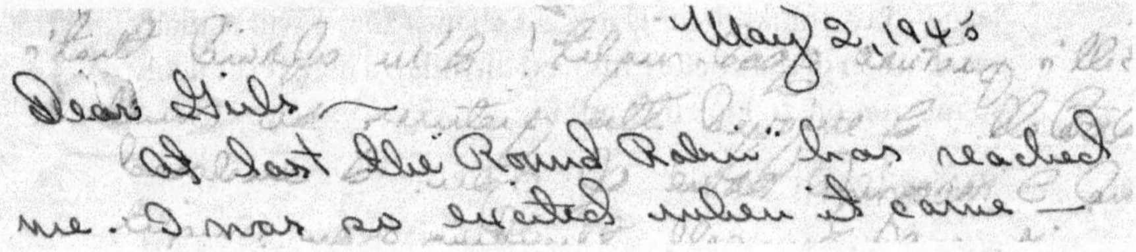
May 2, 1940
Dear Girls
At last the "Round Robin" has reached me. I was as excited when it came —

## CHAPTER XVI

# A MOMENTOUS AFFAIR, ROUND ROBIN LETTERS 43–50

As the 508th ended its mission on the German front in early 1945, the last correspondents in the Round Robin were adding their letters and passing the collection along. By the time the package reached Alice Lindquist, wife of Col. Roy E. Lindquist, the regiment was positioned in the area of Hürtgen-Schmidt, readying to assault Hill 400 and clear the area west of the Roer River. Unbeknownst to Alice, the last major engagement of her husband's regiment, a successful night attack, took place on February 10, the very day she contributed to the Round Robin.

Alice Lindquist, Pittsfield, Maine [RR 43]

February 10, 1945

Dear Wives of the 508,

Was more than surprised to receive the Round Robin as I had no inkling that such a thing was going on. It is a fine idea. I have to admit that the first thing I did was to have a good cry—after that was over, I thoroughly enjoyed all your letters.

I can't help thinking what a lot has happened since these letters were first started. It has certainly been a year of anxiety for all of us; let's hope the worst is over, though I don't dare be too optimistic.

We are really having a winter up here in Maine this year—much more severe than last. We are very comfortable, however, and of course the boys love it. They have been in the best of health, which is always something to be thankful for. Roy Jr. broke his arm a month ago at school, but has the cast off now and he is doing fine.

I have no trouble keeping busy—taking care of the house and the boys, doing a little Red Cross work, and I seem to find myself on every drive that comes along—War Bonds, Red Cross, etc. Some young couples who live near me very thoughtfully include me in their parties and good times, so I don't lack for social life.

I hear from Col. Lindquist quite frequently. He is certainly proud of the regiment and has told me many, many times what a wonderful job all the Officers and men have done. He says, "They did just as I knew they would."

The pictures of your babies are adorable—and so many of them! Hope we can keep this going and I shall be looking forward to receiving it again.

My very best to all, Alice Lindquist.

Alice sent the letter to Jean Mendez, the wife of Lt. Col. Louis Mendez, the commanding officer of 3rd Battalion and one of the most beloved leaders in the 508th. Amazingly, he managed to survive the war without a scratch.

Jean Mendez [Bayonne, New Jersey] [RR 44]

February 15, 1945

Dear Girls—

It was more than delightful to receive all your letters—I enjoyed reading each one so much! I would like to extend my sincerest sympathy to you who have lost your husbands. Your letters displayed so much courage and fine spirit. May you all find the happiness you so richly deserve.

Congratulations to you who have had new babies! The pictures are all darling. Of course, my favorite subject is "babies," and I am so thankful for the three I have. Pamela Clare was three in November, Judith was two in January, and Louis III is seven months old today.

**Jean and Louis Mendez III, age three months, 1944. Picture included in RR #44. Gurwell Collection.**

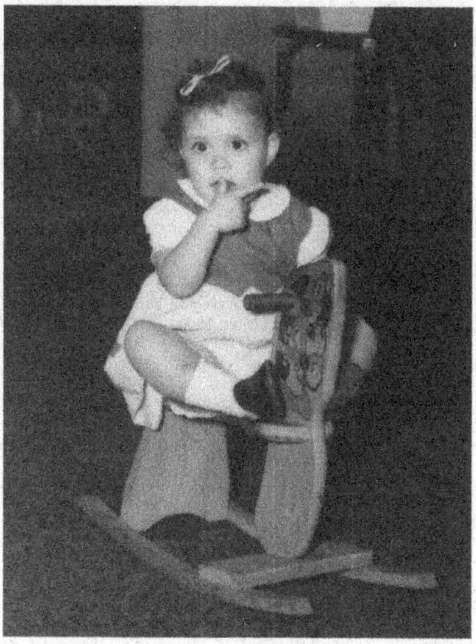

**Judith Mendez, age two, 1944. Picture included in RR # 44. Gurwell Collection.**

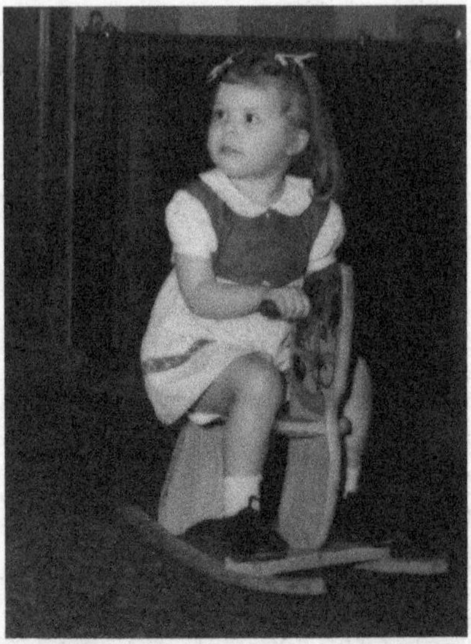

**Pamela Clair Mendez, age three circa 1944.
Picture included in RR# 44. Gurwell Collection.**

We almost lost our son. He underwent a major operation when he was a month old for the removal of a stomach obstruction—you gals who are nurses will recognize pyloric stenosis—and he was hovering with the angels for about six weeks. In the enclosed picture, taken at three months old, he still shows traces of his illness. But you should see him now! He weighs twenty-one pounds and is twenty-seven and a half inches tall!

During October and November, I took two trips to Washington, D.C. to visit one of Louis' men—Sgt. John Rooney, I Company, who lost a leg in Normandy. He was a patient at Walter Reed and was in the bed next to a boy from my hometown. Even under the circumstances, it was a thrill to talk to one who had been with Louis a short time before. Rooney now has his new leg and is doing beautifully.

Last month I received a surprise visit from another of Louis' men—Corporal Jimmy Murphy, H Company. He was fortunate enough to be one of two men from the Battalion to be sent home on furlough. He spent the whole day talking "508"—it was really wonderful. Our men now have two Presidential

Citations and the Combat Infantryman's Badge. Louis was awarded the Distinguished Service Cross for his work in Normandy; and a few months ago, the War Department released a story to our local newspapers concerning Louis and his "Nazi-chasers" and describing some of the battles Third Battalion fought in Holland. Louis certainly has been blessed. He writes that he is in excellent health and has never received a scratch. Thank God!

I have a feeling that we shall see our men soon. They have certainly earned "thirty days"! [A misconception that a unit would receive a thirty-day furlough after fighting three campaigns.] Goodbye for now, gals. The best of everything to all of you! Sincerely, Jean Mendez

Jean sent the batch of letters from northeastern New Jersey back to Helen Moss, who had written the initial Round Robin letter. They arrived at her door in Richmond, Virginia over a year after the venture first kicked off. The Round Robin had come full circle, becoming a great morale booster that had kept the band of sisters updated and close at heart. Yet the circle would be widened still: due to the letters' somewhat irregular itinerary, some intended recipients had not been "kept in the loop," and four more "508th Paratrooper Girls" needed to receive the package before it began a new round. Helen added her second letter with copious instructions on how to forward it, then sent it on its way.

Helen Moss [Richmond, Virginia; 2nd letter] [RR 45]

March 19, 1945

Dear Gals,

At long last the letters came my way and I had more pleasure reading them than I've had in a month of Sundays. Some are masterpieces. I treasure each and every thought. It's been said over and over again, but I want to express also that those who have lost husbands have my deepest sympathy. I pray that your future life will be a fuller one, and that though you have lost in one way, you'll have gained in another—strength and faith. Jane [Creary], you should be mighty proud of Hal [killed in action on June 7]; I know I am, and I'm proud to consider myself and Clint a friend of his.

I want to ask a favor of all of you. As soon as you receive this Round Robin for the second time, please take your letter out and send it to me. I plan to have them printed and bound in book form for myself, if you don't mind. I really think they're all worth keeping—for the human-interest side, if for nothing else—but personally, they are very dear to me, and I want to keep them in a durable form. If any of you would like a copy, I'll find out the price once I get mine done, and have the same done for you. I know Clint would like to see them, and I want Nancy (my baby) to read them in the future. Through them, she'll learn lessons in faith, bravery, and strength that she'll never learn otherwise in a million years. So please do that for me. Beth, when you send me yours—send mine too—the first letter I wrote—I'm leaving it in for the four [last recipients of the first round].

Now to my news. Clint is in a hospital in England, and he gets no news; I have to get it from the girls I correspond with—and believe you me, their news is large and keeps me pretty well posted. Harriett Peterson writes Mel is in Germany and has been to a nearby hospital (in France) to see Charlie Krebs (those of you who were first with the outfit will remember Captain Krebs, adjutant at the time of activation). He was getting along fine and talking up a storm as usual, so he must not have been seriously injured. As to further notices of death, I understand Garry [RR 49], Mitchell, and DeWeese were lost in Normandy. [Helen is mistaken; all three were killed in action in Holland].[184] I want to tell you Mrs. Garry, how sorry I am, and Clint feels the same, as he wrote in a letter.

Clint was taken with kidney trouble in Belgium and sent to a hospital. From Paris he was flown to England. I received a letter today and he says his three months of hospitalization expire March 21, and then I don't know what happens (except his jump pay may stop). Who knows, maybe they'll send him home. They gave him over 150 sulphur pills and that didn't work, then they gave him penicillin shots and that didn't work. Then they decided to try a different kind of morphine, and they're on that now. He has some infection, and they can't find out what causes it or why, but it is not serious—so Clint says. I truly hope he can come home to a specialist, or something good happens so I can know the score. Maybe when I find out you all will hear via the grapevine.

The other day, I was thrilled to death by a call from Clinton, Iowa, from a Capt. Faulkner who said he'd been in the hospital with Clint for two months, and Clint had asked him to call me and give me his love. It was really a thrill to hear almost directly.

Enclosed is a picture of myself and Nancy—not so good, but the only one handy. [Used with RR 1] Also enclosed is an Associated Press article by Clint—didn't know of it til it was published—and an article by Mark C. Watson (*Baltimore Sun*) sent by Doris Mathias. It was indeed a surprise. That was when Clint was public relations officer in Holland.

I'd better close now because I'm running on too much. Please try to keep this letter moving so we'll get it quicker. I'm typing all the names we have in geographical order, and we'll keep it just that way now and add no more. My name is at the top and the four names we skipped are at the bottom. Keep it rolling! Love, Helen (Mrs. R.C. Moss)

P.S. I've also written in changes of address. If any of you have any to change, do so. Nancy Graham—send your copy to Beth Pollom—name under mine—and then we'll have it straight again.

P.P.S. Had to add this—Clint sent me quite a few things like the rest of you received, but among them was some French Chantilly lace (10 yds. and it's impossible to get anywhere now). I had a white satin gown made (trimmed in lace) and a chiffon negligee (white, trimmed in lace), and Ooh la la, I'm waiting for his return to use it.

I should have just written a letter of postscripts and maybe I'd have done better. I thoroughly neglected to tell you about the thing that's keeping me most alive. I'm teaching two classes, ballet and denishawn [modern dance], taking class one night, and also doing some local concert work. It really keeps me moving, along with volunteer YWCA, church, bridge, the baby. If it weren't for dancing, life would be too, too dull without Clint. Anyone interested in taking a class? Ha! I have students [aged] 29–35 keeping trim and in shape for their hubbies overseas. H.

Naomi Gillespi, the first of the remaining four Round Robin correspondents, was married to 2nd Lt. Charles T. Gillespie, an initial cadre member (trainer and organizer) of I Company. Unlike Jane Creary, who hoped against hope that the news of her husband's death had been mistaken, Naomi was happy to report good news, as she wrote below.

Naomi Gillespie [Meridian, Mississippi] [RR 46]

March 25, 1945

Hi Girls,

Gee, was I excited and, I must admit, a little mystified when I received a large envelope in the mail yesterday morn. I couldn't imagine what could be in it. Was I delighted when I opened it to find letters from all you girls!

To you who have lost your loved ones goes my deepest sympathy—you are as brave as your husbands, and I admire you immensely. I noticed a Gillespie among the names in the "killed in action" list on the back of Bernie Shankey's letter. I'm happy to report it is not my Joe. There were two Gillespies in the 508th. [1st Lt. Fred E. Gillespie was killed in action, June 6, 1944]. My last letter from Joe was dated March 9. He is fine and was in France at the time, planning a trip to Reims. Yesterday, March 24, our boys made another invasion. Oh, I pray to God our casualties are few and this will be the last one. [Naomi is mistaken; the 508th did not participate in Operation Varsity, the jump across the Rhine River into Germany].

Enclosed is a picture of our pride and joy, Kathleen, taken on her first birthday, March 11. That *gorgeous creature* with her is me! If you look closely, you will see the candles on the cake. She is a darling and I don't know how I would ever have gotten through these 15 months without her. Like so many of you have already said [about your children], she keeps me plenty busy and from worrying so much about my husband.

**Naomi and Mary Kathleen Gillespie, one year old.
Picture in RR #46. Gurwell Collection.**

Maybe you have heard, but I'll pass it on just in case—Lt. Tomlinson is not with the 508th anymore, but is a Company Commander in the 513th Parachute Infantry. Sis (his wife) and I call each other every month. She paid a visit in Jan. with their little boy, Lynn C. Jr. He is the cutest little fellow. Of course, you know what she and I talked about mostly!

Say girls, if any of you are ever down this way, please come to see me or call. I would be delighted to see you and talk 508!
Love, Naomi, Mrs. C.T. Gillespie

While news from the front was encouraging, tension was still high within the regiment and for families back home. Amid soaring hope that the war would soon be over, the last of the Round Robin correspondents struck a note of nostalgia, as they returned in thought to the times and places that forged their bonds. Reba Holmes wrote of her husband, Lt. Col. Otho E. Holmes, CO Second Battalion after Normandy.

Reba Holmes, Wilmington, Ohio [RR 47]

April 5, 1945

Dear Friends—

It seems easy to write "Dear Friends" because your grand letters prove just that. When the Round-Robin was delivered, I did a good month of crying all in one day.

Many times, I've wondered which way I would turn if I were to receive a telegram from the War Department. After reading the wonderful letters from you girls who did receive those telegrams, I know life can go on—somehow! There's so little else I can say that hasn't already been expressed.

As I read each letter, once more I was in Pinehurst, and on Garren Hill (where Dot Driggers and I lived). My, how we griped, but I'd give anything to be back again.

The summer I was at Pinehurst our son was expected, and I absolutely cared nothing about seeing people or making friends. I've been sorry ever since, and these letters made me more so. As I write this letter, our boys may or may not be in combat across the Rhine—I've heard no news and can add none.

I'll attach a clipping about that husband of mine. Perhaps from it some of you might remember me; also, a snap of our son, Roderick, whom his daddy saw only a few hours when I flew to New York with him, way back in December 1943. Roderick was three weeks old.

**Roderick Holmes, sixteen months,**
**Picture included in RR #47. Gurwell Collection.**

Thanks to Mary Casteel for all her information and to Jeanne Thomas for telling me of Ott's Silver Star. I enjoyed every picture and clipping. Rosemary Guillot, I've often remembered our chat together in the club one afternoon—have you? Perhaps someday we could have a reunion—wouldn't it be grand? Sincerely, Reba Holmes

Censorship often made it hard to keep up with all the war news. A case in point is Nancy Graham, who had no idea that the 508th had been detached from the 82nd Airborne as of April 4, 1945 and was being held in France on standby. With news that the 82nd had gone back to the front, she assumed that the 508th had gone too, but her husband Capt. Chester Graham, Hq2, was with the 508th in Camp Sissonne.

Nancy Graham, Piedmont, California [RR 48]

April 19, 1945

Dear Girls,

It has been so good to read all your letters that I completely forgot to listen to the nine o'clock news, and even postponed writing my daily epistle to Chet—however, I just did that, and now hasten to add my bit and get this to Mrs. Garry in Florida. Mrs. Garry, Sr. phoned me that she had just received these, and that her daughter-in-law had returned to Florida. As she is in San Francisco right across the bay from Piedmont, it seemed better to have me write before sending it back to the East Coast.

Some of the news was so shocking and saddening as I hadn't heard about some of our boys. I have thought so many times of you who have suffered the loss of your dearest one. I can only add my inadequate words that you have been much in my thoughts.

We saw our boys didn't go in on the 24th [in Operation Varsity, the airborne component of the assault across the Rhine, March 24, 1945]; but did go in some time later. Today, I had a letter written in April in France, but I did hear in a list of divisions at the front that the 17th, 82nd and 101st were in. The news now is so marvelous, and my hopes are higher than ever that it won't be long now. [The 82nd had been trucked 250 miles north to move toward the Elbe River, and the 101st went to Bavaria in southern Germany, while the 508th was on standby in France].

A good friend, Louise Hatch, and I compare notes constantly as her Jim is in the 101st, and after being all over [the men] finally got together in Belgium. It is so good to know and be able to talk to fellow paratrooper wives. Every time I see a paratrooper on the street, I practically knock him down I'm so glad to see him. One day I actually raced into one from the 508 who knew Chet. He hadn't seen him in seven months, as he was wounded in Normandy, but that sounded recent to me. I hear from Leeta Berry often—some of you remember her, I'm sure. Maj. Berry is now in the 505th. Leeta has a little girl.

As to my life—I have no trouble keeping busy, what with our seven-month-old Vicki. I guess she's the youngest of our 508 babies! Vicki and I live with my Mother and Father. I don't know what I'd do without them and feel so fortunate.

**Nancy and Victoria Graham, March 1945.**
**Picture included in RR #48. Gurwell Collection.**

Chet has sent several boxes, the latest containing wonderful French perfume, a German helmet, knife, and various other things, including a pair of wooden shoes for Vicki.

Taking care of Vicki and helping around home take most of my time, but I have done Red Cross work and am doing Grey Lady work at the Oakland Naval Hospital.[185] There are many of us at home, and we have a monthly bridge club, go to movies and such! Well, this San Francisco area is a hub and with the coming [peace] conference, let us hope a lasting peace is built—it has to be.

I'll be anxiously awaiting the letters again—very best wishes to all of you. Sincerely,

Nancy Graham

We interrupt the progress of the Round Robin to insert a personal letter by Jeane's good friend, Barbara Martin. An earlier Round Robin correspondent [RR 7], Barbara wrote a private letter to Jeane in April 1945, just a few days after Nancy Graham sent the Round Robin along. Like the rest of the band of sisters at this point, Barbara knew all too well that "safe" was a relative term, and death could strike at any time and place. Holding her breath as the end of the war approached, she sent all the news she had been able to glean about the husbands of her friends. As George had commented, one by one the men he had trained and fought with were leaving the 508th; Barbara's husband, Captain Harold M. Martin of F Company, first wounded in France, had been wounded again in Belgium.

April 23, 1945

From: Barbara Martin, Robinson, Illinois

To: Jeane Gurwell [Portland, Oregon]

Dear Jeane,

Don't faint! It's really me! I've long been trying to get your Christmas card answered, and my persistence has finally paid off....

Med [Harold M.] is still with the 508th. Was in the Holland fray and didn't get a scratch. Then in the "Battle of the Belgian

Bulge," when they were back off the front lines, there was an explosion in the Company CP. He was the least hurt of anyone but was in the hospital three weeks with a couple pieces of metal in the side of his head. Anyway, it was only slight. He wasn't bed-ridden, but it did save him from some fierce fighting. By the time he got back with the outfit, they were back in France. So, he's been a very lucky boy. Oh, yes, he got his captaincy in October.

Don't know if you've kept in touch with many of the other gals or not. Terry, Beth and Helen are my only "steadies." Deane Tibbetts got shrapnel in his jaw in Holland and now one side of his face is temporarily paralyzed so he's on non-combat status. Winner Pollom has something wrong with his back, so he likewise is out of action. Clint Moss has kidney stones, but the infection has cleared up so he may rejoin the outfit. Do you remember Pauline Paddock at the hotel? Her hubby was a Lt. Col. in the 17th [John W. Paddock, 155th AAAB, Airborne Anti-Aircraft Battalion]. She had a baby girl in Jan. and told me that Judith Flicker (wife of the bald-headed, red-haired Dave who's a psychiatrist) had a boy, Robert, in Dec. She had the baby, Stephanie, remember?

Something tells me my child will soon be waking, so I'd better get his bath water hot. Write soon now Jeane and let me know what's going on in your neck of the woods. Oh, yes, Terry sent me a snap of Jimmy at Christmas and he's darling, believe it or not! The image of Deane. Really a handsome boy.
Love, Barbara

Life had greatly changed from the Pinehurst days for the wives whose husbands had died in the war. By the time the Round Robin reached Nancy Garry, she had officially been notified of her husband's death. First wounded in action in Normandy on June 20, 1944, 1st Lt. William J. Garry, H Company, survived, only to be severely wounded in Holland on September 18, 1944. He died two days later in a Nijmegen hospital after one of his legs had been amputated by the regimental surgeon, Doc Klein. He was posthumously awarded the Silver Star.[186]

Nancy Garry, Jacksonville, Florida [RR 49]

May 2, 1945

Dear Girls—

At last the Round Robin has reached me. I was so excited when it came—I couldn't imagine what it was! Thank you so much for including me because I have enjoyed every word. Helen, you are certainly wonderful for starting the Round Robin. I received the letters a few days ago, but with everything that has happened around here lately, it took a few days to write. Little Bill fractured his collar bone, and it so frightened me I couldn't do anything all that day, and my sister, who is nine, cut her foot and has had tetanus shots and sulfa drugs. On top of that, Dad has been in bed with a cold. Oh, I guess Mother and I will live through it all right!

**Nancy Garry, August 1944. Her husband, 1st Lt. William Garry was WIA in Normandy, June 20, 1944, and KIA September 20, 1944 in Holland. Picture included in RR #49. Gurwell Collection.**

I want to express my deepest sympathy to you who have lost your husbands. I had no idea we had lost so many.

Our baby, William James Garry, Jr., was born May 8, 1944, in San Francisco (he is better known as "Bill"). He kisses Bill's picture good night. I enjoyed the pictures and recognized some of you. I enclosed a picture of myself, thinking you might recognize me. The one of little Bill isn't a very late one.

**Bill Garry, Jr., January 1945, eight months old. Picture included in RR #49. Gurwell Collection.**

I stayed in San Francisco with Bill's family from the time the boys left until January '45. On my way out, I was stranded in New Orleans for *one whole day* and in Los Angeles another day, then on my way back I was taken off a flight in Kanas City and spent the day there struggling to get a flight out, and also lost a day in Atlanta. Now this makes me *very angry*!! *Now* I know that some of you girls were in all these places and we could have been talking "508," but instead I sat in dirty old stations twiddling my thumbs. I'm planning a visit to San Francisco the first of next year and hope to see some of you. If any of you are ever stranded in Jacksonville, Florida, please give me a ring because I wouldn't miss seeing you for the world. We have lots of bed space, too. My telephone no. is 2-2093. Now don't forget!

My news of the boys is probably old by now, but here goes—Dot Richard got a letter from Hal [1st Lt. Harold V. Richard, A Co.]. He said that Junior Hughes [Pfc. Howard T. Hughes, E Co.], 1st Lt. Temple W. Tutwiler II [D Co.], 1st Lt. Earl Carlson [D Co.], 2nd Lt. Adam B. Young [C Co.], Master Sgt. Leon E. Lavender [C Co., rank should be 1st Lt.], and 1st Lt. Joseph R. Raub [Hq1] were with him as prisoners of war.[187] Hal's letter was dated December 10. He also said that [Pfc. Joel] Lander [HqHq] and Capt. George A. [should be Charles J.] McElligott [Hq1] were with him.[188]

As you know, Terri Dowling [Ferne Dowling, RR 17] and Jerry Hardwick [RR 16] are here in town. We have dinner together and go to the Little Theatre monthly. We never can remember what we've eaten for talking "508." I have been corresponding with Doth Hartsough and Dot Richard and I received a sweet letter from Claire Tracey a while back.

If any of you have pictures of Bill, I would love to have copies, as my pictures of him are few.

If you want to see paratroopers in action, see *Objective, Burma!* with Errol Flynn. It's all about the 503, I believe. Am anxiously awaiting the Round Robin.

Good luck to you, Nancy, Mrs. W. J. Garry

Nancy forwarded the Round Robin on to her sister Floridian, Beth Pollom. The recipient of Helen Moss's first letter back in January 1944, Beth was now the first to receive the complete set of letters, amplified by a second letter from Helen and correspondents along the way who had not been on the original list. Penning her second letter in mid-May 1945, Beth was the first—and, as it turned out, the only—correspondent to add to the Round Robin after V-E Day, marking the end of the war in the European Theater of Operations on May 8, 1945. She revealed a tempered response to the day, knowing that the war in the Pacific was far from over and loved ones were still far from home.

Beth Pollom, Jacksonville, Florida. [RR 50]

May 15, 1945

The 508'er Gals—

It was certainly a pleasant surprise when I received the Round Robin to find that it had grown into such a momentous affair. If I remember correctly, when it was thought up about five of us were going to write each other that way to save our time, but this has grown into a volume of priceless information for all of the 508th.

I, like a lot of the others, had a good cry and a lot of sad moments reading of the bravery of all those girls who have lost their husbands. Their spiritual magnitude places their names on the honor roll right next to their trooper husbands'.

Enjoyed all the pictures of the girls and their darling babies. I regret that I cannot add one, but you all know I don't have a child, and by golly, not even a dog to keep me company. That isn't all: I don't have any Irish linens, jewelry, or any other things to brag about. I have received a couple bottles of perfume from France and a pair of doe skin gloves. Understand that my Pappy [husband] is sending a couple of unique beer steins from Germany soon. Those I am a bit excited about and I am hoping for some more, so I can start a collection.

Since I received the letters from you all V-E Day has come and passed without a great deal of celebration here in Kansas City, which I thought was as it should be. I hope that by the time this gets around the next time, the war with the Nips will also be over and we shall be working on readjustments to civilian life.

The other night while dining out I ran across an officer from the 101st. I have forgotten his name, but he told me he was a prisoner of war for a long time with 1st Lt. Junior Hughes [Charles R. Hughes, B Co.], 1st Lt. Lavender [Leon E., C Co.], and 2nd Lt. Young [Adam B Co.]. This last name is not familiar to me, but no doubt it will be to some of you. This fellow said I could quote him that they were all there right up to January 22. On that day he was liberated by the Russians, for he was one of the ill who was left behind while the others were marched farther into Germany because of the nearness of the Russian armies.[189]

Am enclosing a copy of the citation my husband won early in the war, of which I am proud [Silver Star citation, action near Chef-du-Pont, 10 June 1944]. I have some newspaper copies of it, but they are in my paratrooper scrapbook, and I hated to part with those.

At present, I am living in an apartment hotel with two girls I knew from college. One is married to an officer in the South Pacific and the other is unmarried. I am not working at all, for I have lost quite a bit of weight, thank God. The Dr. thinks I need to rest for a month or so, and brother they only need to say that to me *just once*.

At the moment I cannot think of anything else to write, but no doubt tomorrow after this is on the way once again, I shall think of jillions of things. So long to you all for now, and the best of luck to all of you and yours.

As always, Beth Pollom (Mrs. L.W. Pollom)

Picking up the original order of Round Robin correspondents, Beth Pollom sent the package anew to Jeane, whose name followed Beth's on the list. Postmarked May 17, 1945, the package was addressed to her parents' house in Hood River, Oregon. And here, for whatever reason, the Round Robin stopped.

At the time, Jeane was very busy, completing nursing school and living in Portland. We know she received and read the letters, however, because she wrote to George about them. While we do not have that letter, we do have George's reply.

15 June 1945 [Frankfurt, Germany]

Hello, My Adorable One, Received two letters from you today, the first in almost two weeks. They were so good. The day has been a bearcat. Everything coming at once. Managed to finish up about 10:30 tonight. It has been a full day since six this morning. Work, work, work, and more work.

Your words about the 508th Round Robin have me wondering. I often feel that way about this old unit. There is a pride

> in us that will always be there, but a bitterness along with it. So many have come and gone—old friends, new men, and replacements in one hour and gone the next. I would like to read it.[190]
>
> I thank God each night that He has made it possible for us to be together again. At least the chances are very good now. There were many times though, Jeane, when the chances weren't worth much. Such is war.
>
> There is no word of the 82nd going home. We are no longer a part of the 82nd. A separate regiment again. Seems as though we were only attached to them for insufficient rations and casualties. Sweetheart, this letter will have to be short tonight, my eyes just won't stay open. Maybe tomorrow night will be better. Your Devoted Husband, George.

By the time the Round Robin arrived at Jeane's parents in Hood River, many changes had taken place in the writers' lives. As the letters circulated from January 1944 to May 1945, the optimistic young women who had faithfully kept them going had modulated into mature wives and widows who had passed through their own baptism of fire as they bravely waited, and often mourned, news from the front. Nobody, including the correspondents, could have envisioned how sharing news about babies, daily activities, and the special gifts their husbands sent from abroad would spontaneously grow and develop into a network of mutual support. Often eliciting a "good cry" from its recipients, the Round Robin became a lifeline for vital information and encouragement, reassuring its readers that somebody understood. They were not alone: they were "paratrooper girls" in the 508th family, a "band of sisters" who sustained each other through the darkest times. For some, the ties lasted a lifetime; for many, they turned into memories as husbands returned, families grew, and the challenges of getting on with life loosened the bonds of the past.

Sue's thoughts: There must have been a weariness not only for the men but for the women of this remarkable family. The pride of accomplishment endured, as did the unity forged by long training and combat. But as Dad expressed at the end of the war, a sense of bitterness arose when the 508th was detached from the 82nd Airborne Division. The old unit was no longer the same. Too many lives were gone; too many ghosts were present. Wartime bonds and friendships were unique, a part of life never to be forgotten, but it now was time to heal and look forward to a brighter future.

Neither Mom nor Dad ever mentioned the Round Robin letters. We were astonished to discover them neatly tucked into their big, olive drab-colored envelope, filed away with my parents' personal wartime correspondence. The Round Robin letters were found close to chronological order, except for Jane and Hal Creary's tragic masterpieces, which were moved closer to the front.

Why Mom chose not to pass them on we can only speculate. When the final envelope landed in her parents' mailbox, she was in Portland, busy with exams, hospital rotations, and raising her son. New priorities took precedence, and life-changing events were afoot. She had shared much of the Round Robin in letters to Dad, and he had voiced his desire to read them. She possibly tucked them away for that very reason, but the war was over, her husband was coming home, and the Round Robin had more than fulfilled its initial purpose. The time to pass it on had slipped by.

The Round Robin letters, never individually folded and always sent as a group, were part and parcel of the war. Yet the meticulous care with which they were cataloged, along with thousands of other ephemeral documents Dad had collected throughout the war, and the pristine condition in which they were preserved, communicated the belief in their historical importance, not just for their correspondents, or for our family alone, but for posterity.

Red Devils Honor Guard At Frankfurt

Devils' Digest

WEDNESDAY, JUNE [illegible] 1945 — VOL. II—NO. 3

## Assigned Special Occupation Duties

508th Parachute Infantry, famed in the combat histories of Normandy, Holland and Belgium, has been ordered to Frankfurt-on-Main to serve as honor guards of American headquarters, Allied Control Council, it was announced today by Colonel Roy E. Lindquist, Red Devil regimental commander.

Selected for this distinctive role in the military occupation of defeated Germany, the Regiment will begin duties in Frankfurt a little more than a year after it spearheaded the invasion of France dropping into the hedgerows and fields of Normandy in the early dawn of D-Day.

It is expected the Red Devils will provide special escorts for visiting [illegible]

## Lt. Col. Mendez Is Executive Officer Of 508

Lieutenant Colonel Louis G. Mendez, Jr., who led the Third Battalion since activation of the 508th Parachute Infantry Regiment in October 1942 is assigned regimental executive officer, it was announced at headquarters today. He succeeds Lieutenant Colonel Thomas J. B. Shanley who is leaving to assume new duties with [illegible]

American, British Awards

# CHAPTER XVII

# GUARDING IKE: OCCUPATION DUTY IN FRANKFURT, GERMANY

The 508th returned from Chartres to Camp Sissonne on May 30, 1945. No longer on standby jump status, the regiment had been chosen to guard the headquarters of General Dwight Eisenhower, Supreme Commander of Allied Forces in Europe in Frankfurt am Main, Germany. George arrived at Sissonne ahead of the main group to prepare for the regiment's return to the old French army complex and the transfer to Germany. Foreseeing a long period ahead before he could go home, he penned a letter to Jeane on 508th Parachute Infantry Officers' Club stationary as the "dreaded downtime" again settles in on him.

**George with a formal picture during the occupation, summer, 1945. Gurwell Collection.**

26 May 1945 [Camp Sissonne, France]

Your letter of May 12 reached me today telling me that your Mother's Day present arrived. I am so glad that you liked the roses. You just had to have them—dark red roses for the most adorable wife and mother in the world.

It might be quite some time before we are together again. We have been chosen as General Ike's guard at his headquarters in Germany. Still don't know what that means. If our battle stars come through the way they should, I might even transfer if it looks like we might stay here for a long time.

Just looked at my watch—after eleven. Must bring this to a close—more work tomorrow, Sunday or not. Just another day over here.

In addition to writing to Jeane, George found solace and another "safe space" in nature. Long walks called upon all his senses and spontaneously elicited positive thoughts of home, as in the letter below. Instinctively employed, these habits temporarily "took him out of" the war, and proved to be a strong resource against the symptoms of PTSD that invariably returned as days of tedium stretched out before him.

28 May 1945 [Camp Sissonne]

Today has been busy again. A little more pleasant though, with no rain up until a short while ago, so I took off my shirt this afternoon and worked a little more on my tan.

After dinner tonight I took a long walk. It was lovely out. Warm, and the woods smelled so good. I saw all kinds of strange flowers and bugs. Just made up my mind to come in when I found a patch of wild strawberries. Gee, Darling, they tasted good—the first strawberries that I have had for heaven knows when. Reminded me so much of home, though. We have loads of them around Seaside and Gearhart.[191]

I am enclosing a clipping from the *Stars and Stripes*. It has reference to our coming job here in the European Theater of Operation. Sweetheart, I want to come home so darned bad. Maybe someday, though—who knows?

29 May 1945 [Camp Sissonne]

It has been pouring—great bucketsful of water all over the place. Have been soaked most of the day. Managed to dry out about five o'clock this afternoon for the first time. Went to a show this evening after supper, Objective, Burma! Made me sweat just to watch those guys in the plane getting ready to jump. Very good picture, though, tense and dramatic all the way. Stopped by the Officers Club on the way back to find it jammed and extremely noisy. Played a couple of games of ping pong—won both. Couldn't stand the noise any longer, so I wandered up to the Company. Nothing doing again, so back here, with darkness just closing in, to write a letter to the most wonderful wife in this world.

About German guns [requested by Jeane's father]—I have some, but I can't promise how good or what condition they are in. Lugged them around with the idea of sending your Dad one—but moved to the airport and stored them [at Sissonne], and now I am afraid to look. Probably all rust. Promise to look tomorrow though.

I wonder how long I will be able to stand this life away from you. Might tell someone off one of these days and wind up heaven knows where. Well, my Darling—I must close—a long day again tomorrow. The Army and its red tape—records and what not. Sometimes I feel like giving up completely. Just kidding, Sweetheart—I always remember that poem I sent you:

Through the muck and through the mire
Through the shells and small-arms fire
V-1, V-2
Things is rough, I'm telling you.

Makes me laugh, probably because it's true. Goodnight, Sweetheart, and pleasant dreams.

As the war in Europe came to an end, some wives had to face the fact that their husbands would never come back; others like Jeane, whose spouses had made it so far, struggled to remain optimistic while they now wondered if their husbands would be sent to fight the Japanese. Battling her anxiety with typical irony, Jeane told George that at this rate, he would be lucky to get home in time to help with his grandchildren.

30 May 1945 [Camp Sissonne]

Received your letter of the 17th. It contained a very good talking to and a rather pessimistic mood as to whether I would ever get home. Sometimes, Sweetheart, I wonder myself. It seems as though the army is taking great delight in keeping us apart. Officers' status is never clear [on coming home]. We not only have to be in excess, but also non-essential. I know that the army doesn't need me. If I could just be certain that they knew it! I have to go on, powerless to do a thing, and afraid I might make the wrong move and jump from the frying pan into the fire. Things are still very unsettled over here—just a lot of confusion.

The company pulled in today. Getting them settled is no easy job. All the other officers disappeared, collecting their luggage and stuff. Consequently, I have been jumping from pillar to post and taking each new trouble under my wing. Just realized that it is midnight again—past my bedtime. Good night, Sweetheart, pleasant dreams.

May 30, 1945 [Portland, Oregon]

My Darling George— How are you and the doldrums? If you think of any ways of banishing them, pass them along please, Sweetheart, because they're pretty constant here without you, too. We should only be glad that V-E Day came and that you're safe—each hour of the day I thank God for that. It's long and wearing and more, but it just *has* to end sometime.

Hear that the 101st landed in N.Y. and there is very carefully no word of the 508th. Felt like using a little profanity at that point. Please Darling, can't you nose around and get an idea as to what seems most likely to happen to you? Who all is left that I remember? Have a fair idea—guess it isn't many. I must go to bed now and pray for your return soon—real soon, somehow. Good night, Sweetheart.

Jeane was certainly right: by the time the regiment returned to Sissonne, the 508th was nothing but a shell of its former self. Of the 135 captains and first and second lieutenants who had sailed to Europe on the *James Parker*, thirty-four (25 percent) had been killed in action and seven were listed as prisoners of war. Another thirty-four officers had transferred, returned to the States (usually injured or wounded in action), or would be hospitalized before war's end. These absences weighed heavily on George as he prepared the camp to receive an influx of replacements.[192] George also begrudged having to serve as Eisenhower's Honor Guard—an assignment with too much pomp and paperwork to suit his disposition, especially as the duty prolonged the seemingly interminable time before he could go home.

2 June 1945 [Camp Sissonne]

Ran around all day getting things set up for a Company beer party. Wound up getting there late myself. Drank beer and sang songs until almost dark. Walked to the Officers' Club—had two more drinks—read about two pages of my book and folded up. Went home and right to bed.

This morning was a hectic affair—getting some undesirables [soldiers convicted of serious offenses] ready to leave. There are so many new faces in the Regiment. The Company seems to have lost all my friends and the old officers seem fewer each day. The young kids coming in don't show much except a noisy attitude. Just losing faith in the outfit, I guess. Not the crack outfit you used to know. That, coupled with the army itself, makes me have one hell of an outlook. If I hadn't grown up with the 508th, I think I would leave tomorrow. Have never felt quite so low. Frankfurt smells too much like a regular Army show. Trying to impress everyone and not a thing to do. Your husband just wasn't made for things like that.

Really, my Adorable One—I don't know what I am going to do to keep from going crazy. Refuse to start drinking heavily again—so that leaves work. Wish to high heaven that I could tell you something definite, but we don't know a thing.

We have to buy more clothes for this dress parade [for a review by Supreme Headquarters Allied Expeditionary Force (SHAEF) staff and later in July by President Truman], so don't be surprised if I send some things that won't be of use to me anymore.[193] Two leather jackets, my Darling, one for each of us—might have to cut yours down—and other odds and ends too numerous to mention.

The regiment arrived in Frankfurt, Germany, on June 10, 1945.

11 June 1945 [Frankfurt]

These past five or six days have been a nightmare. Doing triple duty until at last we are settled or almost so, here in Germany. During the move, and for about five days before, I had the Company plus all of my other little odd jobs. Worked several nights until three or four in the morning. Sorry, my Darling, to have missed those days in my letter-writing—was in a pretty bad mood besides. This honor guard, or whatever you call it, for General Ike just doesn't appeal to me.

We have nice quarters, regular seven-room apartments with furnishings still in them [at 2 Im Burgfeld, Frankfurt]. Some really beautiful furniture—pianos, etc. Hot water, electric stoves, potted plants, and everything but the most important—you, Sweetheart. What good are decent quarters except to make us realize more each day that nothing matters except those we love? I have two offices, both with beautiful desks. Each apartment has a cute little garden behind it, with a great

> variety of things growing in them. Have even managed to get strawberries and cherries. Quite a treat—they are the first since coming over.
>
> Jeane—I wonder how long I can stand this being away from you. It isn't easy, sitting here trying to put up a front. So many youngsters and newcomers around that seeing an old officer is something of a treat. This place [Frankfurt] must have been really something until our Air Corps worked it over. Right now, it is more ruins than anything else.
>
> It's almost dark and already it is 11:30. The petals are from some roses right here on my desk and the pieces of lace are something that I thought you might like. Love you—good night, Sweetheart—pleasant dreams.

Trying to keep it light, George did his best to "put up a front" in his letter to Jeane, too, although weightier matters strained the façade. What he did not tell her was that officers had received an unnerving memo from Col. Lindquist that very same day, with an undated article from the *Infantry Journal* typed into the text, titled "It Takes a Man." "Leadership in the rear areas, far from the enemy, is just as important to the success of the whole Army as leadership in battle itself," the first line asserted. This was precisely the kind of empty "chicken shit" sell job that set George on edge, a resentment shared by many field-grade officers who had performed frontline duty under the duress of combat only to end up in "worthless" ceremonial functions and reams of red tape far away from home.

To a growing degree, this disgruntlement extended to Col. Lindquist and other brass after the army initiated a plan to allow soldiers to return stateside and be discharged. The system accorded points for time in service, overseas duty, combat medals, marital status, and dependents, but honor guard duty was classified as "essential," a status that excluded officers—unlike enlisted men—from benefiting from the system, no matter how many points they had racked up. With eighty-nine points, George qualified as a "high-point man" to no avail.

To make matters worse, senior officers were granted the privilege of furloughs, while from George's perspective, he and fellow junior officers were left high and dry, unable to move on with life. They were tied to their desks, obliged to dress up for useless symbolic displays, and unfairly mired in the snafues, hassles, and deadly boredom of the army's perpetual "hurry up and wait."

14 June 1945 [Frankfurt]

Oh Punkin—I am working on those German rifles. Should have them back in shape before long—then out they go [to Jeane's father]. Have two pistols besides, a Luger and a P-38. Can't send them through the mail, so I will have to keep them with me. The Luger is a beautifully balanced gun, and it will be yours if and when I get home.

16 June 1945 [Frankfurt]

My Darling—today has been another of those full, full days. Supposed to be off at noon, but I managed to finish about 7:30 this evening. Decided to go to the Officers Snack Bar at Headquarters. 508th was very well represented—had a couple of drinks, a sandwich, ice cream and called it an evening.

You should see our mess area—there are literally thousands of German kids around. Some of them are so darned cute. They all look at you with such a curious look in their eyes—"so that is an American soldier." They are a friendly lot, some a little shy, others on the suspicious side. It is just like trying to keep a hoard of locusts away. You chase one out and three more take his place.

It seems so strange to see women, old men, and kids standing in our mess lines. We feed those who work for us. Every day and in every way, we see just what an industrious and intelligent people they are. It is a pity that they have that streak in them that makes them think they are so much better than everyone else. Consequently, we have wars.[194]

So, you see, we are beset by Germans and non-fraternization is not the answer. We are punishing ourselves instead of making the Germans feel it. There isn't anything left here but farms and garden plots. These people are going to have to work and work hard for their mere existence for quite a few years to come. Reconstruction in these larger towns will take years and years. What masses of rubble the bombings have left. It is very good though, because they have really learned the hard way this time.[195]

June 19, 1945 [Portland]

Heard that the 82nd is going into Berlin. What does it all mean? A big show and then home? Going to keep all my fingers crossed and *know* that it won't be long. It's all so worth waiting for, but the thought is a little too wonderful to endure. At present, Sweetheart, I'm having the wonderful illusion of what I'd do if you would walk in now—I could never get my feet on the ground again.

20 June 1945 [Frankfurt]

It was so good to hear from you today. Two letters, my Darling. One with a picture in it, the other gave me some very good news: the first package arrived and with the chute in it. That is our regular chute. It was jumped into Holland—not mine though. They come in very handy, especially since we don't take blankets in with us. Very warm when you wrap up in them.[196]

There is a little German girl just beyond the wall in our Company area who is just about the prettiest girl you have ever seen. About five, and I would like to steal her. Always ready with a smile and a "Guten Tag." She reminds me of a picture that I have seen somewhere. Blonde hair in pigtails, a red dress, very fair complexion and bright blue eyes. She is really adorable. At least we can talk to them. The kids over here are a treat after seeing the kids of England and France.

21 June 1945 [Frankfurt]

My Adorable One—it has been quite sultry all day. Arranged for the Company to go swimming, then wound up too busy to go myself. It certainly gets lonely over here, particularly when we get such indefinite news about officers getting any breakthrough the point plan. Our *Stars and Stripes* listed the 82nd as one of the occupation units. We have a funny status even other than that—our regiment is detached, but we still wear the 82nd patch on our shoulder. Can't quite figure it all out.

It is really something to watch some of these SHAEF officers. They come up and tell you how rough it is here. They have never known anything but this sort of life. The poor kids—ice cream, beer, fancy mess halls, big offices, and beds every night. They start telling us how they used to be in a fighting outfit and kept trying to get back in. What out-and-out lies. We listen to their stories, laugh to ourselves, and agree with them. Really a strange life and not a very pleasant one. Definitely not a paratrooper's life, and believe me, Darling—I resent it.

23 June 1945 [Frankfurt, Germany]

Took quite a long trip yesterday. Didn't get back until 0230 (2:30 a.m.). Rolled right into bed, so consequently—no letter last night. Went after some electric barber equipment for the Company. Bought the equipment ok, but figured the time wrong, so we were late getting back.

Travelled on one of the famous autobahns in Germany. Sweetheart—they are wonderful six-lane highways with three on each side of an island. Very well kept, and the best roads that I have ever travelled on. The area we went to had several ski-jump rigs for winter sports. It was a mountainous country all covered with evergreens. Beautiful little towns, all clean and neatly tucked in the valleys. It made me terribly homesick to see country like that.

Received some good news today—we now wear a fourth Bronze Service Star in our Theatre Ribbon. Five more points, which makes me 89. Enough to at least be eligible for a discharge, 85 points are needed. Doesn't seem to bring me any closer to getting home, though. Still very put-out about this whole set-up. Me and quite a few others.

As the day-to-day routines dragged on, writing about everyday activities was one way to feel connected. Like George, many men now had children they had never met, and reading about them in letters brought the little ones closer.

June 27,1945 [Portland]

How's our Punkin? Two letters from you today again, and you haven't heard from me for a couple of weeks. Can't understand where the mail was held up. Your letters were lovely. "Ricky" and I walked up to the mailbox to get them. Of course, he wanted them, so he carried them back to the house too. We saw a dog on the way, which fascinates him to no end. It was a Boston Bulldog and he didn't quite trust it—wouldn't let it get behind him. He climbs all over the place, and yesterday his sitter Rosie said he almost made his first jump (without a chute). He climbed up on a kitchen chair onto the kitchen table and had one foot out the window preparatory to invading the onion patch. Stopped him just in time.

28 June 1945 [Frankfurt]

The weather has turned much cooler the last two days, sprinkled with intermittent showers. Not even decent to go swimming. This has all the appearance of being a difficult place. No means of transportation to go to shows or anything else. The Snack Bar is about the only place that doesn't entail a sizable job of walking. Even our own Officers Club is a good walk from here [1.6 miles as the crow flies and 4.6 miles by street].

A lot of promises of passes and furloughs have figured down to one thing—at the present high rate, everyone will have had a leave or furlough by at least 1947. The Colonel [Lindquist], however, is gone again on his sixth since coming overseas. A very good average for him. Today marks a year and a half overseas. Three overseas stripes now and starting on the fourth, much to my regret.

Had a very nice letter from you today. Postmarked the 13th of June. I had to laugh at your gardening episode—so the cabbage turned into brussels sprouts. Rather strange, my Adorable One—as a matter of fact, revolutionary.

You overestimate the Army. I haven't had a good physical check since I joined the parachute troops in 1942. Our last physical profile after the war consisted in Major Thomas asking me if I felt warm. But Sweetheart, we aren't supposed to catch bugs. Bugs wouldn't even have a chance in our regular quarters. We have a difficult job ourselves—particularly in foxholes and tents.

German people are of two kinds. One, and at least on the surface the more rare, hate us and show it in a cold, unemotional attitude. The other, and by far the greater percentage, are very friendly, or at least try to be, if we let them. They are a very energetic race, and their standard of living is much like ours. They keep very good gardens—work in them continually—but there isn't much else for them to do. The women are excellent housekeepers. We have two who clean the Company Officers quarters. Boy, what a thorough job they do. It is just too darned bad that they haven't good sense to go with everything else [their good qualities]. They are by far the leaders here in Europe. No one else can even come close, including the English.

5 July 1945 [Frankfurt]

Today has been rather dull and cheerless. Very low, Sweetheart, and as fed up with the 508th as I ever have been. We were promised a lot and we haven't gotten a bit of it. Not even as much as other units. Lindquist doesn't care—he is playing around on leave again. Must be a great life to forget that you have something to worry about and travel around. I feel a crisis or an explosion coming up—all of the officers are ticked off. Gets rather monotonous working your heart out just to be kicked in the pants again.

We are no longer a part of the 82nd. We are a separate regiment, stationed in Frankfurt as General Ike's Honor Guard. Which is short for saying a rather permanent occupation job guarding a lot of worthless brass that are a pain in the neck. Don't let the papers worry you. We are not redeployed, as we should be, thanks to Regiment. Making everyone unhappy trying to put on an elaborate show. Such a waste of time.

After midnight already and a busy day tomorrow. Training schedules, supply, regular daily jobs, three meetings, and a million small things. Guess I will have to go swimming tomorrow afternoon. Keeping my fingers crossed that soon there will be that chance to come home.

As time dragged on, George's restlessness and dislike of garrison life had him thinking, as in previous down times, that combat might be better than his current duty.

22 July 1945 [Frankfurt]

Today has been a horrible waste—haven't done a thing but sit around the Orderly Room. Not on duty, just nothing whatsoever to do—so I sit here half asleep, and half awake. Sundays are a terror—a whole day to try and keep busy. Times like these make me feel as though even the South Pacific would be a blessing. We will probably even change our shoulder patches soon to the Army of Occupation patch. They are breaking us down—slow but sure. [Attrition has taken its toll on George: only a few friends are left from Pinehurst days.]

28 July 1945 [Frankfurt]

Days are getting to be years long here. Almost August, almost another year old, and what a year it has been. Last year, my birthday found me sitting in a foxhole congratulating myself that I had survived another jump and wondering if I would see another birthday. Strange how it looks as you look back.

Punkin—nothing new is happening. As a matter of fact, nothing is happening. No information and no news. Good night my Darling—pleasant dreams.

The boredom, uncertainty, and seemingly infinite waiting were all swept away when incredible news broke on August 6, 1945: The first atomic bomb had been dropped on Hiroshima, Japan. Three days later, the second atomic bomb was dropped on Nagasaki. Victory over Japan was declared on August 14, bringing an end to World War II.

While George did not write home in the immediate aftermath, letters from Jeane expressed worry about the use of radioactive materials. Otherwise, she was hopeful, but not ready to celebrate while George was still so far away.

August 6, 1945 [Portland]

George Darling—what effect has the news of the atomic bomb had on you? I, too, feel the tremendousness of it all and the apprehension, but we must not lose faith in its control either. What do you think of it all? Closely akin to such principles is the "Drug X," or radioactive phosphorus that we've [medical staff] been using on the floor [hospital ward] in treatment of cancerous growths. Mighty interesting stuff that yours truly knows little about. What about that chemistry class? Have you decided whether or not to take it if the chance comes?

August 15, 1945 [Portland]

Hello, my Darling—you will probably hear about the tremendous expression of feeling that was displayed here. V.J. Day or not, after the tense waiting it was almost anticlimactic. Many of us worked, but it was hard to concentrate. Got off at 7:30 and several of us went to see the bedlam in town. Bedlam it was, with noise and more noise, but I might as well have been alone, for my heart was over there with you. We left early, and Connie [Jeane's coworker] and I gave up the idea of celebrating, or even getting gloriously drunk. No, there're too many deeper feelings and too much meaning to this—we can't forget the price paid by all of you we love. In fact, that's what everyone really feels. Well, Darling—celebrating and happiness and all good things mean your return, and I will pray that it can be sooner now.

* * *

Although the war was officially over, the 508th PIR remained on "essential duty" in Frankfurt until November 1946. By war's end in August, however, the regiment was almost entirely filled with replacements, which permitted "old timers" like George to begin the elaborate administrative process the army had devised to allow them to return home. Released a few at a time, high-point officers were transferred to the 17th Airborne Division and then to the 101st, at which point they returned to the States. The morning report showed George transferred out on August 18, 1945.

As the high-point men were readying for transfer, "an election was held to select the two men killed in action who were best remembered and best loved by their buddies. In their memory, the privates and noncoms of the 508th named their clubs. The privates' club was called Bartholomew Hall after Technician Fifth Grade Ellsworth Bartholomew, and the noncoms' club became known as Brogan Hall in memory of Staff Sergeant Harold J. Brogan."[197]

One of George's final duties in Regimental Headquarters was to send a cable to Evalyn Ryckman, sister and next-of-kin to his dear friend Bart, requesting a photograph of her brother. She replied with a photo of Bart with his ex-girlfriend and another with Harry Hudec, a buddy from Regimental Headquarters. Our records also contained a concurrent V-mail from Evalyn with the same content.

Mrs. Evalyn Ryckman, Whittier, Calif, USA

August 17, 1945

Lt. Geo. Gurwell, 508 PIR

Dear George,

(Mind the first name? He was Bud to his family always, until he went to Dutch Harbor, Alaska, where the Bart started).... Tomorrow, I'll get a larger photograph and send it—if it's a cut you want, it might be easier to use that one. I have others, as mine is the only large one he had made. It was used for his picture in the paper here after news of his death.

Dear God, my heart is crying out—is there a *chance* he is still alive, and they need this photograph for identification, somehow? But no—I just won't let myself even think it—Such queer things have happened in this war.

About the pictures—we like the one of Bud and a buddy of his (I think Harry Hudec, "Big Stupe"?), but never knew for sure, or who to send it to. I had six made as Bud asked, and was just ready to send them to him at D-Day time. I like it best. The one of him looking at a tall building with a girl he liked quite well looks just like him also but is only profile. It was taken on his last leave in the U.S.

**T/5 Ellsworth Bartholomew and Barbara Duck, 1943. Gurwell Collection.**

I remember Bud mentioning your name a time or two in his letters. It tears me to pieces to read them, and I'm not very well (couple of major surgeries in the last three years plus pneumonia), so I just try not to think about it too much. We lost our mother and father and 15-year-old sister, but somehow this—Ellsworth—has been the hardest to take of anything I have ever had to take. He was nine years younger than I, the baby, and I the oldest of the five of us—so he was like a son to me, as he was only five years old when our mother died. He lived with us off and on after father was killed when he was 14 years old. I nursed him all summer thru a terrible siege of traumatic pneumonia, broken ribs, and punctured lungs—at the time of the accident when my father and sister were killed, and Bud and Fred were both hurt.

I miss his letters and the bits of poetry he wrote me—so much—and now that peace has come, I am rejoicing with all you swell fellows in the grand job you've done, but I just can't keep back my tears to think of so many coming home, and our Bud not with them.

Now that it's over—Can't you or someone tell me more about him—how it happened—when he died, where he is buried? Wonder if they left his wristwatch on, or if it was broken or if he gave it to someone. Just for sentimental reasons, I'd love to have it. And his wings—do they leave them on when they bury him? He had just written that *he* was the one to mark white crosses, and that he sorta had it figured out which names he'd have to put on them! Sometimes he seemed to think he'd never come back, but we all scolded him for talking that way, so he quit. Did he ever talk that way to you or fellow soldiers? Can you tell me about the jump over France?

Somehow, I seem to feel you are the Lt. he used to speak of. (I looked you up in the Organization Day booklet with all the Reg's names).[198] He was so very fond of you, and acted as your "aid de camp" and took walks with you sometimes. What was the Special Detail he went ahead to England to do? Our grandparents were born in England and we have relatives there (unless Hitler's bombs got them). Bud was so happy to see some of it. He wrote such beautiful descriptions—When I can, I want to try to put a lot of his writing together and have it published.

God, you are no doubt rushed to death nearly and have no time to answer a sister's questions. Why not come and see me? Stay with us a day or two and tell us all about it. We have a son, Don, 11 years-old, who adored his Uncle Bud. We do hope to meet you and any or all of the other fellows in Bud's company. Is Capt. Abraham still living? Bud said he was such a swell fellow. And the one he called "Christy" and Harry Hudec and George Fredrick. I am answering Abraham's letter to me very soon, am so ashamed I haven't before. Do come and see us—home dinner—bring any other of your Co. you wish.

Most Sincerely, Evalyn Ryckman.

On the back of the photograph of Bart and the young woman, Barbara Duck, Evalyn wrote: "T/5 Ellsworth Bartholomew and Barbara Duck, Delaware, Fall, 1943. On his last furlough—not long enough to come home to Calif, from N.C. Paul Zills, Del. "Barbara Duck" was their neighbors' girl. Beautiful, but Bud said too young for him, tho he loved her. He did not become engaged to her."

While searching documents in the Gurwell collection, we located an unfinished letter George had started to Evalyn:

[To: Evalyn Ryckman, Whittier, California ]

31 August, 1945

Dear Evalyn,

Received your very lovely letter yesterday, and I only wish that I could bring "Bart" back for all of us. He has been selected as one of the two outstanding men in our Regiment. We needed a picture so that the regiment could have a plaque made. Your letter was delayed in reaching me since I too have moved. On the way home to Portland, Oregon. I am keeping your address and promise to write and possibly visit you when I get home.

Yes—you were quite right. I am the one who used to work with "Bart" in Tenn. I was very proud to say that he and I were the best of friends. In parachuting there is very little rank except when responsibility comes into the picture. Bart was a man and Loved and respected by all of us.

It also fell to George to write the official tribute to his friend for the dedication of Bartholomew Hall. We were very moved to discover among George's war documents three sheets of paper covered in block print that show his repeated attempts to capture the spirit and honor the sacrifice of his buddy. We can only imagine what an ironically bittersweet task this must have been, as George himself was on the verge of a long-awaited homecoming and a new phase of life with a wife he dearly loved and an infant son he'd not yet met.

We here reproduce the drafts as we found them. Crossed-out sections are in the originals.

Sheet one:

> T/5 Ellsworth Bartholomew
>
> To forget why he died is to forget the meaning of civilization. ~~Bart personified an American in every sense of the word.~~ He died unshaken in his belief that a true democracy of the world is within our reach.

Sheet two:

> Bart—A smiling, cheerful guy. Tolerant and understanding; sincere in his beliefs and purpose—~~a friend and buddy to all who knew him. He and millions with him died that a lasting peace might become an actuality, others might live in perpetual peace.~~
>
> ~~No job too great, no job too small. Loved by many and respected by all.~~ An inspiration and friend to all.

Sheet three:

> To Bart—An American
>
> No job too great, no job too small. Loved by many and a friend to all. A smiling, cheerful guy—tolerant and understanding, sincere in his beliefs and purpose. ~~May his cheerful, tolerant and understanding soul remain embedded in our memories.~~ The sooner conceit is knocked out of mankind, the sooner the world will be free—livable and free!
>
> May his cheerful, tolerant and understanding soul find its way into the hearts of the next generation so that the world will truly find perfect peace.

George's last war letter to Jeane, written at the end of August after he had transferred to the 101st Airborne, described the hectic pace of being on the move and expressed the certainty that a hope long deferred would finally become a reality.

30 August 1945

Hello, my Adorable One—by the time this reaches you, you will know that I am no longer with the 508th. Finally cut the ties, hoping that I might get home a little earlier. No definite news as to when yet, but I have made a start. Ripper is with me—we have been in so many units these past two weeks that it isn't even funny. No return address and continually on the move has prevented any letters to you. Three Divisions—82nd, 17th, and 101st—plus about nine different outfits will give you some idea how much we have been moving.

Finally received some mail from you today. Probably the last for some time because one of the officers picked it up back at the 508th. We are moving again Sunday—please don't worry. As soon as I settle down, I will send my address. The real prize is that I am at the moment assigned to the 321st Field Artillery Battalion in the 101st Airborne Division. Me, an infantryman, in the artillery.

I have been Company Commander of a Division Artillery N.C.O. School. Boy—what a life. *Please*, don't write to me at the return address on the envelope. We are moving again Sunday. We don't know where yet. I am hoping against hope to get away by October. Seems as though I have travelled over at least half of Germany and about three-quarters of France. France is our home right now.

Our celebration was the relieved expression on most faces and the question *when do we get home?* in every heart. We listened to the celebrations in the States and got a laugh while comparing the two. It still seems difficult to believe that both wars are over.

Take wonderful care of yourselves for me. Good night, Sweetheart—pleasant dreams, and I should be home by Christmas, too.

# CHAPTER XVIII

# SAILING HOME ON THE S.S. *MADAWASKA VICTORY*

Although the 508th remained in Frankfurt until November 1946, several officers were blessed to return home well before then. Two of the lucky couples who benefited were Jeane and George, along with Jerry and Don Hardwick.

On returning to the United States as a unit, the 508th Parachute Infantry Regiment was deactivated at Camp Kilmer, New Jersey, on November 26, 1946. The war was over, but the price had been high. Regimental statistics show 613 Killed in Action/Died of Wounds; 13 Died in Training Accidents; 3 Died of Injuries; 1,274 Wounded in Action; 526 Injured in Action; 254 Missing in Action. George felt fortunate to make it home with all his parts attached.

HEADQUARTERS, U. S. A. T. JAMES PARKER WHN/eo

VOYAGE NO. 19
28 Dec. 1943

MEMORANDUM:

TO : All Officers.

The following Dining Room table assignments are made as of Breakfast 29 Dec. 43.

| NAME | GRADE | 1st Sitting | 2nd Sitting |
|---|---|---|---|
| LINDQUIST, ROY E. | Colonel * | | 7 |
| EKMAN, WILLIAM E. | Lt. Col - SOS | | 7 |
| HARRISON, HARRY J. | Lt. Col. - States | | 7 |
| MENDEZ, LOUIS G., JR. | Lt. Col * | | 7 |
| SHANLEY, THOMAS J. B. | Lt. Col * | | 7 |
| CASTEEL, JAMES R. | Major * | | 5 |
| HOLMES, OTHO E. | Major * | | 5 |
| SHANNON, JACK T. | Major - OSS | | 5 |
| THOMAS, DAVID E. | Major * | | 5 |
| WARREN, SHIELDS, JR. | Major * | | 15 |
| ABRAHAM, ROBERT | Captain - transf. | | 6 |
| ADAMS, JONATHAN, B. | Captain - Hosp | | 12 |
| BELL, ALTON L. | Captain * | | C |
| BREEN, JOHN A. | Captain K.I.A | | 3 |
| BRIDGEWATER, ERLE H., JR | Captain - transf. | | 4 |
| CREARY, HAL M. | Captain - K.I.A | | 4 |
| DOWLING, JAMES A. | Captain - transf. | | 3 |
| DRESS, HILLMAN C. | Captain - * | | 6 |
| DRIGGERS, JAMES C. | Captain - States | | 6 |
| ELDER, JAMES L. | Captain * | | 12 |
| FLANDERS, FRANCIS E. | Captain K.I.A | | 4 |
| GRAHAM, CHESTER E. | Captain * | | 12 |
| HARVEY, WAYNE K. | Captain K.I.A | | 3 |
| KING, EDWARD F. | Captain K.I.A. | | 15 |
| KLEIN, JAMES C. | Captain * | | 3 |
| MATERNOWSKI, IGNATIUS P. | Captain K.I.A | | 10 |
| MILAM, ROBERT L. | Captain * | | C |
| MONTGOMERY, GEORGE E. | Captain - transf. | | 10 |
| NATION, WILLIAM H. | Captain K.I.A | | 15 |
| NOVAK, FRANK J. | Captain - transf. | | 10 |
| PETERSON, MELVIN V. | Captain * | | 15 |
| SILVER, WALTER H. | Captain * | | 9 |
| SIMONDS, GEORGE W. | Captain K.I.A | | 9 |
| SNOW, HAROLD E. | Captain transf. | | 6 |
| TAYLOR, ROYAL R. | Captain * | | C |
| THORNQUIST, JOHN J. | Captain PW | | 9 |
| ZAKBY, ABDALLAH A. | Captain - transf. | | 3 |
| ANDRES, FRANK J. | Captain — | | 2 |
| SPRADLIN, WALTER C. | 1st Lt. — | | 2 |
| WILDE, RUSSELL E. | 1st Lt. * | | 9 |
| ABBOTT, EDGAR R. | 1st Lt. K.I.A | | 11 |
| ALBRIGHT, BARRY E. | 1st Lt. * | | 11 |
| AXELROD, DAVID | 1st Lt. — transf. | | 11 |
| BAILEY, HARRY C. | 1st Lt. * | | 11 |
| BEAUDIN, BRIAN N. | 1st Lt. * | | 12 |
| BEAVER, NEAL W. | 1st Lt. * | | 14 |
| BELL, BRUCE E. | 1st Lt. K.I.A | | 14 |
| BERRY, PAUL N. | 1st Lt. — Hosp | | 14 |
| BODAK, MICHAEL C. | 1st Lt. - Hosp - K.I.A | | 14 |
| BRANNEN, MALCOLM D. | 1st Lt. * | | 16 |
| BRUMFIELD, MELBOURNE L | 1st Lt. K.I.A. | | 16 |
| DALY, JOHN J. | 1st Lt. K.I.A | | 6 |
| DAVIS, DONALD A. | 1st Lt. - States | | 16 |
| DeWEESE, RALPH E. | 1st Lt. K.I.A | | 16 |
| DIETRICH, JAMES D. | 1st Lt. * | 6 | |
| DOERR, WILSON D. | 1st Lt. - transf. | | 17 |
| EGLICK, PAUL G. | 1st Lt. - transf. | | 17 |
| FARRELL, JOSEPH F. | 1st Lt. * | | 17 |
| FRASER, HUGH W. | 1st Lt. - transf. | | 17 |
| FOLEY, JOHN P. | 1st Lt. * | | 1 |

- 1 -

| NAME | GRADE | | 1st SITTING | 2nd SITTING |
|---|---|---|---|---|
| GARRY, WILLIAM J. | 1st Lt. | K.I.A. | | 1 |
| GILLESPIE, CHARLES T. | 1st Lt. | * | | 1 |
| GILLESPIE, FRED E. | 1st Lt. | K.I.A. | | 1 |
| GOODALE, HOYT T. | 1st Lt. | K.I.A. | | 19 |
| GRABBE, VICTOR | 1st Lt. | Dow | | 19 |
| GUILLOT, GERALD P. | 1st Lt. | * | | C |
| HAGER, ERNEST J. | 1st Lt. | * | | 19 |
| HARDWICK, DONALD W. | 1st Lt. | * | | 19 |
| HETLAND, EUGENE C. | 1st Lt. | * | | 10 |
| HOFFMAN, HERBERT | 1st Lt. | – Hosp | 5 | |
| HOLDEN, LEWIS M. | 1st Lt. | States | 5 | |
| HUGHES, CHARLES R. | 1st Lt. | – PW | 5 | |
| JAMPETERO, JOHN J. | 1st Lt. | – K.I.A. | 5 | |
| JOHNSON, DONALD J. | 1st Lt. | K.I.A. | 5 | |
| JONES, HOMER H. | 1st Lt. | * | 6 | |
| KOLISCH, PAUL D. | 1st Lt. | — | 6 | |
| LAMM, GEORGE D. | 1st Lt. | – States | 6 | |
| LAVENDER, LEON E. | 1st Lt. | – PW. | 6 | |
| LeFEBVRE, HENRY E. | 1st Lt. | – * | 4 | |
| LING, WALTER J. | 1st Lt. | – States | 4 | |
| MacVICAR, NORMAN | 1st Lt. | * | 4 | |
| MAHAN, FRANCIS L | 1st Lt. | – Hosp | | 4 |
| MARTIN, HAROLD M. | 1st Lt. | * | 4 | |
| MATHIAS, ROBERT D. | 1st Lt. | K.I.A. | 4 | |
| McDUFFIE, JAMES H. | 1st Lt. | * | | 15 |
| McELLICOTT, CHARLES J. | 1st Lt. | — PW. | 3 | |
| McREYNOLDS, LOYLE O. | 1st Lt. | * | | D |
| MERRIAN, ARMAN L. | 1st Lt. | — States | 3 | |
| MILES, GEORGE E. | 1st Lt. | * | 3 | |
| MILLSAPS, WOODROW N. | 1st Lt. | * | 3 | |
| MITCHELL, ROBERT N. | 1st Lt. | K.I.A. | 3 | |
| PLUNKETT, WOODROW C. | 1st Lt. | — | | 4 |
| POLLOM, LESTER W. | 1st Lt. | – Trans | C | |
| QUAID, JOHN A. | 1st Lt. | K.I.A. | C | |
| RICHARD, HAROLD V. | 1st Lt. | PW | | C |
| RUDDY, GERALD H. | 1st Lt. | K.I.A. | C | |
| SANDERS, RAYMOND J. | 1st Lt. | * | C | |
| SCHWANK, BERNARD J. | 1st Lt. | * | C | |
| SHANKEY, JOSEPH I. | 1st Lt. | K.I.A. | | 5 |
| SHAVITCH, EUGENE H. | 1st Lt. | K.I.A. | D | |
| SMITH, CARL A. | 1st Lt. | * | D | |
| THOMPSON, CHARLES J. | 1st Lt. | * | | D |
| TOTH, LOUIS L. | 1st Lt. | Hosp | D | |
| TUTWILER, TEMPLE W. II | 1st Lt. | — PW. | | C |
| VANCE, HAROLD H. | 1st Lt | * | D | |
| GRAVE, FRANKLIN N. | 2nd Lt. | — | | 2 |
| LaROCCO, JACK A. | 2nd Lt. | — | | 2 |
| ALSMAN, RICHARD C. | 2nd Lt. | — | 12 | |
| BENNETT, EDWIN E., JR | 2nd Lt. | — * | 12 | |
| BOLGER, FRANCIS J. | 2nd Lt. | — States | 12 | |
| CAPONERA, NELLO F. | 2nd Lt. | — States | 12 | |
| DAVIS, GEORGE C. | 2nd Lt. | — KIA | 10 | |
| DELFS, HAMILTON O. | 2nd Lt. | — States | 10 | |
| EVANS, JOHN W. | 2nd Lt. | — Trans | 10 | |
| FITZPATRICK, JOSEPH | 2nd Lt. | — Trans | 10 | |
| FRICK, HERMAN L. | 2nd Lt. | * | 9 | |
| FRIGO, LIONEL O. | 2nd Lt. | * | 9 | |
| GURWELL, GEORGE L. | 2nd Lt. | * | 9 | |
| HAGEL, VINCENT | 2nd Lt. | — | 9 | |
| HAMILTON, ELBERT F. | 2nd Lt. | — KIA | 11 | |
| HARTSOUGH, JOSEPH E. | 2nd Lt. | * | 11 | |
| HAVENS, ROBERT N. | 2nd Lt. | * | 11 | |
| HORNE, KELSO C. | 2nd Lt. | — States | 11 | |
| McATAMNEY, RICHARD W. | 2nd Lt. | — " | 14 | |
| McCONNELL, REEVES E. | 2nd Lt. | * | 14 | |
| MEADOWS, BENJAMIN F. | 2nd Lt. | — KIA | 14 | |
| MEHMAN, PAUL E. | 2nd Lt. | — KIA | 14 | |
| MORANN, MARJORIQUE G. | 2nd Lt. | — KIA | 16 | |
| MOSS, ROBERT C., JR. | 2nd Lt. | — | 16 | |
| MURRAY, LAWRENCE F. | 2nd Lt. | * | 16 | |

- 2 -

| NAME | GRADE | 1st SITTING | 2nd SITTING |
| --- | --- | --- | --- |
| POLETTE, LLOYD L., JR | 2nd Lt. — KIA | 16 | |
| RUSSELL, JAMES F. | 2nd Lt. | 17 | |
| SCUDDER, WILLIAM S. | 2nd Lt. — KIA | 17 | |
| SHEEHAM, VINCENT L. | 2nd Lt. — KIA | 17 | |
| SKIPTON, ROY K. | 2nd Lt. — States | 17 | |
| SNEE, ARTHUR F. | 2nd Lt. — KIA | 1 | |
| STEVENS, ARTHUR R. | 2nd Lt. | 1 | |
| TIBBETTS, JAMES D. | 2nd Lt. — | 1 | |
| TOMLINSON, LYNN C. | 2nd Lt. — | 1 | |
| TRACEY, DAVID J. | 2nd Lt. | 19 | |
| TRAHIN, JEAN H. | 2nd Lt. | 19 | |
| WEAVER, ROBERT J. | 2nd Lt. — | 19 | |
| WILLIAMS, GENE H. | 2nd Lt. — KIA | 19 | |
| YOUNG, ADAM B. | 2nd Lt. — PW | 2 | |
| ALBRECHT, DENVER D. | 2nd Lt. — | C | |
| BARGER, ROY S. | W. O. | | D |
| ALLEN, SIMEON L. | W. O. — States | 2 | |
| FLANAGAN, JAMES J. | W. O. | | D |
| MARGOLIN, OLIVER | W. O. | 2. | |

Only two meals will be served daily with the following schedule in effect:

| | | |
| --- | --- | --- |
| FIRST SITTING | BREAKFAST | 0730 Hour |
| SECOND SITTING | BREAKFAST | 0815 Hour |
| FIRST SITTING | DINNER | 1700 Hour |
| SECOND SITTING | DINNER | 1745 Hour |

The first sitting will have moved out of the room by 0805 and 1735 in order that the second sitting can be served. Smoking will be allowed, provided it does not cause lingering and delay in clearing the room by the time specified.

Meals aboard this transport are not chargeable to officers. Tips to waiters are not required but at the end of the voyage it is customary to give tips to the waiters at your tables.

Before officers will be admitted to the dining room, beginning Breakfast, 29 Dec. 43, they must have table assignment cards. These cards can be obtained from Transportation Office on Prom. Forward Deck (deck above state rooms).

By order of the TRANSPORT COMMANDER:

WILLIAM H. NATION
Captain, Infantry
Adjutant.

- 3 -

**Officers' mess seating assignment on the USAT James Parker on the way to England, January 1944. We imagine that George wrote his recollection for the fate of each officer on the journey home in 1945. We found only one error, 1st Lt Michael Bodak was not KIA, but survived the war despite severe wounds that left him paraplegic the rest of his life.**

Dated September 4, 1945, George's orders for return to the States put him in charge of Group Number RE 3216-40 on the SS *Madawaska Victory* for the first leg of the long journey home. Members were scheduled to arrive at the reinforcement depot near the port of Le Havre, France by September 10, 1945. The ship and its 1,986 passengers finally set sail for New York City on September 26, 1945.

Known as "casuals," Group RE 3216-40 consisted of George and five enlisted men, each from a different unit. The group had only one thing in common: all were headed from France to Oregon or Washington in the great American Northwest. Other homebound veterans of the 508th, including George's good friend the Ripper, were also aboard, all assigned to groups based not on their unit but their destinations in the U.S.

Of the more than 3,200 transportation ships constructed by the United States during World War II, 500 were "Victory Ships" like the *Madawaska Victory*, which had been converted, like many others, from a cargo ship to a troop carrier, and named after a town in one of the States. Named for Madawaska, Maine, the ship that George and the Ripper boarded on September 26, 1945, carried at least three other 508th officers and five enlisted men: 1st Lt. Gerald P. Guillot, Chaplain James L. Elder, 2nd Lt. Russell J. Palmerton (E Co.), Pvt. John Sklanka (Hq1), Pvt. James A. Fitzgerald (HqHq), Pvt. Carmelo Costa (A Co.), Pfc. Joseph V. Ricci (H Co. and HqHq), and Pvt. Julius G. Benda (C Co.).[199]

National news was available via six issues of the *Seasick Daily: It Brings Everything Up*, the newsletter published under the supervision of 1st Lt. Guillot of the 508th. The first issue was published on September 27, after the ship had traveled 451 miles on its first day out. George saved all six issues, just as he had saved every issue of the newsletter published on board the *James Parker* when he sailed to Europe in December 1943. We seem to have the only set of these newsletters: no others have been located to date.

Sample news throughout the eight-day voyage included word of many strikes: an elevator operators' strike in New York City, a rubber workers' strike in Ohio, and strikes throughout the States by oil workers, lumber workers, coal miners, electrical workers, and auto workers. As George's letters show, the strikes did not sit well with him, a sentiment he shared with many other veterans. An ominous report originating in Saigon announced that rioters in Indo-China had killed a major in the American Army, and that the death toll had risen to nineteen in hand-to-hand fighting between French and Indo-Chinese troops who strongly opposed the return of French colonial rule. Better news of a far different sort announced the cancellation of V-mail, set for December 1945, after 11.5 million letters had passed through the program. And the best news of all was found in the last issue, dated October 3: Only 235 miles to go before arrival the next day in New York Harbor!

One of the chaplains on board was Captain James L. Elder, who had been with the 508th from Camp Blanding and had accompanied the men through every battle, including the combat jump into Holland. A training injury prevented him from jumping in Normandy, but he had arrived on D+1, (one day after D-Day). George had nothing but praise for the chaplain and had sought his guidance as well. Titled "A Fresh Start," his shipboard "Chaplain's Notes," published on October 3, 1945, describes the combat veteran:

> "[We have] returned from the war to civilian life with clearer vision and greater courage than we would have had otherwise. Anyone who has passed so close to death, feels that he has been given, for some unknown reason, a fresh start in living. Most of us are going home with that conviction. Having been brushed by death, we feel that there is less to fear from life. Such a feeling will make for a stronger, straighter, more satisfying life.
>
> "The attraction of the Christian gospel is that it too furnishes men with a fresh start. The new life becomes so different from the old that Paul does not speak too strongly when he says, 'It is not I that live, but Christ liveth in me.' The keyword of the Christian experience is forgiveness. That means God is willing to wipe out the past and improve on the future if we give our cooperation. It means a new, clean leaf on the calendar of life....
>
> "Immediately before us lies the threshold of a new day. Equipped with the courage and cheerfulness of knowing God's forgiveness through Christ, we are ready to meet life with victory assured."

Chaplain Elder is mentioned affectionately by Selma Abbott [RR 34], a Gold Star wife, knowing that her husband had been buried by the Chaplain himself. Elder not only provided religious services, but he was also "a veteran of all the Red Devil campaigns.... He was awarded the Bronze Star medal for meritorious service while the Red Devils were mopping up in Normandy. After both the Graves Registration officer and his assistant had been killed, Chaplain Elder volunteered to do the job which was accomplished only by working hour after hour without assistance....

"Most of the time while the unit was in combat, he was to be found around the Aid Station giving what assistance and help he could to the attendants and offering comfort to the men who had fallen before the Nazis' guns. When the fury of the firefights lessened and men could crawl out of their foxholes, he held services within sight of the front lines. 'The most valuable thing a soldier has is the will to keep strong and active in everything connecting him with the good things of life.'"[200]

Being a chaplain was dangerous duty. Chaplain Joseph P. Kenny joined the 508th after the Normandy campaign, replacing Chaplain Ignatius P. Maternowski, who was KIA in France. The Catholic chaplain for the 508th was known for "carrying religion to the foxholes, befriending the lonely, cheering the down hearted and burying those that will fight no more." [201]

Chaplains like Elder and Kenny played critical roles in providing the regiment with spiritual guidance and assurance of forgiveness for deeds done and witnessed. Combat like that experienced in World War II and later wars injured the moral values of American combatants raised in a culture where human life is valued.

Our friend and instructor on all things related to the M1 rifle was Gerald J. "Hook" Boutin of the 95th Division during the Battle of the Bulge. He was a sniper with the 101st Airborne in Vietnam. While talking with Jack about the finer points of modifying the M1 for accuracy, Hook suddenly asked, "Doc, am I going to hell? I've killed so many people."

This hardened soldier was at heart still the boy that grew up in the woods of Maine. Late in life, Hook found solace that indeed proved that "the keyword of the Christian experience is forgiveness."

Today's veterans often tell of the chaplain being the only source of guidance, since there still exists an unspoken culture of avoidance when it comes to seeking help from a mental health professional while in service. Many current veterans experience moral injuries that parallel those of the World War II veteran and struggle with meaning in their lives, having served the country for up to twenty years or more, only to witness the hurried and disorganized withdrawal from Afghanistan. Sue's daughter and son-in-law, both veterans of Afghanistan, are not strangers to grappling with this issue. Many find peace in service to other veterans, the community in general, and other activities that are in the broad sense "spiritual."[202]

Going home as a unit is often helpful in reintegrating the veteran. That did not happen for the experienced men of the 508th, who trickled home in small groups, many not having the opportunity to decompress on the voyage home. Paperwork for George and his group of travelers received on October 4, 1945, stated that they were to arrive at Camp Shanks at 11:00 a.m. Almost immediately, they got into trouble.

George, at least, had a friend. As he remembered it in 2001, "Ripper and I almost got locked up the first night we got back. We went into a bar, and they would not serve us a drink. It seems they had some other boys in there that had gotten drunk and caused trouble, so they weren't going to serve us. Ripper went on one side of the guy, and I went on the other. We got us a drink. We almost got in a fight because we overheard this bunch of civilians complaining about how bad they had it in the war with rationing and shortages of this and that. We just lost it and the cops came and took us away. They didn't lock us up but told us not to go back."

Group RE 3216-40 proceeded by government vehicle to Transcon Center, Camp Kilmer, New Jersey, "on or about 5 October for further movement by air to Separation Center No. 42, Camp Beal, CA."[203] George flew most of his journey home, very glad to know he would never again have to jump out of a perfectly good airplane. His discharge papers record his final day of active duty as October 9, 1945. After one year, nine months, and seven days of foreign service, 1st Lt. George L. Gurwell finally made it home.

The army did little to prepare returning veterans for reintegration into civilian life. Civilians could not conceive of the unseen wounds that George, Ripper, and other combat veterans carried with them. The two old friends and brothers-in-arms who had drunk their way across Europe, but could only scrounge up a drink with a fight once they arrived in New York, must have said an emotional goodbye. George later told us that the two of them kept in touch a couple of times a year for the rest of their lives.

George's ghosts persisted, but they did not impair his day-to-day functioning, as they did with some returning veterans, although he did tell us that Jeane used to recount "a wild night in Portland," shortly after he arrived home. "I had a few and was singing with the orchestra, and just jumped on stage. I wouldn't let her drive home, and she got pretty scared by my driving. I guess we were pretty lucky." And yet, despite George's evident PTSD, such incidents remained very rare. As much as he talked and wrote about alcohol during the war, Sue never saw her father drink more than an occasional glass of wine or bottle of beer, and never witnessed him to be intoxicated. George showed great resilience in overcoming the PTSD symptoms he described in his wartime letters.

Jeane and George lived a full life after the war. Their firstborn, Rick, was followed by three sisters, and Jeane pursued a full career in nursing and eventually became a nursing instructor. George finished another B.S. and a M.S. in chemical engineering, then worked in the nuclear industry at Camp Hanford,

Washington, building nuclear weapons for the Cold War. His true passions, however, were his family, the Richland Light Opera (a local theatrical group), his church, and working as a hospice chaplain.

George died in 2004, and Jeane in 2016.

Hi! George

4-9-84

Read on - Sure would be nice to meet again

Harry

1942 1945

508th Parachute Infantry Regiment Association

## EPILOGUE

# FINDING HARRY

The memorial service for George was held on October 6, 2004 in Richland, Washington, just after his granddaughter and ROTC Cadet, Kristen Dodds (nee Harris), graduated from "Warrior Forge," the army's advanced leadership training course at Fort Lewis, Washington. During the service, family and friends shared their memories of how George had touched their lives. Sue reminisced on the many years she and her dad had spent directing, producing, acting, singing, and dancing in Richland Light Opera Company musicals. Kristen, wearing her ROTC uniform, expressed how her grandfather's military service had inspired her. Jack spoke to the gathering about George's war years. Many were in tears, especially local theatre friends: they had not known he was a veteran, much less a D-Day paratrooper.

**Susan Gurwell Talley, Kristen Dodds Harris (Sue's daughter) and Jeane Gurwell, Richland, Washington, 2004. The family gathered for George's memorial service.**

**1st Lt. Kristen Dodds Harris 2009 Kandahar, Afghanistan, 2009. Kristen's experience of war was in stark contrast to her grandmother's.**

During this visit home, Sue discovered several letters stashed away in George's belongings that held special importance to him. A collection of papers and a photograph of Ellsworth Bartholomew were prominent. Letters from army buddies, including one from Capt. Robert Abraham, were easily distinguished from other letters, since they were mostly written on unprocessed V-mail forms.[204] We also came across 508th and HqHq newsletters from the 1980s sent by Harry Hudec, inviting George to association functions.

In the 1983 letter, which was addressed to the veterans of the regiment, Harry wrote a personal note to George. Signed "Big Stoop" and "Harry and Dort" [Dorothy], it mentioned that George had been located by his wartime buddy, Charlie Yates. The only reunion we are certain that George and Jeane attended took place in 2000, in San Antonio, Texas. Also finding registration information about a future meeting, we made plans to attend the upcoming 508th Parachute Infantry Regiment Association reunion in Florida. It would be their sixtieth and final reunion, and the association would be retiring their colors in the place the regiment had originated in October 1942.

The reunion was held in Gainesville and Camp Blanding, Florida, from October 17–21, 2004, just a few days after we returned to Georgia.[205] Once we checked into the hotel and picked up our packet of materials, we were guided to the Command Post (CP), where tables were set up for each company in the regiment. A bar was close at hand. The local 101st Airborne Association supplied all the liquor at the reunion, a wonderful gesture from the "Hundred and Worst" to the "All-Alcoholics."

We found our way to the table marked HqHq, where about a dozen 508th troopers were seated, and who did we find sitting there? Harry Hudec. Strangers to the group, we were not immediately invited to sit down. Jack looked over at Harry's name tag.

> Jack: "Harry Hudec," now that's a name I remember.
>
> Harry: What cha gonna do with that camera?
>
> Jack: Take pictures. There. Gotch ya.
>
> Harry: Take that camera and cram it up your ass!
>
> Jack: Well, how far up do you want me to cram it, sir?
>
> Harry: As far as you can!
>
> (Laughter all around)
>
> Jack: (Introducing Sue) This is Lt George Gurwell's daughter. Does anyone remember Lt Gurwell?
>
> Harry: (Completely changing tone) You're Little Georgie's daughter? [George was 5'7", a foot shorter than Harry.] Well, I'll be! He was one of the best officers we had.

Harry wiped back tears and went around the table to hug Sue.

We were then welcomed to join the group. Pfc. William Tritt quickly made a comment to the effect that we should be careful about the kind of questions we asked. Once assured that we knew how to "behave around veterans," everyone became more relaxed. With the change in mood, we met other 508ers at the table, including Zig Boroughs, Stanly Kass, and Ray O'Connell.

Harry complained about the type of drinks at the CP and left to retrieve a large yet unopened jug of Rossi red wine. He came back fifteen minutes later, poured himself a glass from the jug, and sipped on it slowly. Harry again asked us who we were. Sue explained she was Lt. Gurwell's daughter. Harry repeated his emotional display and statement that "Little Georgie" was one of the Company's best officers.

While writing this book, we kept coming across Harry's name in actions where someone reliable was needed for assistance when 508th troopers were killed. At 6'7", T/5 Harry Hudec was bigger than life. A "gentle giant" who drew the camera like a magnet, he was nicknamed "the Big Stoop" because he had to stoop to hide his height, which was greater than regulation for paratroopers.

(That, at least, is the official story.) He also had to stoop down to get into the C-47 aircraft.

Harry served in the demolitions platoon under Lt. Donald Hardwick, aka "the Ripper," in Regimental Headquarters Company, HqHq, the same company as George. Like George too, Harry was with the 508th all the way from Camp Blanding through Germany. Awarded the Purple Heart for a wound to the leg in Normandy, he was later assigned to attend to Pfc. Hartman's body along with those of three fellow soldiers who were killed when a direct hit from an artillery shell exploded in their fighting hole in Holland. We had read about this episode in George's copy of *The Devil's Tale*, and he later told us personally in 2001 that, for him, that day had been one of the toughest of the war.

Harry was present during another incident when regimental headquarters was attacked by a German Tiger tank at the end of the Battle of the Bulge near Lanzerath, Belgium, in January 1945. When Captain William Nation was killed in the attack, Harry had attended to his body as well. We knew to ask Harry about this incident since we had read Captain Abraham's letter recounting Nation's death. Harry affirmed he had retrieved Captain Nation's mangled remains.

Due to George's assignment of inventorying and shipping KIA possessions home, it is not a stretch to say this duty would have also included handling Capt. Nation's effects, which among them was twenty-three canisters of eight-millimeter film that he took throughout the war. Believe it or not, Bill Nation's grandmother saved a letter documenting how the films were sent home through regular channels, which was highly unusual, since unprocessed film was typically confiscated. George most likely had a hand in preserving the now digitized ninety-minute movie that 508th veterans loved seeing at previous reunions, shown by nephew Bill Nation.[206]

The next day we set up a display of our M1 rifles in an adjacent room. We took several wonderful photos of 508th veterans with ear-to-ear grins, holding "my old M1."

**Staff Sergeant Herman Jahnigen, Co. A, holding Sue Talley's Winchester M1, 2004 Reunion.**

After securing our display, it was back to the CP to hear tales from George's company. Harry returned with his jug of Rossi, nearly full. It was clear that he did not remember having met us the day before. Based on Jack's training and experience, it seemed to us that Harry was suffering from Alzheimer's disease.[207]

Subsequent events confirmed our suspicions. During the next few days, Harry displayed irritability, loud verbal outbursts, and memory lapses. He quit asking who we were. One day near lunch time, he stated he was going to walk to a restaurant "just down the road that has good chicken noodle soup." Harry wanted nothing to do with ordering lunch at the hotel and was determined to walk to get his soup. Rather than argue with him, Jack offered to take him to the restaurant. They drove for at least a mile, with no restaurant in sight. Finally seeing a Chinese place, Harry proclaimed, "They have good chicken soup there."

They walked in and Harry told the waiter, "I want a large bowl of chicken noodle soup," to which the waiter responded that they did not serve chicken soup. Jack quickly intervened by saying he would order for both of them, and got Harry a bowl of egg drop soup, "just like chicken noodle." Harry was satisfied. Upon finishing, he complained loudly about the tab, so Jack took care of it and drove them back to the hotel. Other 508th veterans complained that Harry "drinks a bit."

After talking with other relatives of HqHq veterans of our generation, Deb Abraham, daughter of Captain Robert Abrahm, and Bill Nation, nephew of Captain William Nation, we assigned a rotation to keep an eye on Harry. "Harry duty" included sitting beside him to calm him down at meetings; going to his room to escort him to breakfast; and Jack's duty: walking him to his room at night, since he could not operate the magnetic swipe cards to enter his building and room.

Harry had arrived at the reunion two days early, and one morning, he yelled to the entire assembled group that he could not get more coffee. Now, hearing complaints that Harry was drinking awfully early, Jack decided to tell the conference commander, Ernie Lansom, his suspicions. Harry was not drunk: he was showing the confusion, irritability, and memory lapses of Alzheimer's. We all kept a closer eye on Harry. Given his service to the 508th during the war, and all the work he had done afterwards to organize and keep the 508th Parachute Infantry Regiment Association going, it was an honor to assist him.

At the next gathering at the CP, Sue told the story of her dad driving a load of rations to the front under artillery fire in Holland, only to find that the men had killed a cow and were butchering it. Stan Kass piped up, "I was the butcher!" The eight-millimeter film Captain Nation took during the war does indeed capture Pfc. Kass chopping away at the cow.

We knew to ask the group about one last episode, because we knew of Harry's friendship with another trooper killed in action, Ellsworth Bartholomew. In 1945, Bart's sister, Evalyn Ryckman, had mentioned Harry by name in a letter to George, seeking to know the circumstances of her brother's death in June 1944, in France. One afternoon during an unusual lull in the conversation, Jack took the opportunity to ask if anyone had known Ellsworth Bartholomew. Stanley Kass piped up immediately: "Sure, my buddy Bart." He could not believe we had a picture of him. We showed the group the photo of Bart and his girlfriend, Barbara Duck: "Yep, that's him," said Stanley. When we explained our finds in George's estate, Stanly added: "I can tell you exactly how he died. Bart was famous for making one-man patrols. One night he went out on his own, and the next morning we found him up against a tree shot to hell, with dead Krauts laying all around." Bart was listed as wounded on June 14, 1944, and died of wounds two days later.

This revelation motivated us to look for Bart's relatives after we got home. Evalyn's 1945 letter mentioned her son, Bart's eleven-year-old nephew, Donald Ryckman. Donald would be seventy years old in 2004. We found his phone number and gave him a call, hoping he was still alive so we could tell him about his uncle's heroic death. We got an answer on the *first* call—it was Donald's widow, Rose Marie Ryckman of Healdsburg, California.

Donald and Rose did not have children, but there were nieces and nephews in the family. Rose Marie knew that Uncle Bud (Bart) was killed in World War II, but knew nothing of his famous paratrooper unit or his participation in D-Day. We wrote her a letter of explanation and sent copies of all our letters and documents, including the account of Bart's death, even though we are certain that George contacted Bart's sister after the war.

On the next-to-the-last day of the reunion, we all boarded buses for the short ride from Gainesville, Florida, to Camp Blanding, where the 508th originated. For miles, the route out of Gainesville was filled with flag-waiving citizens who had gathered to show their appreciation to the 508th veterans. Awaiting the start of the ceremony, when the association would lower its flag for the last time, we saw Harry looking confused, wondering what to do next. Sue invited him to come over and sit with us, which he did. Jack took a wonderful picture of the two of them together. It was an honor to be with him during the ceremony and hearing him sing "God Bless the USA" in his deep baritone voice. It is still a cherished memory.

**Sue with Harry Hudec, the 508th Association 60th reunion, 2004, Camp Blanding, FL.**

The solemn occasion of retiring the 508th's association colors was officiated by none other than Command Sergeant Major (CSM), Kenneth "Rock" Merritt, a corporal on D-Day who stayed in the service and served all the way through Vietnam. When he was over ninety years old, he was given the rank of Honorary Command Sergeant Major of the Army—quite an honor. Rock's daughter, Dianne Merritt Pflueger, told us in 2019 that if her dad was anything, he was "by the book."

On a crystal clear, shirtsleeves-wearing fall day, Rock introduced a representative from twelve of the thirteen companies, but after a pause, it became clear that no representative from Regimental Headquarters Company would be called. Harry noticed this slight and became highly agitated. He yelled, "Where's regimental headquarters?" so loudly, we thought for sure they could hear him in Atlanta. Rock defended the ceremony, explaining that no one had nominated a company representative, despite repeated requests. Harry yelled his complaint again, but to no avail. We thought for certain that he was going to join the assembled group himself, but he did not, and stayed beside Sue. After a moving ceremony, we reboarded the buses for Gainesville for one last gabfest in the CP.

**508th PIR, HQHQ group picture, Gainesville, FL. Front Row, L to R: Ray O'Connell, Geoff Brand, Jack Talley, Susan Gurwell Talley, Andrew Smith, Deborah Abraham, Rob Gawel. Second Row L to R: Zig Boroughs, Stanley Kass, Harry Hudec, Charlotte Apple, Lyle Smith, Mary Grieshammar, Ed Anderson. Third Row L to R: Chuck Oehler, Bill Nation, Helen Sakowski, Frank Sakowski, Grace Brand, George Brand, Darrell Apple, William Tritt, Lawrence Grieshammar, Carol Anderson. Purchased Reunion Photo.>**

On our last night in Florida, we made a plan to assist Harry on his journey home. Jack would escort him to his room and Deb Abraham would get him to the airport and contact his children. The other veterans had said that Harry always traveled with a large framed picture of Dort after she passed in 1998. Later, Jack walked Harry to his hotel and unlocked the door to his room. Entering, he saw the jug of wine still nearly full, his small bag already packed, and the 8.5" x 11" framed picture of Dort sitting on top of his bag. Jack had to hold back a tear. The two men shook hands. Then Jack took a step back and came to attention. Harry did the same.

Jack: Harry, I have one last thing to say to you.

Harry: What's that?

Jack (shouting): Airborne!

Harry: All the Way!

## APPENDIX I

# WIVES AND OFFICERS—ROUND ROBIN LETTERS

Unless otherwise noted, all biographical information was found on 508pir.org.

RR 1—Helen Moss. 2nd Lt. Robert C. Moss, Company H. The troopers in his plane were badly misdropped on D-Day. Lt. Moss survived the war, living until 1985.

RR 2—Beth Pollom. 1st Lt. Lester Pollom, Hq2, was awarded the Silver Star for action on June 7, when he led two enlisted men on a patrol to Chef-du-Pont from the surrounded Hill 30 area to obtain life-saving blood plasma for the many injured and cut-off paratroopers. He lived until old age.

RR 3—Jeane Gurwell. 2nd Lt. George Gurwell, HqHq.

George died in 2004 at the age of eighty-three.

RR 4—Bonnie Hetland. Capt. Eugene Hetland. Company E. He was in the same company as Robert Mathias. He lived until 1990.

RR 5—Dottie Quaid. 1st Lt. John Quaid, Company H, was badly misdropped on June 6, 1944. He was declared missing on June 9 and declared Killed in Action on June 23, 1944.

RR 6—Anne Klein. Capt. James Klein. A regimental surgeon, Capt. Klein was awarded the Purple Heart for the wound he received on June 7, 1944. He was able to return to duty throughout the Normandy campaign. Dr. Klein died in 1976.

RR 7—Barbara Martin. 1st Lt. Harold Martin, Company F, was promoted to captain prior to the Holland invasion, and was the CO of F Co.

RR 8—Terry Tibbitts. 2nd Lt. James "Dean" Tibbetts, Hq2, was wounded on D-Day near Picauville, attempting to reach a wounded machine gunner. He was wounded again in Holland.

RR 9—Lauren Dress. Capt. Hillman Dress, Hq3, was WIA in Normandy on July 3, 1944, in the assault on Hill 131, just before the 508th was pulled off the front line and sent back to base camp in Nottingham, England. He lived through the war and died in 1965.

RR 10—Mary Skipton. 2nd Lt. Roy Skipton, Company B was wounded in December 1944 during the Battle of the Bulge and received the Purple Heart Medal. He survived the war and lived until 2010.

RR 11—Edith "Sis" Tomlinson. 2nd Lt. Lynn Tomlinson, D Co, was third platoon leader and only found one of his men early on D-Day. He has a story like the one depicted in *The Longest Day*, where a group of Americans passed a group of Germans going in the opposite direction with a hedgerow between them, and they just smiled at each other. See Nordyke, *Put Us Down in Hell*, page 89. He passed away in 2010.

RR 12—Mary Williams. 1st Lt. Gene Williams, Hq3, was KIA in Normandy, June 20, 1944. In keeping with censorship rules, George did not mention Lt. Williams in subsequent letters and did not respond to Jeane's question about the news of the twins' birth. Gene Jr. and Jack Williams would both later serve in special forces in Vietnam.

RR 13—Doris Daily. 1st Lt. John "Jack" Daly, Hq3 and commanding officer of Company I.

RR 14—Mary Casteel. Maj. James Casteel. George worked closely with this officer, who was in charge of supply and logistics for the regiment. Major Castell was Wounded in Action on D-Day and received the Purple Heart, according to Special Order #54, Gurwell Collection.

RR 15—Ruth Beaver. 1st Lt. Neal L. Beaver, Hq3, received the Purple Heart on D-Day when he was hit in the jaw with a spent tracer round just as he jumped. Ruth most likely had not been informed of her husband's wounding when she wrote her letter. He passed away in 2007. See Boroughs, *The 508th Connection*, page 112.

RR 16—Jerry Hardwick. 1st Lt. Donald Hardwick was George's best friend throughout the war. He lived until 2002. Jerry and Donald Hardwick had twin sons, Bruce and Craig, who both served in Vietnam. Bruce's son, Major Clay Hardwick, is an instructor at West Point [Personal communication, Bruce Hardwick, 2018]. Lt. Hardwick was Wounded in Action on September 26, 1944, in Holland.

RR 17—Ferne Dowling. Capt. James A. Dowling, Service Company, is mentioned in the historical record for earning the Combat Infantryman Badge for the Holland campaign. He died in 1998, after forty-one years of service in firefighting and rescue.

RR 18—Dot Driggers. Capt. James C. Driggers was CO of HqHq Company on D-Day.

Captain Driggers wrote George from Ft. Benning on October 27, 1944: "Will you please send me a copy of the orders awarding the Combat Infantry Badges and also the Unit Citation [for Normandy]? So far, I haven't been able to secure those although I asked for them thru channels quite some time ago. Please give my kindest regards to all the officers (tell Hardwick we have heard from his wife) and Sgt. Cooper [HqHq] and all the men."

Capt. Driggers wrote again from Ft. Benning on July 22, 1945: "Dear George, just a note to tell you that I'm still fighting a 'paper war' here at Benning that several of the people have come in and that we are thinking of you often and wishing it were possible to be with you. Merriam, Lamm, and Mahan and Morann are back here now and several enlisted men: Sgt. Williams, Co B., Sgt. Berris, Hq3 and Sgt. Flaherty, Co I.

My year is just about up now so I should be sent out as a replacement to the Pacific soon, I hope. Be careful with the little frauleins and write me when you can. Best of luck to all the boys. Sincerely J. C. Driggers.

RR 19—Helen Bell. Capt. Alton Bell, Hq3, worked closely with Lt. Col. Mendez, commanding officer (CO) of the Third Battalion. Promoted to Major prior to the Holland invasion, Bell was a key communication officer in the command post. His code name was "Dingdong." He lived until 1983. See Nordyke, *Put Us Down in Hell*, page 357.

RR 20—Doris Mathias. 1st Lt. Robert P. Mathias was assigned to Company E. He died at the age of 28. See Ambrose, *D-Day June 6th 1944*, pages 22–24.

RR 21—Harriett Peterson. Capt. Melvin V. Peterson led the forty-eight soldiers that comprised the 508th band and served as Col. Lindquist's assistant or adjutant.

RR 22—Eleanor Thompson. Capt. Charles J. Thompson stayed active training paratroopers until his retirement in 1982. He died in 2013, and is buried with his wife Elanor in Arlington National Cemetery.

RR 23—Doris Novak. Capt. Frank. J. Novak became S-3 of the Third Battalion on June 22, 1944. The Third Battalion Diary reports him as wounded on July 4. He died in 1995.

RR 24—Madelon Merriam. 1st Lt. Armon L. Merriam was in Service Company, then A Company. He was one of the original cadre members, and was wounded in Holland on September 30, 1944. He passed away in 1962.

RR25—Bernie Shankey. 1st Lt. Shankey, Hq3 was wounded in the arm or shoulder shortly after the drop on D-Day. His group rounded up some prisoners, but in the confusion and rapidly changing fortunes of battle, they themselves fell captive to the Germans. They were then taken to a chateau two miles north of Picauville that served as the headquarters for the German 91st Airlanding Division. Early the next morning, the troopers were loaded into trucks to be transported to the German fortress in Brest, Brittany. The convoy consisted of one truck with officers and about six others with enlisted men, many of whom were wounded. Heading south and west along the road St. Sauveur-le-Vicomte-La Haye-du Puits, the trucks were sighted and repeatedly strafed by a flight of Thunderbolts [American P-47 fighter-bombers].

Lt. Shankey was killed instantly, along with about twenty other troopers. Vincent Barry (C Co), who had been grievously wounded during a predawn skirmish, recalls the trucks were in flames from the attack. The ranking American captive, Lt. Col. George V. Millett, 507th PIR, insisted that the dead be buried, and their graves properly identified. Allied troops who later overran the area located the graves. Lt. Shankey, posthumously promoted to Captain, was re-interred in the Brittany American Cemetery. He is buried in Plot C, Row 15, Grave 12. See http://508pir.org/honors/docs/shankey_jl.htm.

RR 26—Cheryl Hoffman. 1st Lt. Herbert Hoffman, Hq1, S1, was wounded and received the Purple Heart for action in Belgium, on December 24, 1944. He passed away in 1985.

RR 27—Edna Taylor. Captain Royal Taylor. Captain Taylor's WWII awards include the Bronze Star with Oak Leaf Cluster. He later served in the Korean war and achieved the rank of colonel in 1968. He lived until 1992.

RR 28—Rosemary Guillot. Lt. Gerald P. Guillot was initially commanding officer of A Co., then Hq1. He landed 400 yards north of the Douve River on D-Day within a stone's throw of Montessy, where he assembled a small group of about thirty men who penetrated the village and quietly entered the German command post, slashing the throats of four officers. Paratroopers had been ordered to use knives and bayonets as much as possible to avoid revealing their position, and SLA Marshall reports in *Nightdrop* that Guillot surprised the Germans while sleeping, slit their throats, and captured a clerk. Rock Merritt, who was in Guillot's platoon on D-Day, later confirmed these actions to us in our 2018 interview.

RR 29—Evelyn Milam Captain Robert L. Milam had been assigned as Commanding Officer of C Co. on D-Day but was replaced due to his injury. He was Wounded in Action in Belgium on February 24, 1945 but survived the war.

RR 30—Betty Hagar. Initially assigned to C Company on Organization Day, November 4, 1943, 1st Lt. Ernest J. Hager received the Purple Heart for a bullet wound on June 6, 1944. He survived the war. See 508th PIR Organization Day Program and General Order #54, Gurwell Collection.

RR 31—Jeanne Thomas. Maj. David E. Thomas, CO of the Medical Detachment, was captured in Normandy on June 10, escaped on June 13, and rejoined friendly forces on June 15, 1944. He retired as a brigadier general, having participated in World War II, Korea, and Vietnam, and was the attending physician of both President Eisenhower and President Johnson. He died in 2002.

RR 32—Anne Havens. 2nd Lt. Robert N. Havens, Hq2, S-1 (Personnel), was awarded the Bronze Star for action in Holland. He died in 1993.

RR 33—Jane Creary. Captain Hal Creary was Commanding Officer, H Company on D-Day. He was killed in the same incident noted previously involving P-47 fighters where 1st Lt. Joseph Shankey and 1st Lt. Francis Flanders were killed as well on June 7, 1944. Killed-in-Action dates vary due to differences in identifying physical remains. See also Boroughs, *The 508th Connection*, pages 158–160.

RR 34—Selma Abbott. 2nd Lt. Edgar R. Abbott was assigned to Hq1 on D-Day as the mortar platoon leader. He was killed in action June 17, 1944 and awarded the Bronze Star Medal.

RR 35—Helen Flanders. 1st Lt. Francis E. Flanders was CO, F Co. on D-Day. He died on June 7, 1944, in the same incident noted previously involving P-47 fighters where 1st Lt. Joseph Shankey and Capt. Hal Creary were also killed. See Boroughs, *The 508th Connection*, pages 73–84.

RR 36—Jeanette Foley. 1st Lt. John P. Foley was the leader of First Platoon, A Co., on June 6, 1944. He was involved in the entire Normandy battle, including the heavy fighting for Hill 131. He was awarded the Bronze Star for valor for action—who along with others—that kept his company from being destroyed. He was awarded the Distinguished Service Cross for action in Holland three months later. He lived until 2008. See Boroughs, *The 508th Connection*, page 247.

RR 37—Marrion Farrell. 1st Lt. Joseph F. Farrell was assigned to C Company and was Wounded in Action on D-Day. He also earned the Bronze Star. During a training jump, the C Co. First Sargent, Leonard Funk, did a test jump with Lt. Farrell's dog. Farrell died in 2001.

RR 38—Dorothy Hamlin. CWO Arthur N. Hamlin was the assistant adjutant for Service Company. He worked closely with the Regimental S1, Captain William Nation. Assisting Captain Milam with typing orders for new transfers in Nottingham, England, July 1944, Hamlin keyed the following:

> Our Battle Cry: Diablo. Our Aim: To Give the Enemy Hell. Our Morale: Always the Best. Our Convictions: We're the best Regiment, attached to the best Division, in the best Army, of the best country in the World. Fellows—you've really hit the jackpot. Dig in and join the Regiment with everything you've got. By order of Captain Milam: /s/ ARTHUR N. HAMLIN, CWO, USA

Hamlin survived the war.

RR39—Dottie Delfs. 2nd Lt. Hamilton O. Delfs was initiated at a "Prop Blast" party when he earned his jump wings on August 28, 1943. He served with Company E. He was the assistant platoon leader (with 1st Lt. Robert Mathias as the platoon leader) on D-Day. He was wounded in the Normandy Campaign. He lived until 2001.

RR 40—Jean Snee. 2nd Lt. Arthur F. Snee enlisted as a private in February 1941, but by November 1941, he was commissioned as a second lieutenant. Snee served with F Company and was Killed in Action on June 6, 1944.

RR 41—Virginia Johnson. Capt. Kenneth L. Johnson was the regimental munitions officer according to the Organization Day Program, Gurwell Collection. He died in 1990.

RR 42—Dorothy Scudder. 2nd Lt. William S. Scudder, Company G, was Killed in Action on July 3, 1944.

RR 43—Alice Lindquist. Col. Roy E. Lindquist was the commanding officer of the 508th PIR from its inception through the end of WWII. He wrote Field Manual, 23–5, for the United States Rifle, Caliber 30, M1 (The Garand). He ended his Army career at the rank of Major General. He lived until 1986.

RR 44—Jean Mendez. Lt. Col. Louis Mendez was the commanding officer, Third Battalion, (G, H, and I Companies). He was awarded the Distinguished Service Cross for the Normandy campaign along with many other medals during the course of his service. Of the twelve battalion commanders of parachute infantry that made the D-Day jump, Col. Mendez was the only one that was not wounded or seriously injured. He lived until 2001.

RR 45—Helen Moss. Second RR letter. See RR1.

RR 46—Naomi Gillespie. 2nd Lt. Charles T. Gillespie was initially a cadre member with Company I. Later he was the assistant regimental intelligence officer and was Wounded in Action on June 6, 1944. He returned to duty on June 29, 1944. He lived until 2005.

RR 47—Reba Holmes. Maj. Othoe E. Holmes was the regimental Intelligence Officer (S-2) on D-Day. Later he became the commanding officer of Second Battalion, just before the Holland invasion, and promoted to Lt. Col. During his time with the 508th he was awarded the Bronze Star, Silver Star, and Purple Heart Medals. He died of leukemia in 1959.

RR48—Nancy Graham. Capt. Chester E. Graham was the commanding officer of Headquarters Company, 2nd Battalion on D-Day. During the Normandy campaign, he was the third of four commanding officers for the entire 2nd Battalion. He was relieved of command on July 4, 1944, objecting to an attack over open space rather than taking advantage of nearby woods for cover. Col. Mark J. Alexander also gives a stirring account of this battle. See Alexander and Sparry, *Jump Commander*, page 224. Chet passed away in 2015.

RR49—Nancy Garry. 1st Lt. William J. Garry was killed in action in the Holland campaign while single handedly covering his platoon's withdrawal. Nancy was awarded Lt. Garry's posthumous Silver Star in a ceremony after the war.

# BIBLIOGRAPHY


Alexander, Mark J., and John Sparry. *Jump Commander: In Combat with the 505th and 508th Parachute Infantry Regiments, 82nd Airborne Division in World War II*. Philadelphia: Casemate, 2010.

Ambrose, Stephen E. *D-Day June 6th 1944: The Climactic Battle of World War II*. New York: Touchstone, 1994.

Atkinson, Rick. *The Guns at Last Light: The War in Western Europe, 1944-1945*. London: Picador Books, 2013.

Bando, Mark. *Avenging Eagles: Forbidden Tales of the 101st Airborne Division in World War 2*. Ann Arbor: Mark Bando Publishing, 2006.

Berry, Adam G.R. *And Suddenly They Were Gone: An Oral and Pictorial History of the 82nd Airborne Division in England, February–September 1944*. Boston: Overlord Publishing, 2015.

Beevor, Antony. *D-Day, the Battle for Normandy*. New York: Penguin Books, 2009.

Beevor, Antony. *The Battle of Arnhem The Deadliest Airborne Operation of World War II*. New York: Penguin Random House, 2018.

Blair, Clay. *Ridgeway's Paratroopers*. New York: The Dial Press, 1985.

Boroughs, Zig. *The 508th Connection*. Bloomington, IN: Xlibris, 2013.

Boroughs, Zig. *The Devil's Tale*. Summerville, GA: ESPY Publishing Co., 1992.

Burns, Dwayne T., and Leland Burns. *Jump Into the Valley of the Shadow: The War Memories of Dwayne Burns Communications Sergeant, 508th P.I.R.* Philadelphia: Casemate, 2006.

Carrell, Paul. *Invasion! They're coming*! Atglen, PA: Schiffer Military History, 1995.

Doubler, Michael D. *Closing with the Enemy: How GIs Fought the War in Europe, 1944–1945*. Lawrence, KA: University Press of Kansas, 1994, 179–95.

Drez, Ronald. *Voices of D-Day: The Story of the Allied Invasion Told by Those Who Were There*. Baton Rouge: Louisiana State University Press, 1994.

Fauntleroy, Barbara Gavin. *The General and His Daughter: The Wartime Letters of General James M. Gavin to his Daughter Barbara.* New York: Fordham University Press, 2007.

Gavin, James M. The James M. Gavin Papers, Box .8, Personal Diaries, 1939–September 45, June 1958–May 1960. United States Army History Institute, Carlisle Barracks, Pennsylvania. Copy supplied by Gayle Wurst.

Gavin, James M. *On to Berlin: Battles of an Airborne Commander 1943–1946.* New York: Viking Press, 1978.

Green, Bob. *Once Upon a Town: The Miracle of the North Platte Canteen.* New York: Harper, 2003.

Grossman, David. *On Killing: The Psychological Cost of Learning to Kill in War and Society*, New York: Back Bay Books, 2009.

Hanson, Victor Davis. *The Second World Wars: How the First Global Conflict Was Fought and Won.* New York: Basic Books, 2017.

Kershaw, Alex. *The Longest Winter: The Battle of the Bulge and the Epic Story of World War II's Most Decorated Platoon.* Boston: Da Capo, 2004, 132–135.

Langdon, Allen L. *Ready: The World War II—The History of the 505th Parachute Infantry Regiment, 82nd Airborne Division*, ed. Rev. George B. Wood, Indianapolis. IN: 1986, 121.

LoFaro, Guy. *The Sword of St. Michael: The 82nd Airborne Division in World War II.* Cambridge, MA: DaCapo, 2011.

Lord, William G. *History of the 508th Parachute Infantry Regiment.* Washington, D.C.: Infantry Journal Press, 1948.

McCann, John P. *Passing Through: The 82nd Airborne Division in Ireland 1943–44.* Newtownards, N. Ireland: Colourpoint Books, 2005.

Marshall, S.L.A. *Night Drop: The American Airborne Invasion of Normandy.* New York: Bantam Books, 1962.

Millett, Allan R. "*Blood Upon the Risers.*" In Penrose, Jane., (Ed.) *The D-Day Companion.* Oxford: Osprey, 2004.

Murphy, Robert M. *No Better Place to Die: The Battle for La Fière Bridge: Sainte-Mère-Église, June 1944.* Philadelphia: Casemate 2009.

Nordyke, Phil, *All American, All the Way: The Combat History of the 82nd Airborne Division in World War II.* St. Paul, MN: Zenith Press, 2005.

Nordyke, Phil. *Four Stars of Valor: The Combat History of the 505th PIR in World War II*, St. Paul, MN: Zenith, 2006.

Nordyke, Phil. *Put Us Down in Hell: The Combat History of the 508th Parachute Infantry Regiment in World War II.* Historic Ventures, LLC, McKinney, Texas: 2012.

Reeves, Richard. *Daring Young Men: The Heroism and Triumph of the Berlin Airlift, June 1948–May 1949.* New York: Simon and Schuster, 2010.

Ryan, Cornelius. *The Longest Day: The Classic Epic of D-Day, Collector's Edition.* New York: Simon and Schuster, 1959, 2014.

Ryan, Cornelius. *A Bridge Too Far*, New York: Popular Library, 1974.

Sutherland, Jon and Diane Canwell. *The Berlin Airlift: The Salvation of a City.* Gretna, LA: Pelican, 2007.

Van Lunteren, Frank. *Blocking Kampfgruppe Peiper: The 504th Parachute Infantry Regiment in the Battle of the Bulge*, Havertown, PA: Casemate, 2015.

Vlahos, Mark C. *Men Will Come: A History of the 314th Troop Carrier Group 1942–45.* Hoosick Falls, NY: Merriam Press, 2019.

Zaloga, Steven J. *Battle of the Bulge 1944 (1): St Vith and the Northern Shoulder.* Minnetonka, MN: The History Channel Club, 2005.

# ENDNOTES

## INTRODUCTION: THE JOURNEY BEGINS

1 V-Mail, an official 8.5 x 11-inch form with space for the date and address at the top, was devised to decrease the weight of letters shipped overseas. The message was restricted to an 8 x 8-inch box. The form was photographed and placed on a roll with thousands of other letters at special processing centers; at the overseas processing center, it was printed onto a 4 x 4-inch note and put in a small envelope.

2 In WWII, a parachute infantry regiment had a company of about 150 men assigned to regimental headquarters company, (HqHq Co.). Each of three battalions had a separate headquarters company, labeled Hq1, Hq2, and Hq3. Each battalion had three "line" companies, labeled Companies A, B. and C for 1st Battalion (Co. A, Co. B, Co. C). 2nd Battalion was Companies D, E, and F (Co. D, Co. E, Co. F). 3rd Battalion was Companies G, H, and I (Co. G, Co. H and Co. I). Special Services Company handled logistic functions for the regiment, such as mail and the medical detachment. Headquarters for the regiment and each battalion had four staff officers who were specialists: S-1 (personnel), S-2 (intelligence), S-3 (plans and operations), and S-4 (logistics and supply).

3 The 82nd patch has AA on it, meaning "All Americans." 82nd members also use the AA as a greeting/parting phrase. One veteran initiates the phrase with "Airborne" and is answered by "All the Way!" This was the motto of the 82nd.

4 Post-Traumatic Stress Disorder and World War II Veterans David Grossman, *On Killing: The Psychological Cost of Learning to Kill in War and Society* (New York: Back Bay Books, 2009), 97.

5 Antony Beevor, *D-Day: The Battle for Normandy*, (New York: Penguin, 2014), 67. See also Mark Bando, *Avenging Eagles: Forbidden Tales of the 101st Airborne Division in World War 2* (Ann Arbor, MI: Mark Bando Publishing, 2006), 104–111.

## PTSD AND WWII VETERANS

6 Ralph Thomas, "Voices of the Past," 4–17–2002, http://508pir.org/voices/t/thomas_rh_03.htm As Thomas reports, this verbal order was not always followed. Recounting his discussion with Col. Linquist about whether to execute the twelve to fifteen prisoners (numbers vary) captured at La Fière Bridge on D-Day, the Germans were spared because the 508th had a building in which to lock them up. George was present at the Manoir

at La Fière when the Germans surrendered; this incident and worse were ingredients for the PTSD stew that we have learned so much more about since we first spoke to George in 2001.

7 *Letters from Captain William H. Nation, 508th Parachute Infantry Regiment, 82nd Airborne Division, United States Army, January 1941–January 1945*, Edited by Bill C. Nation (1998, Bill C. Nation), 179. Private collection. Thanks to Bill, who granted us permission to quote from his uncle's letters.

8 The U.S. Department of Veterans Affairs, National Center for PTSD, Treatment Basics, "Understanding PTSD Treatment": https://www.ptsd.va.gov/understand_tx/index.asp.

9 Conversation with Phil Cronin, Family and Friends of the 508th PIR Association Reunion, Columbus, OH, June 25, 2021.

## CHAPTER I: PRELUDE TO LOVE AND WAR

10 In British slang, a "ripstitch" is an "unruly, wild, reckless person."

11 Lt. Donald Hardwick's nickname later morphed from "Ristitch" to "the Ripper." He was known as Ripper throughout the war.

12 *Letters from Captain William H. Nation,* September 20, 1942, 75.

13 Rick Smith from 508th PIR HqHq, Reenacted, has located a document from the estate of First Sgt. (later Lt) J.D. Kelley, Jr. that attributes the authorship of the song to Kelley and Herbert Malloy, in 1943, at Camp Blanding, FL, in honor of Joseph Singletary. Records from the 508th indeed place Kelley at Camp Blanding in early 1943. (Source: daughter Trish McLoud).

## CHAPTER II: PINEHURST AND CAMP MACKALL, NORTH CAROLINA

14 This information was located in an unnamed, undated newspaper clipping in the Gurwell Collection, doc109.

15 This quote is from an undated newspaper clipping in the Gurwell Collection, doc132.

16 The Holly Inn, Franklin Flats, and Woodbine Cottage are listed today as National Historical Sites. Pinehurst boasts the first 18-hole golf course in the United States and has hosted the North and South Open, the North and South Amateur Golf Championship, the PGA Championship, the Ryder Cup, and the U.S. Open.

17 George was a jump master on night training jumps. In another lesson, "Lt. Gurwell will show you how to swim thru burning oil." *Devil's Digest,* Vol.1, No. 7, p. 4, September 2, 1943. Gurwell Collection.

18 Colonel Roy E. Linquist, Headquarters 508th Parachute Infantry, Office of the Regimental Commander, "History of the 508th Parachute Infantry," National Archive, p. 3. Cited in: Phil Nordyke, *Put Us Down in Hell: The Combat History of the 508th Parachute Infantry Regiment in World War II* (Historic Ventures, LLC, McKinney, Texas: 2012), 23.

19 Frank Schouers is not listed on 508pir.org, the Organizational Day Roster of November 11, 1943, or on the Officer's seating list for the voyage across the Atlantic on the *James Parker.*

20 Capt. Graham amusingly recounted how he and his superior officers ducked out of duty: "During a three-day rest period out in the woods on Tennessee maneuvers, Col Shanley told me that he would be gone for 24 hours and that Maj Shields Warren would be

in charge of the battalion. An hour later, Maj Warren told me that he would be gone for 24 hours and that I would be in charge of the battalion.... [My wife]...had been in California. We had a baby boy who died after one day.... But now she was in Nashville and I was in the woods on bivouac. I told Lt Tibbetts that I would be back in twenty-four hours and that he was in charge. With walnut stain on my face and in a dingy jumpsuit I got a ride to Nashville and spent the night with her. Maj Warren found out about my little escapade and thought it was bad but funny. He told Col Shanley, and I found out many years later that Col Shanley had written a scathing report about the incident." http://508pir.org/pdf_files/memoirs_graham_chester_e.pdf

21 Shoes were rationed during the war, requiring a ration stamp to buy a pair.

22 Jeane wrote a private letter to George, thus the unrestricted tone. Helen and Jeane wrote to each other throughout the war offering information, friendship, and mutual support. While we do not have any of the letters between Jeane and Helen, Jeane mentions "letters from Helen" in six of her letters to George during the European deployment.

23 As a rigger, Lt Thompson specialized in packing parachutes. Once the regiment had completed its jumps, his part in maneuvers was over, which meant he could return to base earlier than most.

24 Jimmie Davis: singer-songwriter of country and westerns and blues, known for "You Are My Sunshine;" *The Philip Morris Playhouse* (a 30-minute dramatic radio series on CBS from 1939–1934); *Fibber McGee and Molly*: long-running situation comedy on NBC radio featuring the adventures of a working-class storyteller and his wife, by the husband-and-wife team Jim and Marian Jordan; Bob Hope: stand-up comedian, vaudevillian, actor, singer, dancer and author, whose radio career began in 1934, and who made over fifty tours for the United Service Organization (USO) to entertain active-duty American service personnel; Red Skelton: American comedy entertainer whose 70-year career included a regularly scheduled national radio act between 1937 and 1957.

25 The Western Front in the European Theater of Operations, which opened with the invasion of Normandy on June 6, 1944, and was fought in France, Holland, and Belgium; the Axis powers had been fighting the Soviet Union on the Eastern Front since June 22, 1941.

## CHAPTER III: LEAVING PINEHURST: SENDING THE 508TH TO WAR, RR 1–7

26 Women who served in the US Navy in an auxiliary capacity in WWII.

27 Bob Greene, *Once Upon a Town: The Miracle of North Platte Canteen,* (Harper, New York: 2003).

28 In case the mail was intercepted and fell into enemy hands, censorship was in place for information contained in letters to and from overseas. Officers censored their own letters, but enlisted men had to have an officer sign off on all mail sent. All letters were subject to spot checks. Mail was required to be censored and sent out within forty-eight hours. The War Department decreed ten prohibited subjects:

Military information of Army units—location, strength, materiel, or equipment.

Military installations.

Transportation facilities.

Convoys, routs, ports (embarkation or disembarkation) time in route, naval protection, or incidents in route.

Unit or ship movements.

Plans for future operations.

The effect of enemy operations.

Any casualty until released by proper authority (full name only).

Do not formulate a system or code for your letter.

Your location unless authorized (new locations were generally authorized after fourteen days).

29 Prior to America's entry into the war after Pearl Harbor, there was a strong anti-war, isolationist movement that lingered well into the war years.

30 John P. McCann, *Passing Through: The 82nd Airborne Division in Northern Ireland 1943-44*, (Newtownards, Northern Ireland, Colourpoint, 2005) 44.

31 We found only one letter from George's mother, dated March 22, 1944, from San Francisco, which says she got his address from Babe, and asks George repeatedly to write. As of March 1944, it appears he had not.

32 Both the press and the public had a naïve expectation that the war would be over by Christmas, 1944. The war ended in Europe on May 8, 1945.

33 While labor organizations pledged no strikes during the war, "wildcat" strikes such as ones by coal miners still occurred.

34 Forty-eight women of the 508th wrote fifty Round Robin (RR) letters as the first two writers each wrote a second letter. Throughout the text we use the abbreviation "RR" and a numeral to designate each Round Robin letter.

35 508th PIR Organization Day Program, Gurwell Collection. This document lists all the officers and enlisted men of the 508th by company as of November 4, 1943. The Appendix lists the Round Robin writers and their husbands.

36 An old saying, meaning you were so poor and walked so much that you had worn out the bottom of your shoes and were walking on the "uppers."

37 As the famous "Rosie the Riveter" advertisement attests, the need for wartime labor propelled many women into the workforce for the first time. Like Beth, many were encouraged to take manufacturing jobs in factories, where the pay was typically higher than that of a secretary.

38 "Latrine rumors" were so-called because they were full of _ _ it.

39 Daylight savings time was instituted in 1942 and remained yearlong until the war ended.

40 An "A" card was a square sticker on your windshield, indicating the lowest level of gasoline rationing, four gallons per week. The "fatherly gentleman" must have had a higher ration card, such as B or C. https://carcoachreports.com/gas-rationing-gas-ration-stickers/#:~:text=The%20%E2%80%9CA%E2%80%9D%20sticker%20is%20the%20most%20common%20of,and%20was%20worth%20about%20eight%20gallons%20a%20week.

41 Double daylight savings time.

42 Dwayne T. Burns, and Leland Burns, *Jump Into the Valley of the Shadow*, (Casemate, Philadelphia, 2006) 26, 184, 208. Martin was Burns' CO.

43 We found no information on the Paddocks.

## CHAPTER IV: PRE-INVASION JITTERS: THE 508TH IN NORTHERN IRELAND AND ENGLAND, RR 8–14

44 Ralph Thomas, quoted in John P. McCann's Passing Through: The 82nd Airborne Division in Ireland 1943–44. Newtownards (N. Ireland: Colourpoint Books, 2005) 57.

45 Morning reports for HQHQ, 1942–1945, courtesy of Rick Smith, *508th Regimental Headquarters Company, Reinacted.*

46 These two officers are mentioned often in this period, and are most likely George's roommates.

47 Adam Berry, email to Jack Talley, May 12, 2020.

48 According to Adam Berry, large numbers of men from the 505th and 507th PIRs—as well as the 508th—either failed to find their drop zones or landed with their planes during this exercise. The failure foretold the difficulties the division would experience due to cloudy weather for Operation Eagle, the last full-scale division exercise on May 12, and more critically, the difficulties with clouds in the early morning of June 6. Berry, email and unpublished manuscript to Jack Talley, May 12, 2020.

49 Phil Nordyke, *Four Stars of Valor: The Combat History of the 505th Parachute Infantry Regiment in World War II*, (St. Paul, MN: Zenith 2006).

50 Adam G.R. Berry, *And Suddenly They Were Gone: An Oral and Pictorial History of the 82D Airborne Division in England, February–September 1944* (Boston, MA: Overlord Publishing, 2015), 99.

51 Zig Boroughs, *The 508th Connection* (Xlibris: Bloomington, IN, 2013), 31-33.

52 "Hymie" was a derogatory nickname for a German. See Berry, p.152.

53 Women's Army Corps.

54 The Williams letter does not include a home address. We have made an educated guess about the state and town, based on Sis Thomlinson's letter.

55 The term "D-Day" applied to the start of any assault or invasion.

56 Mr. Fredrick Mitchell was Lord Mayor and Mr. Francis Carney was Sherriff. This photo was not in George's archive, but we did find pictures of both officials with other soldiers. https://library.uta.edu/digitalgallery/img/20032089

57 General James Gavin's war diary, entry of June 4 1944. Untitled, unpublished, unpaginated document.

58 Guy LoFaro, *The Sword of St. Michael*, (Cambridge, MA: DaCapo, 2011), 191.

59 Gavin talked of his soldiers killed in battle as "his boys lost along the way." (Kenneth "Rock" Merritt, personal communication, Ft. Walton Beach, FL, 2018.)

60 See Colonel Mark C. Vlahos, *Men Will Come: A History of the 314th Troop Carrier Group 1942–45* (Hoosick Falls, NY: Merriam Press, 2019), 176-179.

## CHAPTER V: D-DAY AND THE BATTLE FOR NORMANDY

61 George was wounded on June 6, but the Army listed him as WIA on June 9, the date he was sent to the rear and was not present for morning report.

62 The 508th was stationed on standby jump status in Chartres as a quick reaction force in the case the Germans began to execute POWs. George was extremely thankful they did not have to make any jumps.

63 On D-Day, the German air force was practically absent. Only two sorties, both FW-190 fighters, flew strafing runs on the beach, according to interviews by Cornelius Ryan. See his *The Longest Day: Collector's Edition* (New York: Simon and Schuster, 1959, 2014) 201.

George could have seen either the 190 piloted by Wing Commander Josef Priller or that of his wingman, Sgt. Heinz Wodarczyk. They strafed the beach low and fast, going from the British sector to the American sector, then turned inland, consistent with what George described. George possibly saw one of 10 other aircraft that were "intercepted straight away and were forced to drop their bombs prematurely." The Germans had about a hundred operational fighters on D-Day, compared to the Allies' 5400. See Paul Carrell, *Invasion! They're coming!* (Atglen, PA: Schiffer Military History 1995) 80.

64 Capt. John I. Dolan, A Co., 505th PIR recalled that "I went down to the bridge and found that we had received an assist from some of the 508th PIR…there were about ten or twelve Germans holed up on the second floor of a stucco-type farmhouse…. [The firing] lasted about twenty minutes with about ten or twelve Germans surrendering. About a squad of men from the 508 made the actual capture." Dolan, "Letter to General Gavin," cited in Robert M. Murphy, *No Better Place to Die* (Havertown, PA: Casemate 2009), 148-149.

65 George's account closely parallels the testimony of 1st Sgt. Ralph Thomas, who identified the farmhouses as the Manor near La Fière Bridge. 1st Sgt. Thomas' account included calling up a bazooka team, had a similar number of German casualties and prisoners, and reported the rare sighting of a German fighter. http://508pir.org/voices/t/thomas_rh_03.htm

66 John McCrae. "In Flanders Fields." https://www.poetryfoundation.org/poems/47380/in-flanders-fields.

67 Although Edson Raff reported that General Ridgeway stood during attacks by 88 millimeter flak cannons that were drawn in by triangulating on radio transmissions, Lt. Gurwell reported at least one episode where the general took cover. Raff cited in Clay Blair, *Ridgeway's Paratroopers* (Annapolis, MD: Dial Press, 1985), 265.

68 The bicyclists George describes are reminiscent of the photographs, now lost, of "men and bicycles lying around on the ground" that Sue discovered at her grandparents' as a girl. Capt. William H. Nation recorded how the 508th resourcefully put the bikes, like all confiscated German materials, to good use: "We have captured enough equipment to mobilize our outfit nearly. The only transportation we have of American make is three jeeps and the remaining thirty vehicles are captured materials. They sent down some bicycle outfit against us and now everybody has them a bicycle, an automobile, or some type of German equipment. We had for a while some German horses and one boy has one of their dogs. If it weren't for their equipment we would be walking everywhere." Nation, 178–79. German Company 243 was a bicycle unit, as identified by Nordyke in *Put Us Down in Hell*, 41.

69 The town was most likely Cauquigny, on the eastern end of La Fière Causeway.

70 LoFaro, *The Sword of St. Michael, 242.*

71 Nordyke, *Put Us Down in Hell*, 242

72 "Warren R. Wilkins Update", *Devil's Digest*, September 2015. http://508pir.org/archival/508_chapter_newslrs/pdf_files/2015_09USPS.pdf

73 LoFaro, *The Sword of St. Michael, 244, 267.*

## CHAPTER VI: MEN LIKE THAT NEVER DIE, RR 15–25

74 See Appendix I for two wartime letters from Capt. Driggers to George.

75 http://508pir.org/voices/h/hamm_cj_01.htm

76 Nordyke, *Four Stars of Valor*, 410.

77 Nordyke, *Put Us Down in Hell*, 168.

78 http://508pir.org/deweese_diary/index.htm

79 Zig Boroughs, *The Devil's Tale* (Summerville, GA: ESPY Publishing Company, 1999) 9, 130.

80 http://508pir.org/deweese_diary/index.htm

## CHAPTER VII: GHOSTS, MEMORIES, AND A HORRIBLE LONLINESS

81 The casualty statistics break down as follows: "307 killed in action, 26 died of wounds, 3 died of injuries, 487 wounded in action, 173 injured in action, and 165 missing in action. Many of those missing in action were later reported as prisoners, a few of which escaped and returned to the regiment." Nordyke, *Put Us Down in Hell,* 245.

82 Allan R. Millett, "*Blood Upon the Risers.*" In Penrose, Jane., (Ed.) *The D-Day Companion.* Oxford: Osprey, 2004.

83 A small notebook carried on an officer's person that functioned as a formal to-do list.

84 Lt. Col. Dave Grossman (USA, Ret.), a Ranger, paratrooper, law-enforcement trainer, and a specialist in the psychology of killing, has demonstrated that the closer a person's physical proximity to physical killing, the greater the likelihood that PTSD and emotional distress will result. See Grossman's *On Killing.*

85 George's depiction of characteristic paratrooper qualities is confirmed throughout the literature of the 82nd Airborne. Here is General Gavin describing his men's extraordinary performance in Normandy: "These parachutists have been nothing short of remarkable in their fighting. Admittedly I am very biased, but I believe that the violence and savagery of their combat technique is without parallel in our military history. The germans [sic] fear them now and give them lots of elbow room." See Barbara Gavin Fauntleroy, *The General and his Daughter* (New York: Fordham University Press, 1007), 11.

86 Special Order 110, July 14, 1944: payroll and other duties, including serving on court martial boards. Gurwell Collection.

87 In the first half of 1944, George wrote on average twenty letters home a month. In the latter half, he averaged eight letters a month, including fifteen written over six weeks of non-combat duty in England after being WIA in Normandy.

88 Highly decorated service members and celebrities spearheaded major US Government bond drives to finance the cash-strapped War Department: From April 1943 to January 1944, George bought a fifty-dollar bond every month, reducing the amount only if his growing family needed cash. In January 1944, even George's little brother Dick and his Boy Scout troop got into the action: "In scouts [sic] we're gonna sell enough bonds to buy a P-51 Mustang," he proudly wrote to George.

89 News of various, wide-ranging strikes that reached the troops through the national news did not sit well with them. They included an elevator operator's strike in New York City, a rubber worker's strike in Ohio, and strikes by oil workers, lumber workers, coal miners, electrical workers, auto workers, rubber workers, and many others.

90 Our records do not indicate the type of cases George had to process, but they could have ranged from public drunkenness to murder. Bored, misbehaving, and no doubt suffering from undiagnosed PTSD, the men were getting into serious fights and legal trouble. In addition to brawls between rival paratroop units, significant racial incidents took place between the 82nd and the African American Aviation Engineer and Quartermaster units. Well established near Leicester before the 82nd arrived, the Black troops were dating local English women; the paratroopers objected, and fights, stabbings, near-riots, and even deaths occurred. The incidents were largely covered up, or even classified, at

the time. See Berry, *And Suddenly They Were Gone,* for a discussion of racial tensions between Black and white American troops stationed in England in 1944.

91 Sue comments: My parents were married on April 11, 1943, and never would a month go by that they did not acknowledge the 11th as special.

92 Maj. Gen. James Gavin, a well-known womanizer, had just assumed command of the 82nd Airborne Division on August 8, 1944. George's letters elsewhere mention that extramarital activities were a favorite pastime for numerous junior officers as well. As the Round Robin letters show, their wives were far from duped. Or, as Jeane so pointedly put it to George in her letter of August 4, "We all check up, you know."

93 Jeane would turn 24 on September 26, 1944.

94 The September 23, 1944 morning report states George's promotion to First Lieutenant to be effective as of 1 September.

95 Sue comments: After Dad died, we sent a copy of this poem to Dick O'Donnell, the webmaster of the official 508th website, for inclusion in the archives. Later, a beautifully printed copy of the same poem was found in the effects of James Blue (Pfc, A Co.), who died in May 2004.

It was thanks to Dick's research that the author of the poem and his place of death were identified. http://508pir.org/archival/poems/ellifrit.htm We and all family and friends of the 508th owe Dick a tremendous thank you for his labor of love in developing and maintaining the excellent 508th website.

96 Matthew B. Ridgway, Memorandum, "Reported Loss of Transport Planes and Personnel," Headquarters, 82nd AB Division. Quoted in LoFaro, *The Sword of St. Michael*, 103.

97 Conversation with Rock Merritt, Family and Friends of the 508th PIR Association Reunion, Ft. Walton Beach, Florida. November 2, 2018.

## CHAPTER VIII: OPERATION MARKET GARDEN: THE JUMP INTO HOLLAND

98 Berry, *And Suddenly They Were Gone*, 225.

99 Nordyke, *Put us Down in Hell*, 253.

100 Nordyke, *Put us Down in Hell*, 253–54, 259, 273.

101 Gurwell Interview, 2001. This is the canopy that George sent to Jeane and that the young Sue and her siblings enjoyed as a tent, now in the Camp Blanding Museum in Clay County, Florida.

102 Guy LoFaro, *The Sword of St. Michael*, 387.

103 The term originated in a discussion between Lt. Gen. Frederick Browning, Deputy Commander, First Allied Airborne Army, and Field Marshal Bernard Montgomery at the final conference on Market-Garden at Montgomery's headquarters on September 10, 1944. Weighing the likelihood that the British 1st Airborne could seize the crucial bridge at Arnhem and hold it long enough for XXX Corps to arrive, Browning said: "Sir, I think we might be going a bridge too far." Quoted in: Cornelius Ryan, *A Bridge Too Far* (New York: Popular Library, 1974), 9.

104 British 1st Airborne statistics in Antony Beevor, *The Battle of Arnhem* (New York: Viking Books, 2018), 337.

105 While George enjoyed sharing "the cow story," he never mentioned any names. Not until Sue recounted the tale in 2004 at the 508th 60th Reunion did we learn the name of the butcher, when Pvt. Stanley Kass of Regimental Headquarters Company spoke up to claim the honor.

106 The Gurwell family joked for years about Jeane's propensity to burn food when cooking. Some things, even potatoes, would get burned a second time. George would patiently rescue the good parts from the burnt ones, and cooking would continue. He never gave Jeane any grief, and the family laughed and gave thanks for the "burnt offerings."

107 We were moved to discover the following letter with George and Jeane's personal correspondence. It is dated Jan 2, 1945 and postmarked from Cumberland, Maryland.

Dear Sir: As the parents of PFC George E. Hartman, 33009218 Reg. Hqrs. Co. 508 Prch Inf, who was Killed in Action in Holland 1 October 1944, we are very anxious to learn as much as possible regarding the circumstances leading to his death. We hope and pray that you can spare time to give us what information you can about how he was killed and where he was buried. We hope to have him returned after the war is over.

Yours Respectfully, Mr. & Mrs. C. W. Hartman, Parents of George E Hartman

George's friend Harry Hudec attended to the remains of his fellow troopers (Boroughs, *The Devil's Tale*, 206).

108 George's personnel file. He mailed his official documents home with Jeane's old letters.

109 Chemical munitions in World War II included phosphorous and colored mortar/artillery rounds, as well as the poisonous gas rounds in the German arsenal (which were never employed).

110 Pvt. Steve Schmelick wired the sound equipment. [Cpl. Matthew] Bellucci and [Pvt. Richard H.] Nelson set up a generator for electric lights. Zig Boroughs, *The 508th Connection*, 308.

111 The photograph is missing from our archives.

112 George's freehand drawing shows Jeane where to attach the "jump star" on the wings. It was a lovely surprise to discover the heather still in the envelope.

113 *Paraglide* (sometimes appearing as *Para-glide*) is still the 82nd Airborne Division official newsletter. The issue in question was published October 17, 1944, Gurwell Collection.

114 Memorial Service Program dated November 25, 1944, Gurwell Collection.

## CHAPTER IX: SEEMS LIKE A BAD DREAM, ROUND ROBIN 26–32

115 Edson D. Raff, *We Jumped to Fight*, (Washington D.C.: Eagle Books, 1944).

116 Colonel Raff commanded the 2nd Battalion, 509th PIR in the first American combat parachute drop, which seized the Tafarquay Airport in Oran, North Africa, on November 8, 1942, during Operation Torch. He later commanded the 507th PIR in the Ardennes Campaign.

117 Dr. Thomas was put to work treating the German wounded. At one point the guards were busy building defensive positions and stopped watching him. "I strolled through a gate into a pasture, wandered a few steps along a hedgerow and, to be polite, relieved myself standing up. Still having attracted no attention, I slowly sauntered along the hedgerow until I reached the corner, dove into the ditch beside the hedgerow, and started crawling away." The entire account is in Boroughs, *The 508th Connection* 174–179.

## CHAPTER X: DREADED DOWN TIME

118 General Gavin's war diary, entry for November 18, 1944.

119 George mailed the *Paraglide*, the Division newsletter, with a letter to Jeane's parents on November 26, 1944, the day before he wrote to Jeane. Designed to be sent back home, the

issue took the form of a large, folded souvenir circular with a small place for a personalized letter. Dated October 17, 1944, a month after the invasion, it was largely devoted to brief, sanitized information about each regiment's role in the Holland campaign. The issue also contained a more disturbing article by journalist William F. Dawson that lay out the case for dispelling overly optimistic reports that Germany was all but defeated.

120 The Commander of Base Section, Loire Section, Communications Zone, ETO, during World War II, U.S. Army Brig. Gen. Charles O. Thrasher was the Commanding Officer of the United States Forces of U.S. Army forces stationed in France.

121 Order #8 was signed by the Regimental S-1, Capt. William H. Nation. The regimental Supply Officer was Major James Casteel. George's copy of the order and several letters from wounded soldiers who wrote to retrieve their belongings are in the Gurwell Collection.

122 In 2001, George was still praising Roach for the clever ways he managed to procure alcohol. Loewi was killed in action in Belgium on January 1, 1945, less than one month after their trip.

123 We speculate that the clubs also served to keep the men from drinking and brawling in town.

124 Col. Raymond D. Millener died December 7, 1944. "Raymond Davis Millener" https://www.honorstates.org/index.php?id=324156.

## CHAPTER XI: WE CANNOT GIVE UP THE JUMP, RR 33–36

125 The dates of death may vary, according to when physical remains were located and identified. While Creary clearly died on June 7, his official KIA date is July 1, 1994, the date his status was changed from MIA to KIA in the morning report.

126 Nordyke, *Put Us Down in Hell*, 145, accounts by Private Jack Schlegel (Hq3) and others. See also Boroughs, *The 508th Connection*, 159–160. On 28 November 2009, the following post left by Alice Felts appeared on "Find a Grave": "Jane Copas Creary was Hal's widow. He was the love of her life. She mourned for him daily, in her own quiet way, until her death in 1983."

127 1st Lt Edgar R Abbott, mortar platoon leader assigned to Headquarters Company, First Battalion on D-Day, was officially listed as Killed in Action, June 17, 1944. He was awarded the Bronze Star and is buried in the Normandy American Cemetery, Plot C, Row 16 Grave 30. Long after the war, Honorary Command Sergeant Major of the Army Rock Merritt (ranked as Corporal on D-Day) still recalled the striking demeanor of Lt. Abbott on D-Day: "Prior to moving toward Hill 30, I received my first combat order. Lieutenant Abbott turned to me and said, 'Corporal, take two men with you and go knock out that machine gun.' I guess it was the calm way Lt. Abbott ordered me to knock out that machine-gun nest, like 'Take two men and go fill up the water cans.'" Nordyke, *Put Us Down in Hell*, 111.

## CHAPTER XII: THE ARDENNES CAMPAIGN: JUMPING FROM A TRUCK INTO THE BATTLE OF THE BULGE

128 William G. Lord II, *History of the 508th Parachute Infantry Regiment* (Washington, D.C.: Infantry Journal Press, 1948) 60.

[129] Going into the Bulge, the XVIII Airborne Corps consisted of the 82nd and 101st Airborne Divisions, the 1st and 4th Infantry Divisions, and numerous combat and logistical support units.

[130] Women who volunteered to work overseas in mobile units or Red Cross Clubs.

[131] Nordyke, *Put Us Down in Hell*, 409.

[132] Alex Kershaw, *The Longest Winter: The Battle of the Bulge and the Epic Story of World War II's Most Decorated Platoon* (Boston: Da Capo, 2004), 132–135. Kershaw points out the defensive stands by the 99th Infantry Division, and their 349th intelligence and reconnaissance platoon in particular, as deserving of praise, 43.

[133] Frank van Lunteren, *Blocking Kampfgruppe Peiper: The 504th Parachute Infantry Regiment in the Battle of the Bulge* (Havertown, PA: Casemate, 2015), 41.

[134] Nordyke, *Put Us Down in Hell*, 406.

[135] Nordyke, *All American, All the Way*, (St. Paul, MN: Zenith Press, 2005), 683.

[136] Lord, *History of the 508th Parachute Infantry Regiment*, 65–68.

[137] LoFaro, *The Sword of St. Michael*, 480–81.

[138] Buzz bombs were V1 rockets, the first functional cruise missile. Shaped like an airplane, these unpiloted, crudely navigated devices would run out of fuel and fall to the ground with nearly a ton of explosives. https://en.wikipedia.org/wiki/V-1_flying_bomb.

[139] A kind of tree fiber.

[140] George either had some advantages over troopers in rifle companies, such as first access to winter gear, or was telling a tale to assuage Jeane's fears. After their hasty mobilization on December 18, 1944 many troopers lacked warm gear until January 11, 1945 when "everyone drew new combat suits, gloves and galoshes." Lord, 73. Cold weather injuries, and especially frostbitten feet, caused a steep rise in casualties in Belgium.

[141] Hunting game this close to the front lines means George and his men were lacking in hot chow.

[142] George identified the "large shell" from its sound. Artillery shells are heard when fired and go slowly enough to produce an audible whistling sound that alerts listeners of incoming fire. The German 88mm flak gun fired a flat trajectory round that traveled faster than the speed of sound. The explosion of the 88 round and the crack of its sonic boom occurred without warning: the sound of the round being fired came last. We have heard the "crack" of rifle fire thousands of times in the target pits during our days in marksmanship competition.

[143] The keepsake "coin" is a commemorative medal awarded for donating to the Orphans' Charity Fund. Dated 1914; the King and Queen of Belgium, Elizabeth and Albert, are pictured. https://en.wikipedia.org/wiki/Elisabeth_of_Bavaria,_Queen_of_Belgium. See also https://en.wikipedia.org/wiki/Albert_I_of_Belgium.

[144] Lt. McKillop, 517th PIR, was awarded the bronze star. We were unable to find the origin of the newspaper article. https://www.google.com/books/edition/517th_Parachute_Regimental_Combat_Team/ZtAAXnd1LvQC?hl=en&gbpv=1&dq=Edward+F+McKillop&pg=PA105&printsec=frontcover, 41, 105.

[145] *What a Diff'rence a Day Makes,* written in Spanish by Maria Greven, 1934, English lyrics by Stanley Adams, and English recording by the Dorsey Brothers, 1934.

[146] Jeane was engaged in optimistic thinking: There was no rotation home until the war was over. Morale was certainly diminished by the fact that the only way home was by injury or a coffin. Francis C. Steckel, *Morale Problems in Combat: American Soldiers in Europe in World War II*, https://www.jstor.org/stable/26304183?seq=1#metadata_info_tab_contents.

147 In his war diary entry of January 18, 1945, Gavin himself proudly employs such terms: "Our paratroop infantry is superb, close quarter killers." Paratroopers were professionally trained, in contrast to draftees or replacements, who were thrown into the fray after eight weeks of training.

148 Joseph Kassane's Diary, http://508pir.org/pdf_files/memoirs_kissane.pdf.

149 Abraham quoted in Boroughs, *The 508th Connection*, 412.

150 Conversation with Harry Hudec, 508th PIR Association Reunion, 2004. Sgt. Jack Johnson, Service Company, offered a different eyewitness account, stating that Johnson had driven Captain Nation in a jeep to the F Company command post, and had just stopped next to the CP when a shell hit the front of the jeep, killing Captain Nation and wounding Johnson, who was thrown out of the vehicle. Cited in Nordyke, *Put Us Down in Hell*, 476–77. We met Bill C. Nation, Captain Nation's nephew, in 2004 at the 60th 508th reunion, the same one where we talked with Harry Hudec. Bill had talked with Harry previously. We were able to share Captain Abraham's account with Bill at the June 2021 508th Family and Friends Reunion in Columbus, OH. Taking all the information into account, Bill favors Sergeant Johnson's account.

151 Nordyke, *Put Us Down in Hell*, 477.

152 George was accustomed to getting letters from soldiers' families asking about their loved one, but not decades after the war, when one last such request came in March 2000 from Bill C. Nation, the namesake and nephew of Capt. Nation. George did not answer Bill's letter from 2000 even though they had met at a 508th reunion in San Antonio, Texas. One year later, George told Sue, "How can you tell a family member that I found his uncle all dead and mangled? I just couldn't talk to him about it."

153 While the western allies were attacking from the west, Russia was attacking Germany from the east with a massive army. George was betting the Russians would reach Berlin first, which happened in April 1945.

154 In 2020, Ellen Peters, a former secretary and treasurer of the 508th Association, described to us a conversation she had with Captain Abraham, who summed up his state thus: "I was very concussed and went a little coo coo after that." He was listed as a non-battle casualty, possibly a combination of traumatic brain injury from the concussion from the explosions and the cumulative effects of battle fatigue/PTSD. The morning report of March 12, 1945 states he was transferred to the 10th Traffic Regulating Group on March 7.

## CHAPTER XIII: THE ARDENNES CAMPAIGN: HORROR IN THE HÜRTGEN FORREST

155 Rick Atkinson, *The Guns at Last Light: The War in Western Europe, 1944–1945* (New York: Picador Books 2013), 325.

156 General Gavin's entry of April 29, 1945 shows he was no stranger to PTSD-related intrusive memories. "I came across a pig eating a dead kraut. The noise that he made was more bothersome than the act. I could hear it at lunch. I have seen enough war for a lifetime."

157 Caroline and Lowell Eddy remained lifelong friends with Jeane and George, and Sue remembers spending time with them over the years.

158 George's discharge papers indicate he received a Purple Heart with Oak Leaf Cluster (two awards for two wounds). We know he was first wounded on June 6, but his report

about seeing the medics for an eye problem, when he avoided medics at all costs, is the only indication of a second war wound. Sue's sister, Linda Odenborg, recalled that George received a second Purple Heart that he did not want to accept. By the end of the war, he must have been happy to have it since it added to the points he needed to go home. He never wore the second award on his dress uniform.

159 Attrition had taken its toll: The 508th phone directory, published in Frankfurt around July 1945, lists only 21 of the 45 Round Robin officers who jumped on June 6 were still with the unit. The others had been killed or wounded in action, injured, had died, or been hospitalized due to illness. Battle fatigue and harsh weather conditions also contributed to attrition, and cases of frozen feet and frostbite would be especially devastating in the Ardennes.

160 Nordyke, *Put Us Down in Hell*, 483.

161 Lofaro, *The Sword of St. Michael*, 521_22.

162 Alan Langdon, *Ready: The History of the 505th Parachute Infantry Regiment, 82nd Airborne Division, World War II*, ed. Rev. George B. Wood (Indianapolis, IN: 1986), 121.

## CHAPTER XIV: THE GRANDEST PEOPLE I'VE EVER KNOWN, RR 37–42

163 The Kenny Method, a polio treatment, used hot compresses to ease muscle spasms. The paralyzed muscles were then exercised, instead of being immobilized during the acute phase of the disease.

164 1st Lt. William H. Preston died of wounds in Holland on September 9, 1944.

165 One of Shorty's "qualifying jumps" was conducted with 1st Sgt. Leonard Funk (C Co.), who was awarded the Medal of Honor for action in Belgium.

166 The 508th was stationed at Camp Sissonne, just north of Rheims, the heart of the Champaign region. Champaign was reputedly the cheapest drink around, and many a hungover trooper roused from bed in the wee hours of January 18, 1945, began the Battle of the Bulge with a blinding Champaign headache.

167 Sgt. William G. Lord II was sent to OSC and commissioned as a second lieutenant on June 7, 1945. He authored the official *History of the 508th Parachute Infantry* during the occupation of Germany.

168 Capt. Droge was transferred to the 541st PIR and served in the Pacific Theatre.

169 http://508pir.org/taps/graves/s/snee_af.htm

170 Norman Kennedy was a well-known magazine illustrator at the time Jean met him.

171 http://508pir.org/obits/obit_text/j/johnson_kl.htm

172 Tacky party: a festive occasion where everyone dresses as ridiculously as possible.

173 http://508pir.org/taps/graves/s/scudder_ws.htm

## CHAPTER XV: ON STANDBY: RESCUE MISSION FOR ALLIED POWS

174 http://508pir.org/obits/obit_text/g/gundlach_rc.htm

175 http://508pir.org/obits/obit_text/y/yates_ca.htm

176 Ineffective Japanese high-altitude balloons with an explosive payload that rode jet stream winds to the west coast of the U.S.

177 The United States 17th Airborne and the British 6th Airborne executed the last airborne assault of World War II in Operation Varsity, dropping into Germany, east of the Rhine, on March 24, 1945.

178 "Patriotic" teenaged girls and young women who offered companionship and often sexual favors to servicemen.

179 Nordyke, *Put Us Down in Hell*, 485.

180 1st Lt Harold Feuerheim, the new CO of HqHq Co., was promoted to 1st Lieutenant on July 9, 1943. While newer to the 508th, the new CO did outrank George and Hardwick (promoted to 1st Lieutenant on Sep 1, 1944 and Nov 16, 1943, respectively).

181 George's sentiments were consistent with a comment about the 508th by CSM Rock Merritt in 2018: "If you were a good officer, you couldn't get promoted."

182 We were unable to identity the mysterious princess. "Chouchou" is akin to "sweetie" or "cutie" in French.

183 To a growing degree, this disgruntlement extended to Colonel Lindquist and other brass after the army initiated a plan to allow soldiers to return stateside and be discharged. The system accorded points (eighty-five needed) for time in service, overseas duty, combat medals, marital status and dependents. Honor Guard duty was classified as "essential," a status that excluded officers—unlike enlisted men—from benefitting from the system, no matter how many points they had racked up. With eighty-nine points, George qualified as a "high-point man" to no avail.

## CHAPTER XVI: A MOMENTOUS AFFAIR: RR 43–50

184 1Lt. Robert M. Mitchell, I Co. KIA in Holland, September 19, 1944. 1Lt. Ralph E. DeWeese, G Co. KIA in Holland, September 23, 1944.

185 The "Gray Ladies" were American Red Cross volunteers who offered non-medical services to the sick, injured, and disabled, including thousands of U.S. servicemen. The service began under a different name at Walter Reed in World War I and continued until the 1960s. An affectionate nickname coined by WWII veterans because of the color of the volunteers' uniform, "Gray Ladies" was officially adopted as the name of the service in 1947.

186 Nordyke, *Put us Down in Hell*, 360.

187 Nearly an entire platoon from D Co. was captured on September 17, 1944, including the three men on this list. These troopers might have been interned at Stalag 12-A, near Küstrin-Kietz, Germany. We discovered that another Co D. trooper captured the same day was imprisoned there, Pfc. James H. Talley (no relation).

188 We were able to verify all the troopers listed were POWs except Mr. Lander, who insisted that he was not a POW when we contacted him by phone on January 10, 2022. Joel "Jody" Lander was the only 508th member with that surname in our sources.

189 These officers were listed on the Officers' Seating Assignments on the *James Parker* in December 1943. George had correctly labelled them as "PW." Gurwell Collection.

190 Green replacements coming to the front were dumped straight into battle and frequently killed before anyone knew their names. It was a bitter time for the "old men."

## CHAPTER XVII GUARDING IKE: OCCUPATION DUTY IN FRANKFURT, GERMANY

191 The love of nature is a gift that George also passed on to his children. Discovering her father's letter of May 28, 1945 brought the taste of wild strawberries to Sue in turn when it elicited a memory of a childhood walk with her father: "My dad was intrigued with

nature and the beauty surrounding him. Throughout his whole life, he shared his fascination with birds, bugs, plants, and all of God's creation with his family. He taught us as kids how to find wild mushrooms, catch crayfish or, as he called them, crawdads, and where to pick wild huckleberries and gather wild asparagus where the old fields had been. I remember all of these adventures fondly, but one of the best was picking wild strawberries. One summer vacation, as we were leaving the beach at Seaside, Dad stopped while crossing a sand dune and burst out laughing with delight. Wild strawberries so small you would miss them if you weren't looking closely were growing along the path. He pointed them out to me, and I remember them even now as the best and sweetest strawberries I have ever had."

[192] Statistics are garnered from the Officers Seating Assignments on the *James Parker*. George had carefully written the status of each man next to his name after the war. Gurwell Collection.

[193] "It is expected the Red Devils will provide special escorts for visiting military officials and civilian dignitaries, guard highly restricted areas and lend color to formal ceremonies to be staged at the American occupation capital, headquarters of Supreme Commander Dwight D. Eisenhower. Special uniforms including additional clothing and tailor-made garrison caps, gloves, scarfs and jump boots are either being issued now or will be when they are available." *Devil's Digest*, Vol. II, No. 3 (June 6, 1945), 1. Gurwell Collection. Officers had to buy their dress uniforms.

[194] At the end of the war, Germans were scraping by on a starvation diet of 1,200 calories a day out of a recommended 2,500. Jon Sutherland and Diane Canwell, *The Berlin Airlift* (Gretna, LA: Pelican, 2007), 72.

[195] Less than four years later, Jack's father, Corporal Walter J. Talley, was stationed near Frankfurt at Wiesbaden Air Force Base. A flight engineer in the new Air Force, Walt was part of the huge effort to supply Berlin during the Berlin Airlift, when Soviet forces blockaded West Berlin in an attempt to force the Allied forces out of the city. Walt bombed the children of Berlin with candy and raisins as the USAF supplied West Berlin by air with food and fuel for a year.

[196] Sue comments: This was the parachute that I played with as a child. It was kept in a box in the basement, and we used it as a tent in the backyard. Later, Dad explained that his own chute had blown a panel, and he'd gathered this one up for future use. He wrapped up in it along with his bedroll during the Battle of the Bulge and it literally kept him from freezing to death. According to his wishes, we donated the chute to the Camp Blanding Museum in Florida.

[197] Lord, *History of the 508th Parachute Infantry Regiment*, 92.

[198] We have made extensive use of George's copy of this booklet.

## CHAPTER XVIII: SAILING HOME ON THE S.S. *MADAWASKA VICTORY*

[199] We are very grateful to Dick O'Donnell, the webmaster of the regimental website, 508pir.org, for researching and identifying the enlisted members on the ship. His support has been an invaluable resource and source of knowledge throughout the entirety of our project.

[200] *Devil's Digest*, Vol. II, No. 4 (August 7, 1945), 7–8. Gurwell Collection.

[201] Elder and Kenny's biographies are featured in the *Devil's Digest*, Vol. II, No. 4 (August 7, 1945), 7–8. Gurwell Collection.

202 PTSD: National Center for PTSD, "Moral Injury," https://www.ptsd.va.gov/professional/treat/cooccurring/moral_injury.asp.

203 The estimated date of arrival on the travel orders October 5, 1945.

## EPILOGUE: FINDING HARRY

204 Jeane gave us these finds in 2004 and later the bulk of the Gurwell Collection after granddaughter Julie Rathbun uncovered them in 2007.

205 After the 508 Parachute Infantry Regiment Association was retired, we attended the initial meetings for the new group, the Family and Friends of the 508th PIR Association, which remains active today.

206 The film is in the hands of Captain Nation's nephew, Bill C. Nation, who inherited them from his father. He explains: the shipment "would have arrived in 22 small canisters each with 25 feet of raw film that was then split down the middle (lengthwise). After, the film was developed and spliced together to arrive at a film of 50 feet in length" and returned to the "same canisters that the film was originally packaged in. After Dad got them developed, he spliced the 50-foot reels so that they fit on 250-foot reels." Email, Bill C. Nation to Jack Talley, February 19, 2022.

207 After battling Alzheimer's, Harry Hudec made his final jump in 2007.

# ACKNOWLEDGMENTS

Without a doubt, our biggest acknowledgment goes out to Sue's parents, George and Jeane Gurwell, and the brave men and women of the 508th Parachute Infantry Regiment (PIR) who started this journey by sharing their life experiences through correspondence during WWII. If it wasn't for George and Jeane's desire to hang on to these very precious items and tuck them away, this book would not exist. Our deepest gratitude goes out to two very special women, Sue's maternal grandmother, Delpha Slonaker, for continuing to keep these boxed items safe over the years, and Sue's niece Julie Rathbun, who found them, bringing these treasures once again to the light of day.

Very heartfelt and special recognition goes to our editor, Gayle Wurst, at Princeton International Agency for the Arts, for being willing to take this extraordinary journey with us. Without her editing expertise and love of the subject, we would still be trying to figure out the best way to tie all the history and story lines together. She took our initial manuscript, and through careful guidance, helped us weave it all into this amazing book.

Many other people were also integral to bringing this project together. One stands out above the rest—Dick O'Donnell, webmaster *extraordinaire* of the regimental website 508pir.org. There are not enough words to express our gratitude for the love, dedication, and persistence Dick has shown in keeping the 508th story alive. He has tirelessly gathered and pieced together their history, and single-handedly created one of the best regimental websites out there. It has been a constant source of invaluable information to us in the course of writing this book.

Sincerest gratitude is owed to a host of others who contributed in various ways: Mike Lefevre, who spent three months scanning our letters and documents; Rick Smith, who supplied copies of the Regimental Headquarters Morning Reports and other documents; Carl Mauro, for the beautiful maps; our British contact, Adam Berry, who shared information about the 508th in Nottingham, England; Thulai van Maanen, our Dutch friend, for giving us valuable insight into the 508th while in Holland and Belgium; and a truly special friend, Bill Nation, who allowed us to use pictures, information, and excerpts from his uncle's letters. Thank you from the bottom of our hearts for your support, encouragement, phone calls. Thanks as well for being a great sounding board and sharing the excitement of discovery with us.

Our recognition and gratitude also go to the veterans of the original 508th PIR, who privileged and honored us by sharing their time and personal stories. Thank you Kenneth "Rock" Merritt, Harry Hudec, Stanley Kass, Ray O'Connell, Zig Boroughs, John Coates, Dwayne Burns, Bob Chisolm, Ernie Lansom, and Joel "Jody" Lander. At the time of this writing, I'm happy to say Jody is still with us.

A big thank you to the amazing members of the Family and Friends of the 508th PIR Association who offered their encouragement along the way: Diane Merritt Pfluegar, Ellen Peters, Liberty Phillips, Jim Farrell, and Troy and Donna Palmer, just to name a few. A special thanks to Chris Harris for giving us the opportunity to present our book at the 2019 and 2021 508th PIR reunions. Thanks also goes out to Museum Technician Ralph Alvarez and Director John Aarsen of the 82nd Airborne Museum at Fort Bragg for their expertise.

To family and friends who shared our excitement along the way, listening to our stories and keeping us motivated as we saw this project through: Sue's sister, Linda Odenborg, who clarified family history, and Sue's daughter, Kristen Harris, who first suggested this book was truly a journey. Others took time to read the manuscript and offer valuable feedback and suggestions. A special thanks to our good friend Tim Lemming, a retired 82nd Airborne paratrooper, for reviewing the PTSD chapter, and to Jerry Green, who shared his knowledge about the North Platte Canteen during World War II.

We also want to thank our publisher, Roger Williams; our managing editor, Aleigha Kely; and our publicist, Devon Brown at Post Hill Press for their part in bringing this project to completion. Thank you from the bottom of our hearts to all of you, and always remember—"never give up the jump."

# INDEX